the knot
complete guide to
weddings

*The ultimate source of ideas, advice & relief for
the bride & groom & those who love them*

carley roney
and the editors of TheKnot.com

CLARKSON POTTER/PUBLISHERS
NEW YORK

Copyright © 1999, 2004, 2012 by The Knot, Inc.

All rights reserved.
Published in the United States by Clarkson Potter/Publishers, an imprint of the
Crown Publishing Group, a division of Random House, Inc., New York.
www.crownpublishing.com
www.clarksonpotter.com

Previous editions of this work were published in the United States by Broadway Books,
an imprint of the Crown Publishing Group, a Division of Random House, Inc., New York,
in 1999 and 2004.

CLARKSON POTTER is a trademark and POTTER with colophon is a registered trademark
of Random House, Inc.

Library of Congress Cataloging-in-Publication Data
Roney, Carley.
    The Knot complete guide to weddings / Carley Roney and the editors of
TheKnot.com.—1st rev. ed.
        p   cm.
        1. Weddings—Planning.   2. Wedding etiquette.   I. Knot (Firm)   I. Title.
III. Title: Complete guide to weddings in the real world.
    HQ745.R66 2012
    395.2'2—dc23   2012012480

ISBN 978-0-7704-3338-3
eISBN 978-0-7704-3339-0

Printed in the United States of America

Front cover photographs (clockwise from top left): Kris Drake Photography, Nate
Henderson Photography, Evoke Photography, Kristin Spencer Photography, Heather
Waraksa Photography, Elizabeth Messina, Katie Moos, and Philip Ficks • Back cover
photographs (left to right): Jesse Leake Photography, Kristin Spencer Photography,
Nessa K Photography, Justin & Mary

10   9   8   7   6   5   4   3   2

Second Revised Edition

contents

you're engaged!
. . . now what?

protect your ring

Don't forget to insure your engagement ring . . . just in case. When you shop for a "ring rider" policy, read the fine print: A good policy will cover every potentially ring-threatening situation, from theft and damage to accidentally dropping it in the garbage disposal. Go to TheKnot.com/ engagementrings for everything you need to know.

If you're reading this book, you probably have a ring sparkling on the fourth finger of your left hand. (And if you're the groom, or both of you are grooms or brides, we hope you will ignore the pronouns and appreciate the book just as much!) One thing is certain—you've signed up for the adventure of a lifetime: getting married. First off, congratulations! Get ready for some exciting times ahead.

Now, we know visions of gowns and cakes are dancing in your head, but before you start obsessing, stop and savor the moment with your fiancé (don't you just love how that sounds?), because there's nothing better than the first few weeks after you get engaged. Have fun breaking the news to your friends and family (read our advice for whom to tell first!) and celebrating your next adventure with a soiree or two (more on that, as well). And above all, enjoy!

In the next months (or longer), you'll be playing many new roles—event planner, family referee, professional juggler, marathon decision maker, accountant, and more— as you pull together a party for fifteen or five hundred. Before you hop on the nuptial roller coaster, think about how long a ride you want to take (and can handle). A typical engagement lasts from six months to a year, but we've seen amazing weddings that were five years in the making and beautiful ones that have been pulled together in just six weeks. In general, a yearlong engagement is about right. It gives you time to get your dream wedding dress (which can take six to nine months) and your perfect wedding reception venue (some are booked a year in advance!) yet doesn't drag out the engagement—and planning process—too long.

Once you do begin, you'll be faced with hundreds of decisions and even more options. Start with the big-picture elements (think season, setting, size, and style). These will shape your entire wedding and inform all those more detailed choices going forward.

If at any point you're considering tossing this book and eloping, take a deep breath. Yes, there's a lot to do, but by simply reading this book, you're equipping yourself with the know-how you need to take on your new roles and plan your perfect party. And this book is just one of the many resources we've created to get you through the planning with as little stress as possible. In every chapter, you'll be pointed to a variety of tools on TheKnot.com designed to make the entire process easier. If you haven't already, sign up for our planning newsletters and create a profile on our website to get customized articles, advice, and ideas at every stage. Bottom line: Between our website and the book, we have you covered from the proposal to the last dance (and beyond!).

Ready? Let's get started.

ETIQUETTE
meet the parents

Introductions are made by the groom's parents, who reach out to the bride's parents and convey their excitement. But it's also completely acceptable for the bride's parents—or you two—to make the first move. If either or both of your parents are divorced, schedule separate introductions. Regardless of who initiates contact, we highly recommend getting both sides together at some point before the wedding weekend. Trust us, at that point, you're going to have enough to stress over without worrying about whether your parents will get along. If a face-to-face meeting is impossible (maybe your parents live on opposite sides of the country or world), your parents should exchange phone numbers and e-mails so they can communicate about the engagement party, shower, and wedding plans. See if you can get everyone together a few days before the wedding for an introductory dinner or lunch.

complete planning timeline

12+ months before   BY _____ / _____

- [ ] Announce your engagement and spread the word.

- [ ] Get organized. Create a system to keep all wedding-related communication and research together. Go to TheKnot.com/planner for easy access to all your online planning tools (inspiration board, checklist, budgeter). (See chapter 1.)

- [ ] Envision your wedding style and colors. (See chapter 1.)

- [ ] Draw up your wedding budget. (See chapter 2.)

- [ ] Insure your ring.

- [ ] Choose a wedding date and time. Finalize it after okaying with important guests (parents, grandparents). (See chapter 3.)

- [ ] Start researching ceremony and reception sites. (See chapter 3.)

- [ ] Start outlining the initial guest list. (See chapter 4.)

- [ ] Create your wedding website. (It's free at TheKnot.com.) Add your "how we met and got engaged" story and photos. Then update it with venue and hotel info later as you make your choices. (See chapter 4.)

- [ ] Book any priority vendors (that is, if you know there's a particular band or photographer you have to have). (See chapters 6, 9.)

- [ ] Interview and book a wedding planner. (See chapter 6.)

9–11 months before   BY _____ / _____

- [ ] Reserve your date at your house of worship, or start looking for a civil ceremony site. (See chapters 3 and 13.)

- [ ] Book your wedding reception venue. (See chapter 3.)

- [ ] If a priest, minister, or rabbi at a house of worship isn't marrying you, choose and book an officiant. (See chapter 13.)

- [ ] Having an engagement party? Set a date, draft a guest list, and order invites. (See chapter 1.)

- [ ] Choose your wedding party. Also consider roles for other very important friends and family. (See chapter 5.)

- [ ] Settle on wedding colors and style (if you haven't already). (See chapter 1.)

- [ ] Decide on a caterer and start thinking about the reception menu. (See chapter 11.)

- [ ] Start shopping for wedding dresses. (See chapter 15.)

- [ ] Finalize your guest list. (See chapter 4.)

- [ ] Research photographers and videographers. (See chapters 9 and 10.)

- [ ] Start researching musicians. (See chapter 12.)

- [ ] Set up appointments with florists in the area to discuss options. (See chapter 8.)

- [ ] Research lighting and rental places (if you're having an outdoor wedding or want to add a few extras). (See chapter 7.)

6–8 months before   BY _____ / _____

- [ ] Order your wedding dress. (See chapter 15.)

- [ ] Register for gifts. (See chapter 14.)

- [ ] Plan out the ceremony with your officiant and talk about any religious requirements (such as premarital counseling). (See chapter 13.)

- [ ] Book your florist. (See chapter 8.)

- [ ] Book your photographer. (See chapter 9.)

- [ ] Book your videographer. (See chapter 10.)

- [ ] Book your reception band or DJ. (See chapter 12.)

- [ ] Have engagement photos taken (if you want). (See chapter 9.)

- [ ] Start planning your honeymoon. (See page 414.)

- [ ] Research hairstylists and makeup artists. (See chapter 18.)

- ☐ Interview and book a cake baker you love. (See chapter 21.)
- ☐ Think about and then nail down your bridesmaid dress pick and tell your bridesmaids so they can schedule fittings. (See chapter 17.)
- ☐ Set aside a block of hotel rooms at nearby hotels (put that info on your wedding website and make sure it's easy to find, especially if it's a destination wedding). (See chapter 4.)
- ☐ Order save-the-dates and send them out as soon as possible if it will be a destination wedding for most guests. (See chapter 19).
- ☐ Start planning the rehearsal dinner. (See chapter 24.)
- ☐ Order your invitations. (See chapter 19.)
- ☐ Map out the menu with your caterer. (See chapter 11.)
- ☐ Confirm that your bridesmaids have ordered their dresses. (See chapter 17.)
- ☐ Research wedding insurance. (See chapter 2.)
- ☐ Browse centerpieces and figure out which ones you like. (See chapter 8.)

4–5 months before   BY _____ / _____

- ☐ Finalize your flower proposal. (See chapter 8.)
- ☐ Decide on formalwear for all the guys. (See chapter 16.)
- ☐ Reserve a calligrapher (if you're using one for your invites and stationery). (See chapter 19.)
- ☐ Finalize your rental list (tables, chairs, extras) for the reception. (See chapter 7.)
- ☐ If you're having a welcome party, finalize those details. (See chapter 24.)
- ☐ Make honeymoon travel reservations. Make sure passports are up-to-date. (See page 418.)
- ☐ Address those invitations or drop them off with the calligrapher. (See chapter 19.)
- ☐ Book your wedding-night accommodations. (See chapter 25.)
- ☐ Book the rehearsal dinner site and finalize the menu. (See chapter 24.)

- ☐ Sign up for professional dance lessons. (See chapter 12.)
- ☐ Brainstorm the design for a groom's cake and commission it. (See chapter 21.)

2–3 months before   BY _____ / _____

- ☐ Choose accessories for your bridesmaids; confirm their dress deliveries. (See chapter 17.)
- ☐ Decide on a marriage contract (*ketubah* or any other contract required) for the ceremony. (See chapter 13.)
- ☐ Buy or rent the decorations that aren't included in your flower proposal (aisle runner, program basket). (See chapter 7.)
- ☐ Make all prewedding beauty appointments (facials, haircuts, color). (See chapter 18.)
- ☐ Attend prewedding counseling (if required). (See chapter 13.)
- ☐ Shop for and buy your wedding rings. (See chapter 19.)
- ☐ Decide on wedding favors. (See chapter 22.)
- ☐ If you're planning to host a bridesmaid luncheon, finalize the details and let your bridesmaids know. (See chapter 24.)
- ☐ Arrange for day-of transportation for you, your wedding party, and your guests (if needed). (See chapter 23.)
- ☐ Confirm the delivery date of your dress and schedule your dress fittings. (See chapter 15.)
- ☐ Purchase your under-the-dress essentials in time for your first fitting. (See chapter 15.)
- ☐ Have your bridal shower. (See chapter 24.)
- ☐ Figure out ceremony readings and reach out to the people you want involved. (See chapter 13.)
- ☐ Work on the ceremony (see chapter 13) and start writing your vows (if you're writing your own).
- ☐ Draw up reception song lists (including the must-play and do-not-play lists). (See chapter 12.)

2 months before   BY _____ / _____

☐ Send out wedding invites. (See chapter 19.)

☐ Start working on the ceremony programs. (See chapter 19.)

☐ Have your bachelorette party. (See chapter 24.)

☐ Buy your wedding veil, shoes, and all accessories (in time for your final fitting). (See chapter 15.)

☐ Decide on your "something old, new, borrowed, and blue." (See chapter 15.)

☐ Make a plan for kids at your reception and arrange a babysitter, if necessary. (See chapter 20.)

☐ Research local marriage license requirements. (See chapter 25.)

☐ Confirm out-of-town guests' hotel reservations and check with the hotel to make sure you don't need to block out more rooms. (See chapter 25.)

☐ Have your first dress fitting. (See chapter 15.)

☐ Schedule hair and makeup trial appointments to take place three to four weeks ahead of the wedding. (See chapter 18.)

☐ Get going on thank-you notes for those gifts received already. (See Epilogue.)

1 month before   BY _____ / _____

☐ Attend the final tasting and finalize the menu with your caterer. (See chapter 11.)

☐ Finalize the ceremony. (See chapter 13.)

☐ Finish your ceremony programs. (See chapter 19.)

☐ Send out rehearsal dinner invites (if you didn't include them in the invites). (See chapter 24.)

☐ Work out a day-of schedule. (See chapter 25.)

☐ Plan night-before activities with friends. (See chapter 24.)

☐ Purchase gifts for parents and each other. (See chapter 5.)

☐ Order or plan in-room welcome baskets. (See chapter 22.)

1–2 weeks before   BY _____ / _____

☐ Call guests who have not yet returned their invitation response cards. (See chapter 25.)

☐ Put the seating chart together and give it to your caterer, manager, and planner. (See chapter 25.)

☐ Give your caterer, cake baker, and reception venue the final head count. Include vendors, who will expect a meal. (See chapters 11 and 25.)

☐ Supply the reception site manager with a list of requests from other vendors (such as a table for the DJ, setup space needed by the florist, and so on). (See chapter 25.)

☐ Work on escort cards. (See chapter 19.)

☐ Confirm transportation for the day. (See chapter 23.)

☐ Shop and pack for the honeymoon. (See page 374.)

☐ Confirm all final payment amounts, details, delivery times, and locationswith your vendors. Also, compile their phone numbers to distribute. (See chapter 25.)

☐ Confirm and distribute the day-of schedule and contact list to all parents, attendants, and vendors. (See chapter 25.)

☐ Prepare your wedding toasts. (See chapter 20.)

☐ Practice walking in your wedding shoes. (See chapter 15.)

☐ Have your final dress fitting. (See chapter 15.)

☐ Put together an overnight bag for the wedding. (See chapter 25.)

☐ Leave a copy of your honeymoon itinerary with close friends and family. (See page 000.)

☐ Put final payments and cash tips for vendors in labeled envelopes and give to a friend to distribute on the wedding day. (See chapter 25.)

☐ Give a must-take photo and videography list to your pros. (See chapter 9.)

☐ Apply for a marriage license together. (See chapter 25.)

- ☐ Give your DJ or bandleader a list of special song requests. (See chapter 12.)

- ☐ Get one last haircut or trim and hair color touch-up. (See chapter 18.)

- ☐ Arrange airport pickups for key family members and guests who can't or won't be renting a car. (See chapter 23.)

2–3 days before   BY _____ /_____

- ☐ Confirm transportation to the airport for your honeymoon. (See page 377.)

- ☐ Organize your day-of emergency kit. (See chapter 25.)

- ☐ Have your dress steamed. (See chapter 15.)

- ☐ Wrap thank-you gifts for parents, attendants, and each other and write special thank-you notes. (See chapter 22.)

- ☐ Touch base with ceremony and reception venues. (See chapter 25.)

- ☐ Determine the order of bridesmaids and groomsmen. (See chapter 13.)

- ☐ If the caterer will be arranging place cards, table cards, menu cards, and/or the guest book, hand them off. (See chapter 25.)

- ☐ Reconfirm that the florist received your (correct) flower order and knows where and when the flowers should be delivered. (See chapters 8 and 25.)

- ☐ Confirm all locations and pickup times with the limousine company or driver. (See chapters 23 and 25.)

- ☐ Deliver welcome bags to out-of-town guests. (See chapters 22 and 25.)

- ☐ Confirm all toasts with your bridal party and family. (See chapters 20 and 24.)

day before   BY _____ /_____

- ☐ Get your manicure and/or pedicure. (See chapter 18.)

- ☐ Bring ceremony accessories to the site. (See chapter 13.)

- ☐ Rehearse the ceremony. (See chapter 13.)

- ☐ Give your marriage license to your officiant. (See chapter 25.)

- ☐ Have fun at your rehearsal dinner or welcome party. (See chapter 24.)

- ☐ Give attendants their gifts at the rehearsal dinner. (See chapter 24.)

- ☐ Go over the hair and makeup schedule with the bridesmaids. (See chapter 18.)

- ☐ Get a good night's sleep! (See chapter 25.)

day of   BY _____ /_____

- ☐ Shoot to get to your hair and makeup session early. (See chapter 18.)

- ☐ Present parents (and each other) with gifts, or at least a big hug and kiss. (See chapter 5.)

- ☐ Give the best man and/or maid of honor your wedding rings. (See chapter 13.)

- ☐ Give your father or the best man the officiant's fee envelope, to be handed off after the ceremony. (See chapter 13.)

- ☐ Introduce your reception manager and consultant or maid of honor (if that hasn't happened already) so they can deal with any questions during the party. (See chapter 25.)

- ☐ Have fun and enjoy your day! (See chapter 26.)

postwedding   BY _____ /_____

- ☐ Drop off your dress for cleaning and preservation. (See page 402.)

- ☐ Freeze the top layer of your cake. (See chapter 21.)

- ☐ If preserving your bouquet, send it to a preservation service. (See page 403.)

- ☐ Send each of your vendors a thank-you note.

- ☐ Keep a gift log (see page 406) and send out those thank-you notes as soon as possible.

laying the groundwork

1

envisioning your event

TIMELINE

PLANNING

12+ months before
Send formal engagement
announcements (optional)

Submit engagement
announcement for
publication (optional)

Think about dates
and locations

Create inspiration boards

Consider your colors

Have your wedding ring
appraised and insured

9–11 months before
Celebrate at your
engagement party

The very first thing you're going to be doing will be announcing your engagement—and even the way you do it will give your friends and family a cue about the type of wedding you're having. As you decide how to let the world in on your newly engaged status, start thinking about what your dream wedding looks like and what you want from your day. In this chapter, we'll walk you through the options, show you how to spread the news in style, and help you draw up a blueprint of your perfect wedding.

ANNOUNCING YOUR ENGAGEMENT TO THE WORLD

You probably feel like shouting the news to everyone you know, from your cube mate to the guy who makes your soy lattes. But if you haven't started shouting yet, keep in mind that recipients of any mass "We're engaged" e-mails will likely expect to be invited to the wedding. In other words, be careful whom you include (and tell your mom and future mother-in-law that the same goes for them). If you have kids from a previous relationship, they should be the first to know. They're the ones who are getting a new parent (and maybe a step-sibling or two). Then share the news with your immediate families. If you want to get technical, the bride's parents have first dibs on the news (even if they were in on the surprise, they should still get the first call).

Once your parents know, your inner circle is next, starting with siblings and close relatives, followed by friends. Warning: Your friends will notice who gets the news first.

Formal engagement announcements

For more traditional duos, pairs with old-fashioned folks, and couples with longer engagements, there's always the option of a formal mailed

---

CLEVER IDEAS

creative ways to spread the news

with a soiree

Keep the secret long enough to gather your nearest and dearest for a "Surprise! We're engaged!" party. Host it at a favorite restaurant or bar, or even at your home, and share your good news with a toast.

with turkey or tinsel

Consider holding off until the next holiday or family gathering when your loved ones are already together and your good news will only add to the festive atmosphere of the day.

with a wedding website

Build a wedding website and include the proposal story, a few postengagement pictures, fun details (like how and where you met), and even some of the wedding info (like the planned locale and month and year). Then e-mail the link to your friends and family. (See chapter 4 for tips on creating your wedding website.)

with a video

If you snapped a few post-proposal shots (or had someone videotape the proposal), send an e-mail with the subject line "Save the Date" or "Status Update." Then just include a link to the album or video and let the footage speak for itself.

formal engagement announcements wording ideas

Spreading the news the old-fashioned way? Here are options for wording printed announcements.

MR. AND MRS. JOHN DOE
ANNOUNCE THE ENGAGEMENT
OF THEIR DAUGHTER

Jane Annette

TO

Mr. Jack Smith

the bride's parents announcing

Ms. Jane Annette Doe

AND

Mr. Jack Smith

ARE PLEASED TO ANNOUNCE
THEIR ENGAGEMENT

announcing the news yourselves

announcement. Though the mailed announcement has pretty much been replaced by the save-the-date, we think the former can be a nice touch (kind of like handwritten thank-you notes).

Traditionally, formal announcements are sent by the parents of the bride, though it's totally acceptable for you two to send them or for his parents to send them. Unlike save-the-dates, they don't typically include specific details like when or where the wedding is happening. In olden days, handwritten announcements were de rigueur, but nowadays, unless you have the time (and the impeccable handwriting), take this opportunity to test out wedding stationer candidates and have cards printed. (Flip to chapter 19 for the rundown on finding a stationer.)

Published engagement announcements
There are any number of ways to announce your newly "altar"-ed state, but for old-school couples (or parents) who want to make the proclamation public, publishing an announcement in your respective local newspapers or alumni magazines is the traditional route. Printed engagement notices run well in advance of the wedding—around three to eight months prior. (Wedding announcements, on the other hand, run shortly after the wedding.)

SAMPLE

published engagement announcements wording ideas

Want to submit your status update to the local newspaper? Here are some
standard engagement announcement wordings for publication.

the bride's parents announcing

Mr. and Mrs. John Doe of Little Rock, Arkansas, announce the engagement of their daughter, Jane Annette, to Jack Smith, son of David and Beth Smith of Tishomingo, Oklahoma. Ms. Doe, a graduate of Vassar College, is a professor at Barnard College in New York City. Mr. Smith graduated magna cum laude from Princeton University, attended law school at New York University, and works at Smith, Golden, his mother's law firm, in Fort Lee, New Jersey. A June wedding is planned.

single parent announcing

Ms. Janet Jones announces the engagement of her daughter, Jane Doe, to Jack Smith, son of David and Beth Smith of Tishomingo, Oklahoma. Ms. Doe, a graduate of Vassar College, is a professor at Barnard College in New York City. Mr. Smith graduated magna cum laude from Princeton University, attended law school at New York University, and works at Smith, Golden, his mother's law firm, in Fort Lee, New Jersey. A June wedding is planned.

(NOTE: There's no need to mention the other biological parent if he or she wasn't involved in raising you, but you can add this line close to the end: "Ms. Doe is also the daughter of John Doe of Sioux City, Iowa.")

announcing the wedding yourselves

Jane Doe, a professor at Barnard College in New York City, is to be married to Jack Smith, a partner at the law firm of Smith, Golden in Fort Lee, New Jersey. Ms. Doe is the daughter of Mr. John Doe of Sioux City, Iowa, and Ms. Janet Jones of Little Rock, Arkansas. Mr. Smith is the son of David and Beth Smith of Tishomingo, Oklahoma. A June wedding is planned.

Start by contacting your publications of choice to get the submission details, including lead time, writers' guidelines, any standardized forms that need to be filled out, the lowdown on whether they accept pictures, and their pricing policy (some charge a fee, some don't). Also, check to see if your announcement will run online as well as in print.

Published announcements typically mention career details about the two of you, your parents' names and places of residence, and your educational credentials (space permitting). Obviously, include only what you'd like the world to know. Haven't nailed down your wedding date? You can include something like, "A June wedding is planned" or "No date has been set for the wedding." If you want to submit a picture with your announcement, a professional shot isn't usually required, but you may want to consider scheduling an engagement shoot for the occasion. (See "Engagement Shoots," page 7.)

The engagement party

It's time to celebrate your newly engaged status with the first of many parties to be thrown in your honor: the engagement party. People will want to congratulate you, and, well, a party's a lot more fun than a phone call. It's also a great time to introduce key people from your lives who are going to be seeing a lot of each other (and possibly working together) over the next nine months or so. Some might even shower you with gifts. (Flip to chapter 14 for everything you need to know before you register.)

Tradition dictates that it's the bride's parents' prerogative to host the first official celebration. Then the groom's parents can throw their own party, or maybe both sets of parents will come together to cohost an event. These days, more and more couples are throwing the fete themselves (just keep in mind that if you're doing the inviting, it's your responsibility to foot the bill). Friends can also host (and may even volunteer to!), but before you ask, be conscious of the financial implications.

THE TIMELINE The engagement party typically falls within a few months of the proposal, right in the sweet spot between carefree, just-engaged life and the start of serious wedding planning. You'll want to give guests about a month's notice, so about nine to eleven months before the wedding is the ideal time frame. Here's what else you need to know.

THE GUEST LIST It used to be that you weren't supposed to invite anyone to the engagement party whom you weren't inviting to your wedding—case closed. But now, with larger networks and friends and family scattered across the country, and with the formality of engagement parties evolving, expectations have changed and your guest list really depends on who's hosting.

Now that so many couples live and/or host their nuptials far away from all their families and friends and more informal engagement parties are becoming increasingly popular, engagement parties often include people who aren't invited to the wedding. If your friends want to put together an informal bar party and just e-mail the invitation a few weeks before, it's totally fine to include people you aren't sure will end up making the wedding guest list (coworkers, newer friends, college roommates). And if your parents' good friends want to host a cocktail party at their fancy home in your honor, let your parents invite mutual friends and business associates you might not have room for at your wedding.

If, on the other hand, either you two or your parents are hosting the engagement party, the old rule sticks. When the wedding hosts send the engagement party invitation, it's considered part of the official wedding parties and guests assume they're invited to the wedding, too. To avoid a sticky situation later, choose your bridal party (see chapter 5) and have your guest list loosely mapped out (see chapter 4) before you send out engagement party invitations. Also, make sure you (and both sets of parents) have a built-in script for addressing the wedding plans with guests that may not be invited to the wedding (you haven't started thinking about the wedding plans yet, but it's going to be a small celebration).

As for which of your wedding guests should be on the engagement party list, typically, close family members and friends of both sides should be invited (even if they live far away and you know they won't be able to attend), as well as your own close friends. But the location of your party will also influence your guest list. Say you live in New York City, but most of your family and friends live in Chicago. You may decide to have your party in your hometown (and enlist someone local to help you plan), host it in your current locale, or even throw two parties. Just beware of tiring out your guests and bridal party with too many invitations before the wedding day is even close! Also, when picking the party location, consider where you plan to have your wedding—you may not want to ask guests to travel twice.

THE INVITATIONS Feel free to keep the invites simple, make them yourselves, or even send them out via e-mail. If you've chosen your invitation designer already, see if she'll give you a special rate if you order engagement party invites from her, too. Don't worry if you haven't chosen a color palette or don't have a wedding date in mind yet—your engagement party invitations don't have to match the rest of your stationery.

THE SCENE Let this definition bring you down to earth if you start to get stressed out.

En•gage•ment par•ty: Both your families coming together with friends to celebrate how psyched you guys are to be marrying each other. It's not a wedding.

In fact, your engagement party should be much more low-key than the wedding (you don't want to upstage the big day, right?). Depending on how many people you want to invite, you can make an engagement

engagement shoots

Engagement photo shoots are a great way to try out potential photographers while getting professional photos that you can submit to your local paper with your engagement announcement, post on your wedding website, incorporate into your save-the-dates, use creatively in your wedding-day décor, or frame and give as gifts to your families. It's also an opportunity to increase your comfort level in front of the camera.

ASK CARLEY

REGISTRY TIMING

We just got engaged two weeks ago. Is it too soon to register?
It's perfectly acceptable to register as soon as you get engaged, especially if there will be any prewedding celebrations in your honor. While gifts are optional for engagement parties, some of your guests may want to give you something to commemorate the occasion, so register for at least a few items beforehand so they don't have to ask (or guess) what you'd like. One thing to note: Do not include registry information in your engagement party invitations or in any other formal manner. Word of mouth is really the only way to inform guests about your gift wish list, though it's also okay to include registry details and links on your wedding website.

party work almost anywhere—the club (cocktails!), a restaurant (good friends and food!), or even your backyard (low-key and easy). While of course it's fine for the décor and details to reflect your wedding colors and theme, like your invites, don't feel like you have to rush to choose them just so that your engagement party can match.

SKETCHING THE BIG PICTURE

Once the excitement of your engagement settles and you get used to that ring on your finger, the realization that you have to plan your wedding sets in (that's why you're reading this book, right?). The trick to pulling it all together is getting organized, staying grounded, and defining and maintaining your overall vision, including a style and color scheme. Then all the other details will fall into place.

As soon as you step into the world of wedding planning, you'll face a zillion choices about everything from the event locale right down to the color of your champagne (seriously). Making all those decisions can be overwhelming without a clear vision for your day. Settling on an overarching concept and sticking to it is crucial for a wedding that feels unified and totally you—and trust us, it'll make your life a lot easier as you weed through all the options in the months (or weeks!) to come. The guiding principle for your day could be as simple as a pink-and-green palette or as specific as a modern-day *Great Gatsby* party. Where you start—and how far you carry the concept—is entirely up to you. No matter how elaborate you get, simply having a common thread will pull the whole day together. So before you try on a single gown, book a band, or sample a bite of cake, you need to look at the big picture and determine what kind of style and vibe you want to set on your wedding day.

Begin dreaming
Throw all price tag considerations out the window along with any notions about what your mom or anyone else might think. Close your eyes and picture your fantasy wedding. What do you see? Is it a candlelit ceremony in the fall? Are you walking barefoot on a beach in the summer? Or maybe it's a snowy mountaintop and you're in a fur stole. Go nuts and don't worry if your ideas don't mesh or if you can only picture your dress at this point. This kind of free-form fantasizing will help you identify your dream scenario and the details that will be at the foreground of the party you plan, making it easier for you to narrow down the options and figure out your wedding

what's your wedding style?

My bridal style icon is:
A. Grace Kelly
B. Bianca Jagger
C. Carolyn Bessette-Kennedy

My dream wedding locale is:
A. A grand ballroom
B. A sleek loft
C. A vineyard

For our grand entrance, we'll:
A. Pull up in a vintage Rolls-Royce
B. Cruise in on a Vespa
C. Walk hand in hand

I'm envisioning my bridesmaids in:
A. Coordinating satin gowns
B. Stylish black cocktail dresses
C. Sundresses in a fun hue

Pick a meal:
A. Five-course plated dinner
B. Cocktails and passed hors d'oeuvres
C. Buffet dinner

For my wedding flowers, I want:
A. Lush peonies and roses
B. Orchids
C. Whatever is in season

My dream honeymoon:
A. Vino and romance in Venice
B. Beach and culture in Bali
C. Sun and margaritas in Mexico

If I were a drink, I'd be . . .
A. A flute of champagne
B. A martini
C. A glass of pinot grigio

Our reception music will be:
A. A twelve-piece band
B. A DJ
C. A six-piece band

Choose a first-dance song:
A. A classic like "At Last" by Etta James
B. A unique choice like a Beatles song
C. A song that's meaningful to you

Mostly A's: Classic
"Good taste never goes out of style" is your motto. You want a traditional and timeless feel for your wedding.

Mostly B's: Contemporary
A modern fete is more your style. You prefer a minimalist approach with sleek lines and sophisticated hues to keep your wedding from feeling too . . . well, wedding-y.

Mostly C's: Casual chic
Frill-free and pared down but still sophisticated—your outdoor wedding will be just like you. Think natural and understated yet elegant.

priorities. While you're picturing your perfect wedding, here are some key questions to consider:

- Big (everyone you know) or small (just close friends and family)?
- Outdoors or in?
- Home (one of your hometowns or your current city) or away (a destination wedding)?
- Modern, classic, romantic, vintage, rustic, or all-out glam?
- Fancy, casual, or somewhere in between?
- Spring, summer, winter, or fall?

Get Inspired

To help you get a better idea of what you want (as well as what you don't want), spend some time gathering inspiration and researching your options. Check out bridal magazines, books, blogs, and, of course, the collection of real wedding photos on TheKnot.com, where you can browse photos by style, color, season, and venue. But don't just limit yourself to the obvious sources—something as unlikely as a wallpaper pattern, a scene from a movie, or a terra-cotta urn can spark your creativity. Gather everything that catches your eye—from fabrics, color chips, and stationery to pictures of cakes and gowns you love.

Creating an inspiration board is one of the best ways to get your wedding color and style ideas out of your head and into something more concrete. It will help you to identify common threads and visualize how various elements will look together. All you need is a bulletin board, a sketchbook, or a virtual inspiration board (see "Personalized Inspiration Boards," above left). Then just add any images, fabric swatches, quotes, or pictures from real weddings that inspire you. Soon, you should see a common style, theme, or color palette emerging, which you can then use to build your vision. You may want to make one board, or you may want to organize your inspiration into different boards for each category—ceremony, reception, and dresses, for example. These boards will also help you give your vendors a better idea of your style and preferences. Since your definition of "classic" may not be the same as your planner's or stationer's or cake baker's, visual examples are essential for making sure you and your vendors are all speaking the same style language.

Settling on a style

There are many ways to define your wedding style, from the reception site to the season and the time of day, so you'll want to begin thinking about those now. For example, if you love the idea of having an evening reception in a grand hotel, that may dictate a more classic, elegant, or old-world style. On the other hand, if you're drawn to a sleek new art museum, you may want to complement that space with a modern, minimalist look.

The setting of your nuptials can also dictate the vision—a beach wedding calls for a more laid-back, seaside vibe, while a ranch wedding has a more rustic feel and a city wedding might have a more modern, urban slant. And don't forget your own personal styles and the type of atmosphere that best speaks to you two as a team. For instance, do you prefer hosting intimate dinner parties, getting all decked out and hitting the town, or throwing low-key poolside picnics? Are you into art? Are you interested in a particular time period? Do you have a signature personal style (preppy, glamorous, hipster)?

STYLE DICTIONARY If the idea of your wedding style still feels too abstract, let these ideas inspire you.

Preppy Chic At a yacht club or country club; bright but classic colors; playful motifs like lobsters, nautical elements, and seashells

Glamorous In a ballroom or grand hall; jewel tones, lacquer, metallics, and lots of sparkle

Elegant At a museum or estate; simple but pretty décor with personalized accents

Classic At a country club, historic building, or mansion; timeless, traditional colors and décor

Modern In a loft or gallery space; sleek, minimalist décor that emphasizes clean lines

Romantic In a castle or a botanical garden; lace, pastels, flowers, and candles galore

Rustic On a ranch, on a mountaintop, or at a winery; nature-inspired décor and seasonal colors

Retro At a hip hotel or restaurant; a throwback to a different era; playful details, bright colors, and bold graphics

Artsy Chic At a posh gallery or warehouse space; South Beach–inspired décor with a black-and-white palette and mirrored accents

Beachy In a beachfront setting; nautical or tropical elements; blues and greens

Vintage At an estate or winery with old-world charm; lace, muted colors, antiques, and whimsical details

REAL BRIDE ADVICE
style inspiration

"Use something personal to inspire your day. We were on a European tour and my fiancé proposed in Paris (the last stop). So we decided to have a travel-themed wedding."
—VANESSA

Figuring out formality

Consider how fancy or casual you want to go, as that decision will affect the number of guests, the food, the decorations, the entertainment, and the debits to your wedding fund, as well as your wedding style. Personal preference is a key element in determining which degree of formality best suits your wedding. But the formality of your wedding will be reflected first and foremost in the location (ballroom vs. beach, for example), as well as the time of day and season. Consider the dress code here, too: If, for example, you've decided on a beach wedding, going informal, or at least semiformal, probably makes more sense than asking your guests to don gowns and tuxes in the heat and hot sand. On the other hand, wearing a tux and ball gown might feel a bit . . . well, awkward if you get married at noon, but totally appropriate if you do so around dinnertime. Whatever you decide, you'll want to carry your chosen formality through every part of your wedding. There may be six degrees of separation between any two people, but there are only four degrees of formality when it comes to getting married. Think about which one best suits your personalities and vision.

ULTRAFORMAL A ballroom or grand hall type of setting, complete with a twenty-four-piece band and over-the-top centerpieces. This kind of überfancy style (think state dinners and the Oscars) only works in the evening and requires the most formal of all dress codes, with white (tails) or black tie for guys and full-length gowns for the ladies.

FORMAL A late-afternoon or evening affair that's slightly less formal than a black-tie event and might be at a museum, historic building, or picturesque estate. A tuxedo isn't required, but the event is still formal enough for one to be appropriate; it's just casual enough for a formal dark suit and tie to be suitable, as well. Women can choose a fancy cocktail dress or a floor-length gown. "Black tie optional" and "cocktail attire" dress-code instructions both fall under this category.

SEMIFORMAL A late-afternoon or evening affair that could take place anywhere from a country club or loft to a winery or restaurant. "Cocktail" attire is de rigueur, with a suit and tie for the gents (dark or light depending on the season and time of day) and a cocktail dress or a dressy skirt and top for the ladies.

INFORMAL Anytime and (almost) anywhere affairs (think stylish backyard ceremony, rustic barn, mountaintop lodge, or beach), with ties optional for the men and sundresses or skirts for the women.

ASK CARLEY

BLACK TIE VS. BLACK TIE OPTIONAL

I'm confused—what's the difference between black tie and black tie optional?

Black tie optional leaves a little more room for interpretation—a tuxedo isn't required, but the wedding is formal enough that one would still be appropriate. Otherwise, men should go with a dark suit and tie. Women also get a little more leeway—long dresses still work, or they can wear a dressy suit or something cocktail-length (but still formal) instead.

Incorporating a theme

The more specific you get with your vision, the easier it will be for you to choose all your details and convey your ideas to your vendors. The tighter your theme, the better. Instead of stopping at "glam," decide whether you want "Art Deco glam" or "old Hollywood glamour," for example. Or if you're picturing a garden party, think about whether you want an English garden party or a rustic country garden party.

Your theme can be anything from a favorite era, hobby, or place in the world to your heritage or culture, the season, or even something inspired by your wedding locale (like a lobster or lighthouse for a seaside affair). Just make sure whatever theme you choose meshes with the formality you've selected (a New England clambake doesn't exactly scream "formal").

Aside from having a gorgeous event, you want your guests to celebrate who you and your spouse-to-be are as a couple. Choose a theme that shows what makes you you, whether it's your ethnic backgrounds or your shared love of books, modern art, or skiing. Remember: Your wedding should reflect both your personalities and preferences, so you may need to . . . yes, compromise. But by compromise, we mean choose one concept that applies to both of you. It's fine if you like Broadway musicals and your groom is into football, but trying to incorporate both ideas into your wedding day is going to lead to a weirdly disjointed affair.

Be strategic with your décor and don't brand every detail with your chosen theme. Even a vintage-style wedding can go from elegant to Grandma's attic if you're not careful. The last thing you want to do is force a thirties-style wedding to the point where you feel like you're throwing a costume party. To keep your wedding from feeling like a theme party, or worse, a kid's birthday party, go for a subtle interpretation. Let your chosen theme inspire your selection of colors and details, but don't hit your guests over the head with the concept.

Picking a palette

Color is another unifying factor between all your wedding elements, from the invitations to your bridesmaids' dresses and table linens. Your wedding colors can inspire your wedding style, help create the right vibe, and even be used as your theme.

RESEARCH THE RAINBOW Peruse magazines, art galleries, paint stores, friends' weddings, and Pantone books to find color combos and shades you like. You can also search real weddings by color and check out hot color combos at TheKnot.com/color.

CLEVER IDEAS
wedding themes

time periods
If you long for a bygone era, wrap your wedding around your favorite (think fifties, Roaring Twenties, or the Victorian era).

a favorite item
A single element, like something you collect, a design you love, a favorite flower, or a piece of lace from your mother's wedding dress that conveys a vintage-meets-romantic vibe, might set the tone for your day.

your passions
What interests or (healthy) obsessions really say who you are? Nature? Movies? Sports?

the seasons
Time of year can influence your wedding food, music, flowers, favors, decorations, and even wardrobe.

going green
Infuse your wedding with your passion for the planet by using eco-friendly elements; a seasonal, organic menu; and an outdoorsy setting.

SET THE MOOD Though yellow may be your favorite color, it might not be the ideal shade for an evening wedding on New Year's Eve. Likewise, shimmering metallic silver might not set the right tone for an afternoon garden reception in a New England town. Figure out which emotions you want your celebration to evoke. A peaceful, Zen-like retreat? A regal, romantic affair? A jumping, high-energy party? A vibrant summer yellow mixed with chocolate brown (think sunflowers and bees) is perfect for a country-chic wedding—add gold to the mix and the combination becomes more reminiscent of regal France.

LOOK TO YOUR LOCALE Your venue's décor (or lack thereof) will affect your choice of colors, so consider your venue first (skip ahead to chapter 3 for help choosing a locale). For example, lime green and hot pink won't work at a country club with navy and maroon carpets. For best results, play up the prominent colors of your site or setting (read: for a seaside affair, the natural choice is blue).

Jeanna & Tyler
JULY 17
PEAKS ISLAND, ME

Having both grown up on the coast of Maine, Jeanna and Tyler didn't have to think twice about where to wed. And their wedding style came just as easily: The couple paid tribute to the coastal setting with nautical décor elements like a boat-paddle guest book, lobster traps, ocean rocks, and striped patterns. Tall glass vases topped with fresh white blooms, dark-wood chiavari chairs, and luxe touches elevated the look.

LET MOTHER NATURE BE YOUR GUIDE Light pastels and barely-there hues like blush might be pretty in spring but can look washed out in the fall and winter. Dark colors like burgundy work well in fall and winter but are best reserved for accents if you're having a summertime fete. Choose your wedding date, or at least the season, first (turn to chapter 3 for help picking both); then think about the colors most commonly associated with that season (pink and yellow for spring; oranges, reds, and browns for fall) and let those guide your palette.

KEEP YOUR FLOWERS IN MIND The most obvious way to add color to your wedding is with your flowers. Get familiar with the different types of flowers and the colors they come in before choosing your palette. If you want an all-blue wedding, your petal picks will be more limited than if you go with a pink celebration, and the season will also influence the colors and types of flowers that will be available.

DON'T FORGET YOUR GIRLS Not all colors are easy to wear, and you've got bridesmaids to think about. Jewel tones are almost universally flattering, while neutrals like beiges, nudes, and light pastels are tricky for most girls to pull off.

Combining colors

Most couples choose one main color and an accent color, or two equally prominent complementary colors (colors that are directly opposite each other on the color wheel, like green and pink or yellow and purple) for a bright contrast. But you could also choose an analogous scheme—putting together three colors that fall side by side on the color wheel, like blue, periwinkle, and violet, to bring out the subtle nuances of one color family. Monochromatic weddings use a single dominant color with variations for accents, or varying shades of the same hue (like brown and beige; indigo and blue; yellow and yellow-green; or pale pink, bubblegum pink, and fuchsia). Sticking with two or three colors will keep the look coordinated. The easiest way to choose is to nail your signature color first: deciding on the main color will make the accent much easier to figure out. Pick one general color—say, blue—and then think about shades and tints (aqua, robin's egg, navy) or other colors to accent it with. For a complete guide to color, see the photo insert.

Now choose an accent color. Don't let your colors compete. Pair a neutral or metallic accent color with a bolder hue for a fail-safe pairing, or if you prefer a brighter palette with two heavy hitters like yellow and orange, encourage their richness to play off, rather than against, each other. Translation: Decide which one will be the showstopper and which will play the sidekick in every scenario.

While there are no hard-and-fast rules about which colors work best

---

DÉCOR IDEAS
classic color combos

White and ivory

Black and white

Pink and cream

Purple and pink

Blue and pink

White and green

Gold and silver

---

together, the easiest way to ensure a coordinated combination is to stick to wedding colors of the same intensity. Keep your palette toned down with lavender and baby blue, or dial it up with deep red and slate gray, but avoid dark/light pairings like royal blue with light brown, which can be hard to pull off. Remember: Every color comes in thousands of shades, so if you're afraid classic red and navy will look too nautical, deviate from the traditional tones, opting for aqua and cherry instead.

ORGANIZING IT ALL

Once you have a solid vision of your wedding in mind, you're almost ready to launch into planning mode. But before you start creating a budget and researching venues and vendors, we've got a little housekeeping exercise for you: setting up a system to organize and track all the inspiration and ideas you are starting to gather, as well as the contracts, proposals, contacts, and other related documents and notes you will collect as you make your way to the altar. Trust us, getting organized from the start will make your lives a lot easier down the planning road. Plus, the more organized you are, the less chance there is that something will go wrong.

Filing all the paperwork
Being organized means that you can easily find ideas or information when you need it and, if something goes wrong, you can return an item or look up an idea or agreement. Here's what you'll want to keep together:

- All vendors' contact information
- Copies of vendor proposals and notes from your meetings
- Copies of contracts
- Receipts (these come in handy as you plan and track your budget, enabling you to stay on top of all the expenses that will pop up along the way)
- Ideas and inspiration (so you can pull them out when you meet with vendors)

Luckily, there are tons of options these days for keeping all your wedding information and contacts organized and at your fingertips. Whether you are an old-fashioned planner who prefers to keep a paper trail or you're the type who stores everything digitally for easy access from your laptop or mobile device, choose whichever method works best for you. If you're not into creating your own filing system—digital or paper—there are tons of kits, binders, and online tools out there to help you stay organized and on top of it all (see "Organizer Options," page 18). Here are some tips to store the massive amount of information, papers, and more you will gather over the next several months (or weeks!).

USING ONLINE FILING SYSTEMS Eliminate the paper with online storage and planning apps: One of the best ways to keep your information organized, readily accessible, and off your kitchen table is to go digital, using your computer, your tablet, your smart phone, and online tools and apps to store and access the majority of your documents, notes, and information. Keep all your vendors' contact information at your fingertips by storing phone numbers and e-mail addresses in your phone. And you may even want to create a wedding "in-box," designating one e-mail address for all wedding-related correspondence, so that all your conversations with various vendors will be in one easily searchable spot.

When searching for tips and advice, real wedding inspiration, and gowns on TheKnot.com, use our Real Wedding Notebook to gather it all in one place—and organize it by category (go to TheKnot.com/tools). You can also track your to-dos, budget, guest list, and ideas—and update them on the go with mobile planners.

KEEPING EVERYTHING IN ONE PLACE Okay, the reality is: Even in a digital world, there's still a ton of paper to manage in the process of planning a wedding. Buy a three-ring binder where you can compile all your correspondence, contracts, receipts, meeting notes, ideas, and photos you want to show your vendors. File them into separate sections for each part of your wedding day (flowers, décor, dresses, hairstyles, cakes).

Staying on top of your to-dos
Yes, planning an affair of this size and scale, with so many details and decisions to attend to, can feel overwhelming. But it doesn't have to be. The key is breaking down all those to-do's into manageable pieces, mapping out a planning timeline, and then checking in regularly to keep yourselves on track.

TAKE IT ONE STEP AT A TIME Put together a wedding planning schedule and do things one by one, in a logical order, so you don't take on too much too fast and end up with everything snowballing around you. Don't hire any vendors before you've confirmed your date; don't check out too many vendors in one day; don't design your cake before you've envisioned your flowers; don't book a band before you've settled on a space. For a detailed list of planning tasks in order of when they should be done, turn back to pages x–xiii for a yearlong timeline.

REAL BRIDE ADVICE
staying sane while planning

"The more you can get done in advance, the more time you'll have to enjoy your engagement, and the more money-saving opportunities present themselves."
—TWINKLE82576

---

organizer options

WEDDING BINDER

best for Old-school organizers who want to keep every piece of paper, receipt, and swatch.

the basics This is the best way to keep your wedding ideas, notes, and contracts all in one place. Use dividers to separate sections and make finding entries simple.

WEDDING APP

best for On-the-go brides and grooms and anyone who doesn't want stacks of paper.

the basics Save all images and ideas virtually, and use Web-based tools to track to-dos and guests. You can even scan all contracts and save them in a folder accessible from any device. Check out our planning apps at TheKnot.com/planning.

WEDDING BOX

best for Busy people who don't have lots of time to organize their papers.

the basics Keep a container for storing samples of invites or favors, or clips of images that you like. That way they'll all be in one place, and when you're done collecting, you can easily pick out favorites.

STOP PROCRASTINATING Get as much done as possible in the first few months so that the last few won't be hectic. One mistake that many couples make is basking in the glow of their engagement until six months before their wedding date. Then they try to cram all of the planning into too short a period of time. Choose a day of the week when you'll focus on the wedding details—or several days, if you're on a short timeline.

SET DEADLINES Once you determine your wedding date, set specific days by which you want to get things accomplished, using our planning checklist as a guide. For example, you got engaged in June, and your wedding date is April 24. Mark August 31 as your goal date for having the ceremony location and reception hall reserved.

2

the budget

It's essential to determine who's contributing to the wedding costs and how much you have to spend from the start (read: before you fall in love with a venue, dress, or other detail that's outside your budget). Because as momentous as your wedding may be, it's still only the first step in your voyage through life together—and that journey will, of course, involve many postwedding expenses (honeymoon, home, kids), which couples often forget about during the thrill of planning a wedding. That said, whether you have $100,000, $10,000, or $1,000 to spend, with careful organization, zealous budgeting, and a few money-saving tricks, you can have the wedding you always wanted.

> TIMELINE
> ## PLANNING
>
> **12+ months before**
> Assess your finances
>
> Talk to your parents
> about budget
>
> Set your spending priorities
>
> Decide how you will
> track expenses
>
> Consider creating a
> separate bank account for
> wedding expenses

We're several months into planning our wedding, and my future in-laws have not yet offered to make any contribution. I don't want to offend them, but we definitely could use their help. Can I bring it up?

The way you interact with your brand-new family members while planning your wedding can set the tone for how you'll get along once you're married, so it makes sense to be sensitive. Each of you should approach your parents alone, since money is a notoriously touchy issue. Consider a light but direct opener, such as, "You know, Mom and Dad, we were talking about how great it would be if you could help us pay for the wedding so we can invite everyone on both our lists and not have to cut people who are important to you and us." If money is an issue for your in-laws, figure out some nonmonetary aid they can give you (researching vendor prices, reserving hotel rooms, addressing and mailing invitations). Regardless of their response, just be gracious.

WHO PAYS?

Before you nail down your budget and begin allocating dollar amounts for different wedding elements, you need to figure out who will actually be paying. Because those who pay also have a say in how much you'll have to spend—and how you'll spend it. In the days of yore, it was the bride's family who paid for the wedding—and made every decision. Today, the division of financial duties is much more fluid.

Splitting it with your parents
With the one-third approach, the bride's family, the groom's family, and the couple—yes, you—each contribute. You're getting the best of both worlds: You're not flying solo (and possibly dipping into your nest egg), but you're also not completely relinquishing financial control (and the creative authority that goes along with it). The three-way split is also a surefire way to make both families feel like significant partners in your wedding preparations. There are two ways to work out this arrangement: You can approximate the total dollar amount you're going to need and then split it three ways, or you can designate specific things that each party will pay for, based on how much they can contribute.

Paying for it yourselves
Legions of modern couples are opting to pay for their weddings themselves. Some don't have families able (or around) to help out; others are making lots more money than their parents; still others simply don't want anyone else's input in the planning of such a personal, momentous event. The upside of this option is total control over every decision. The downside: All the financial and planning responsibilities fall on your shoulders.

Bride's parents pay all
Never *expect* your parents to pay for your wedding. Contrary to popular belief, it's not a birthright. If you're among the lucky few whose parents are prepared to foot the entire bill, you may still have to deal with one potentially sleep-disturbing problem: You have to listen to their opinions and honor their wishes for the wedding, too. Even if you trust your parents not to become wedding control freaks, set some ground rules early on. Be frank with them about the things you're absolutely not willing to budge on, as well as the areas where you're totally open to their input.

Before you approach your folks about making a contribution, get an idea of the costs involved. Ask for estimates from venues and vendors you're considering and check out TheKnot.com/budget to get a better feel for the average costs of things. That way, everyone involved will have a

the budget breakdown

Here's a list of the traditional wedding expense allocation. It can give you a rough idea of how you might want to split your budget up, but as with any wedding tradition, you should feel free to deviate from it as much (or as little) as you want.

bride's side

Reception costs (including food, drink, decorations, rentals, and music)

Wedding planner or coordinator

Bride's dress, veil, accessories, hair and makeup, and trousseau (read: lingerie and honeymoon clothes)

Stationery (invitations, announcements, postage, thank-you notes, wedding programs, and all other paper elements)

Photographer and/or videographer

Ceremony costs (house of worship donation or site rental, sexton, organist)

Floral arrangements for ceremony (including huppah, if you're having a Jewish wedding ceremony) and reception, plus bouquets and corsages for bridesmaids and flower girl and groom's boutonniere

Transportation of bridal party to and from ceremony and reception

Groom's wedding ring

Bridesmaid and other attendant gifts

Wedding gift for the groom

All tips (for waitstaff, band or DJ, photographer, parking attendants, etc.)

Bridesmaid luncheon

groom's side

Bride's rings and wedding bands

Alcohol for reception

Honeymoon, including transportation to the airport

Wedding gift for bride

Marriage license

Groomsman gifts

Bride's bouquet and going-away corsage, boutonnieres for men (other than the groom), and corsages for mothers and grandmothers

Officiant's fee

Groom's attire

Travel and lodging expenses for groom's parents

Rehearsal dinner

Wedding gift for newlyweds

Bachelor's dinner

realistic idea of the financial requirements—and you won't have to deal with the stress of dropping last-minute bombshells ("Mom, Dad, the caterer's bill was four thousand dollars more than we thought—sorry!").

It's also a good idea to sit down with your parents and come up with a spending cap now, so you won't have to ask for another check later.

COST CONSIDERATIONS

If you're planning on a formal candlelit dinner in the grand ballroom of that amazing hotel downtown, your budget is clearly going to have to be much bigger than if you've sketched out an afternoon tea and dessert party in your parents' pretty backyard. In general, there are several major factors that will really affect what you'll need to set aside.

Guest list size
There's a per-head cost for food and liquor, and these two are typically the biggest expense in the whole wedding, so changing the size of the guest list is the surest way to increase or decrease your costs. On top of that, you'll save on all your other details, including décor, stationery, favors, and rentals, because you won't need as much of everything.

Wedding setting
Some cities and towns are just more expensive than others. New York, Chicago, and Los Angeles are the obvious culprits, but small towns and remote destinations can entail greater costs if things like flowers and talent have to come from afar. Tourist towns can also up your wedding price tag during peak season. Likewise, certain venues are more expensive than others. Some—such as a city park—come with no (or low) fees. Others might cost you the equivalent of a year's college tuition. Also, be aware that many popular locations have head count minimums, meaning they won't host a wedding that's too small, and some may also have a per-head minimum.

Date and time
Highly sought-after seasons and days of the week are pricier for obvious reasons. An evening reception is usually more expensive than a brunch or afternoon reception, not only because of higher catering costs for dinner but also because people tend to drink less during the daytime, and many couples choose to go more low-key on elements like lighting, music, and décor during the daytime.

Wedding style
The more formal the affair, the more expensive, because you'll have to match the site, food, and musical entertainment to

the overall upscale tone. The outlay for a full six-course meal is typically greater than for a cocktail soiree with mostly hors d'oeuvres; the fee for a twelve-piece band is greater than that for a DJ or a quartet; all-out décor like lighting, specialty linens, and dramatic floral displays also will run up the bill. Plus, fancier affairs tend to be larger.

THE BUDGET BREAKDOWN

Once you know how much money you have to work with and where it's all coming from, it's time to figure out how you're going to spend it. You have to break the big number down, allocating parts of your wedding budget to each of the various elements—flowers, favors, music, food, etc.—based on what's most important to you. There's a detailed budgeting worksheet in the appendix, but we've listed the traditional breakdowns here as a general guideline for getting you started. Use it to estimate your spending but you should also adjust the breakdown based on your priorities.

Wedding planner
If you intend to hire a wedding planner, you'll also want to subtract that cost from your total budget before you break it down into other categories. A full-service wedding consultant will cost approximately 10 to 15 percent of your total budget (for more on how planners price their services, see chapter 6).

Reception
Assume that about 50 percent of your total budget will go toward your reception, including the site rental, catering, bar, cake (and cutting fee), rentals, as well as tax and service fees. Even if you're having a home-cooked backyard brunch, chances are that the cost of buying ingredients, renting chairs (and possibly a tent), and hiring servers will eat up about half your budget. About 40 percent of that will go toward the catering (hors d'oeuvres, the meal, and any additional food items like specialty bars and late-night snacks), beverages, the cake, and service charges, with the remaining 10 percent going toward renting out the reception site, plus any of the standard rentals you'll need that aren't covered by your venue (like tents, chairs, tables, dinnerware).

Documentation
Devote at least 10 to 15 percent to documenting your day, including photography and videography (shooting fees, as well as the actual end product of prints, albums, or edited video), plus any other elements you decide to include, like an engagement shoot or a photo booth.

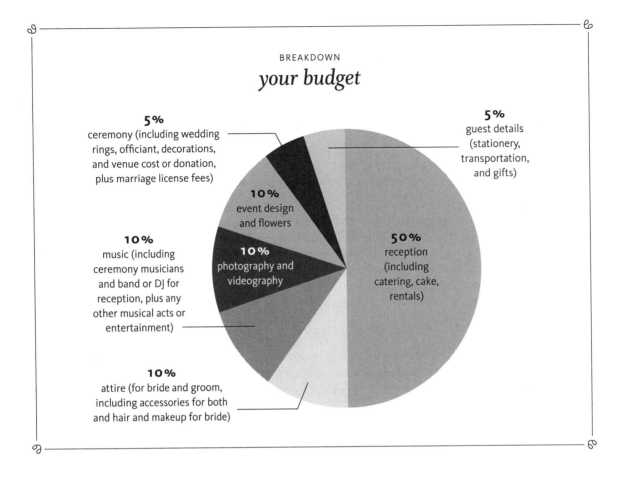

BREAKDOWN
your budget

5%
ceremony (including wedding rings, officiant, decorations, and venue cost or donation, plus marriage license fees)

5%
guest details (stationery, transportation, and gifts)

10%
event design and flowers

10%
music (including ceremony musicians and band or DJ for reception, plus any other musical acts or entertainment)

10%
photography and videography

50%
reception (including catering, cake, rentals)

10%
attire (for bride and groom, including accessories for both and hair and makeup for bride)

Attire

About 10 percent will go toward your wedding dress and formalwear. That includes alterations, headpiece/veil, hair/makeup, shoes, lingerie, and other accessories, plus the groom's attire and going-away garb for both of you. Professional hair and makeup costs are included in that 10 percent as well. (In most cases, the bride's attire will make up the majority of that 10 percent, but if your groom will only settle for a bespoke suit, adjust the budget accordingly.)

Flowers and event design

About 10 percent will be needed to cover flowers (the bride's bouquet, bridesmaid bouquets, boutonnieres, corsages, and ceremony and reception arrangements), plus, additional design components like lighting, specialty rentals (linens and chair covers), and decorations (signage and votives) will also fall within this budget.

Music and entertainment

About 10 percent will go toward both the ceremony music (vocalists, string quartet, organist) and the reception music (band or DJ), as well as any additional entertainment or music you will include in your wedding.

Ceremony and officiant

Overall, about 5 percent of your budget should be reserved for your ceremony, including the ceremony venue fee, officiant, and décor. About 2 percent will go toward the ceremony location and officiant fees or a donation, plus programs and accessories like an aisle runner or ring pillow, as well as marriage license costs. The remaining 3 percent of this will go toward wedding rings for both the bride and groom (note: This does not include the engagement ring).

Invitations and guest details

This final category tends to be where wedding budgets vary the most, but reserve about 5 percent of your budget for the smaller details (some of which you may not include). That 5 percent will cover all stationery elements, transportation and accommodations, gifts, and any extras. To break it down even further, 2 to 3 percent of your budget will go toward wedding stationery—invitations, announcements, save-the-dates, thank-you notes, menus, and any other wedding paper you choose to have. About 2 percent will go toward transporting you and your crew (including your rides to the ceremony and to the reception, transport for the rest of the wedding party, and guest shuttles and parking)—plus the expense of the "bridal suite" for the wedding night (or weekend). Depending on the size of your bridal party and guest list, anywhere from 1 to 2 percent will go toward attendants' gifts, welcome bags, and favors.

Taxes and tips

We all know that there are taxes on almost everything and that certain services call for a tip, but most couples don't realize how much they'll end up spending on both when all is said and done. Fact is, things cost more than you think, and it's easy to get caught off guard by costs you may not have considered. The good news is, if you know what to expect, you can pad your reception budget accordingly. By now, you're probably aware that your reception bill will be far heftier than, say, the price of a pair of jeans, and you should prepare yourself now for the fact that the taxes will probably also be proportionately large. Taxes aren't typically factored into your original venue and/or caterer quotes, so always ask, and make sure to account for them in your reception budget.

ASK CARLEY
TIP GUESTS OFF

Gratuity is included for the bartender at our catering hall. At the reception, should we put up a sign by the bar that says, "The bride and groom have provided all gratuities for the evening," so guests know they don't need to tip?
Even if gratuity is included, as the hosts, you should cover all tips—for valet, coat check and bathroom attendants, as well as bartenders. Guests shouldn't be expected to open their wallets for anything related to your reception. Most wedding guests know that the bride and groom take care of the tips, so a sign isn't necessary. But make sure to let your caterer (and reception manager) know that you'll cover all tips and that tip jars shouldn't be displayed anywhere. Have it written into your contract to confirm it won't be an issue.

breakdowns for three different budgets

Not sure how to divide up your budget? Check out these sample breakdowns for three different-sized budgets.

category	average wedding budget ($30,000; 100 guests)	luxe wedding budget ($50,000; 150 guests)	blowout wedding budget ($200,000; 250 guests)
PLANNER/ COORDINATOR	$1,000	$3,000	$25,000
CEREMONY (including officiant fee, location fee, accessories)	$780	$750	$1,200
RECEPTION VENUE (including rentals, tax, tip & service charges)	$2,400	$4,000	$12,000
CATERING	$11,400	$15,500	$70,000
CAKE	$750	$900	$3,500
FLOWERS & EVENT DESIGN	$2,400	$5,000	$13,000
MUSIC AND ENTERTAINMENT	$1,400	$2,000	$20,000
TRANSPORTATION	$750	$1,800	$4,500
ACCOMMODATIONS	$150	$250	$1,000
PHOTOGRAPHY & VIDEOGRAPHY	$3,600	$5,000	$22,000
INVITATIONS & STATIONERY	$900	$1,800	$6,000
FAVORS & GIFTS	$900	$1,000	$2,000
ATTIRE	$2,670	$5,000	$14,000
HAIR, MAKEUP & GROOMING	$300	$1,000	$1,800
WEDDING RINGS	$600	$3,000	$4,000

As with taxes, many couples don't realize how much they'll end up owing for service charges and tips when all is said and done. The "service charge" is not a tip for the event staff—it's actually an additional fee that venues charge to cover their own cost of hiring servers, coat checkers, and bathroom and parking attendants, which typically amounts to 20 to 25 percent of the event's total food and drink fee. Though your tax bill will depend on the total amount of money spent, as well as the location of the event (taxes vary from city to city), it's a good bet to set aside a third of your total reception bill for both taxes and tips. Once you get the proposed fee, add the service charge percentage and the tax estimate, so they're already accounted for in your reception bill.

You should also set aside at least $800 for gratuities (the additional amount given to your vendors for their hard work). As with a waiter or your hairdresser, tips are generally expected unless you're unhappy with the service. (See "Tipping Guide," right, for whom to tip and how much to give.)

Extra expenses and forgotten fees

You'd assume that the rental companies would include these fees in the per-item costs (do they honestly think you can fit 150 chiavari chairs in your own car?), but surprisingly, they don't. The price you're given is almost always a product-only price. Tax, tip, and delivery, which can run from $100 to $500 or more, are additional and should be included in your budget from the outset. Ask the rental company what their shipping, packaging, and setup fees are up front—if the cost is too high for your budget, shop around a bit. You might find that you'll actually save money by renting items from a more expensive company that includes delivery costs at no extra charge. Also, keep in mind: Your cake baker and florist may not include delivery and setup in their quotes, either.

PICKING YOUR PRIORITIES

The guidelines for breaking down your budget that we just mapped out for you are a good jumping-off point, but every couple's priorities are different, and your budget should be allocated according to yours. The point is to take your vision (and those of any contributors) and break it up into realistic pieces so it can actually happen. This means considering things like whether you absolutely must have all five hundred guests on your list, how much hot weather matters when it comes to your dream day, and if having a cake and a dessert table is important to you two.

CHEAT SHEET
tipping guide

Main reception contact:
$200–$300

On-site coordinator:
$200–$300

Wedding planner:
15 percent of the fee

Catering manager:
$200 plus

Chef: $50–$100

Waitstaff: $25–$30 each

Bartenders: 10 percent of total bar bill (to be split among them)

Hair and makeup team:
15–20 percent of the total bill

Delivery and setup staff: $15–$25 per person

Reception staff:
15–20 percent of the reception bill (to be divided by site manager)

Coatroom attendants:
$1–$2 per guest

Parking attendants:
$1–$2 per car

Officiant: $75–$100 donation or tip

Florist: $100 plus

Reception Band/DJ:
$25–$50 per musician; $100–$200 for a single DJ

Ceremony Musicians:
15–20 percent of the total fee

designate a tipper
The host of the event,
one of the dads, the best
man, or the wedding
consultant usually
handles this job.

plan ahead
Have tips ready in sealed
(labeled) envelopes, and
give them to the
designated distributor
before the ceremony to
distribute at the end of
the wedding. Most likely
you'll want to go ahead
and tip everyone who
did a great job, but you
won't want to have to
think too hard about it
when it comes time.

don't tip owners
If any of the vendors
working on your
wedding own their own
company (i.e., if the
person photographing
your wedding also owns
the studio, your band
doesn't work with an
agency and manages
themselves, or your
consultant owns her own
planning business), you
are not expected to tip
them though a gift is a
thoughtful way to
express your
appreciation.

Throughout the budgeting process, the goal is to chip away at the extraneous details that you can forgo so that you can stay within your budget without having to sacrifice the wedding elements that are the most important to you. If there's no question in your mind that your beverage bill is going to be huge given your passion for fine wines, maybe you should rethink the couture dress. If your hearts are set on the waterfront venue in prime wedding season, perhaps you can scale back your expenses by opting for a four-piece band over a sixteen-piece band and a basic photography package instead of a paparazzi extravaganza.

Start by mapping out all the possible elements you may wish to include in your nuptials. Some—like the officiant's fee and the refreshments—are musts; others—like $700 stilettos, a shuttle for your guests, or a string quartet for your ceremony—are optional. Then it's time to choose which items on your list are the most important to you and which you could live without if you had to.

What happens if your priorities don't align? Once you've both listed them in order of importance, each of you gets your top two items. Then find a middle road, taking into account where your money will go the farthest and make the biggest impact (see "Worth the Splurge," page 30). It's easy to get carried away as you start planning, but think about whether it's worth going into debt or dueling with each other over minutiae. Maybe you'd be fine if that glorious send-off with a white-dove release turned into an enthusiastic sprinkling of birdseed instead.

STAYING IN THE BLACK

It's easy to get tempted by all the options that will be thrown your way and to lose track of what you're spending when there are so many line items involved. If you aren't careful, you could end up running over budget before you're even halfway there, leaving you to skimp on (or skip) some of the most important things (you do want to take a honeymoon, right?). The key to staying on budget is staying organized.

Get organized
To help you stay organized, use an online budgeting tool or an old-fashioned spreadsheet with four columns: expense category (reception, photography, flowers), percentage of budget (estimate) it will cost, the total dollar amount, the deposit amount, and the remaining balance due.

Once you have all your information in one easy-to-read document, you're ready to build a budget. Take the total dollar amount you have allocated and calculate the percentage of your budget that you're willing

wedding insurance coverage

Every insurance policy and every wedding scenario is different. But here's a general picture of what you can expect to be protected by your wedding insurance plan.

WHAT'S COVERED

site Check to see if your ceremony and reception sites (and caterer, if hired separately) are already insured. If not, wedding insurance can cover the cost of an unavoidable cancellation (such as damage or inaccessibility to the site) if, say, your reception hall is unable to honor your reservation because it has burned in a fire, experienced an electrical outage, or closed down. Sometimes this policy covers the rehearsal dinner site, too.

weather This applies to any weather conditions that prevent the bride, groom, any relative whose presence at the wedding is essential, or the majority of the guests from reaching the premises where the wedding is to take place. Insurance covers rescheduling the wedding and all the details involved, such as ceremony flowers, tent rental, and reception food.

vendor no-show A wedding insurance policy usually covers cancellation or postponement of the wedding if key vendors—the caterer or the officiant, for example—fail to show up.

sickness or injury Wedding insurance may also include sickness or injury to the bride, groom, or anyone else essential to the wedding.

military or Job Insurance can cover postponement of the wedding if the bride or groom suddenly gets called to military duty. This can also apply to a last-minute corporate move—that is, the bride's company suddenly relocates her to another city.

WHAT'S NOT COVERED

a change of heart In other words, cold feet don't count.

jewelry Accessories like watches, jewelry, or semiprecious gemstones or pearls (even if they're attached to your dress) may not be covered.

your engagement ring While your wedding rings may be covered by the policy, your engagement ring probably won't. So take out insurance for your engagement ring as soon as you get engaged.

---

to spend on each expense to get the dollar amount for each category. That way you'll know what you really can—and can't—afford when meeting with vendors.

Track your spending

Enter every payment commitment you make and every item you buy along the way into your budgeting tool or spreadsheet, and check in regularly to see how it's all adding up. If you go over in one area, cut something from another.

Protecting your investment

For just about everything from a sudden cancellation owing to a hurricane to a no-show vendor

worth the splurge

Make sure your dollars are devoted in meaningful ways.

the photographer

Your amateur photographer friend may take great photos, but a professional wedding photographer will know the exact details to capture and the right angles from which to do so. You'll cherish your photos from the wedding forever, so make the investment.

music

If you splurge on a great band or DJ who will have you and your guests dancing all night, you'll look back on it as money well spent.

the dress

Okay, we're not about to give you a free ride to remortgage your home so you can walk down the aisle in a $25,000 dream gown. But we will say that your dress—*the* dress—is a definite "spend." And regardless of what you pay for the dress, don't skimp on the alterations.

food and drink

Your guests don't expect you to serve filet mignon and lobster at your wedding, but if you serve food fit for a cafeteria, they will remember your reception for all the wrong reasons. And no matter what, do not have a cash bar. Limit your drink choices to beer and wine and cut costs elsewhere.

and a damaged gown, wedding insurance can help protect you against financial losses and give you some serious peace of mind.

A basic insurance policy covers loss of photos, videos, attire, presents, rings, and deposits (translation: reimburses you for a percentage of the costs after the fact), while general liability insurance covers accidents, like if a guest slips and breaks his leg. Couples can also take out supplemental policies to recover damage to those wedding-related items. For example, you might take out a separate policy that would pay to have the photographs retaken after the fact if the photographer fails to appear or the files are corrupted or otherwise damaged. You can also take out an additional policy that would pay for the costs of buying a new wedding cake and new flowers if yours are damaged or a no-show on your wedding day and you're able to replace them.

top ten cost-cutting tips

1
Cut the guest list. This will slash your catering costs and save you money on all the details like invitations, favors, rentals, and the number of centerpieces.

2
Be up-front with your planner (if you have one), site manager, and vendors from the very beginning. They can help you find ways to stretch your dollars, and they will appreciate your not wasting their time by having them pitch options outside of your price range.

3
Hold your ceremony and reception in one spot—it will cut travel time for vendors you pay by the hour and eliminate transportation and additional site rental fees.

4
Getting married during a slow time of year will give you negotiating power. If you've always wanted a June wedding, then consider having it during the week, or during the day if a weekend is more suitable for you and your guests.

5
While researching reception venues, look for a space with built-in décor you love, as well as nice tables, chairs, and dinnerware to cut down on your rental costs.

6
Consider a Friday, Sunday, or even Thursday wedding instead of Saturday. There will probably be better availability and you may be able to get a lower rate on the space and your vendors.

7
Serve only beer and wine plus a signature cocktail instead of having an open bar.

8
Choose a full-service venue, like a resort, wedding hall, or private club, where they have all the essentials and will include them in a package.

9
Scale back on the number of courses (serve three instead of five) or type of meal (skip the surf and turf in favor of chicken and fish and a pasta dish).

10
Consider an afternoon or brunch reception. People tend to drink less during the day, brunch fare tends to be less expensive, and some vendors and venues charge lower rates for daytime functions.

BONUS TIP: Go to TheKnot.com/save for tons more budgeting tips and tricks for everything from your flowers and your dress to your venue and band.

3

when and where

"You're engaged?! Congratulations! When and where are you getting married?" If you haven't been asked this yet, get ready, because it's going to be the question you hear over and over again (and debate with yourself quite a few times). These decisions are trickier than you may have thought and the answers are different for each couple—after all, they'll arguably have the biggest impact on your wedding.

A lot of factors, from personal preferences to family and friends to holidays and budget, play a role in deciding where and when to marry. While some couples choose their date first and let that help determine their venue, others prefer to pick the place first. Regardless of how you answer that age-old question, you'll want to get going on both pronto, because top venues and vendors book up to a year in advance.

TIMELINE

PLANNING

12+ months before
Start scouting venues

Check date availability with
key vendors and key family

10–12+ months before
Finalize your date

Book your venue

DIVINING A DATE AND TIME

Choosing a date will affect some of the most important elements of
your wedding, including who will come, how much it will cost, and
where you'll have it. Like everything in life, there will be pros and cons
to virtually every date you consider. To pick the right one, prioritize the
factors that are most important to you. Then, after you've settled on
your ideal date, choose two or three backups just in case the venue or
caterer of your dreams is otherwise committed or your best friend can't
possibly make it.

Calendar considerations

The exact wedding date you select
will depend on several variables and people. First and foremost, keep
engagement length in mind and think about how much time you'll need
to prepare for your dream wedding (as we initially mentioned, we find
about a year is about right for most couples). Also, consider the style
sketch you created in the first chapter, as well as the budget you created
in the second one. Here's what else to consider.

BLACKOUT DATES Consult a clergyperson about religious
restrictions surrounding certain dates. Often, there are blackout
periods when it is not acceptable to get married. For example, some
rabbis will not perform weddings between Passover and Shavuot, and
many ministers are reluctant to officiate ceremonies during Lent.

KEY PEOPLE Check with family members and friends whom you
couldn't live without at your wedding, like siblings, grandparents,
best friends, and beloved godparents or mentors, before setting
anything in stone.

SIGNIFICANT DATES You may want your wedding date to have
sentimental value, commemorating your first kiss, your grandparents'
anniversary, or Valentine's Day—or not. On that note, you may
not want to schedule your special day for a date that is sentimental
to someone else in your family or inner circle, like your parents'
anniversary or your sister's thirtieth birthday. You're totally entitled to
share this day with no one if you want.

SITE AND VENDOR AVAILABILITY Is there a church or venue
you've had your heart set on since childhood? Is there an amazing
photographer or DJ you just have to have for your wedding? If so, his
or her schedule is going to influence—and may even dictate—yours.
Run potential dates by any possible ceremony and reception sites or
preferred vendors before you decide.

dates to think twice about

From major and religious holidays to big-time sporting events to days of remembrance, you'll want to consider the following before choosing your date.

Martin Luther King Jr. Day (always the third Monday in January)

Chinese New Year (exact date changes every year, but it's always in January or February)

Super Bowl Sunday (changes every year, but it's always sometime in late January or early February)

Valentine's Day (February 14)

Presidents' Day (always the third Monday in February)

Oscar night (always a Sunday, but exact date changes every year; usually around February)

March Madness (exact dates change every year)

Ides of March (March 15)

Saint Patrick's Day (March 17)

Palm Sunday (always the Sunday before Easter)

Easter Sunday (changes every year, but falls around the spring equinox, typically in late March or early April)

Passover (begins at sunset the night before; exact date changes every year, but typically in late March or early April)

April Fool's Day (April 1)

Tax Day and the weekend before (April 15)

Mother's Day (always the second Sunday in May)

Memorial Day (always the last Monday in May)

Father's Day (always the third Sunday in June)

Fourth of July

Labor Day (always the first Monday in September)

September 11

Rosh Hashanah (begins at sunset the night before the first day of Tishri in the Jewish calendar—typically in September or early October—and can last for two days)

Yom Kippur (begins at sunset the night before the tenth day of Tishri in the Jewish calendar—which typically falls in late September or early to mid-October—and lasts eight days)

Columbus Day (always the second Monday in October)

Halloween (October 31)

Thanksgiving (always the fourth Thursday in November)

Hanukkah (begins at sunset and lasts eight days; always starts on the twenty-fifth day of the month of Kislev and goes to the second day of Tevet in the Jewish calendar—typically sometime in December or late November)

Christmas Eve and Day (December 24/December 25)

Kwanzaa (always December 26 through January 1)

Pearl Harbor Remembrance Day (December 7)

New Year's Eve and Day (December 31/January 1)

Friday the Thirteenth

BUDGET Some times of year are generally more expensive than others. Likewise, certain days of the week, times of day, and even specific dates are pricier. Depending on how cost-conscious you need to be, this may be a factor in your decision.

WEDDING STYLE Certain kinds of weddings work better during specific seasons and/or times of day. Formal clothing is much more fun when it's not 95 degrees outside; family affairs—with lots of wee ones—are best scheduled during the day.

LOCAL HAPPENINGS Research local conventions and events taking place in your wedding location during your wedding weekend. Events like the New York City marathon or the Taste of Chicago can make it hard for your guests to get around and find hotel rooms. Similarly, think about the tourist season where you're marrying—you'll either want to wed during the off-season or plan far enough in advance that your guests will be able to find flights, accommodations, and anything else they need before the crowds do.

WEATHER This one's completely out of your control, but if you know where you're getting married, you should take the elements into consideration. There are no guarantees, true—but if you know that it usually rains twenty-eight out of thirty days in April in the area where you want to host your outdoor wedding, then you should probably rethink your plans. Just remember: According to some traditions, rain on your wedding day is good luck.

DAYS IN DEMAND Saturday nights are the most popular—and expensive—times to wed, and venues and vendors can book up to two years in advance for Saturdays, especially during peak wedding season—summer, spring, and fall. The attractions of a Saturday wedding are obvious: Out-of-towners have ample time to get to your wedding without missing work, and guests have roughly twenty-four hours to nurse any hangovers before heading back to the office.

Still, increasingly more couples are choosing off days, like Friday, Sunday, or even midweek days, for their weddings, as they find that being flexible about the day of the week can make a big dollar difference on both—up to 30 percent. With Fridays and Sundays, it's more of a scramble to get to and from the wedding, and with Sundays there's no chill-out day—but they're still far more convenient than a weekday. Note: Friday night weddings are becoming increasingly popular, so you'll want to make sure you settle on a date well in advance if you're planning to marry on a Friday or Saturday. While a midweek affair is not advisable if you're inviting a lot of out-of-towners or are planning

an all-night bash, it's a great way to cut costs and get a better pick
of vendors.

You may also save on hotel rooms for out-of-town guests, depending
on your locale and the hotel: Hotels that are popular with business
travelers will be pricier during the workweek but may offer great deals
on weekends, while B & Bs, hotels, and resorts that are popular for
weekend getaways and vacations may have higher weekend rates and
better deals during the week. Religious considerations also can come
into play. For example, many Jewish weddings take place on Sunday in
deference to the Jewish Sabbath, which lasts from sundown on Friday
until sundown on Saturday.

MAJOR HOLIDAYS Holidays like New Year's Eve and Halloween
are perfect for couples looking to build a wedding with a theme (and
to celebrate their anniversary on a holiday every year). Remember,
however, that some vendors are in high demand for certain holidays.
While a Valentine's Day wedding may sound romantic, getting a florist
to give you great service at that time may be a nightmare, and bands
are tough to book for New Year's Eve. Plus, prices go up and availability
goes down during holidays. Also, make note of holidays that change
dates every year, like Jewish and Muslim holidays, the Chinese New
Year, Easter, and Thanksgiving. Even if you'll manage to just miss them
for the wedding day itself, potential conflicts with your anniversary
may be an issue.

LONG WEEKENDS While a three-day holiday weekend like
Memorial Day or Labor Day may seem like a great idea when it comes
to accommodating your legions of long-distance guests, your local pals
may begrudge your interfering with three days of much-needed R & R.
Plus, getting to your chosen locale will be more of a hassle (think
traffic) and expensive (airfares tend to go up over long weekends). If
you do choose a holiday weekend wedding date, be sure you give your
guests plenty of notice before they make other plans.

MONSTER MONTHS These are the months when it seems like
everybody and her cousin is getting hitched. The big four are May,
June, July, and October, with August and September hot on their heels.
The more popular your wedding month, the less choice you'll have in
terms of the site, vendors, and exact timing. Competition for services
may drive up your wedding expenses, too. By opting for an off-season
month (November; January through April), you're bound to get more
personalized service from your vendors and have more control over the
minutiae of your event. The catch is that many vendors take time off

during these months, so check that your date doesn't line up with your top-choice photographer's vacation.

BUMMER DATES Beware of scheduling your wedding for "bummer" days—any day during the week before Tax Day (April 15), the anniversary of your father's death, or a date that may be associated with a less-than-happy time for family and friends (like 9/11). Superstitious couples may want to avoid days associated with bad luck, like the Ides of March (March 15), and if you don't want any funny business on the altar, it's best to avoid April Fool's Day (April 1), too.

MAJOR SPORTING EVENTS Unless you don't care if half the room is looking down at their phones to check the score during the ceremony, avoid scheduling your wedding on the day of a big sporting event. Think Super Bowl Sunday, March Madness, and the U.S. Open.

LUCKY DATES In certain cultures, different dates and days of the week are luckier than others. For example, in Chinese culture, dates that include lucky numbers like eight and two, and even numbers (which are considered luckier than odds) are considered fortuitous. Likewise, Chinese astrology says that certain dates are luckier than others per the Chinese almanac. And according to English folklore, Wednesday is actually the luckiest day to get married and Saturday brings "no luck at all."

Power hours If you're thinking black tie or an adults-only dance party, clearly nighttime is your best option. But the earlier the festivities, the more budget flexibility you'll have. A brunch, lunch, or afternoon tea will cost substantially less than an evening dinner reception, there probably will be less demand for that time slot, and these are good choices if you're inviting lots of children. Keep in mind that some churches and synagogues have strict times for when they'll hold ceremonies in order to clear the congregation for evening services, so you may need to consider an early reception or plan activities to entertain guests between the ceremony and reception.

THE LOCATION
You won't be able to book your venues (or any vendors) until you know the city you're getting married in, so the two of you should decide this not-so-minor detail as soon as possible. It used to be a given that couples would say their vows in the bride's hometown. For many, that's

TIMELINE
reception

Breakfast:
8 a.m.–11 a.m.

Brunch:
11 a.m.–3 p.m.

Luncheon:
1 p.m.–5 p.m.

Tea:
3 p.m.–6 p.m.

Cocktail:
6 p.m.–11 p.m.

Evening:
7 p.m.–11 p.m.

Dessert:
9 p.m.–11 p.m.

Midnight Snack:
10 p.m.–1 a.m.

NOTE: The ceremony is typically held thirty minutes to an hour earlier if it's held on the same site as the reception. If you have two separate sites, build in extra time for travel, padding an extra 15 minutes for traffic when determining your ceremony start time.

still true, but today's couples are just as likely to wed in the groom's hometown, in their college town, in the city they live in now, or even at their honeymoon destination. And some couples are hosting two or more receptions so they can celebrate with loved ones scattered across the country or around the globe.

Picking a place
Before you start scoping out possible sites in your chosen locale, think about what you want in your ultimate venue: Blank walls (like a loft) or ready-made design (such as a hotel ballroom)? Indoors or out? To help you decide what type of venue is right for you, consider the following factors.

RECEPTION AND CEREMONY First, you have to determine if you need one location or two. If you're getting married in a house of worship, you already have one covered, and your next consideration will be where you want to celebrate after—and how you and your guests will get there (see chapter 23 for transportation options).

PROS AND CONS

going to the chapel . . .

Whether it's a church, a temple, or a mosque, many couples still choose the traditional route of a religious ceremony in a house of worship. Here are some factors to consider when deciding whether you want to host a religiously grounded ceremony.

PROS

personal significance: A religious institution may have special meaning to you or your families, and hosting your wedding there will allow you to incorporate your faith.

free décor: Many churches and temples are beautiful and already fully decorated. Plus, you don't have to worry about setup since most have a built-in altar and seating.

ceremony music: Many houses of worship provide music.

CONS

time constraints: Your timeline may be limited based on when the church and/or officiants are available for wedding services. Many Catholic churches only host afternoon services on Saturdays, so you'll have to coordinate with your reception space or figure out a plan for guests who don't live nearby during downtime.

double the work: You'll have two venues to book, two venues to potentially decorate, and the extra costs associated with both.

transportation: You'll need to book a separate reception venue and coordinate transportation there if it's not within walking distance.

If you're not having a religious ceremony, you'll have to decide whether you want to host your ceremony and reception in the same spot, taking out the need for additional transportation and extra hours for vendors. If you're choosing two different spots, you'll want to consider whether the distance between locations is walkable. If not, you'll have to arrange transportation from your ceremony to the reception site for you, your wedding party, and your guests, or provide plenty of parking if you expect your guests to coordinate transit themselves.

INSIDE VS. OUT While outdoor weddings would appear to be the cheaper option—after all, you have effortless décor courtesy of Mother Nature, and you're not paying for a fancy reception hall—rentals, such as a tent, a generator, a dance floor, and even a kitchen, can really add up. (See chapter 7 for more on throwing an outdoor reception.) Bottom line: The main reasons to wed under the sheltering sky are beauty and drama, not dollars and cents.

Outdoor weddings tend to be more casual and inspired by their surroundings (garden, ranch, beach), while indoor parties offer more flexibility in terms of formality and can either come with ready-made style or be completely transformed to fit your vision. For certain wedding styles, such as black-tie glamour, an indoor locale like an ornate ballroom or castle is really your most fitting option, and modern weddings often work best in indoor spaces (modern lofts, art galleries, or urban warehouses).

BUDGET While budget may play a role in every decision you make, it's especially important when it comes to choosing your venue—about 50 percent of your total budget will go toward your venue (if it includes the catering as well as tables, chairs, and dinnerware). You'll want to consider what other elements are or aren't included with the venue in addition to food. If you have to bring in tables, chairs, linens, china, and a dance floor, even if the site is inexpensive (or free), you could end up spending just as much, if not more, than what you'd spend for a grand hall or hotel where everything is included.

AVAILABILITY If you're set on a certain date or time of year, availability will likely be more limited. So you may have to do a more extensive search to find a spot that's available for your chosen date, especially if you're getting married during a peak season. Start looking as soon as possible to increase your chances of getting your dream venue for your dream date.

GUEST LIST There's also some debate as to whether you should get a grip on the approximate number of guests you'll invite before settling

"I asked about my venue in wedding message boards on TheKnot.com and also checked the reviews by brides at WeddingChannel.com Reviews. No better way to hear the real story than from another bride."
—VERBRIDE

"I called the Better Business Bureau to check the scores of the venues I was considering."
—JESSIESGURL33

"When you see a venue, take a moment to stand at the altar. Can you picture your fiancé standing next to you? Can you see your family? If you can't, move on."
—DIZZINEA

on a venue or vice versa. We say it depends on what's more important to you: the space or having everyone you want there. (Flip to chapter 4 to start with your guest list.) As a rule of thumb, allow for twenty-five to thirty square feet per guest. That may seem like a lot, but it's not if you count the space you'll need for the tables, chairs, bustling waiters, band, lounge setups, and dance floor.

PARTY SPACE Don't forget you'll need enough room to dance and for guests to eat, drink, and hang out. The best all-in-one locations have at least three separate and workable spaces—for the ceremony, cocktail hour, and dinner/dancing. It's an added bonus if they have space for an after-party and lounge. If a room is too small to separate into sections accordingly, you may feel cramped. If it's shaped like an "S" (or another oddball figure), that could compromise your party's flow, as well.

WEDDING STYLE The setting plays a major role in shaping the feel of your day. If you're having a black-tie affair, a castle, historic mansion, grand hall, ballroom, or even country club is typically more suitable than a rustic ranch, balmy beach, or trendy restaurant. On the other hand, if you're going more casual, a beach might be just right. And for a party somewhere in between, a botanical garden, museum, or loft wedding may be your best bet. While you can make any space your own with the right draping, lighting, and rentals (see chapter 7), it's always easier and more cost-effective to work with what you have and find a venue whose décor fits your style.

THE LOOK Do you want gorgeous interiors and/or exteriors that you won't have to add much to or a blank slate you can make your own? The place doesn't have to be done in the exact colors of your planned decorations, but the walls, carpets, chairs, and curtains shouldn't conflict with your party's mood or theme. If the space allows, you can use draping, lighting, and carpeting to disguise wallpaper and flooring you don't love and completely change a room's look, but it'll cost you extra if it's not part of the location's wedding package (see chapter 7 for tips on transforming your space).

PARKING Make sure the site is near a good parking lot, a garage, or a big, empty (safe) street that's okay to park on. If parking is a problem, look for other ways to get everyone there, like booking a shuttle bus or fleet of vans to take guests from the ceremony to the reception. Inadequate parking isn't necessarily a deal breaker, but it may mean you'll need to spend more time and money figuring out a viable transportation alternative for you and your guests.

PRIVACY   If you're having a daytime event in a public spot, such as a park or botanical garden, be prepared for strangers to trek past your ceremony and even smile and wave. If you're not crazy about that idea, opt for a lovely lawn on a private estate or club. Or hold the reception at a restaurant or gallery that will post a "Closed for Private Party" sign. But don't assume you'll get total privacy just because you're indoors. Banquet halls and hotels often hold more than one affair at a time. If there will be other events going on simultaneously in rooms close to yours, you may hear another party's music or meet them over the hand dryers in the bathroom.

TIMING   If you're relying on natural lighting to create a mood, make sure to visit the site at the time of day that you're planning on having your wedding. Don't assume that just because there are beautiful floor-to-ceiling windows in the room that you'll have sunlight or a view of the sunset. A couple of things to find out when considering a space: What kind of exposure does the room have? (Look for a room that gets southern exposure to get the most light for the longest amount of time.) What time does the sun set during the time of year that you plan to get married?

GOOD VIBRATIONS   If the place is too echoey, it could give some weird reverb to the band, not to mention make it difficult for guests to hear each other talking. A tile or wood floor, for example, will amplify sounds, while a thick carpet will muffle them. Try to visit the room during an event to see what the acoustics are like. Also, make sure your room has lots of places to plug things in and the capacity for all the electricity you'll need for your band/DJ, lighting, caterers, and more—especially if you're celebrating in a place that's not accustomed to hosting weddings.

THE "YOU" FACTOR   Don't just look for the trendiest or prettiest place. The best weddings are the ones guests walk away from saying, "That was so them." Maybe your first date was in a funky Mexican restaurant—a hacienda-style hotel may be a perfect reception venue. If you're both outdoorsy, consider a waterfront or mountaintop setting. If you met and then fell in love during college, wed on the university's gorgeous grounds.

Reception venue options   Still not sure where to wed? Here are some of the most common options to consider—and the pros and cons of each. Regardless of which you choose, ask about any restrictions

on party times, décor, and vendors when visiting spaces. Some sites prohibit candles or draping, require you to use an in-house chef or stick to a preferred list of vendors, and others don't let parties run past a certain hour.

BANQUET HALLS, BALLROOMS, HOTELS, AND COUNTRY CLUBS If these traditional reception locations have one thing, it's experience. They know what's supposed to happen at a reception; they know how long one typically lasts. They've set up dessert buffets and band lighting a million times. They can offer suggestions on things you're unsure about. Another plus: These spaces come with all the necessary tools (tables, chairs, linens, and a bar), plus a staff. If something goes wrong, there are maintenance and cleaning staff there to fix it.

Packages often include a coordinator to help with the details or a list of vendors they know and love. This can make everything incredibly easy for you—but it also can be a hassle if you want to bring in vendors from outside. So find out from the venue or catering manager exactly what the establishment will take care of, from food, drinks, and décor to the waitstaff. And ask about all additional fees beyond the per-head

CLEVER IDEAS

venues from a to z

More ideas for hosting your wedding.

Aquarium, arboretum

Boardwalk, bed-and-breakfast, bowling alley

Castle, cave, covered bridge, casino

Disco, Disneyland, dock on a bay, dunes

Empire State Building

Farmhouse, football field

Gallery, greenhouse, golf course

Historic estate, Harley-Davidson showroom

Ice-skating rink, inn

Jazz club, Japanese garden

Knoll, Kibbutz

Lighthouse, library

Museum, mountaintop

Nature reserve, national park

Oceanside, orange grove, over the Grand Canyon

Poolside, prairie, park

Quarry

Rodeo, ranch

Ski slope, stables

Train station, toy store, theater

Under the stars, underwater

Vineyard

Windmill, wine cellar, (in the) woods

X-act spot where you first met

Yacht, yacht club, yard

Zoo

costs for food and beverages, such as cake-cutting fees, valets, and coat check and bathroom attendants.

LOFTS, WAREHOUSES, AND BLANK SPACES Ideal for city dwellers who love the downtown lifestyle, the open space of a loft is both romantic and sophisticated. The best part: It's a blank canvas. From lighting and linens to drapery and other décor, you can turn a loft (or similar space) into your dream locale. Just beware: Unlike hotels or reception halls, lofts often lack kitchen space and don't have chairs, tables, or other basics that you need for a wedding. Be sure to budget for rentals if you go this route.

MANSIONS, CASTLES, AND OTHER HISTORIC BUILDINGS The biggest advantage of renting a landmark location? The photo backdrop. Many historic mansions, estates, and castles come complete with beautiful grounds and ornate interiors. Make sure to find out exactly what the restrictions are on the space: Which rooms of the house can you use, what parts of the grounds are off-limits, which precious porcelain vases can't your guests touch? Otherwise, just enjoy—often these sites are so picturesque and romantic, not much extra decoration is necessary, but you may need to bring in tables, chairs, a dance floor, and other rentals—many do not come party-ready.

NOT-SO-TYPICAL PARTY SPACES Consider other venues, public or private, that host special events—museums, aquariums, train stations, nightclubs, university buildings. Some will have a special-events staff ready and willing to help you plan the event. Others won't, so you'll be bringing in your own caterer and other wedding professionals. Prices will vary. If you want to wed at a popular museum in a major city, be prepared to pay for the honor. But your favorite nightclub may cut you a great deal, particularly if you can be out before their normal business begins at midnight. And if one (or both) of you is an alumnus of the college whose space you're looking at, you may get a preferred rate. When scouting spaces, consider the layout—configuring furniture can be tough in rooms that aren't designed for events.

HOME WEDDINGS Marrying at home sounds perfect, especially if you, your parents, or a family member has a big, gorgeous house with beautiful grounds. This is about the most personal wedding location there is, and the smaller space also creates instant intimacy. But don't think it's just that easy—home weddings come with a set of considerations all their own. And they aren't less expensive (unless you're inviting very few people and going completely casual). Like nontraditional wedding venues, you'll have to bring pretty much everything in—tables, dishware, linens, tents, bathrooms, and more.

You also need to think about the nitty-gritty of infrastructure: Will the electrical system be able to handle the load? How will you provide ample (and legal) parking? Are the caterers cooking in your kitchen? What about bathrooms? You might need to rent some porta-potties (don't worry—they're luxurious these days!). You also have to make sure your neighborhood (and the city) will allow for a raucous good time; there could be some noise ordinances that would prohibit that seven-piece band you're planning on.

THE GREAT OUTDOORS An outdoor wedding pretty much guarantees a stunning backdrop as well as a built-in theme and décor. For the reception, consider staying under the stars with tables set right beneath a collection of trees, or put up a tent with windows to overlook a field or a lake. (For details about hosting a tented reception, flip to chapter 7, page 96.)

Amanda & Franck
OCTOBER 6
CHAMBORD, FRANCE

Amanda and Franck were lucky enough to be the first wedding to take place at Château de Chambord, in France's Loire Valley, a spot the bride had fallen in love with during their engagement trip. With the castle already providing a dramatic backdrop, the couple needed little additional décor to pull off their romantic, fairy-tale wedding. Though planning from their home in New York proved challenging, the final event was well worth it.

Some outdoor public spaces may have rules limiting noise, alcohol, and the time of the party. If you're thinking beach, public park, or forest preserve, you can't just congregate—you'll need to reserve the area with the local parks and recreation department. You may also need to get a permit, which will limit your wedding size, number of guests, and décor.

Going on site visits

Using magazines, online listings, and your families' personal wedding and party-guest experience, start to develop a list of venues to visit. Have a clear(ish) vision of your desires and requirements: approximate guest count (one hundred vs. three hundred vs. five hundred), your preferred wedding date(s), as well as special requests (Kosher catering).

Looking for something off the beaten path? Check the website for the chamber of commerce in the town where you're marrying for popular public event spaces, as well as some alternative ideas, like the zoo or a sculpture garden owned by the city. Both the articles and advertisements in local magazines and on websites are good places to find out about party venues, as well as to see them in their full glory. If you're thinking about a historic mansion, castle, or estate, get in touch with the historical society in your wedding area for a list of all the local landmarks that allow special events on their grounds.

Talk to your wedding planner (see chapter 6 for how to find one first) and any other vendors you may have locked in at this early date, especially the photographer (chapter 9) or florist (chapter 8) for their favorite places and ask for their opinions on the ones you're considering. They have likely been to more receptions than Liz Taylor's closest pals and have probably seen every location within a fifty-mile radius.

Once you've narrowed down your list, call the places that interest you and ask to speak to "the person in charge of weddings or special events." Find out if your date is available, make sure it's in your price range (just ask for the average cost of the weddings they host), and ask about customization capabilities (bringing in your own alcohol, décor, food). If everything fits, make an appointment for a site visit and meet with the site manager.

Booking a venue

Once you've seen enough to give you an idea of what's out there, make a list of "musts" ("has to hold a hundred and fifty guests") and "wants" ("should be ornate enough that we don't need to spend a lot on decorating"). Whichever one meets all your musts and

ASK CARLEY
DOUBLE-BOOKED

Our venue double-booked, and now they're trying to drop our wedding. Do we have any rights? Computer glitches and miscommunication do happen, though they are extremely rare. If you haven't signed a contract or given the reception venue a deposit yet, you're out of luck. But if you did, at the very least, your deposit should be refunded, as should any other payments you've already made. Be sure to look at your contract closely—it may have a clause in it protecting either you or the venue in the event of a double booking. Hopefully, the venue will work with you to find a solution that you'll be happy with. Otherwise, get a lawyer involved to protect your deposit and rights, and ensure that you're the one who gets to keep the date. Another option: Have the venue rebook your wedding for another wedding, and eat the price difference.

site visits

It seems so straightforward: "Is Saturday, September nineteenth, free?" But there are a lot
of points to talk through before you make your final decision to reserve a reception site.
Take this list of what to look for with you when you scout potential venues.

☐ Is there a reception "package"? Exactly what is included?

☐ How many people can the space hold for a sitdown dinner and dancing? A cocktail reception?

☐ Is my date available?

☐ Is there a flat fee or do you charge per person, or by the hour? How much of a deposit do you have to put down to reserve the space? What's the payment plan? Can I get a detailed list of what's included in the cost (bars, rentals, waitstaff)—and what's extra?

☐ How many weddings do you host per year? What's the time limit for renting the space?

☐ Do you have liability insurance? [In case someone gets injured during the party, you don't want to be held responsible—or if you're going to be, you want to know about it.]

☐ Is there a rental fee? For how many hours will we have the site? Is there an overtime fee if we stay longer? Is there a minimum amount of time we have to rent it for?

☐ Will we be required to leave everything "as is," or can we move things around and/or decorate to suit our purposes?

☐ Are tables, chairs, plates, glasses, and so on available, or will we have to provide (rent) those ourselves?

☐ When will we have access to the site for setup and deliveries? [If you want to set up a tent or install flooring or draping, you may need access to the site more than twenty-four hours in advance, so you'll want to make sure that's possible and check if there are additional fees for early setup.]

☐ Are there guidelines about what kinds of decorations we can use? Do you have styles to choose from, and can we alter those? Do you completely customize service and décor options? (Get a sense of whether they're open to changing the look of the space.]

☐ Are there kitchen/cooking facilities? [Caterers will charge you extra if they have to haul in things like refrigerators and stoves.]

☐ If there's parking, is it free? If not, what are the rates and/or gratuities for valets?

☐ Will there be, or can we set up, a coatroom? Are there bathrooms nearby? [Look at them to make sure they're nice!]

☐ If there's no bar, can we set one up? Do you have a liquor license? Can we bring in our own alcohol, and if so, is there a limit and a corkage fee?

☐ Is ours the only reception scheduled for that day? If not, will there be another one during our reception? Will we be sharing any spaces, like the cocktail-hour area, bathrooms, or lounge areas? Will we be able to hear their music during your reception?

☐ Will the site manager be present during the reception? Will someone who works at the location be there to supervise during our wedding? [This really should be the person you make all your plans with, not someone you've never met until that day.]

☐ What is the staff-to-guest ratio? (See chapter 7.)

- [ ] How long do you need to change over the space (if your ceremony and reception will be held in the same room)? Do you have staff that will handle this?

- [ ] What is the backup plan for any outdoor elements of the event (if applicable)?

- [ ] Are there restrictions on photo and video? [Some churches and museums have rules against flash photography, for example.]

- [ ] Are there permits required and do we need to handle them?

- [ ] Is there any specific additional insurance we need to get?

- [ ] Is there enough power to support a band or DJ, catering and lighting, or do we need backup generators?

- [ ] Will there be coatroom and restroom attendants? Servers? Bartenders? Valets? What are the charges for each?

- [ ] Is there a bridal suite where I can get ready with the bridal party before the ceremony? What about the groom and groomsmen—is there a room where they can hang out before the ceremony? Is there an extra fee to use them?

- [ ] Is there a private room off the main room where we can change or just be alone for a few minutes during the reception? [This is a nice perk.]

- [ ] Is there a dress code that we'll need to inform guests of—coat and tie after six p.m., for example?

- [ ] Are there any restrictions or regulations about what kind of music we can play and/or a time by which it must be turned off?

- [ ] Will we have to hire our own security guards, or do you hire them or have them on staff? [The point is to find out just how safe the place is and to decide whether you're comfortable with its level of security.]

- [ ] What's the cancellation policy? [This is important to know, because some places will give you most of your deposit back if you cancel far enough in advance, since there's still a chance they can rent the space for another party. But after a certain date, you may not be able to get your deposit back, or at least not all of it.]

destination weddings

Whether you want to elope in Vegas, have an intimate affair in a European city, or head a few states away to Hawaii for a spectacular setting, destination weddings are a hot option. But before you start, here's what you need to know. If you are considering a destination wedding, also pick up *The Knot Guide to Destination Weddings* and visit Theknot.com/destinationwedding.

IS A DESTINATION WEDDING FOR YOU?

If your guests are split between three cities, your hometown and current residence aren't exactly to-die-for wedding locales, or there's a special place where you've been dreaming about getting married, a destination wedding may be perfect for you. Here's what else you should consider before deciding to take the plunge away from home.

pros: From the convenient beaches of Florida and Mexico to the snowy mountaintops of Vail, Colorado, from the rolling hills of Napa Valley, California, to the romantic elegance of Rome, a destination wedding has a ready-made theme. Other perks include the setting, the smaller guest list, the chance to gather your favorite people together in one spot for a few days, and the built-in honeymoon.

cons: Obviously, aside from the added travel expense and fact that some people may not be able to attend because of the added travel time and expense involved, the big drawback of having a wedding away from your home is that you'll be coordinating everything from afar. That means that you have to take extra measures to get what you want and rely on a team of pros to pull off your vision. Fortunately, our wired world makes the task immensely easier. You can research your vendors online, as well as browse photographers' portfolios and see potential cake designers' finest works of art. Still, we always recommend meeting with potential vendors in person when possible, which can mean making room in your budget and schedule for at least one or two planning trips.

Also, be sure you know the ins and outs of getting a marriage license in your chosen locale, including how many days you have to wait to get married once you arrive and any other legal stipulations.

WHERE IN THE WORLD TO WED?

The location of your wedding determines not only the mood but also the travel, time, and expenses required to pull it off. Whether you already have a place in mind or need help pinpointing the right spot, here are some factors to consider before settling on a destination for your nuptials.

accessibility: Budget and time will be a consideration for most guests, no matter how much they love you. Figure out how much it typically costs to reach any potential destinations from your friends' and relatives' departure cities to get a sense of the travel time and costs involved. Also, consider how often flights leave and how many airlines fly to your location. The most important detail is whether flights are direct. Two-flight destinations create additional hassles—missed connections, lost luggage, long layovers, and added travel time—that may affect your guests' experience and ability to get there.

marriage requirements: The legal side of marrying in a different country or even state can be complicated. Know these details before you set your heart on a destination: You may need to take a blood test, and many countries have "residency requirements," which means you must reside in the country for a certain length of time before your ceremony. Although this is usually just a few days, it can be longer (anywhere from fifteen days to nearly six weeks): France requires at least one of you to arrive at least forty days before you marry.

PLANNING LOGISTICS

While faraway destinations can give you the exotic, exclusive vibe you're going for, they can also make planning far more difficult. If the location doesn't have the resources you'll need, like a local florist, cake baker, photographer, resort, or venue experienced in throwing weddings, you'll need to import almost all your vendors, décor, and equipment, which can make planning much more difficult, time-consuming, and expensive. Hiring a planner to be on the ground to coordinate and even hire vendors for you is really a must for a destination wedding. On the other end of the spectrum, of course, it will require a greater financial investment for your guests.

budget: If done right, a destination wedding can cost no more—and maybe even less—than hosting the same party at home (depending on where you live, of course). For example, if you live in a U.S. metropolitan city where event facilities are in high demand, like New York City, then holding your wedding in Mexico will likely be less expensive than doing it at home, even when you factor in airfare, hotel expenses, and planning trips. But there are extra expenses you'll need to factor in for a destination wedding, including importing key vendors and décor, welcome bags for guests, additional activities for guests, and travel costs for you and your immediate families (including the planning trips, not just the big day).

special spots: Choose a place that means something to you for a really personalized wedding. Did he propose on vacation in Paris? Then a swank wedding on the French Riviera may be for you. Are you both foodies? Think about having your crew gather in a place like Tuscany or California wine country for the food and, well, wine. Are you nature lovers? Bring everyone to an eco-friendly spot like Costa Rica, where guests can zip-line through the rain forest before your rehearsal dinner.

weather: Don't just assume that the weather in the Caribbean, Hawaii, and Mexico is gorgeous year-round. Hurricane season lasts from July through October in the Caribbean and can put a major damper on your nuptials, while the rainy season makes marrying in Hawaii dicey from November to March, and Mexico can be uncomfortably hot in July and August.

timing: Unfortunately, the best weather in popular vacation destinations tends to correlate with tourist season. If you choose to marry then, you'll want to reserve hotel blocks and venues immediately and send out save-the-dates ten to twelve months in advance so guests can book their flights and accommodations before prices skyrocket and accommodations book up. If you choose the shoulder season (right after high season), you may be able to save yourself and your guests some money and still enjoy great weather. While the off-season will mean fewer crowds, the weather can be iffy, and you may find that many stores, venues, and vendors close up shop.

venue

Make sure the following key points are included
in your written agreement.

- ☐ Your names and contact information
- ☐ Reception company's name and contact info
- ☐ Exact date and time of your wedding
- ☐ Exact location of the wedding (for example, "in the main gallery," "in the Presidential Ballroom")
- ☐ The name of the site representative who will be on hand on your wedding day, as well as the name of an acceptable substitute
- ☐ A detailed description of your reception space, including the décor (color of walls, type of flooring, chandeliers), plus any amenities like a stage or bridal suite

- ☐ A detailed list of everything the place is providing (e.g., tables, chairs, linens, amplifiers)
- ☐ Total cost and a line-item breakdown of what's included (factoring in taxes, service charges, gratuities, and overtime fees) in the package and what's à la carte
- ☐ Anything else you agree about orally that you want to ensure happens
- ☐ Amount of deposit and when it was paid
- ☐ Balance and when it's due/ payment schedule, in what form, to whom, and due dates
- ☐ Cancellation/refund policy

the highest number of your wants should be your winner. Even if you're overjoyed with one space, don't feel rushed to reserve it on the spot. We know the threat of losing the space is going to nip at you, but give yourselves time to compare and contrast prices, notes, and impressions. You'll also want to take the time to call references and ask couples if they were happy with the overall service, if there were any problems and how they were resolved, if requests were accommodated, if the site looked like what they'd envisioned, and what their guests had to say.

4

the guest list

TIMELINE

PLANNING

ASAP
Start drafting your
guest list

12+ months before
Finalize the guest list

9–11 months before
Finalize your guest list

6–8 months before
Send out save-the-dates

3 months before
Send out A-list invitations
(if you're having a B-list)

Reserve hotel room blocks
for out-of-town guests

6–8 weeks before
Send out invites (or B-list
invitations)

When everything is said and done, it's the people—the friends and family members who come together from all walks of your lives—who make the party. But as you remember from chapters 2 and 3, it's also the people who make the budget grow and your venue options shrink. That's why assembling the guest list is one of the most stressful parts of planning. It can make or break your big day, not to mention your friendships. Whether your biggest challenge is trying to decide who to cut or finding a way to even out the sides, in this chapter, we'll crack the code to figuring out how many guests you can afford, how many invitations each family gets, and who to put on the list.

SETTLING ON A SIZE

You've probably heard horror stories about families torn apart and friendships ruined over wedding guest lists. So we understand why you might feel a little nervous about creating yours. But deciding whom to invite to your nuptials doesn't have to be stressful—we swear. There's a formula to picking the perfect party crowd, and it takes 99 percent of the drama out of the guest list. Of course, you have to think about cost (more on that in a minute), but the number of guests also impacts the mood—and even the venue. Do you have your heart set on a specific locale, such as a local winery that fits only one hundred people, tops? If so, decide what's more important: more friends and family, or the winery.

Your religious, ethnic, and cultural background may also dictate who makes the cut. In some communities, it is customary to invite everyone—the entire neighborhood, congregation, social network, etc. And if supersocial or supertraditional Mom and Dad are adamant about inviting throngs of friends and extended family, you're going to have to hear them out—especially if they're footing a major part of the bill. Your mantra here: compromise.

Finding your number
Your guest list maximum is set by two main factors: your venue and your budget. If your venue can only fit one hundred, then you know you can't go higher than ninety-eight (don't forget to include you two!). Just double-check if the numbers the venue gives you are for a seated dinner and dancing or for a standing (cocktail-style) reception—they are not the same.

Even if your venue can fit eight hundred, your budget may not. So you'll want to figure out your budget before you start on the guest list. Then you can use the percentages we mapped out in chapter 2 to help you estimate how much you'll have to devote to the reception. If you plan to stick with our parameters, then 50 percent of your budget will go toward the reception. Subtract any reception rental fees (if applicable) from that figure, and you'll have a rough estimate of what you can devote to guests. The final piece of the equation: the per-head estimate. You can get this number from your venue (banquet halls, hotels, and other all-inclusive venues that include the catering, rentals, etc. can give you this) or from your caterer (if you're bringing in your own).

Now it's time to plug those numbers into the guest list equation. If you're more mathematically inclined, here's the equation:

$$\frac{(50\% \text{ of total budget } - \text{ venue rental fee})}{\text{Per-head cost}} = \text{guest list cap}$$

DIVVYING UP THE LIST

Once you've got your guest-list limit, it's time to decide who's in and who's out. You and your wedding cosponsors have to slide in everyone you love under the quota you calculated above. That means splitting it up among you two and your families. To minimize confusion and infighting, wait to request your parents' guest lists until you have given them their target numbers. Traditionally, the bride and her family and the groom and his folks each invite half of the guests, with the parents on both sides—usually the major check writers—getting a majority vote. But if you and your fiancé are underwriting most of the reception costs, it's definitely acceptable for you to determine the bulk of the guest list.

For the most drama-free approach, we say play fair: Regardless of who's footing the bill, divide the invitee rations three ways—between you and both sets of parents. So if you're having two hundred guests, you get seventy spots total, and each set of parents would get sixty-five. (Divorced parents should split their family's set evenly.) Sticking with that strategy gives you a bulletproof defense against accusations of favoritism. Of course, if one of you is an only child and the other comes from a big family, you can reevaluate how you want to split up the numbers. Remember, the strategy is: Play fair.

ORGANIZING YOUR LIST

When you give them their numbers, send your (computer-savvy, we hope) parents a spreadsheet to fill out with all their guests' details. Otherwise, you'll get incomplete information and another big project on your to-do list! There's a premade spreadsheet you can download on TheKnot.com/guestlistmanager, but if you want to make it yourself, here are the required fields:

- Full names (including any titles)
- Gender/salutation
- Address

- Phone number
- E-mail address
- Spouse or guest information (including full name, gender, and address)—you can send the invitation to the same address even if the couple lives separately, but you should always include the guest's name instead of just writing "and guest"

Trust us, they won't give you back a complete list, but at least you'll have gotten them started early. Use this organizational structure for your own list, too. Eventually, you'll need an aggregated spreadsheet (that includes everyone's lists) with this level of detail to upload into a guest-list management tool to track RSVPs. Having your entire list online means you always have access to it, whether you happen to be at home, at work, at your parents' house, or in the invitation store. You'll use those names and addresses a gazillion times, from meal selection and seat assignments to the many, many save-the-dates, invites, and thank-you notes you'll send along the way. Trust us, you'll be glad you did the legwork early on when your wedding date wasn't hanging so heavily over your head.

DRAFTING YOUR LIST

Once you've gotten your parents started, it's your turn to create a list. Begin with a "fantasy list"—everyone you and your fiancé would invite if money and space weren't a consideration. Distant cousins, friends you used to be close with but haven't talked to in ages, sorority sisters and fraternity brothers, colleagues—feel free to include them all for now. We're not saying they'll all get an invite, but if you get enough "no" RSVPs, they just may.

Making the cuts
Now that you've finished your fantasy list and combined your list with your parents', you've probably noticed that there are way too many people. Sorry to be your reality check, but at some point between the free-form list of names you jotted down and the engraved envelopes you send out, you'll need to trim. Eliminate repeat names and then get ready to wield the pen and cross out more names until you're within budget and capacity limits. To minimize drama and hurt feelings, make cuts across the board. In other words, don't delete a dozen people from your in-laws' list but only one from your own parents' list. You need to be as fair as possible (noticing a theme?), which means cutting yours, too.

You may want to relegate these cuts to what's known as the B-list (of course, you would never admit to your guests that such a list exists). The reality, though, is that you're pretty safe assuming that 10 to 20 percent of your final list will not come, so it pays to be ready with a second string in case you dip far below your target number.

The B-list is an extension of your original guest list. It's for the people who don't fit on your initial list for space or budget reasons but whom you'd really like to be there and are hoping to add on later if you get enough regrets from the A-list. While you don't have to limit your B-list, keep in mind that unless you're throwing a destination wedding or a small wedding, or getting married during a busy time or over a holiday, you probably won't get more than ten to twenty regrets from your A-list, so you may want to tailor your B-list (and expectations) accordingly.

So, for example, if you have two hundred people on your guest list, it's pretty safe to assume that 20 percent will decline. So once you get more than forty A-list regrets, you can start working down your B-list, sending out a few invites at a time until you get two hundred acceptances. Just don't wait too long to send your B-list invites out—no one wants an invitation the week before an event (you might as well tell them they're second-tier). A good timeline to follow: Send your A-list invites three months before the wedding. Then, as the no's come in, there's still time to send out the B's six to eight weeks before. (Out-of-town guests are an exception since they need advance time to make travel arrangements.)

If you decide to have a B-list, be careful not to make it obvious to those people that they're on the B-list (sending an RSVP card with a date that has passed, for example, is a dead giveaway). A safe strategy: Create a second set of reply cards with a later RSVP date so you don't raise the red flag that they're your second-choice guests. Warning: This strategy can backfire if your other friends are digital (or real-world) big mouths and post: "Hey, got the invite. Yay!!" So, how do you decide whom to cut?

FOCUS ON THE PRESENT A wedding is not an excuse to round up every friend you've ever known—focus on people who matter now.

If the issue at hand is the potentially hurt feelings of the uninvited, remember that remote cousins often feel as indifferent toward you as you do toward them and may be fine with not coming. The same goes for distant friends. Invite that sorority sister you've stayed in touch with but not necessarily the entire house if you haven't seen half of them since college. And if you've never spoken to, met, or heard the name of a particular guest previous to the list building, he gets cut, even if Dad swears they're close as clams.

guest list drama

Your fiancé has a friend you can't stand, you have relatives he considers extraneous,
and your mother expects all her friends to make the list. Here's how to deal.

stand your ground

Listen, we know this can be tricky, especially
if one set of parents is footing the bill and
demands a greater slice of the guest pie. But
when it comes down to it, this is your event. If his
mom wants to invite all of her bridge partners but
there's just not room, he needs to explain to his
mom that even though she's generously paying
for the fete, this is a celebration for everyone
involved, and everyone must participate on an
equal footing. It may not be easy or pleasant,
but if you start to bend now, you may be in for
a tidal wave of last-minute requests.

figure out the ex factor together

While there are no hard-and-fast rules when it
comes to inviting exes, we will say this: There's a
reason many couples who are on very good terms
with exes still decide against inviting them. Most
feel it would just be too weird. If thinking about
having a former flame at the wedding causes one or
both of you to stress, just don't include that person.
If you do invite him, make sure he can bring a date.

nix unwanted guests from the get-go

More often than you might think, even
when couples are clear about making out an
invite to one person and one person only,
the RSVP comes back with two names
crammed onto one line.

You can avoid the awkward conversation in
which you try to explain to your ex-roommate
why her boyfriend of three weeks can't come
to your wedding by asking your calligrapher to
write the full names of the invited guests on the
RSVP card. After their names, have her include
a blank line where they can indicate whether
they're attending or sending their regrets. That
way, there's almost no way for guests to force
an unwanted invite on you. And if someone still
sends in an RSVP with a plus-one (or three—
all the kids who were not invited!), have the
planner or a non–family member call to
explain the circumstances.

DON'T LET GUILT DETERMINE GUESTS It's your party. If you
don't want them there, don't feel guilted into sending an invite—even if
you were invited to their wedding or they're friends with lots of people
who will be invited to yours.

CUT CATEGORIES To make trimming your list easier, create a
set of criteria for cutting your list that makes sense to both of you. To
avoid hurt feelings, adopt the all-or-nothing approach. In other words,
establish a no-exceptions policy, like "no significant others unless
they're engaged or living together" or "no children under eighteen." If
you have a clear best friend at work, it's fine to invite just that person;
otherwise, if you're planning to invite one member of your team, invite

all of them. The other exception: You can invite just your boss. It's totally acceptable to invite no one from work (and still gab about your wedding at lunch).

Now that you have your final guest list (okay, there may still be some changes along the way—but it's pretty darn near finalized), break out the bubbly. Completing this task is well worth toasting!

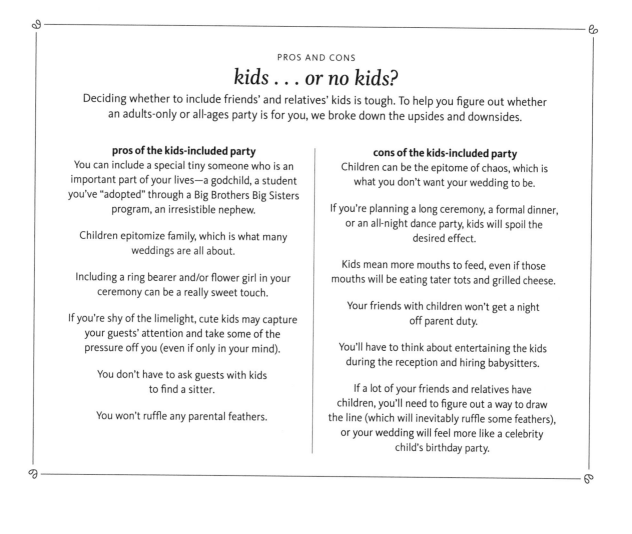

kids . . . or no kids?

Deciding whether to include friends' and relatives' kids is tough. To help you figure out whether an adults-only or all-ages party is for you, we broke down the upsides and downsides.

pros of the kids-included party

You can include a special tiny someone who is an important part of your lives—a godchild, a student you've "adopted" through a Big Brothers Big Sisters program, an irresistible nephew.

Children epitomize family, which is what many weddings are all about.

Including a ring bearer and/or flower girl in your ceremony can be a really sweet touch.

If you're shy of the limelight, cute kids may capture your guests' attention and take some of the pressure off you (even if only in your mind).

You don't have to ask guests with kids to find a sitter.

You won't ruffle any parental feathers.

cons of the kids-included party

Children can be the epitome of chaos, which is what you don't want your wedding to be.

If you're planning a long ceremony, a formal dinner, or an all-night dance party, kids will spoil the desired effect.

Kids mean more mouths to feed, even if those mouths will be eating tater tots and grilled cheese.

Your friends with children won't get a night off parent duty.

You'll have to think about entertaining the kids during the reception and hiring babysitters.

If a lot of your friends and relatives have children, you'll need to figure out a way to draw the line (which will inevitably ruffle some feathers), or your wedding will feel more like a celebrity child's birthday party.

GETTING GUESTS THERE

If you have scores of out-of-town guests (or are hosting a destination wedding), you have extra issues to think about—namely, where they'll sleep, how they'll get around, and what they'll do with their spare time. This isn't just the biggest day of your life; it's also a party for your friends and family (whom you may be asking to take time off work and to spring for plane tickets and a hotel room, plus that state-of-the-art cappuccino maker on your wish list). Take steps now to help them get there and have a good time once they arrive.

Keep them informed
This is a party, not a game of Clue. Don't make your guests use their super sleuth skills to find you the right gift, get to your wedding, and dress the part. Let them know early on what the dress code is, when to RSVP by, where you're registered, how to get to the ceremony and reception, and the dates and times of any extra

Zeina & Shawn
SEPTEMBER 13
KAPOLEI, HI

Since they already live in a tropical paradise, getting married in their home state was a no-brainer for Zeina and Shawn. But because most of their seventy-five guests flew in for their Hawaiian nuptials, the couple incorporated subtle nods to the locale, like straw fan programs. More prominent touches like white, gauzy draping and lush, feminine arrangements kept the overall vibe of the beachfront wedding glamorous and romantic.

parties or activities they're invited to. You can include this info on your wedding website and send it along with your invitations (except where you're registered—that's word of mouth or on your wedding website only). Your wedding website is also a good place to list local information and the weekend's itineraries and activities, too.

Reserve rooms

Though you're not expected to pay for guests' overnight accommodations, you should offer suggestions for where they can stay. Recommend a few places at different price points. To get the best deals and ensure everyone has a room, call nearby hotels to ask about group rates and reserving room blocks for your wedding weekend. Reserve rooms as early as possible for out-of-town guests. Begin your research up to a year in advance, and make sure your block is booked at the eight-month mark.

Include the hotel information with your save-the-dates, invites, and/ or wedding website—the address, phone number, website, and details for cashing in on any special rate. Reserving a block doesn't mean you'll have to pay for the rooms; you're just setting them aside. Your guests will need to put down their credit cards when they call to book their rooms. But help your guests out and ask about a discounted group rate if you send all of your out-of-town guests their way. And be considerate of your crowd when choosing lodging. You may want to reserve rooms at two hotels—a more luxurious one for your parents, their friends, and those who want to sleep in style, and a more budget-friendly—and perhaps party-friendly—option for the younger crowd who may want to host after-parties in their suites. You can also check with close local friends or relatives to see if they'd be willing to put up out-of-town VIPs.

Research transportation options

Make it easy for guests to get to your nuptials. Post information on your wedding website about nearby airports, as well as airlines with direct flights to your wedding locale (or the nearest city) and phone numbers and websites of nearby rental-car companies (including other airport shuttle services and limo and taxicab companies). While most rental cars come with navigation systems, it's still a good idea to include driving directions from major airports, as well as nearby cities where guests might be driving from—just in case. If you have lots of guests flying in for the wedding, consider arranging for a hotel shuttle or asking a friend or relative to pick everyone up. It's a nice way to give traveling friends and family a warm welcome.

REAL BRIDE ADVICE
guest list gripes

"We accidentally sent out an invite addressed to my cousin Steve and his ex-wife. Needless to say, his new wife wasn't very happy with the mix-up."
—JENNIELEE229

"We decided to make an A-list and a B-list. Unfortunately, my fiancé decided to keep track by marking an 'A' or a 'B' on the back corner of each invitation. It didn't take long before our guests caught on and the offended calls started streaming in."
—BIRDIEBRIDEYBEE03

"My mother-in-law said she needed additional invites for the wedding, even though we asked for her full list months earlier. I explained that we had no extras, but the next week, my fiancé and I returned to a mailbox full of RSVP cards from people who were not on the guest list. My mother-in-law had made copies of the invites and sent out 87— yes, 87—additional invites."
—MOBRIDETOBE

wedding websites 101

You can create your own wedding website, hire a designer to make one for you, or find customizable templates online. The sooner you have your website up and running, the better. Not only will you get a task out of the way, but an early launch will also allow you to take advantage of more of its features. Here are the things you'll want to consider when building your wedding website.

essentials

A picture of the happy couple (give your guests at least one adorable picture—it will help them know they are downloading directions from the right John and Katie's wedding website)

Nearby airports and airlines

Directions from the major airports and/or major cities most guests are coming from

Rental car or hotel shuttle information

Nearby hotels (also include the phone numbers, links to their websites, rates, and information on room blocks you've set up)

Directions to the ceremony and reception locations (including how to get from the ceremony to the reception)

The complete wedding itinerary, including the times, locations, and addresses, and directions to any peripheral parties that will take place in your honor. (If the entire guest list won't be invited, leave the event off or restrict viewers to the invitees.

Local attractions, restaurants, and activities, including your favorite spots, as well as suggested activities for guests to do in their downtime

Details for any transportation you will provide

Links to your registries

Dress codes for the wedding as well as all the peripheral parties and events (include any information about the weather or location that may affect guests' attire—guests will want to know if it gets cold at night, or if the ceremony will be on the grass or sand, or if a jacket and tie are required at the rehearsal dinner venue)

List of members of the wedding party (consider including pictures and short bios of each so guests can identify who they're seeing up on the altar at the ceremony)

optional extras

Custom domain name (you can purchase a custom domain name like CarlyandDavidGetMarried.com so it's easier for guests to remember your site)

Short story about how you met and got engaged. Your guests will enjoy reading about you and your relationship.

Slide show of pictures of you two, the bridal party, and your families

RSVP information (you can direct guests to your wedding website to RSVP for any peripheral parties like the next-day brunch or welcome party

A guest book

Interactive features like polls and quizzes (for example, you might let guests vote on your first-dance song

Entertain them
Put together an itinerary with the rundown of all the wedding events, as well as additional activities and recommendations for things to do during downtime (if you're having a weekend wedding). Post it on your website and leave a printed version in your welcome bags or at the front desk of the hotel.

If you're hosting a destination wedding or have lots of out-of-town guests, think about organizing group activities. (Although we recommend having your reception right after the ceremony, sometimes it's not possible. If there will be a break between the day of events, it's also a good idea to provide entertainment for guests who don't live in the area.) If you don't have a wedding planner, appoint an outgoing, very loving friend or relative to play "cruise director" and help coordinate those downtime group activities for your guests, since you'll probably be too busy with last-minute preparations to entertain them. Activities can include casual get-togethers, like a barbecue lunch or a margarita happy hour, or a golf game, a tour of the city, a trip to a museum, a baseball game, or a beach day. You set it up and pay for the supplies; the "cruise director" donates her time.

Keep in mind that some of your guests may never have visited the area before, and may want to explore on their own, so add a mini travel guide with highlights of the area, including all your favorite restaurants, activities, and shops, plus any great sights to see, on your website and in your itinerary to get out-of-town guests excited about the journey. If you're having a large number of guests ages ten and under, suggest some kid-friendly activities, too. Also, consider hiring a babysitter to watch the kids during the rehearsal dinner, ceremony (have her sit with small kids in a separate room, if necessary), and/or some of the other not-so-kid-friendly activities to give their parents a chance to let loose.

5

the wedding party

From bridesmaids and groomsmen to the flower girl, ring bearer, and honor attendants (the maid of honor and best man), you have plenty of wedding ceremony roles to fill. Here's the good news: You get to give elevated status to all your favorite people—best friends, childhood buddies, siblings, cousins, even your dog. The bad news? You can't include everyone, or no one will be left to watch the show. Choosing who will play a special role on your day isn't always easy—in fact, when it comes to siblings, it can get pretty sticky. To help, we've prepared a cross-section of the wedding-day cast of characters, plus tips for choosing them, enlisting their help, and dealing with any drama along the way.

TIMELINE
PLANNING

9–11 months before
Pick your wedding party and other VIP roles

2–3 months before
Attend your shower

Have your bachelorette and bachelor parties

1–7 days before
Host a bridal luncheon

ATTENDANTS AND THEIR ROLES

They'll be there to zip your dress and decorate your getaway car; to toast you and roast you; to grin and bear it when you make them wear salmon taffeta dresses and matching ties (please don't). They're your bridesmaids and groomsmen—your team of VIPs. But before you pop the question, check out what they'll be responsible for and make sure your top picks are up for the job.

The bridesmaids

In the distant past, bridesmaids escorted the bride as she traveled to the groom's village for the wedding, protecting her (and her dowry) from attack by highway robbers or scorned suitors. Today, your maids probably won't have to do double duty as a defensive line, but they do have a variety of other challenging tasks. In theory, bridesmaids are the trustworthy friends and family members who form the bride's entourage (and ostensibly also work well together). They're a support team, with duties including:

- Helping to plan (and finance) the shower and bachelorette party
- Spreading the news of where you are registered
- Aiding with general planning tasks—addressing invites, making favors, decorating the reception site
- Paying for their own dresses, shoes, lingerie, and jewelry
- Attending the rehearsal dinner
- Helping you get dressed and hanging out with you before you walk down the aisle, and reminding you to breathe
- Marching down the aisle before you and standing at the front alongside you during the ceremony
- Serving as auxiliary hostesses at the reception, introducing people, and making sure everyone's comfortable
- Offering you emotional support throughout the planning process and on the wedding day

The groomsmen

Back in the days when a groom would capture his bride, literally, and carry her away to be wed, the groomsmen were his trusty warriors who helped fight off opposing forces (families, suitors) trying to get the bride back.

Today, your groomsmen probably won't engage in hand-to-hand combat. But they do more than just show up in a tux. Their chief responsibilities? Supporting the groom and helping the best man plan (and pay for) the bachelor party. Other duties can include:

- Helping to plan (and finance) the bachelor party
- Attending the couple's shower (if there is one)

the knot NOTE

bridesmaid help
We know bridesmaids can behave pretty badly sometimes, but it's not always easy to know what to do, how to act, or what's off-limits—that's why we wrote *The Knot Bridesmaid Handbook* (hint: It makes a great will-you-be-my-bridesmaid gift). If your crew could use some guidance, gift them a copy; then send them to TheKnot.com for tons of information and advice on their new duties, plus shower and bachelorette party tips and ideas.
TheKnot.com/ bridesmaids

how to keep your maids happy

Here's how to make sure there's no love lost between you and your maids after the wedding.

respect their (other) responsibilities

Planning a wedding can feel like a full-time job, but that doesn't mean being a bridesmaid should, too. Remember: While your wedding may be your number one priority right now, your friend who's busting her butt at work or adjusting to life with a new baby may have other priorities.

dress them well

Want happy maids? Pick a dress they'll like enough to wear again, or at least one that they won't mind wearing once. And if you really want to win their hearts and minds, let them pick their own. (For more help choosing their dresses, go to chapter 17.)

keep them in the black

Bridesmaids have to shell out for quite a bit over the course of the wedding—dresses, shower decorations, wedding gifts, the bachelorette party, and travel expenses—which can put a pinch on even the most financially flush of maids. Take their budgets into consideration before choosing their dresses or requesting a destination bachelorette party.

give (and receive) graciously

You pictured an elegant afternoon tea; instead, there's bridal shower bingo and mini crescent hot dogs. You imagined a spa-day bachelorette; instead, you got a night of pole dancing at a strip club. It might be tough sometimes, but you've got to smile and say thank-you. Remember they're doing it for you.

be a good friend

Really obvious, right? But sometimes when you're caught up in wedding-related drama, it can be hard to remember that there's a world outside your wedding. Make it a point to talk to your maids about their lives, too.

keep the meltdowns to a minimum

The occasional bridal breakdown is inevitable—your maids are pretty much counting on it. So don't think twice if, during a particularly stressful week, you cry over boutonnieres or lose your cool over favors—it's par for the course. Just try to keep the Bridezilla moments in check, okay?

say thanks

Show your appreciation for all that they're doing and will do for you by finding a special something that shows how much their attendance means to you. You don't need to spend a lot—it should make sense for your budget—but make it personal and thoughtful.

- Spreading the news of where you are registered
- Renting or buying their own wedding attire, including shoes and accessories
- Attending the rehearsal dinner
- Possibly serving as ushers and helping seat guests before the ceremony
- Serving as information central during the wedding, directing wayward guests to the restroom, chapel, and/or reception site
- Standing at the altar during the ceremony (possibly after escorting bridesmaids up the aisle)
- Offering support and an unfailing sense of humor throughout the preparations and during the wedding

The maid, matron, or man of honor (moh)

The maid of honor, or matron of honor if she's married, is your wingwoman—the person you want by your side throughout the wedding preparations and at the altar. Traditionally, brides choose a sister or a best friend (though you can choose your mom, daughter, or even your closest guy pal—a man of honor). The MOH is responsible for overseeing the rest of the ladies, as well as providing unflagging moral support. In addition to regular bridesmaid duties, the MOH's traditional duties include:

- Helping to shop for dresses (yours and the bridesmaids') and paying for her own dress
- Hosting a bridal shower and/or working with the best man to organize a couple's shower
- Helping smooth over any disputes (with family or bridesmaids)
- Heading up the bachelorette party planning
- Coordinating transportation and lodging for the other maids
- Making sure all the maids get their dresses fitted, get their hair and makeup done, make it to the ceremony on time, and have the right flowers and accessories; she is the last bridesmaid to walk down the aisle before you
- Arranging your veil and train once you're at the altar; holding your bouquet during your vows and the groom's ring until you're ready for it
- Signing the marriage certificate as a witness
- Helping you remove your headpiece and bustling your train so you can start partying
- Giving a toast after the best man, or leading the toasting
- Collecting any gifts and hanging on to them for you (she may deposit checks to your bank account or hold them for you until you return from Bora Bora)

ASK CARLEY
MALE MAIDS

My brother is my best friend, and I want him to stand next to me at the wedding. Is it okay to have a male maid of honor?
It most definitely is. More and more brides and grooms are asking close friends of the opposite sex to be their attendants—and it's about time. If you want him to be your honor attendant, call him the man of honor. If you want him to stand with the bridesmaids, call him a bridesman. Your guy can wear whatever the groomsmen are wearing. Also, let your photographer know that he should be photographed as one of your attendants in wedding party pictures.

The best man or maid (bm)

He's a consultant, bachelor-party master of ceremonies, and commander in chief of the groomsmen brigade. Usually the groom chooses his best male friend, dad, or brother (though a female friend or sister—a "best maid"—can also fill the role). The best man should be someone who's reliable, not too busy to help you with planning the details, and generally pro-marriage (or at least pro your marriage). Not just a glorified groomsman, the groom's number two will also need to fulfill the following special duties:

- Heading up the bachelor-party planning
- Potentially working with the maid of honor to organize a couple's shower
- Helping the groom choose and rent (or buy) his attire

HOT TOPIC

new best man?

post: marriedinmarch
After my fiancé (FI) and I got engaged, he immediately asked an old college buddy (whom I've never met!) to be his best man. Since the pal accepted, the two of them haven't even talked. My FI realizes he jumped the gun, and wants to ask his current roommate to be his best man instead. Is there any way to politely ask the old buddy to resign?

reply: born2bwild
I hate to be the one to break it to you, but there is no polite way to un-ask a best man. Your FI made a mistake and both of you must think of a way to deal with the situation. Have your FI call him, and put it in his court—maybe he'll be relieved to not take on the responsibility.

post: roxbride
Tell your FI to explain to his old friend that he got overexcited and would like for him to be part of the wedding party, but that he and his FI decided a mutual friend should be the best man. That way, the old friend is still involved, and your FI gets the best man he wants.

reply: chicklit
Don't ask the old friend (and current best man) to step down; ask the new roommate/friend to step up. Have two best men!

post: mrsbob2b
Maybe your FI and his old buddy will reconnect and their friendship will be stronger than ever. I say, just stick with it.

the knot
Sadly, there is no graceful way to retract the best man invite. In this situation, honesty is the best policy. Your fiancé's first step should be a frank conversation with his current BM. He could say he got caught up in the moment and made the initial decision without consulting you, but both of you want your honor attendants to be the two people you feel closest to right now. And, as ChickLit said, another option is simply for your fiancé to have two best men.

- Coordinating the groomsmen's wedding attire rentals or purchases; paying for his own attire
- Corralling the other guys and making sure they're performing their duties
- Coordinating groomsmen's wedding transportation and lodging (if necessary)
- Standing next to the groom at the altar and holding the bride's ring until he needs it
- Signing the marriage certificate as a witness after the ceremony
- Handing the officiant his or her fee after the ceremony, and having cash in hand for anyone who needs tipping, paying, or bribing
- Kicking off the reception-time toasting, traditionally
- Collecting any gift envelopes guests bring to the reception and keeping them or depositing them for you
- Possibly driving you to your wedding-night hotel or to the airport after the reception

Calling all kids

So you have twenty-seven little cousins who are so cute, you just have to include them in the ceremony? We love children in a wedding party, not only for the adorable photos but also for the levity they can add to the ceremony. Just be forewarned: Kids will not necessarily do what you want, so if you do choose to have them, you will need to let go a little. And don't expect too much of young attendants: Even your thirteen-year-old cousin might not be able to handle standing still on the altar for the entire ceremony. Here are some roles to consider for the younger members of your families.

JUNIOR ATTENDANTS Include young friends and relatives (ages nine to sixteen) as junior ushers, bridesmaids, or groomsmen. They'll attend all major functions (excluding ID-required bachelor/bachelorette parties, of course) and fulfill many of the same responsibilities as senior squad members depending on their age.

FLOWER CHILDREN These little ones (ages three to eight) walk down the aisle before the bride, scattering flower petals from a basket (or carrying a pomander). Little ladies are the norm, but cute little boys can fill this role, too.

RING BEARERS Traditionally a small boy (ages four to eight), the ring bearer walks down the aisle either before or along with the flower child, holding a small, fancy pillow with your two wedding bands tied to it (usually fakes, in case they are lost, while the real ones wait safely with your honor attendants).

GLOSSARY
bridal party shorthand

MOH: Maid of Honor

BM: Best Man

Maids: Bridesmaids

FI: Fiancé

MIL: Mother-in-Law

FIL: Father-in-Law

FOB: Father of the Bride

MOB: Mother of the Bride

B2B: Bride-to-Be

CLEVER IDEAS
petal alternatives

Forget the title "flower girl." Consider one of these petal alternatives for your flower child to carry down the aisle:

A little lantern

A photo of a special relative to remember

A Bible

A basket of lavender

A favorite toy of yours from growing up

other special ceremony roles

huppah holders

In Jewish weddings, individuals close to the bride and groom (usually family members or close friends) may hold up the huppah (canopy) poles during the ceremony. They might even help make the huppah, if they have the time and creativity.

Shushavim

A Jewish term describing anyone close to the bride and groom who helps them plan and prepare for marriage. In many Jewish weddings, there's no traditional wedding party, but certain members of the *shushavim* (a mom, a sister, a best friend) might perform similar tasks.

Koumbaro/Koumbara

The *koumbaro* is the Eastern Orthodox groom's best man. (The *koumbara* is the female version.) In traditional Greek weddings, the *koumbaro*'s role is highly symbolic. For example, during the Greek crowning ceremony, he places crowns on the bride's and groom's heads, and then switches the crowns back and forth three times, which symbolizes uniting and binding the couple.

Vratimi

Basically, they're Greek groomsmen. In traditional Eastern Orthodox weddings, the *vratimi* is a pack of the groom's male friends who help the *koumbaro* carry out his traditional role and perform various rituals.

Hattabin

A Muslim term for male family or friends who participate in and help prepare the groom for the wedding. Among Moroccan Muslims, it's common for the *hattabin* to propose to the bride on the groom's behalf.

PAGES This traditional English role is usually performed by two little boys, aged six through nine, but girl pages are perfectly fine, too. Pages, also called "train bearers," carry the bride's extra-long wedding-gown train (think of Princess Diana's wedding) as she walks down the aisle.

Roles for other important people Maybe you were voted "Most Popular" by your high school class, college dorm mates, and tennis team. Or perhaps you come from one of those families with a hundred first cousins and two hundred second cousins. Don't inflate your wedding party to a Rockettes-size line—just turn those VIPs into

VIEs (Very Important Extras). You can acknowledge special people in a relatively passive way by giving them corsages, seats of honor, or a place in the family pictures. Or you can make them part of the party by having them do a reading at your ceremony or inventing entirely new roles for them. Just make sure your honor roles are actually honorable—there's nothing particularly appealing about guest book duty or bathroom detail. Here are some other ideas for your VIEs.

USHERS Ask special friends or relatives (male or female) to serve as ushers, walking your guests to their seats, passing out ceremony programs, and acting as general guest guides. Groomsmen often double as ushers, but if it's a huge wedding or there are lots of people you want to include, appoint extra designated ushers to help with crowd control. Dedicate about one usher for every fifty guests.

CANDLE LIGHTERS In some Christian ceremonies, preteens (aged nine to twelve) light candles at the altar just before the mother of the bride is seated. But at any wedding, you can honor someone by asking her to light a candle during the reception.

READERS Have a well-spoken friend or relative do a reading during your ceremony. You can choose the text or ask him to select something he loves. Alternately, you could ask a literary type to write something to be read aloud or to be printed in the program.

PERFORMERS Musically inclined friends or siblings can be a featured part of your ceremony or reception. Ask them to sing a special song or play an instrument during the ceremony. Just make sure they are comfortable in front of crowds and you are both okay with what they're planning.

PICKING YOUR PARTY

Choosing the wedding party can be one of the toughest (read: most political) decisions you make as to-be-weds. Your best buddies, college roommates, siblings, cousins, and even long-lost elementary school friends may be vying for a coveted position on the team. To help you choose the right team, let the duties we've just outlined guide you. Are your best buds up to the responsibility? Think twice about asking friends who live far away or who have extremely hectic schedules if you expect them to be involved in all festivities.

ASK CARLEY
PLAYING FAVORITES

I have two best friends. How do I choose just one to be my honor attendant?
Don't! There's no rule that says you can't have co–honor attendants. If these are the two people you feel closest to and you want them by your side, then give them both the title. Just make sure to divvy up the duties clearly to avoid confusion.

ASK CARLEY

BREAKING THE BAD NEWS

I'm only having five bridesmaids, and I'm afraid the good friends I couldn't include will be mad. How do I let them know?

Call each friend you didn't ask (or make a dinner date) and tell her how much her friendship means to you and how much you want her to be there. Then let her know, straight up, that you were only able to choose a certain number of attendants and you would never want that to affect your friendship. You could ask her to take another special role during the ceremony or reception if you'd like.

Crew considerations Although there are no set rules or guidelines and every wedding party is different, you should want to take these factors into account before choosing your crew.

SIZE While bridal parties can range from a single maid of honor to more than a dozen attendants, one formula you can use for guidance is to have one groomsman and one corresponding bridesmaid for every fifty guests (so if you're inviting two hundred guests, you'd have four bridesmaids and four groomsmen). While you certainly needn't be tied to that formula, keep logistics in mind, too: If you're getting married at a church with a small altar, you may not be able to fit a huge bridal party unless you plan to have everyone sit during the ceremony. Also, more attendants can mean more stress—there are more people to agree on a dress, get measured for tuxes, and decide on a bachelor/bachelorette party date.

SYMMETRY Don't feel like you have to ask a stranger to be in your wedding just because your fiancé has one more attendant than you do. We say, even schmeven—it's perfectly okay to have five on one side and three on the other. Just have one groomsman walk two bridesmaids down the aisle, have one of your honor attendants walk alone, or each member of the party can make the trip down the aisle solo.

It's perfectly appropriate (and frankly, we think, pretty cool) for your best pals to be there by your side—male or female. So if your best friend is of the opposite sex, there's no reason why he can't be a bridesman (or she a groomswoman). With that said, you may want to include siblings or close cousins on the "traditional" side, even if you're not particularly close. It may be easier than dealing with the resulting family drama if you don't.

BUDGET The bigger the bridal party, the more of your budget you will devote to bouquets ($75–250 each), boutonnieres ($25–65 each), and bridal party gifts ($50–500 each). This is no reason to cut out people you love, just bear it in mind. (While we're on the topic: Be mindful of friends who are paying for grad school or who just had a new baby and may not be able to afford the financial burden of being a bridesmaid or groomsman.)

Finalize your wedding party list with your partner—you both have to be happy with who will be standing up for you. Once you make up your minds, you'll want to get the word out quickly—and at close to the same time. (You don't want key friends' feelings getting hurt because they heard you'd chosen people but you didn't ask them until two weeks later.) Asking your VIPs well in advance of your wedding day will also make it easier for them to help you plan.

FITTING IN THE FOLKS

You can't choose your parents, but you can decide what role they play in your wedding. While traditionally the parents were the official hosts, parental involvement today is more a question of comfort and closeness than cash (especially since you two may be putting the whole wedding on your gold card or the groom's parents may be paying more than the bride's). Regardless of who is paying, here are some ways to get both sets of parents involved.

Mother of the bride (mob)

The mother of the bride may serve as wedding planner, guest-list moderator, reception hostess, fashion critic, or cheerleader. Other possible duties include attending the bridal shower and rehearsal dinner, greeting guests in the receiving line, and dancing the night away at the reception. The nature of the bride's mother's role is entirely up to you. If you get along great with your mom (and she has the time), feel free to ask her to help with just about everything, easing your burden and giving you some serious mother-daughter bonding opportunities. If your relationship isn't quite so smooth, give her roles that will make her feel involved—without driving you crazy (like researching hotels for out-of-town guests or making sure your dad and brother get fitted for their tuxes).

Mother of the groom (mog)

The groom's mother traditionally has only a shadow role on the actual wedding day—greeting guests in the receiving line, being escorted down the aisle during the ceremony prelude, taking part in the mother/son spotlight dance, and sitting at the parents' table. Her big event has always been the rehearsal dinner, which she traditionally plans and hosts along with the groom's father. She also typically attends the bridal shower. But she can chip in on any of the traditional mother-of-the-bride tasks as well. (Just make sure the MOB is okay with sharing her duties.)

Father of the bride (fob)

Dad's chores might include wedding planner, contract negotiator, venue scouter, and tipper (to wedding-day staff), as well as a variety of toasting and hosting tasks. Don't assume your dad isn't interested in helping with the planning just because he doesn't offer. Even if he's normally Mr. Take Charge at the office, he may be shy around all things wedding related. Typically, he walks the bride down the aisle.

---

pets in the party

A beloved pet can join the party as a ring bearer or other honored guest. But before you dress Fluffy in formalwear, keep these things in mind.

make sure your wedding site allows pets
Many churches, temples, and catering halls have strict no-pets policies.

assign (or hire) a pet sitter
Make someone responsible for keeping your pet safe and out of trouble. That person will also need to take your little guy home after the ceremony.

do a test drive
If you're expecting your pet to carry the rings on his back or in a basket in his mouth, check that he can do this before you turn down your nephew's offer to be the ring bearer.

brace yourself
Be prepared for things to go haywire.

ASK CARLEY
OBLIGATORY ASK

Do I need to ask a friend to be in my bridal party just because she asked me to be in hers?
No. Weddings are not a time for quid pro quo. Period. If you're afraid of hurting someone's feelings, remember that, as clichéd as it sounds, any true friend will understand whatever decision you ultimately make. Be up-front. Simply explain that there were a lot of people you wanted to include and it was really hard to decide, so you chose only your very closest friends and siblings. Chances are she's been in a few weddings and will be perfectly happy attending as a guest.

Father of the groom (fog)

The groom's dad traditionally pays for—and plans—the rehearsal dinner along with the MOG. He might also fulfill numerous dancing, toasting, and other "fatherly" obligations at the wedding (i.e., escorting elderly guests, moving tables, addressing problematic service).

Stepparents (sp)

When it comes to including stepparents and siblings in the wedding, it's really up to you and your family dynamic. If you're close to your parents and stepparent(s), include them both but make sure you divide the duties. For example, if you ask Mom to walk you down the aisle, maybe your stepmother will be the last person seated before the processional begins. Have a heart-to heart with each mom well before the wedding to let them know you're planning to include both of them and to see what they're comfortable (and uncomfortable) with. Decide together what roles they'll have on your wedding day. Not sure whom to dance with during the father-daughter dance? You could start the dance with your stepdad and then switch halfway through to your dad (or vice versa if you prefer). Just let them know your plan so they won't be surprised. Or do a complete dance with each one; just keep the songs short and spread them out. So you might dance with your stepdad first, immediately following the first dance, and then dance with your dad before the cake cutting. You don't have to do an emotional "Daddy's Little Girl"–type song if it feels fake. Feel free to dance to something fun, like "The Twist"! If you're not close to a stepparent, it's also perfectly fine to save the traditional roles for your parents (or another relative or friend that you feel close to).

6

wedding planners and pros

TIMELINE

PLANNING

12+ months before
Research vendors; book
any key ones

Hire wedding planner

Book officiant

9–11 months before
Book caterer, band or DJ,
florist, and photographer
and videographer

6–8 months before
Book cake baker,
transportation, and
ceremony musicians

4–5 months before
Choose stationer and
calligrapher

Hire lighting designer
and rental company

Planning, organizing, and designing every little detail of your unique wedding vision will take a tremendous amount of time and talent. And no matter how much you plan to do yourself or how skilled your friends are, you will need a team of professionals to help you execute your big day. We're talking about the vendors: wedding planners, cake bakers, caterers, florists, photographers, bandleaders and DJs, videographers, lighting designers, and more. The secret to a successful—and stress-free—wedding is hiring the right key players.

do you need a wedding planner?

Are you already short on time because of work, school, or other obligations?

Y ☐   N ☐

Do you have trouble staying organized and keeping track of paperwork and budgets?

Y ☐   N ☐

Are you getting married in less than a year?

Y ☐   N ☐

Are you planning a destination wedding?

Y ☐   N ☐

Are you on a tight budget?

Y ☐   N ☐

Does the thought of talking budgets and fees with vendors make you cringe?

Y ☐   N ☐

Do you need help creating a wedding vision and tying all the details together?

Y ☐   N ☐

Are you having a big wedding with 200+ people?

Y ☐   N ☐

Are you dreading the family drama that a wedding is sure to cause?

Y ☐   N ☐

Are you throwing a tented, off-site, or other complicated wedding?

Y ☐   N ☐

Mostly Y's: You Need a Full-Time Planner

An experienced event planner can take on a large (or small) amount of responsibility and can also cut out some of the early research and legwork, which can be extremely time-consuming. If you're having a destination or a big (200-plus) or off-site (a tented reception or nontraditional venue) wedding, a planner is really a must to help you handle all the extra components that go with these more complicated affairs.

Mix of Y's and N's: Hire a Part-Time Planner

This more economical choice can pitch in where you need the most guidance and save you time and stress. Plus, he can help you find reliable and skilled vendors.

Mostly N's: Consider a Day-of Coordinator

You may be really involved in wedding planning, but trust us, you'll want someone there the week—or at least night—of your wedding to make sure everything goes off without a hitch.

WEDDING PLANNERS AND COORDINATORS

Wedding planners are professionals whose lives revolve around all things nuptial; they're equal parts party planner, stylist, stage manager, financial adviser, vendor broker, shrink, and all-around wedding genius. They'll help you search for the perfect venue and find great vendors that will fit within your planning budget. (In fact, a successful planner will have relationships with vendors and will often be able to help you negotiate deals you wouldn't be able to on your own.) Once you have booked your vendors, your planner will oversee each relationship (including contracts and budgets) and help pull everything together. The best part is, they plan weddings for a living, so chances are there won't be a problem they haven't encountered before, they'll have experience handling even the stickiest of situations, and they'll know how to keep you calm in the process.

Planning, organizing, and carrying out a unique and gorgeous wedding takes exceptional skill, and you want to make sure you find the right person for the job.

Cost considerations
A planner charges in one of three ways: a flat fee, an hourly rate, or a percentage of your overall wedding bill. Costs vary from 10 percent on the lower end to 20 percent on the higher end of the spectrum. Most planners charge flat fees these days, but regardless of which way your planner charges, if you want a full-service scenario, estimate about 15 percent of your wedding budget. (So if your budget is $100,000, for example, set aside $15,000.) Fees for wedding-day coordination vary widely. While it can seem like a big investment, between private discounts, budget control, and creative solutions, hiring a wedding planner will help you make the absolute most of your wedding budget.

Types of planning services
When it comes to planners, you have many choices, so you'll want to start by thinking about what you're looking for and reading about your different options before meeting with any candidates. Then, be sure to clarify what each planner does. There are a range of professionals who fall under the wedding planner title, who have different skill sets. Not all planners offer design services, and not all event designers handle logistics. Some are more vision-oriented, others are more schedule- and production-oriented.

what a planner can do for you

Here is a list of the general tasks planners can handle.

- ☐ Setting up a realistic wedding budget

- ☐ Devising a wedding master plan that maps out all the little details, from ceremony music to favors

- ☐ Showing you the best and most original locations in the area, considering your wedding size, budget, and vision

- ☐ Finding the top florists, photographers, caterers, bands, DJs, and other vendors in your price range

- ☐ Cutting you choice deals: Consultants bring volume to favored vendors, so often the vendors will reciprocate by slashing prices or throwing in extras

- ☐ Reading over all your vendor contracts to make sure everything is there, correct, and in accordance with your best interests, and negotiating any amendments on your behalf

- ☐ Creating a day-of (or weekend-of) timeline that tells everyone involved in the planning process—vendors, members of the wedding party, you, and your families—when to do what

- ☐ Handling the invitations, from the wording and ordering to the addressing and mailing, as well as tracking RSVPs

- ☐ Counseling you on proper etiquette as well as what's hot on the wedding front

- ☐ Managing the wedding day: supervising vendors, setup, and delivery; handling emergencies; and soothing nerves

- ☐ Serving as your spokesperson, conveying your every whim and desire to vendors or family members when you just can't deal with doing it yourself

- ☐ Helping to plan and book your honeymoon (yep—most planners will handle your travel plans too!)

Be sure you're clear on the extent of the services potential planners are willing to provide when you interview her to make sure you're going to receive all the support you're expecting. Here is a more detailed breakdown of your options—and which one might be right for you. Be forewarned: These terms are not used consistently across the industry; nonetheless, this will give you an idea of the type of service you want.

FULL-SERVICE PLANNERS A full-service planner handles both design and coordination, from start to finish (from designing the overall vision and hiring and meeting with vendors to arranging weekend activities for your guests). This type of planner is great for couples who are having a complex event or simply want a professional to guide them every step of the way and to handle all the details of executing their vision.

EVENT DESIGNERS An event designer focuses on pulling together the overall look of the day rather than organizing all the myriad details (like the timeline or budget). She is like an interior designer for your event, often working with other vendors—from invitation designers to florists and bakers—to bring your vision to life. But don't expect her to handle the organization or logistics.

A wedding designer is not necessary if you would like to work with your venue manager, wedding planner, and/or florist (some florists, called "floral designers," are also design experts who will help you with the décor and design concept, as well as the centerpieces and bouquets) to create your wedding décor concept. Busy brides often turn to event designers to take some of the planning pressure off or to achieve a unique theme idea or concept, or just to make sure their reception looks amazing.

À LA CARTE PLANNERS This part-time pro helps you shape the event by giving you décor suggestions, vendor recommendations, or assistance with specific projects—you contact the planner when you need help and he charges either an hourly rate or a flat fee for each service. An à la carte planner is great for couples who need someone to design a blueprint that they will execute themselves. Basically, if you want to steal his secrets, but don't want everyone to say it was clearly a [insert popular planner's name]'s wedding, an à la carte planner is for you.

DAY-OF COORDINATORS A day-of pro helps to make sure everything runs smoothly on the actual wedding day but isn't really involved much beforehand. Most prefer to begin their involvement at least a month before the wedding to truly make sure all things are in order, and they charge a flat fee. They'll handle all your vendors and setup on the day of your wedding, as well as any type of cleanup or postwedding duties needed so that you and your family members can just relax and enjoy the day. A day-of coordinator is perfect for couples who plan to be very hands-on during the planning process and can handle the contracts and organization but want someone to take care of all the details the week before and want someone to be there the day of.

Finding the perfect planner
Once you know which type of help you want, gather names of local planners. Start with friends who have recently married—and were pleased with their weddings—for the names of their planners. If you've booked your reception site, ask your reception site manager for planner suggestions. A planner who knows

wedding planner

Here are key questions to ask when meeting with potential planners and coordinators.

☐ Are you available on my wedding date?

☐ What's the cost of the average wedding you plan?

☐ What sorts of services do you offer (day-of coordination, full-service event design, or à la carte planning)? Do you create the overall vision, or are you more of a producer who brings in an event designer? Do you handle event styling?

☐ If you do both planning and coordinating, what is your main specialty?

☐ How many weddings have you planned?

☐ How many weddings will you be working on at the same time as mine?

☐ Have you planned any other weddings at our site?

☐ Do you handle vendor services, contracts, and payment processing? [Some planners will request a lump sum and from there handle hiring and paying vendors for you. Others will ask you to cut the checks for vendors yourselves. It's generally best to pay vendors directly instead of through your planner. This way you will have more control over the contract and your budget.]

☐ Are there specific vendors you like to use? What is your process for selecting and hiring vendors? How are we involved? Are you offered client discounts for any vendors that you work with?

☐ Do you handle guest list coordination and RSVPs?

☐ Do you do destination weddings [if applicable]?

☐ Do you handle rentals?

☐ What was the most unique wedding you ever planned?

☐ What are some ideas you have for pulling off our vision [if applicable]?

☐ What is your secret for staying calm under pressure and dealing with day-of disasters and mishaps?

☐ How many meetings will we have? Do you come with us to all our relevant meetings? What are the steps we will go through?

☐ What is the best way to get in touch with you?

☐ How many people on your staff will be at the wedding?

☐ What happens if you're ill or otherwise unable to be there on the day of our wedding?

☐ Do you have references? [Ask for professional testimonials as well as those from recent brides.]

☐ How will you help me stay within my budget (stay away from things I can't afford, find alternatives)?

☐ Do you carry personal liability and professional indemnity insurance?

☐ How do payments work? (A percentage of our budget? A flat fee?) Will there be additional expenses on top of your base fee? (Travel, parking, food?)

your venue will have a better idea of lighting and electricity needs, problem spots that need to be covered, the best way to lay out the room, and any logistical or design details that may not be obvious. Also, use local wedding magazines, websites, and blogs, as well as city guides, to find the names of planners in your area.

Check out prospective planners' websites for photos of recent weddings they have done to help narrow down your list. Notice whether elements seem to have a cohesive look and if there is an overarching style that the weddings share—this is probably what the planner is most experienced with, so decide if it's one you like. If all the weddings that he's planned look over-the-top and glamorous and you're looking for a small, intimate gathering, he may not be the right person for you. Also, look for information about the types of planning services they offer, sites they've worked with, awards, and membership in professional associations (such as the Association of Bridal Consultants).

Call your top three or four picks to confirm the following: types of planning services offered, names of sites they have worked with, wedding date availability, and appropriateness price-wise (ask their typical price range and/or cost of the average wedding they plan). If their answers fit your budget and your vision, set up appointments to meet with each of them.

Bring magazine clippings, photos, and even your inspiration board(s) (see chapter 1, page 10) with you when you meet with potential planners. At your meeting, you obviously want to get a sense of the quality of their weddings by asking them about events they've done and perusing their portfolios, but you're also looking at their personalities: Is this someone you can work with intimately for months at a time? Voice your ideas about your style and colors and see how the planner responds—she should meet them with enthusiasm. Then ask how she'd pull off your vision to get a better idea of how she works. A good planner should be able to listen to your thoughts and hone them to make your wedding something truly unique and memorable.

Sealing the deal
Don't feel pressured to hire a planner you like on the spot. Be sure to call references and ask the following.

- How closely did she stick to your budget?
- Can you e-mail me photos from your wedding? [This is a good way to confirm the overall consistency and professionalism of the wedding. Planners' portfolios are filled with their best work, and, of course, they'll offer brides they know were happy with their work for references, so search online for other real weddings they've done as well.]

EXPERT ADVICE
wedding vendor list

These are the professionals you need to bring your wedding vision to life:

Ceremony officiant (unless a friend or relative will be marrying you)

Planner/Coordinator

Caterer

Band or DJ

Photographer

Florist

Stationer

Cake baker (unless caterer is designing your cake, too)

Videographer

Transportation company and drivers

Ceremony musicians

Rental company

Hairstylist and makeup artist

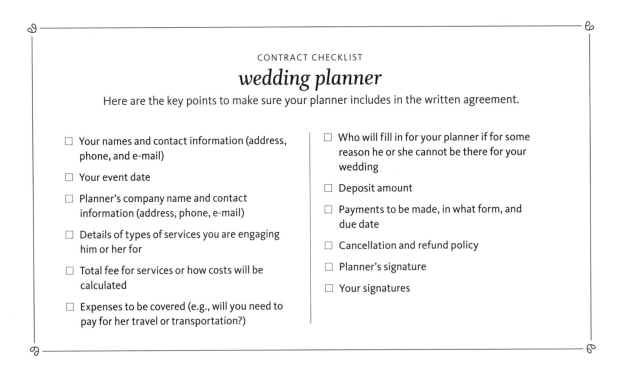

CONTRACT CHECKLIST

wedding planner

Here are the key points to make sure your planner includes in the written agreement.

- ☐ Your names and contact information (address, phone, and e-mail)
- ☐ Your event date
- ☐ Planner's company name and contact information (address, phone, e-mail)
- ☐ Details of types of services you are engaging him or her for
- ☐ Total fee for services or how costs will be calculated
- ☐ Expenses to be covered (e.g., will you need to pay for her travel or transportation?)

- ☐ Who will fill in for your planner if for some reason he or she cannot be there for your wedding
- ☐ Deposit amount
- ☐ Payments to be made, in what form, and due date
- ☐ Cancellation and refund policy
- ☐ Planner's signature
- ☐ Your signatures

- How well did she interpret your ideas?
- Were the style and wedding exactly what you wanted?
- What did she take care of for you (guest list, vendor meetings, setup, etc.)?
- Did she have good vendor recommendations? Did she coordinate with other vendors?
- Did she respond quickly to your calls or e-mails? Was she nice to work with?
- Did the wedding go smoothly according to your guests?
- Did anything go wrong, and how did she handle it?

Also, take some time to compare and contrast prices, impressions, notes, and, if provided, formal proposals (some planners may draft their overall vision for your wedding and their intended services in the form of a proposal, which would then work as the basis for your contract). Once you've found your planner, call her immediately to express your desire to move forward and have her prepare a contract (see "Contract Checklist," above). As soon as you've signed the contract and paid your deposit, you'll have your right-hand woman (or man) secured.

OTHER WEDDING VENDORS

If you're hiring a planner, she can help you select vendors, but you will still want to have a say in who is making your centerpieces, decorating your cake, and spinning the tunes. Your vendors will be responsible for making your wedding dreams a reality, and choosing a team you're comfortable working with will make the next several months a lot less stressful.

Finding your wedding pros
Whether you're looking for a florist, stationer, DJ, or cake baker, there are some go-to resources that will become your best friends over the next few months for finding the top vendors in your area.

- Word of mouth is still the number one way to get recommendations. Ask your friends and coworkers who have recently gotten married, and you can also connect with real brides online.
- Your planner and other vendors are also a huge asset, as they work with tons of wedding professionals every weekend and will have great intel on the best wedding pros out there.
- Your next go-to source for vendor recommendations: professionally published wedding magazines and websites, which feature the work and tips of the best in the biz (you can probably see some of their work in their photos).
- Do some investigating on your own, too. Visiting a bridal show is a way to speak briefly with a wide range of vendors and get a sense of prices in your area.

Once you've gotten a list of solid vendors, always do a background check. Check with your local Better Business Bureau to see if any consumer complaints have been filed against any vendors you're considering, and see what other brides had to say about their work by checking out online reviews (like those on WeddingChannel.com). Then visit vendors' professional websites to get a feel for their work, any awards or professional distinctions they've received, their specialties, and venues they've worked with. Pros who have worked at your venue will probably know the staff, layout, and any quirks there, which can make your life easier, and they may even fill you in on potential issues like poor acoustics before they become problems.

Interviewing potential vendors
Aim to personally speak to three vendors in every category before selecting one. You will want to do an in-person interview whenever possible to make sure your

the knot NOTE

vendor listings and reviews
Need help finding a vendor or determining if one is up to par? Connect with thousands of real brides across the country at **TheKnot.com/talk.**

personalities jive and to check out their workspaces to make sure you like what you see. You will be working with your vendors a lot and trusting them for key elements of arguably the most important day of your life, so whether it's your florist, officiant, or DJ, it's key to meet them and make sure you get a good feeling from them. And always, always ask for—and follow up with—references.

The "other" proposal   Once you've narrowed it down to a short list of potential vendors in each category who suit your budget, taste, personality, and timetable, ask them to give you a written proposal, outlining the services they will provide, the vision they have sketched out based on the ideas and preferences you've expressed, and the estimated cost to pull it all off. Then compare potential vendors' proposals carefully. Use these documents in future negotiations as a benchmark, adding or deleting elements to hit the figure that fits your budget. Vendors want your business, especially during down months and on weekdays, so it doesn't hurt to ask (nicely) if they can throw in extra perks or reduce their price quote. Sometimes they won't be able to come down, but most vendors would rather make it work than see you walk away.

WORKING WITH VENDORS

Got your top vendor picks nailed down? It's not quite as easy as calling them up to let them know they got the job. You've got some paperwork to fill out (including a few checks to sign) first. Here's how to lock down your wedding team.

Contracts 101   Once you've squared away all the details, get a contract or written agreement—composed in easy-to-understand language—that spells out everything you've discussed. Have an expert eye (your detail-oriented aunt, a lawyer friend, or even better, your wedding planner) look over the contract to make sure it's kosher and clear and that nothing has been forgotten. Sign the contract only when you're completely comfortable with it. You and the vendor should sign and date two copies (one for each of you to keep) so it will be legally binding.

For every single vendor you hire, from your planner to the rental company supplying your linens, it's crucial that you get a written contract. Professionals should take the lead in drawing up contracts, but if anyone you want to work with hasn't, be sure to ask for one. Even if you're working with a friend or relative, you'll want some form of written agreement! A verbal contract or handshake is not enough, not when you're talking about your money and your wedding. If a vendor refuses to provide or sign a contract, move on. You don't want to work with someone who won't guarantee his or her work.

While there will be aspects of your wedding you won't be able to control (like the weather), contracts are your number one insurance plan against something going wrong and can help ensure you get exactly what you want from your vendors—from the cake flavor you requested and the right-color peonies to a limo driver who shows up on time. Contracts are legally binding, so if your vendor fails to do what is stipulated in your contract, you can take him to court to recover your payment. Likewise, if you don't hold up your end of the deal, he can take you to court to get the rest of his. And until you sign a contract and pay the deposit, vendors aren't obligated to hold the date of your wedding.

CONTRACT CONTENT The basic points that should be in all contracts include dates and times of services, the names of all parties involved in the agreement, the deposit and final payment amounts (as well as the payment schedule), the cancellation and refund policy (on both ends), and contingency plans (if Photographer A is not available to shoot the wedding due to illness, Photographer B will replace him). A detailed description of the services provided and final product you've agreed upon should also be there. Contracts should be as specific as possible, listing particular colors, types, quantities (number of guests to be served, centerpieces to be created, individual flowers in each centerpiece, etc.), and even substitutions (if pink peonies are not available for the wedding, pink garden roses will be used instead).

INSURANCE CLAUSES Some venues will require both you and your vendors to carry liability insurance in case any damage to the space is caused. If this is the case, confirm with your vendor that his or her company is covered (most professional vendors will be) and include a clause in your contract guaranteeing that said vendor will have and will show proof of liability insurance. Another smart addition: a hold-harmless clause, which basically says that you are not responsible for any damage or other issues caused by your vendors.

To protect themselves, your vendors may include an indemnification clause. Translation: If a guest slips and falls and sues you and your venue is named in the lawsuit, you will cover all legal expenses and any other damages the venue is liable for if you lose the case. An indemnification clause is also a good way to protect yourselves from potential lawsuits brought against your vendors, so ask them to include the reverse (or "indemnify you") in the contract as well.

EXPERT ADVICE
vendors to avoid

Anyone who doesn't listen to you, respect your vision or ideas, and insists he or she knows better

Vendors who are not straight about costs and fees

Anyone who is too busy to return your calls or e-mails

Anyone who sends an assistant in his or her place

vendor contracts

From your florist and cake baker to your DJ or band and more, here are the key points
that should be in any vendor's contract before you sign.

☐ Vendor's name and business name, address, phone numbers (cell, office number, and any other numbers where they can be reached easily), and e-mail

☐ Your names, address, phone numbers, and e-mail

☐ The date and time of the service to be delivered

☐ The length of the service: exact start and finish times, including setup and breakdown periods and delivery times

☐ An hourly overtime rate (make sure the vendor will be available for overtime—you don't want wrap-up work interrupting the party if it's still in full swing)

☐ Details, details: a list of everything the vendor will be supplying and doing for you, down to the minutest of minutiae, like the exact measurements of the linens you want.

☐ Contact information and directions for how you want to be contacted throughout the process and the best way to reach your vendor.

☐ Exact prices, including a breakdown of individual items or services, fees for setup and delivery, and the tax; also include a list of any required service charges (a detailed list of expected—but not required—gratuities is optional)

☐ The deposit amount and the remaining fee that is due—if you've paid the deposit, make sure that the payment is noted in the contract

☐ Acceptable payment methods (credit card, personal check, certified check, etc.)

☐ Breakdown for when fees will be due, including deposit and final payments

☐ Any agreed-upon numbers for services, like how many meals or centerpieces

☐ An agreed-upon staff dress code that's appropriate for your wedding's formality

☐ Cancellation and refund policy

☐ A contingency plan, detailing who will fill in if your vendor is unable to perform his duties the day of or what will happen if he is unable to deliver the final product

☐ Setup and return details (make sure it's clear when and where the vendor will deliver equipment, whether they'll handle setup and breakdown, and when you need to give everything back—and how you'll do that)

NEGOTIATING CONTRACTS   It's crucial to read the fine print of any contract and ask questions or make clarifications and/or adjustments before signing. Do not think what you first see is what you get: You can absolutely make changes or add information to your contracts before signing. Just make sure that both you and the vendor initial any changes and that you see a completed contract that includes all revisions you have requested before signing. Any changes discussed via phone or e-mail should be written into the contract, or if they're made after the fact, request an addendum to the contract and keep track of any e-mail correspondence and receipts—just in case.

Deposits   You're not done quite yet—in order to reserve a vendor's services, you will likely need to put down a deposit, too. Until you do, don't consider him booked for your wedding. The deposit is usually a percentage of the total bill (typically about 50 percent, but it varies, and you can negotiate a set amount with your vendor). Most deposits are nonrefundable in the event of a cancellation, change of heart, etc.—but talk to your vendor. Some are willing to return your deposit (just make sure to get it written into your contract!) for special circumstances like loss of a job, illness, postponement (as long as you use their services later), or military deployment. (If they don't offer refunds for your deposit for these special circumstances and they pertain to you, look into wedding insurance—see chapter 2.)

Deposits are a good thing—they commit both you and your vendor to your event from the start. Still, it's smart to use a credit card to pay any deposits. That way, if the vendor goes out of business, ruins your cake, or fails to show up, you may be able to convince the credit card company to reverse the charges.

Keep track of all deposits you make in your online budget tracker (and get receipts!), so you know how much you've spent and how much is due after the fact. A word of caution: Never pay in full just to get another to-do out of the way or to get a discount. You want to wait to see the final product to guarantee that you're happy with the result and that the vendor follows through.

Getting what you want   Your vendors are there to help you, and they truly want you to be happy. So never hesitate to speak your mind if you're not pleased with what you see. Some vendors use process of elimination to get to the root of what you really want, incorporating both your positive and negative feedback into subsequent attempts, so your feedback—the good, the bad, and the ugly—is key.

ASK CARLEY
VENDOR ETIQUETTE

How can I make changes to a vendor proposal without sounding negative?
Vendors want your wedding to be perfect, too, and they like to know how to help. How you communicate is key. Just state the needed changes, and to ease any tension, mention the things you like as well (though we promise, as professionals, they are used to criticism, changes, and nitpicky clients, and won't be upset—they'll actually be grateful for the feedback). Try something like, "I love the lushness of the bouquet, but it would be great if we could use more blue."

The best way to get exactly what you're envisioning? Don't just tell your team what you want—show them. Words like *modern*, *gorgeous*, or *elegant* are largely subjective. Don't expect your vendor to magically re-create something from your imagination when you haven't given him concrete explanations or examples of what you mean. For anything visual, like the flowers or cake, bring images to all of your appointments to show your cake baker or florist what you're thinking—and what you are not thinking. For a DJ or band, make an explicit song list of what you do—and don't—want played. Same goes for your event designer or lighting designer. Remember: One woman's chic is another woman's eek.

TIMELINE

vendors' day-of duties

Here's when to expect to see your vendors the day of your wedding.

vendors whose work will be finished before the wedding
Stationer

Calligrapher

Wedding gown consultant, designer, and seamstress

Tux tailor and rental store

vendors who will just make an appearance the day of or the day before the wedding (to set up or deliver goods or services, for example)
Rental company

Cake baker

Florist

Event designer

Lighting designer

vendors who will work with you in the hours before the wedding
Hairstylist

Makeup artist

(Some brides will ask their hair and makeup pros to stay with them for postceremony touch-ups before taking pictures. Or you may want your hairstylist to stay to help you remove the veil and even give you a new reception hairdo.)

vendors who will stay only for the ceremony
Officiant

Ceremony musicians

Ceremony site manager

vendors who will just be there for the reception
Reception site manager

Reception site staff

Waitstaff and bartenders

Caterer

Reception band or DJ

vendors who will stay for the entire wedding, start to finish
Planner or coordinator

Photographer

Videographer

Transportation providers

the deal with diy

While hiring wedding professionals will reduce your stress and workload and ensure a top-quality final product, taking on some things yourself can help add a personal touch and trim your budget.

DIY DOS

your makeup

If you do your own makeup, you'll be in the privacy of your home or hotel room—and you won't have to worry about booking an appointment. Invest in quality makeup and consider heading to a nearby department store for a (free) lesson at one of the beauty counters. And don't skip the trial run, which helps you to perfect your look in advance.

your ceremony décor

The ceremony lasts less than an hour, so it's a good place to save on décor, especially if the site is pretty on its own. Create hanging baskets or vases filled with locally grown flowers. Or, instead of flowers, buy candles and place them throughout the space.

your favors

Making your favors or just wrapping them yourself is a popular way to save money. If you prefer to stay away from the hot glue gun, sweet treats are a safe choice. Grab a box of your favorite mix and start baking. Pack the treats in colorful boxes or cute bags.

your ceremony programs

Head to a local craft or paper store for a DIY kit or choose stock paper in any color and print programs right off your computer. (You can find directions for easy-to-make programs and other DIY wedding details at TheKnot.com/diy.)

DIY DON'TS

As we mentioned in chapter 2, a professional photographer and band or DJ are definitely worth the money. Here's where else to stick with the pros:

cake

Constructing a cake that can feed 150-plus guests and won't topple over, not to mention looks beautiful, is not easy (bakers go to school to learn how). A wedding cake disaster is hard to fix.

flowers

Creating a gorgeous centerpiece that won't block conversation or start to wilt midway through the night isn't as easy as arranging flowers in a vase. If you need to cut something, hire a florist to make the centerpieces and your bouquet, and make the bridesmaids' bunches yourself.

catering

Catering a large-scale party is a huge undertaking, even for a culinary whiz. You'll be hard-pressed to get enough food together for a hundred people and keep it hot. And, once you get it made, you'll need a reliable staff to serve it. Caterers are trained to make it happen; they have the support staff to serve you and your 200 guests in a timely manner.

invitations

We recommend leaving the invitations to a professional stationer—the look of professionally designed and printed stationery is impossible to replicate with a home office printer. Choose a less expensive stationer, design, paper, and printing technique, and make some of the other paper elements—menus, programs, save-the-dates—yourself if you're looking to spend less.

the big decisions

7

transforming
your space

TIMELINE

PLANNING

6–8 months before
Book an event designer
(if you're using one)

Do an on-site inspection
of ceremony and
reception venues to
assess décor needs

6 months before
Book a lighting designer

5 months before
Reserve tent, porta-potties,
tables, chairs, and other
rentals

3 months before
Pick linens, tableware, and
other décor elements

Review sample centerpiece
with your florist and go
over flower proposal

1–2 months before
Finalize and order (or start
making) any additional
décor details, like signage,
hallway and bathroom
décor, and display areas

6–8 weeks before
Order or make escort cards,
place cards, table numbers,
and menus

1–2 weeks before
Confirm all delivery and
setup details with vendors

You've made your decision. You want a laid-back afternoon affair on a spring Sunday. Or maybe it's going to be a dressed-to-the-nines soiree on a Saturday evening smack-dab in the middle of June. Now the key is making it *your* casual springtime celebration, *your* black-tie ballroom bash.

There are so many different elements—from flowers and décor to lighting and draping—to draw on to personalize your space. Whether you want to give your venue a minor face-lift or put it through major rehab, you can make your reception look like none other. Remember that little exercise you did in chapter 1 (the one where you pictured your dream wedding)? Here's where we show you how to turn an existing space into your dream space.

WORKING WITH YOUR SPACE

Your choice of venue will be one of the main drivers in determining your reception style. Selecting the type of venue that best exemplifies the look and feel you want for the party (see chapter 3) is key to pulling off your vision. It's much easier to work with the style of your space than to transform a venue to your style.

An indoor locale can set the entire color scheme for your reception or merely protect your party from the elements. Some—classic country-club ballrooms, for example—are designed to be more of a blank slate and will require more décor to personalize them; others, like historic mansions and castles, truly exude a certain style through the architecture and permanent fixtures, like fireplaces, wall sconces, and chandeliers. Outdoor weddings come with built-in scenery, rich with texture, and natural décor provided by the surroundings.

The extreme makeover

Using the same space for your ceremony and reception and maybe even your cocktail hour or lounge too? You can make the same room look like two, three, or even four places over the course of your wedding.

A separate spot for the cocktail hour is a must—even if it's just a section screened off from the main room or an outdoor patio. The division will give your catering crew time to set up the dining area and allows for the "big reveal" of your reception décor once guests are called in for dinner. Make sure the venue has enough staff on hand to quickly switch things around if you're using the same spot for your ceremony and reception.

If you can't divide the room in half, wait until after the ceremony to put the reception tables in the room. That way, your centerpieces will remain hidden until the reception. Reuse the same chairs, but add covers and change the lighting (see page 95 later in this chapter) to set a new mood. Move the arch you're getting married under to a different part of the room for the reception—behind your head table, over the cake, or wherever you'd like to draw focus. Use the stage as your altar or for the ceremony musicians, and have the reception band/DJ set up there during cocktail hour. Cover the dance floor with carpeting or a bed of silk flowers during the ceremony.

Ceremony décor

If you're getting married at a house of worship, there may be rules about the type of décor you're allowed to bring in, so check with your venue before choosing decorations. Flowers play a starring role in ceremony décor—we'll cover those in the next chapter. But for a truly unique look, go beyond the altar arrangements and aisle petals.

- Rent specialty seating and extras like arches, aisle runners, a canopied altar, topiaries, and candles to decorate your ceremony.
- Swap traditional chairs for hay bales covered in fabric for a rustic, outdoor wedding, or intersperse regal, tufted sofas with Louis Ghost chairs for a formal indoor affair. And for a more casual, romantic vibe, set out plush blankets and lounge pillows on a lawn or beach with gorgeous umbrellas set around them for guests to sprawl out on and watch your nuptials.
- Decorate chairs with cones filled with confetti or birdseed for throwing as you walk back down the aisle as husband and wife.
- Get creative with your programs, creating ones that double as fans to place on each guest's seat or look like movie tickets for a playful touch. (See chapter 19 for more ceremony program ideas.)
- Line the aisle with rose petals for a traditional romantic look, or shape it in a curving pathway. Place candles along the aisle or order a custom liner embroidered with your monogram or motif, or have it projected onto the runner with a custom gobo light (see "Lighting Lingo," page 95).
- All eyes will be on the altar, so make it worthy of attention, too. Use draping to create a dramatic canopied altar as the focal point for the ceremony, illuminated with specialty lighting for a nighttime affair.
- Spruce up a pergola with blooms, twinkling lights, or pomanders; using two towering floral arrangements is a gorgeous way to make your ceremony stage stand out.

Cocktail hour décor

You've spent hours selecting linens for the dinner tables, but don't let the look of your pre-meal interlude fall by the wayside. Keep things interesting by varying the reception and cocktail-hour décor. Just keep the vibe consistent, changing only the details to give the entire event a cohesive feel. For example, reverse the color schemes, so the accent color at your reception becomes the dominant color at your cocktail hour and vice versa. Use specialty lighting to set a different tone for your cocktail hour and reception. For an outdoor cocktail fete, hang crystal chandeliers or string lights from tree branches. Place smaller versions of the reception centerpieces on cocktail tables surrounded by votives for a more low-key, nightclub vibe. Personalized extras—like monogrammed napkins or barware—can go a long way in making your cocktail hour feel special. Order custom drink stirrers for your signature cocktail, or have your bartender display garnishes in your color palette in clear glass jars set atop the bar. You can also make a statement with a monogrammed ice sculpture.

Any wedding planner will tell you that the key to a successful cocktail hour is the room setup. You want to leave enough room for guests to mingle, while also making sure Grandma has a comfortable seat nearby. Setting up about half as many chairs as guests is a good estimate for heavy hors d'oeuvres. Cut that number in half for a cocktail hour with light hors d'oeuvres that can easily be eaten with one hand. A combination of low chairs with coffee tables arranged in intimate groupings and tall cocktail tables will help give your cocktail hour a different feel from the dinner to follow. This will also allow guests to unwind without having to balance their plates in one hand and drinks (or clutches) in the other.

Even if your venue already includes sitting-room furniture, think about renting a few special pieces to create a stylish lounge for your cocktail hour. If you have the flexibility, plush sofas and chairs arranged in intimate groups along with stand-up cocktail tables is optimal, as it allows for more of a living-room-meets-nightclub feel. Not only do you achieve a sophisticated vibe, but guests are also better able to unwind and converse.

Laying out the reception
The configuration of tables and chairs will affect the feel of your fete just as much as the style of your décor will. You want to create an environment that's comfortable, promotes mingling, and makes sense in your locale. Work with the site manager and your planner to determine the right-size tables and dance floor for your space and guest list, as well as where all the different elements will go (band/DJ, dance floor, cake table, escort card display, guest tables, head or sweetheart table, buffet or food stations, bars, lounge). A good strategy? Divide your room into different areas by activities: dancing, mingling, and eating.

PARTY AREAS Since the band and dance floor will be the focal point of the room (see page 97 for help sizing up the dance floor), determine where your guests will be first and then arrange your tables around them. That way, your guests will be able to see the spotlight dances, speeches, and cake cutting (all of which typically take center stage on the dance floor). Just be careful not to place tables too close to the speakers or the dance floor.

Keep in mind that the music provider(s) will be bringing some hefty equipment and will need access to a large door into the room and a setup space near outlets. Obviously, if there's a stage, that's probably

TIP
dividing your space

Maybe you booked a site for 300 guests, but only 125 are coming, or the venue's smaller room wasn't available on your date. Strategically placed curtains or screens can make a wide-open area feel more intimate. Setting up screens is also a great way to create different environments for dinner and dancing, or to create a separate lounge or cocktail area. To work your colors in, hang fabric that matches your scheme over dividers, or use lighting to change the mood from one area to the next.

the best place for them—it will leave you and your guests more room to dance, and it's an especially great way to showcase the twelve-person band you splurged on. Even if there isn't a stage, your venue probably has one logical spot where your band or DJ can perform, and you can rent a stage if you want to be sure the band is front and center.

EATING AREAS How your guests are seated will have a lot more influence on whether they'll have a good time than you'd think. The size, shape, and setup of tables can maximize your space and encourage mixing and mingling. For example, if you have long banquet tables, your party will have the feel of a regal feast, whereas a room filled with classic rounds will have a more traditional vibe. But keep in mind how annoying it is when you're at a restaurant or dinner party and you have to straddle a corner at a rectangular table, or when your chair backs up directly into someone sitting behind you.

Another focal point to factor into your reception floor plan: where you will sit. Hey, the ceremony may be over, but you're still the stars of the show! The head table is traditionally long and straight and puts the bride and groom and the wedding party on display. You can also set up a sweetheart table for just the two of you—it may be the only alone time you get during the wedding! Either way, all the tables should be strategically situated so that you two are front and center.

MINGLING AREAS There should be plenty of room for guests to circulate during the reception. Since people tend to cluster around the bar, set yours up away from the dance floor, which will encourage movement around the entire room (and keep Cousin Art's vodka-cranberry away from your white gown while you're dancing!). Likewise, make sure there's enough space between the bar(s) and tables to avoid crowding seated guests. A good way to keep everyone moving and mingling: Set up two bars in different parts of the room.

If you're planning to have food stations, fill in your site manager in advance (before you start working on the menu), so he can make sure that they'll fit and the right equipment is available. The placement of food stations will depend on proximity to the kitchen, as well as access to outlets. Make sure there is plenty of room for guests to line up at the buffet and fill their plates without bumping into the tables and chairs, too.

DISPLAY AREAS From photo booths and cigar bars to dessert displays, adding mini parties around the room can fuel excitement. Place your guest book and escort cards on display near the entry so guests can't miss them. Give some thought to where you want your cake to be set up: It can greet guests near the entrance, serve as a focal point at the center of the reception room, or sit on the side near the head table.

When you hand over your seating chart to your reception site two weeks before the wedding, you'll also want to make the staff aware of any additional tables you're planning on having, like one for an ice sculpture, one for your guest book, one for an escort-card display, one for the cake table, and one full of favors near the exit. But confirm that there's enough space in the room or in a room nearby when you book the venue (or shortly after), so you don't create an elaborate escort-card display or cake table that won't fit. The venue staff and/or your designer should not only set up these tables and stations but also decorate and light them.

LIGHTING 101

Lighting is one of the best ways to transform your space, and any event designer will tell you it's worth splurging on lighting and spending less on the rest of the décor because it makes that big of a difference. Use lighting to highlight your favorite features of the venue while hiding the less appealing things. For instance, if you love the Gothic columns throughout the room, placing a light at the base of each one will emphasize their details. Not a fan of the floral rug? Project a pattern on the ceiling to draw eyes upward, or call guests' attention to the dance floor by shining your monogram or motif onto it. You can also totally change the mood with color washes (see "Lighting Lingo," at right). Intense ambers and reds let guests know it's time to party, while cool blues and purples set a soothing, sophisticated vibe.

Hiring a lighting pro
Most venues do not provide specialty lighting, so you'll probably need to bring in an outside lighting designer. Start looking about six months before your wedding. Ask your event designer or florist—many do their own lighting. If not, they may have a lighting pro they regularly work with. Or the coordinator at your reception venue may recommend a lighting company that has partnered with the site before and is familiar with its sore spots, built-in lighting, and power capabilities. Plus, he can show you pictures of the venue transformed by various lighting arrangements to help you home in on what you want.

Once you've shown a potential lighting designer your space, he will come up with a proposal based on an evaluation of the site (see

the tented reception

Found the perfect outdoor setting for your wedding? When the sun goes down, a chic party tent strung with twinkling lights or chandeliers is the perfect place to wine and dine your guests. Here's what you need to know to throw a tented reception.

stake out a space

Tents can be set up just about anywhere. Before you choose one, make a site visit with an expert from the tent rental company, as well as the site manager and/or your planner, so they can help you choose a tent that works on the particular surface—pavement, grass, sand, and so on—and will fit all your guests. The site manager can speak to the stability of the ground (especially if you're having a tent set up on or near the beach) and any underground hazards such as sprinkler systems, wells, or septic tanks that will factor into the placement of the tent.

weatherproof

Just because it's covered doesn't mean you and your guests will be protected from the weather. For a summer wedding, bring in fans and portable air-conditioning units, and keep guests warm in chillier months with tall patio or propane heaters. You may also want to add floor surfaces (to correct uneven ground) and wall panels (to protect against wind and rain). Still, even the sturdiest of tents can't withstand heavy rains and fierce winds. Your best bet is to have an indoor backup plan at a nearby reception space or restaurant. If your area is known for having inconsistent weather, make sure your wedding insurance package covers rain, which could help you recover at least a portion of the fees if your event has to be postponed.

size it right

The size of your tent can make or break your day. You don't want to pack guests into too small of an area or have a space so big that it feels like nobody's there to celebrate with you. To find the right-size tent for your wedding day, multiply the number of guests by 13 for the minimum size in square feet you'll need for a sit-down wedding, or by 15 for the optimum. For example: 50 guests x 13 = 650 square feet; 50 guests x 15 = 750 square feet. So a comfortable range for a wedding with 50 guests for a sit-down dinner would be a tent ranging from 650 to 750 square feet. When measuring your location, add 10 feet to both the length and width to allow room for staking.

tent size cheat sheet

Make sure your tent can fit all your guests with these guidelines.

number of guests	size of tent (in square feet)
50	650–750
100	1,300–1,500
150	1,950–2,250
200	2,600–3,000
250	3,250–3,750
300	3,900–4,500

factor in logistics

Reserve the site for your wedding day and the morning after. Your team of pros will need extra time to set up—and break down—the site, including the tent, rentals (tables and chairs, linens, dishware, etc.), flowers, and décor.

power it up

Have an electrician check out the space before lighting up your tent. Not only will he be able to ensure you pass all the proper inspection laws, but he should also be able to tell you whether you'll need to rent an extra generator and how to safely secure your lighting fixtures. You may want to keep a lighting professional (who has wedding experience) on hand for the actual wedding to ensure everything stays in place—and lit up— all evening. Also, verify that your band or DJ has enough power to supply their equipment. This may mean bringing in an extra generator so you don't lose the lights in the middle of the party. Your DJ or bandleader should be able to suggest options that work for your site.

consult the caterer

Check that any catering companies you're considering have experience running tented events. They'll not only provide all the right supplies (saving you the hassle of having to rent them) and handle setup and cleanup, but they'll also know to have enough waitstaff on hand to take good care of your guests. Schedule a site visit for your caterer to make sure she's well equipped to handle the space. Also keep in mind that in most cases, your caterer will need a separate prepping tent, as well as electricity and running water. Work with your caterer to draw up a detailed floor plan and a list of what she needs.

install flooring

If you set up on the grass or sand, you may have to deal with wobbly tables and chairs. On top of that, if it rains, you'll have to contend with mud. And you'll need a floor to dance on. To pick the right size for your dance party, follow this formula: Divide your number of guests by four to estimate how many couples you can expect to see dancing at any given time. Next, multiply that number by ten for the total number of square feet you'll need for your dance floor. So if you have two hundred guests, you'll divide by four to get fifty couples dancing, times ten for a total of five hundred square feet of dance floor.

provide restrooms

If there aren't any bathrooms nearby (and even if there are a few), you should consider renting porta-potties. The general rule is one stall per thirty-five guests. This way, guests will spend less time standing in line and more time partying. These days, you can rent luxury portable restrooms with amenities like in-room music, granite countertops, and air-conditioning or heaters, depending on the season.

nix annoyances

Bugs (gnats, mosquitoes, flies, and bees) typically swarm during the summer months, often in the evening. To control insects, consider having your site sprayed two days beforehand, renting pest control tanks to alleviate the problem, and scattering citronella candles throughout the space.

tent types

Whether you're going for formal or casual, tents come in all shapes, sizes, and materials.

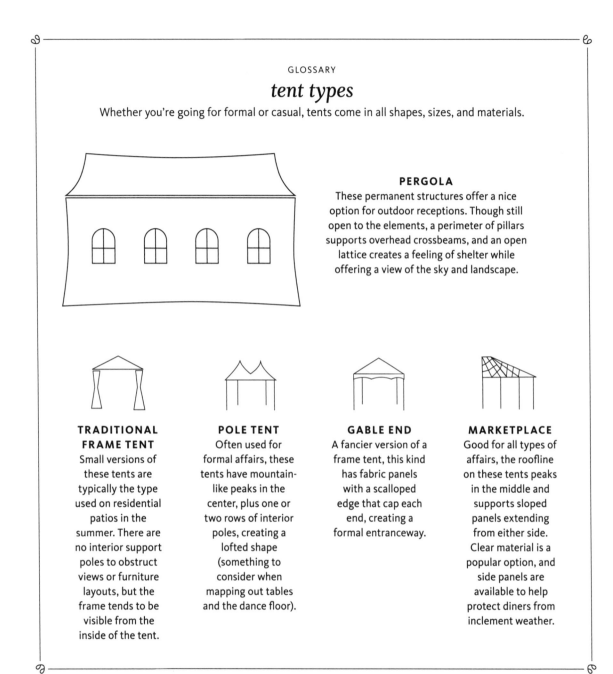

PERGOLA

These permanent structures offer a nice option for outdoor receptions. Though still open to the elements, a perimeter of pillars supports overhead crossbeams, and an open lattice creates a feeling of shelter while offering a view of the sky and landscape.

TRADITIONAL FRAME TENT

Small versions of these tents are typically the type used on residential patios in the summer. There are no interior support poles to obstruct views or furniture layouts, but the frame tends to be visible from the inside of the tent.

POLE TENT

Often used for formal affairs, these tents have mountain-like peaks in the center, plus one or two rows of interior poles, creating a lofted shape (something to consider when mapping out tables and the dance floor).

GABLE END

A fancier version of a frame tent, this kind has fabric panels with a scalloped edge that cap each end, creating a formal entranceway.

MARKETPLACE

Good for all types of affairs, the roofline on these tents peaks in the middle and supports sloped panels extending from either side. Clear material is a popular option, and side panels are available to help protect diners from inclement weather.

"Choosing the Right Type of Lighting," below) and the pricing for each. Professional lighting can run from $1,500 to ten times that amount, depending on what you are bringing in and who you are hiring. Make sure the proposal accounts for lighting setup (for a complicated lighting design, it may be worth it to pay extra to have someone on-site in case anything goes wrong).

Choosing the right type of lighting About four or

five months before the wedding, set up a time to visit your venue with your designer to assess what type of lighting you need. Your lighting designer will be able to recommend types of lighting that will fit your budget and have the biggest impact, and your site manager can fill him in on the venue's power capabilities, plus any restrictions on lighting or equipment. If you're planning an evening reception, visit the site with your lighting pro when it's dark outside.

VENUE CONSIDERATIONS During the site visit, look around the room and see where the fixed lighting is focused. Lights that illuminate the walls, windows, and ceiling can draw attention away from the center of the room—and you want to keep everyone's eyes on the tables, dance floor, and each other. Ask if the site has dimmers for the overhead lights to set the mood, and if there's any fluorescent lighting at all, keep it turned off—it's never flattering. Also, make sure there won't be any service doors kept open, which could flood the space with light and ruin the effect.

If you're hosting a wedding at home or at an atypical venue, discuss how much electricity your lighting designer is going to need. Your band or DJ will probably have to tap into your home's power source for their speakers, and you don't want to risk blowing a fuse. If your lighting expert is concerned that there won't be enough power to go around, he or she may consider bringing a generator, which should be kept well out of earshot (they make a lot of noise). If you're having an outdoor wedding, you'll need to light up the tent (so make sure you have ample power for that), and if your site has a path or steps that people will be using throughout the night, keep it lit with luminarias, twinkling lights, or paper lanterns so that no one trips.

TECHNIQUES The layout of your reception site will help guide how you're going to use lighting techniques. If dinner and dancing are happening in the same room, use a color wash to set the dance floor apart. If your reception site has sprawling ceilings, use pin-spot lighting to keep the focus on certain details. If you have a recurring motif, a gobo light can help tie your reception together. A more low-tech (and cost-effective) approach is to hang beautiful Chinese paper lanterns or to suspend chandeliers, which can also up the elegance factor.

Colors Instead of choosing colors in your wedding palette, which may not put everyone in the most flattering light, opt for colored lights that complement all skin tones, like magenta or a soft rose. Take advantage of the effect color can have on the atmosphere by changing the shades throughout the night. For example, if your cocktail hour starts around sunset, you can splash your room with golden tones. During dinner, consider soft lighting that will mimic flickering candlelight.

RENTAL BASICS

Ask your reception site what will be included and check their wares to see if they fit your style and color palette. For any items that aren't included (see the rental checklist on page 107, for an idea of what you need), get a price quote on rentals before making your final location decision (these things can greatly affect the cost). Your venue doesn't have linens or china you love? It doesn't come with a built-in bar, stage, or tables and chairs? Or maybe the carpet or curtains doesn't match your color scheme? No problem. You can rent everything you need to create the perfect party (and ceremony) space. We're talking anything from an ornate golden tent for your Moroccan-themed rehearsal dinner to a parquet dance floor for a bare loft, right down to gold chargers and linens for your tables to match. You can also rent electronic equipment, entertainment systems, and ceremony extras like arches, aisle runners, candelabras, kneeling benches—whatever your hearts desire.

Finding a rental company Renting the bulk of your
equipment at one party-rental store will make coordinating the logistics much easier (and a package deal could save you money). If the rental equipment company you visit doesn't stock special extras, ask them to refer you to a store or service that does.

 If you're using an event designer or a full-time wedding planner, they'll probably have rental companies that they work with and recommend, but you can also ask your site manager to suggest rental companies who know the space. If you need china and linens, your caterer might be able to hook you up there, as well. Otherwise, you can search online with the American Rental Association.

Setup and delivery

Once you've figured out what you need and have found a place that can supply it all, work out setup and delivery details. When it comes to getting the goods, you have two choices: tailgate or custom delivery. Tailgate is the more cost-effective but labor-intensive choice—the delivery truck pulls up to the party site and unloads the rental items. From there, it's up to you, so you'll probably need to enlist a lot of help from family and the bridal party, or pay the venue's staff to do it. Custom, on the other hand, is just like it sounds— the delivery truck comes to the party site, unloads your order, sets up the equipment before the event, and takes it down afterward. It will cost more, but it means minimal fuss for you (and your wedding party).

Regardless of which service you choose, you'll need to have someone at the site for both delivery and pickup (often a site manager, planner, or parent can handle both). Also, make sure the rental company is available to pick up after hours and find out if they charge an extra fee for doing so—some sites require that all equipment be broken down and removed immediately after the party.

INTERVIEW CHECKLIST

rental requests

Whether you go to Paul's Party Shop in town or the local branch of a huge rental chain, make sure you're working with pros by verifying a few things up front. Your ideal rental center will:

☐ Be a member of a business or trade group like the American Rental Association

☐ Be in good standing with the Better Business Bureau

☐ Show you their inventory: If the china is cracked, dingy, or caked with mashed potatoes from the last party, keep looking; also, make sure they have the types of items you want

☐ Send staff to help with setup and teardown

☐ Accommodate last-minute changes (such as additional tables for unexpected guests or extra tents if it rains)

☐ Offer names of past customers as references (yes—even for a rental company!)

PERSONALIZING YOUR SPACE

No matter what your reception space looks like (or how popular it is), you can use draping, carpeting or temporary flooring, and specialty rentals to completely personalize it. The style of your décor and even the smallest details will also affect the feel of your fete and help bring the look together. Your choice of venue will drive your décor choices, but there's also room for some creativity.

Flooring
Don't let an ornate floral carpet that clashes with your wedding vision dissuade you. Hide that carpet with ground-sweeping linens. Or cover it with a coordinating rental carpet. And if your venue's standard parquet wood floor isn't doing anything for you, you can also change its color and design. A checkerboard floor is the perfect accessory to an Art Deco–themed reception. Or bring in a circular or a triangle-shaped dance floor. Unexpected shapes can make your setup more modern and maximize the dancing area.

Draping
If your reception venue has wallpaper or paint that doesn't match your wedding colors (or even if it does), you can create another world within the room using draping. Not only will it make the same space that your cousin got married in feel unique, but it will create a more intimate environment. Choose a fabric that matches your wedding colors, or pick white for a clean, classic look that will go with anything.

Even draping just the ceiling can also give your venue a fresh look—and it's less expensive than covering the entire room. Light-as-air tulle can be draped artfully over tablecloths or chair backs, or hung from the ceiling in clusters for cloudlike columns. Be careful with the amount of tulle you decide to drape around the room, though—you want it to look soft, not like the place has been hosed down with marshmallow fluff. Other fabrics, such as organza, gauze, and satin can be used for a huppah or an archway for the wedding party's entrance, or spread elegantly on the ground to create a romantic aisle (affix it carefully to the floor so no one—including you—slips on his or her way down the aisle). Just check with the venue manager first—many sites, especially historic ones, will not let you attach anything to the walls or ceilings.

Chairs
With one-hundred-plus guests, you'll have more chairs than almost any other element in the room, so this is a key area to play up your colors and style. Swap out blah chairs for crowd-pleasing chiavaris, or throw tasteful covers over ho-hum seating. Even more subtle décor,

EXPERT ADVICE
complicated installations

You should clear all complicated installations with your venue first and find out about any restrictions or fire codes you'll need to follow. You may need to acquire a permit or ensure that the carpet or fabric is flame-retardant. Also, ask your venue contacts for access to the site a day or two before the event—carpeting and flooring take more time to install.

whether it's a flower cluster, a hanging monogram, or a coordinating ribbon, will definitely get noticed. (See "Take a Seat," page 104, for more chair options.)

Tables

Tables are the single most important design element in your reception area. Not only do they take up the most room and therefore dramatically affect the overall look, but your tables are also the focal point for guests for much of the night as they dine and wander from table to table. Use your table décor to bring out the theme and look of the day, to add color to your space, and to create that wow factor when your guests walk into the room.

LINENS Of any detail, table linens, place settings, and centerpieces make the biggest impact because they're what guests will be looking directly at anytime they're seated or mingling. And your linens are one of the main ways you can bring out your colors at your reception. Bare tables immediately set a casual tone, while covering them in floor-length silk shantung linens dresses them up. In addition to color, focus on material. Burlap runners create a rustic vibe, while silk tablecloths

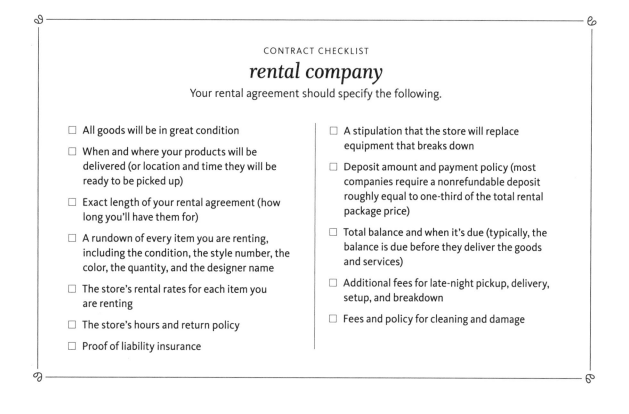

CONTRACT CHECKLIST

rental company

Your rental agreement should specify the following.

☐ All goods will be in great condition

☐ When and where your products will be delivered (or location and time they will be ready to be picked up)

☐ Exact length of your rental agreement (how long you'll have them for)

☐ A rundown of every item you are renting, including the condition, the style number, the color, the quantity, and the designer name

☐ The store's rental rates for each item you are renting

☐ The store's hours and return policy

☐ Proof of liability insurance

☐ A stipulation that the store will replace equipment that breaks down

☐ Deposit amount and payment policy (most companies require a nonrefundable deposit roughly equal to one-third of the total rental package price)

☐ Total balance and when it's due (typically, the balance is due before they deliver the goods and services)

☐ Additional fees for late-night pickup, delivery, setup, and breakdown

☐ Fees and policy for cleaning and damage

take a seat

Know what chairs to rent for your wedding.

**CHIAVARI/
BALLROOM
CHAIRS**

best for formal
and semiformal
ceremonies and
receptions

common colors gold,
silver, white, black,
dark wood, light
wood

**WOODEN
FOLDING CHAIRS**

best for casual
and semiformal
ceremonies and
casual receptions

common colors
white, black, dark
wood, light wood

**BISTRO
STACKING OR
COMPOSITE
LAWN CHAIRS**

best for casual
outdoor ceremonies
and receptions

common color white

**MIRAGE OR
LOUIS GHOST
CHAIRS**

best for modern
receptions

common color clear

have a more formal air. Use different textures and colors with overlays, runners, and swagging (two tablecloths layered on top of each other).

Make sure the tablecloths are larger than your table so the cloth hangs over appropriately. For formal occasions, you want to cover the table legs (unless you've chosen the tables for their design and, therefore, want part of the table to show). For a standard-size 54-inch square table, a 60-inch-by-60-inch tablecloth is required, and a standard 70-inch round table needs a 70-inch-by-108-inch tablecloth.

If you don't want to cover the entire table, or you want to add subtle dimension, another color, or a pattern to your tables, you can also use table runners on banquet tables (long strips of fabric that usually run down the center of a rectangular table, lengthwise, and don't cover the entire table). An overlay, a decorative cloth set atop a tablecloth, can be used on round or square tables to add contrast or dimension. And don't forget place mats and napkins—you can use both to play up the other colors in your palette or add pops of color to an otherwise neutral tablescape.

TABLEWARE If you're having your reception at a venue accustomed to hosting events, your dishes will be taken care of. Otherwise, check with your caterer—most supply basic dishes, glasses, and flatware. For an extra touch, you can rent specialty tableware to fit your style. Think gold leaf chargers, ornate flatware, and crystal glasses for a formal, glam affair, or stemless wineglasses and square bold plates for a modern loft reception.

Ask your caterer what you'll need, but here's a list of basic elements:

- China
- Flatware
- Glasses
- Napkins
- Place mats
- Chargers (large decorative plates that are placed under the entrée and salad plates to add color to your reception tables)

GLOSSARY

table types

Find the right table shape and size for your space.

round
Aside from the conversational benefits, circles are the most popular table choice because they mesh with just about any room and layout, so you can set them up in whatever arrangement you'd like. Dinner (or brunch or lunch) tables are typically round and can seat anywhere from six to ten guests.

square
For a party area that's not so well defined (like a lawn, a patio, or the space under a tent), use square tables to establish borders, which will help create a sense of place. Square tables have a more modern feel and can fit from four to twelve.

banquet
Long, lean tables give more weight to (and help fill) a large, bare room with high ceilings and tall windows. Set them up in organized rows or in a U-shaped formation.

mixed
Eclectic arrangements, with tables of various shapes or sizes, allow you to seat groups of people much more easily because you're not stuck with a set number for each table. They also add visual interest to a room.

high tops
For your cocktail hour or a cocktail-style reception, these tall round tables give the room a night-club feel and encourage mingling, while still giving guests a place to rest their drinks and eat appetizers. They can usually seat two to four if you add stools.

Instead of the standard numbers, try one of these creative ways to identify your reception tables.

Places the bride and groom have traveled together

Flower types if you're getting married in a garden

Names of runs printed on wooden arrow-shaped signs for ski buffs

Hollywood classics for movie fans (include a black-and-white framed image from each flick)

Different wine vintages

Subway stops or roads

Skiing or hiking trails for nature buffs

Photos of the bride and groom over the years

Hobbies or sports

Favorite books or movies

For a big impact without renting the entire tablescape, rent special chargers, glasses for your signature cocktail, and serving platters. Choose place settings that mimic the table's shape for a more symmetrical look. But don't be afraid to mix it up, too: Introduce a rectangular napkin and a square plate on top of round chargers to add interest.

ADDITIONAL TABLE DÉCOR Candles, special accessories, and creative table markers are the finishing touches to the reception tables. Surround your centerpieces with anything that's beautiful to you and that helps bring out your theme or style, be it votives or lanterns, seashells or sailboats. Or use special accents to the bar, cake table, escort card display, and cocktail tables.

For a dynamic look, group arrangements of similar colors and sizes in the middle of your tables. Prevent a potential color overload by using accent hues in a few strategic spots, like on the ballroom-chair cushions, tall candlesticks lining the middle of each table, and the menu or place cards at your table settings. To up the romance factor, place candles on each table and throughout the room. Surround arrangements with low votives or opt for floating candles that look gorgeous reflecting dim light. Majestic candelabra will add drama to a room; traditional lanterns will make any site feel cozier. Place mirrors under flower arrangements, or use these reflective surfaces as long, skinny runners with little candles on top to up the sparkle factor without also upping your budget. Feminine accents like bows and ribbons can be attached to chair backs, wrapped around vases, or mounted on the walls at regular intervals.

TABLE PAPER Table numbers, menus, and place cards are the final pieces of the tablescape puzzle. In chapter 18, we cover the details if you want to order these final pieces of wedding stationery along with your invitations. For a rustic setting, you might write the menu options on a chalkboard. As for table numbers, you can just place printed numbers in elegant frames, or give your reception tables clever monikers that act as instant icebreakers (see "Creative Table Name Ideas," at left).

Focal points
You can incorporate a variety of other special touches throughout your ceremony, cocktail hour, and reception. The right finishing touches can take your wedding to the next level and create a truly unique look.

SIGNAGE You don't want your guests getting lost on the way to the bathroom or reception. Create signs to help direct guests to each wedding spot (the ceremony, cocktail hour, bathrooms, and reception).

If you're having an outdoor wedding, make or buy a wooden sign and paint it with an arrow. For a more sophisticated soiree, consider using printed black-and-white-framed directions in a script font.

THE GUEST BOOK Though they may feel outdated, trust us—you'll be glad you had a way for guests to leave you their best wishes. Cocktail hour is a good time to set it out for guests to sign. Guest books can be ordered with the rest of your stationery for a cohesive look. You can go classic and choose a leather or fabric book with blank pages for guests to write a special wish in. Or you could place printed cards that coordinate with your wedding stationery on a table and ask guests to share their best marriage advice, and have them bound into a book or place them in an album after the wedding. You can even get creative with your guest book by having guests sign a custom graffiti wall.

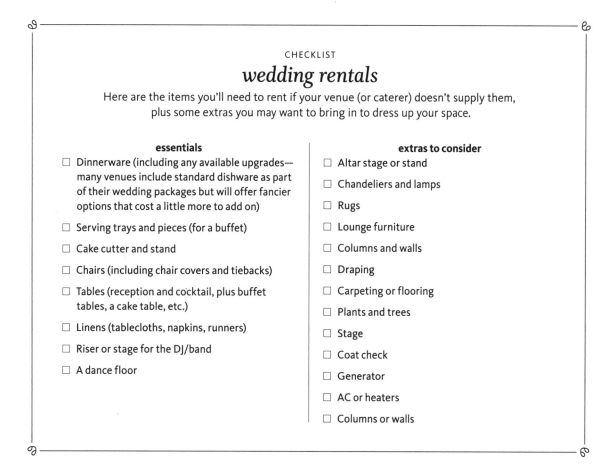

CHECKLIST
wedding rentals

Here are the items you'll need to rent if your venue (or caterer) doesn't supply them, plus some extras you may want to bring in to dress up your space.

essentials

- ☐ Dinnerware (including any available upgrades—many venues include standard dishware as part of their wedding packages but will offer fancier options that cost a little more to add on)
- ☐ Serving trays and pieces (for a buffet)
- ☐ Cake cutter and stand
- ☐ Chairs (including chair covers and tiebacks)
- ☐ Tables (reception and cocktail, plus buffet tables, a cake table, etc.)
- ☐ Linens (tablecloths, napkins, runners)
- ☐ Riser or stage for the DJ/band
- ☐ A dance floor

extras to consider

- ☐ Altar stage or stand
- ☐ Chandeliers and lamps
- ☐ Rugs
- ☐ Lounge furniture
- ☐ Columns and walls
- ☐ Draping
- ☐ Carpeting or flooring
- ☐ Plants and trees
- ☐ Stage
- ☐ Coat check
- ☐ Generator
- ☐ AC or heaters
- ☐ Columns or walls

Jeanne & Oscar
OCTOBER 17
SAN FRANCISCO, CA

Even though their
wedding was in San
Francisco, Jeanne and
Oscar wanted to pay
tribute to New York City,
where they met. The
solution: a 1930s Art Deco
theme with distinct nods
to Manhattan: seating in
a grid pattern and tables
named after streets and
avenues in the city. Even
the centerpieces—vases
filled with a mix of curly
willow, kiwi vine, and
local pistachio branches—
had an artsy, urban vibe
and added height to the
long tables.

THE CAKE TABLE Don't hide your cake in the corner. Dress up
the table with table linens in a complementary color. Add a small
arrangement or have your florist sprinkle the table with small flowers
in your wedding hues.

THE ESCORT CARD DISPLAY Set up near the entrance to your
reception, your escort card display can be a focal point for your cocktail
hour space or a chance to make a dramatic impression as guests enter
the reception. Escort cards are extremely easy to personalize and an
excellent way to bring in your wedding-day colors—from calligraphed
seating cards set atop a textured linen to apples tagged with each
guest's name or small personalized bundles of lavender tied with
string. You could also use your escort cards to highlight your passions
or theme (for example, make library card pockets with each attendee's
name to highlight your love of books or set them in a bed of glass for a
garden wedding). Or incorporate them into your cocktail hour using
personalized stirrers tagged with guests' names.

Overlooked spaces

Sure, you've got your reception décor covered, the cocktail hour set, and your ceremony aisle chosen. But don't forget some of the other areas.

THE BATHROOMS Pay a little extra attention to the restrooms. Think subtle sophistication: A flower arrangement (like bunches of sweet-smelling lavender in small vases or wildflowers bundled in baskets) and personalized soaps will go a long way.

THE BAR The bar itself is often a focal point, so think about ways to make it a showstopper. Top it with blooms (sturdier ones, like orchids, work best, but you can also reuse your ceremony arrangements). Or let the barware do the work: Set out rows of highball glasses on lacquered trays, along with pretty iced pitchers filled with your signature cocktail.

THE ENTRANCEWAYS Wow your guests with a grand entrance. Floral wreaths on doors, colorful votive candles atop entrance tables, hurricane lanterns hanging from trees, luminarias lining the walkways, and other beautiful embellishments will give guests a warm welcome to your event.

THE HALLWAYS Use potted plants, trees, floral garlands, and trellises to make a big impact when guests enter or exit your ceremony or reception space. Or try small, dramatic flower arrangements placed on the ground, like huge amounts of tightly packed blooms lining the hallway leading to the bathroom.

REAL BRIDE ADVICE
personalizing your space

"We added pink uplighting and a huge gobo display of our monogram inside an arch cutout the building already had."
—GIAN&VAN2008

"We got married in a backyard, so we brought in a tent and specialty linens to amp up the décor."
—MRSMOLINA

"Our venue had this hideous maroon and gold draping that really clashed with our silver and black color scheme. So we decided to add our own draping with rich-colored fabric to cover it up."
—SOONTOBESCHLEIFER

8

wedding flowers

TIMELINE

PLANNING

6–8 months before
Start researching florists

5–6 months before
Book a florist

4–5 months before
Review proposal and
centerpiece mock-up

3 weeks before
Finalize order, setup,
and delivery details

3 days before
Confirm venue details

When it comes to wedding décor, flowers are essentially the star, taking a leading role in both your ceremony (you didn't forget about your bouquet, did you?) and your reception (hello, centerpieces!). They help set the mood, enhance the color scheme, and can even carry the entire theme. Flowers are 100 percent romance—so it's no surprise that they've always gone hand in hand with weddings. The good news is, it's tough to go wrong in the flower department—just arm yourselves with a fabulous florist and some key facts.

BLOOM BASICS

Whether you already have definite ideas of your own regarding your wedding flowers or you aren't sure where to start or need help maximizing your style, these basics will help you to better communicate with your florist and get the look you want. It's not as simple as picking your favorite flowers and requesting them in your wedding colors. There's season, style, budget, size, and meaning to consider. Plus, there's some florist lingo you'll want to know.

Durability If you're getting married during the hot summer months or outside where wind can come into play, you'll need your flowers to last a long time (perhaps even for the duration of your weekend celebration), steer clear of blooms that wilt easily, like gardenias, lilies of the valley, tulips, or wildflowers. Ask your florist for long-lasting flowers.

Color Choose blossoms that will suit your wedding style and colors. Keep in mind: Many flowers come in multiple shades, so talk to your florist about what color options are available for your favorite blooms. Pastels are ultrafeminine, vivid shades can have a more modern feel, and soft green paired with white makes for an unfussy, timeless combination. Choose one hue (an elegant choice), a pair to match your palette, or mix a bunch for a casual paint-box effect. Bring a bridesmaid-dress fabric swatch with you when you meet your floral designer so she has a good starting point.

Scent Be sure your bouquet won't be too fragrant—you don't want to sneeze your way down the aisle. Same goes for centerpieces: You don't want your guests' allergies to flare up or for the smell of your flowers to interfere with the experience of the food or wine. Fragrant blooms include freesias, lilies, lilacs, tuberoses, and gardenias.

Availability Local, in-season flowers should be your mainstay. For starters, you're ensured freshness—which means they'll look best. In addition, seasonal blooms will be the most affordable. Talk to your florist to find out what's blossoming in your wedding region around the time you'll be getting married and try to make those flowers the cornerstone of your bouquets and decorative arrangements.

Style Yes, even your flowers can reflect your wedding style. Tighter bunches of classic wedding blooms such as roses and peonies fit a classic

the root of it all

Maybe you don't care what meaning the Victorians ascribed to different blooms, as long as they're beautiful. But then again, you may not want your maids carrying arrangements that connote jealousy (yellow roses). Your maids probably won't know the meaning behind their flowers and it's not going to bring bad luck on your wedding day if your flowers mean something less than glowing. But if you want everything to be rosy, read on for the meanings and the seasons for some of the most popular wedding flowers.

Anemone (fall to spring): expectation

Baby's breath (year-round): innocence

Calla lily (spring/summer): magnificent beauty

Camellia (spring): perfect loveliness

Carnation (year-round): boldness (pink), love (red), talent (white)

Chrysanthemum (year-round): wealth, abundance, truth

Daisy (year-round): empathy, openness

Freesia (spring/summer): innocence

Gardenia (year-round): purity, joy

Gerbera daisy (year-round): beauty

Holly (winter): foresight

Iris (spring): faith, wisdom

Lilac (spring): first love

Lily (summer): truth, honor

Lily of the valley (spring/summer): happiness

Magnolia (spring/summer): love of nature

Orange blossom (fall): purity

Orchid (year-round; imported): love, beauty

Rose (year-round): love; "I love you" (red), "I am worthy of you" (white)

Stephanotis (year-round): marital happiness

Sunflower (fall): adoration

Tulip (spring): love, passion

vibe. Lush arrangement soft big-headed blooms take on a romantic note, while sleek, architectural varieties in minimalist arrangements have a modern look. Loose clusters of wild, vibrant flowers mixed with fruit or vegetables and greenery set in natural containers, on the other hand, exude a rustic feel.

Location   Your wedding locale will greatly influence your floral decisions. If, for example, you're marrying at a park, botanical garden, or vineyard, the flowers can be kept to a minimum (meaning you can make a big impression with fewer flowers). If your space is a blank loft or a simple ballroom, you may have to up the floral factor, so take that into consideration when setting a budget, too.

FINDING A FLORIST

You want the overall look of your wedding to make an impression—and your florist is a key player. As with all vendors, it's important to find one who's reliable, capable, and within your price range. But you also want a florist who's open to your ideas and whose taste you respect. Not all florists are created equal. Some are event designers who will help conceive the overall look of the day—chairs, chargers, and centerpieces included—and others are craftspeople who will bring your bouquets, altar arrangements, and centerpieces to life, but that's it.

The interview Before you venture out and start the meet-and-greets with selected florists, think about the type of service you need. Do you want someone who will not only make your arrangements but also help design the look of your reception tables and ceremony aisle and altar? Then a floral designer is probably more your speed. Already have a planner, event designer, or eye for design? Then just a regular florist

Larissa & Red
OCTOBER 10
MOSS BEACH, CA

The low-key duo rented a house on the beach for a truly intimate wedding—just twenty-seven guests watched from the grass as Larissa and Red exchanged vows with the ocean in the background. A color palette of orange and brown reflected the fall season and blended seamlessly with the location. The floral arrangements included bamboo, orchids, dahlias, and other blooms.

flowers and their roles

leading ladies

These blooms remain the little black dresses of bridal bouquets—classic, elegant, and well paired with just about anything—making them perfect choices for the main bloom in an arrangement.

ROSE
Colors: white, cream, yellow, apricot, orange, pink, red, burgundy, lavender
Season: year-round
Price range: moderate to expensive

TULIP
Colors: white, yellow, orange, pink
Season: November–May
Price range: moderate to expensive

ANEMONE
Colors: white, pink, purple, magenta, burgundy
Season: November–May
Price range: moderate to expensive

ORCHID
Colors: white, yellow, green, apricot, orange, pink, red, burgundy
Season: year-round
Price range: expensive

DAHLIA
Colors: white, yellow, green, orange, pink, red, burgundy, purple
Season: summer–early fall
Price range: inexpensive

RANUNCULUS
Colors: white, yellow, apricot, orange, pale pink, dark pink
Season: November–April
Price range: moderate

PEONY
Colors: white, cream, green, peach, pink, burgundy
Season: late spring
Price range: expensive

HYDRANGEA
Colors: white, green, pink, burgundy, purple, blue
Season: July–November
Price range: moderate to expensive

LILY OF THE VALLEY
Colors: white, pink (rare)
Season: spring (imported year-round in limited quantities)
Price range: expensive

CALLA LILY
Colors: ivory, yellow, orange, pink, red, dark burgundy
Season: year-round (peaks in winter to late spring)
Price range: expensive

supporting actresses

They might not be the stars of the bunch, but these accent blooms can fill the background with style.

STEPHANOTIS
Colors: white
Season: year-round
Price range: expensive

MUMS
Colors: white, yellow, green, orange, pink, red, burgundy
Season: year-round
Price range: inexpensive

COSMOS
Colors: white, pink, burgundy
Season: midsummer–fall
Price range: inexpensive to moderate

LISIANTHUS
Colors: white, cream, pale green, peach, pink, purple
Season: year-round
Price range: moderate

DAISIES
Colors: white (classic daisy); gerbera variety comes in white, yellow, orange, pink, and red
Season: summer–early fall
Price range: inexpensive

the knot

wedding color guide

Your ultimate 101 lesson on choosing
the perfect wedding palette

ivory + sunshine　　melon + pale pink　　fuchsia + celery　　violet + lime　　turquoise + taupe　　sky + cerulean　　mulberry + navy

choosing your colors

Picking your wedding palette isn't exactly as easy as just declaring your two favorite colors and making them the foundation for every wedding detail. Having two (or more) colors work together seamlessly, and creating the right vibe, takes a little know-how. The basics are something you learned in fifth grade art class: remember the color wheel? Here's a refresher course and how it applies to wedding colors. Color combinations that work best are those that are complementary or analogous, or use a color/neutral combo.

Complementary colors are opposite each other on the color wheel. They work because they pair a cool and warm in the same saturation.

yellow + violet

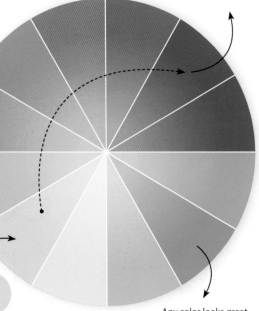

orange + yellow

Analogous colors (aka neighbors) are next to each other. They work because somewhere in their makeup, they share a primary color.

Any color looks great with a neutral.

green + taupe

---

opposites

butter + mulberry   orange + sky

turquoise + coral   grass + honeysuckle

sherbet + cobalt   blush + lime

neighbors

fuchsia + salmon   navy + sky

sunshine + melon   poppy + lavender

celery + turquoise   mulberry + peony

pairing with a neutral

cerulean + taupe   sunshine + white

mauve + gold   seafoam + ivory

lime + silver   violet + gray

gold + ivory

neutral pairing

cobalt + orange

complementary

poppy + fuchsia

analogous

grass + white

neutral pairing

pink

Believe it or not, pink is actually one of the more versatile colors—it can be fresh and feminine, chic and sophisticated, or even edgy, depending on the color with which it's paired.

perfect your pink

Whether you go with soft blush tones or hot pink, there are so many different wedding details that can pick up hints of your color. Almost every flower type comes in pink, and it also looks gorgeous on your cake and stationery. The trick is to keep it as an accent if you're using a more saturated version of the shade.

try these combinations

peony
+
melon

honeysuckle
+
celery

blush
+
cobalt

purple

Cool colors, like purple, are good for creating a relaxed or subdued feel. The deeper shades look royal, whereas lighter lavenders are more girly. When the two are mixed together, a romantic, Victorian vibe emerges.

reign in the purple

This is one of the most popular colors for weddings. When done right, it's completely regal and luxurious. But be careful not to go too garish. Purple shouldn't be used equally with another color of the same saturation. If you want to pair purple with teal, for example, make one the primary and the other the accent.

Table G

try these combinations

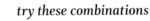

violet + coral

lavender + cerulean

mulberry + gray

Whether as the accent or primary color in a combination, this shade never disappoints. The mood can be formal if it's navy or more casual and light if it's aqua.

The only tricky thing about blue is that your selection of blue wedding flowers is limited: hydrangeas are the obvious choice, but irises, blue sea holly, and delphiniums are all pretty choices too.

try these combinations

cobalt
+
leaf

navy
+
taupe

sky
+
seafoam

white or ivory

Shades of white and ivory are simple, elegant, and timeless, which is probably why white is the quintessential wedding color. Beautiful all on its own, white is also the most universal accent color—everything goes with it.

work your white

Not all whites are created equal. Depending on the style you're going for, such as romantic or modern, you'll want a different shade of white: soft and creamy for romantic; more pure white with a cool undertone for a minimal modern affair. Also, incorporating texture is important when you're working with white.

try these combinations

white
+
gold

ivory
+
sky

cream
+
blush

green

From whimsical to mod, green can be used to create the right mood. Brighter shades like kelly give a more playful, bold vibe while darker emeralds exude elegance, and muted shades like wintergreen set a serene tone.

save the date

TRACY CARDISIO AND NICHOLAS WILSON
will be joined in marriage
08.07.18

gauge your greens

Fresh, fun, and natural, this always-elegant hue can liven up any space, and there's a shade for every style and season. One caveat: There may not be a shade that works for every girl in your group—some greens can be hard to pull off on certain skin tones.

try these combinations

green
+
sunshine

lime
+
turquoise

grass
+
violet

yellow

The key to pulling off such a happy hue: take control and steer it in the right direction. Decide if you want to go bold and bright or soft and soothing. Opt for golden shades of honey or mustard for fall and winter, softer shades like butter and daffodil for spring, and go bright and bold with lemon or sunshine for summer.

will probably do the trick. Figure out which you want, so you can narrow your search.

Have a general idea about your taste, too (look back to chapter 1 if you need help with this). Are you a true minimalist? Or are you looking to do an über-romantic Gatsby-style wedding? Go through your vision for the day. Images are more telling than words (which leave room for interpretation), so bring your inspiration boards, magazine tear-outs, and pictures of arrangements you like, as well as color swatches to help give your florist a sense of what you're looking for.

The design phase
After the initial interview (but before you pay a deposit or sign a contract), where you define your vision and your budget, you'll meet again with your top-choice florist. She will present

---

questions to ask before booking a florist

☐ How many weddings are you handling on the same day or weekend as mine? If you're handling multiple clients, is there enough staff and time to go around?

☐ Have you done many weddings?

☐ Can I see photographs or live examples of your work? [If no, cut to the door.] Have you done weddings at our ceremony or reception site before? [If so, she'll be knowledgeable about what sizes, shapes, and colors work in the space. If not, she should be willing to scope out the venue, so she can take note of any limitations and suggest the most flattering arrangements.]

☐ Can you recommend flowers you think will fit best with my space and style? [Map out any other important details, such as theme, color scheme, floral allergies, and flowers that have special significance to you. This is the time to show your florist the pictures, tear-outs, and inspiration boards you brought, as well as pictures and fabric swatches of what you and the wedding party will be wearing.]

☐ Are you willing to work with my budget? [Let your florist know up front how much you're thinking about spending so she can plan accordingly. Cover everything from the bridal bouquet to reception centerpieces; name specific flowers. A good florist can work with you no matter how much you have to spend.]

☐ What other services do you offer? [These days, florists are actually more like event designers. You may be able to get decorations such as balloons, streamers, lanterns, and chairs from your florist. And this could be a really good thing: Dealing with one vendor rather than four or five may alleviate some stress.]

☐ Who will handle setup and delivery? What about breakdown? How long will you need for both, and what are the fees?

☐ Will you be responsible for working with my venue to find out about any restrictions they may have in terms of décor?

florist

Before you sign, make sure the following items are included in your flower contract.

- ☐ Date, times, and locations of your ceremony and reception

- ☐ An itemized list of all the flower arrangements you're buying—from bouquets to center-pieces—with exact names, amounts, and colors

- ☐ Flower alternatives (in your price range) if a specific bloom is unavailable on your wedding day; also include unacceptable substitutions, if any

- ☐ A list of items the florist will supply—centerpiece vases, trellises, other accessories

- ☐ Arrival times for setup at the ceremony and reception sites and addresses for both

- ☐ Where and when bouquets and boutonnieres should be delivered, if not to the ceremony site (to your home, for example, stating that exact address)

- ☐ Name of the florist who will be on hand during the wedding and for how long (you'll want the florist you've been working with to help set up the arrangements at both your ceremony and reception sites; if you are transporting ceremony flowers to your reception site, you may also want your florist to stay through the ceremony to help transport and rearrange your ceremony flowers for the reception)

- ☐ Floral proposal details

- ☐ Who will be responsible for the breakdown of any installations and when and where that will occur

- ☐ Who will fill in if the florist can't be there on your wedding day

- ☐ Sales tax, delivery fees, and setup fees

- ☐ Deposit amount and due date

- ☐ Balance amount and due date

- ☐ Cancellation/refund policy

an exact proposal based on what you discussed, itemizing the number and types of arrangements, the exact kinds of flowers to be used, and the cost for materials, as well as setup and breakdown. In addition, she'll show you sketches or small models of complex orders, such as a flowering gateway for your outdoor ceremony, the perfect nosegay bouquet, table topiaries (little flower trees or other ornamental arrangements), or the special modern table arrangements you discussed. This is the time to make changes and voice concerns about costs or elements you don't like. Adjust both your floral budget and your plan, ensuring that the two match. Once you're completely satisfied with the proposal, it will be added to a formal contract that you will then sign.

BEAUTIFUL BOUQUETS

While you might think that the dress steals the show, think of the bouquet's role as best supporting actress. Whether it's romantic roses, modern orchids, or the ever-popular peony, what you carry will shape your down-the-aisle look and be a focal point in your wedding photos.

Flower fit
Picking the right bridal bouquet size is all about scale. While the bride's bouquet is usually grander than those of her maids (or at least distinct from theirs), fitting in your wedding flowers with other elements of your wedding day isn't so cut-and-dried. Here's what to consider when sizing up your bridal bunch.

BODY SHAPE A small bride will be overshadowed by a massive cascading arrangement; a scaled-down bouquet (a nosegay or a posy, or even a composite) will be more proportional. A larger bridal bouquet allows full-figured brides to project grace. Also, make sure the bouquet isn't too heavy or too hard to carry.

YOUR GOWN A ball gown calls for a bouquet with an equally grand, impressive shape. If your bouquet is too small, it may get lost in a sea of fabric. Sheaths are meant to feel light and airy, so carry a bouquet that embodies that same spirit, like a small nosegay or a posy. If your wedding dress has slender lines, a bouquet that's too big might hide your shape and weigh you down. Bows, crystals, sashes, and other details can also play a role in how big your bridal bouquet should be. If your gown features a lot of embellishment, opt for a simpler bouquet. If there's some sparkle at the waistline, carry a tight nosegay rather than a cascading collection of blooms, so that you don't hide the dress's detailing.

YOUR VENUE If your ceremony will be held in a large, elaborate space like a ballroom or a grand cathedral, a small bouquet might seem insignificant. Avoid bitsy bunches of flowers and try an elegant, round bouquet. Or if you really have a flair for the dramatic, go all out with a grand cascading bouquet. If city chic is more your style (like a loft), think pretty and petite—a large bouquet might overpower your space.

Getting married outside? Don't compete with Mother Nature. Big or small, choose something that works with your surroundings. An intimate backyard or vineyard gathering calls for a hand-tied bouquet for that natural, just-picked look, while a reception near the beach with the ocean as your backdrop justifies something grander.

bouquet history

Brides in ancient Rome carried bunches of herbs to symbolize fidelity and fertility. The Greeks used ivy to symbolize indissoluble love. Brides today carry floral bouquets as a symbol of fertility and bounty.

bouquet shapes

CASCADE
A waterfall-like "spill" of blooms and greenery that's anchored in a handheld base. Looks like a miniature floral train.

COMPOSITE
A handmade creation in which different petals or buds are wired together on a single stem, creating the illusion of one giant flower.

HAND-TIED
A dense bunch of "just-picked" blooms tied together with wire that's covered with a ribbon.

NOSEGAY
A small, round cluster of flowers, all cut to a uniform length. Usually made with one dominant flower or color, nosegays are wrapped tightly.

BIEDERMEIER
A nosegay made up of concentric circles of different flowers for a somewhat striped effect.

PAGEANT
This bunch of long-stemmed flowers is cradled in the bride's arms.

POMANDER
A bloom-covered ball suspended from a ribbon, perfect for child attendants.

POSY
Smaller than a nosegay but similar in design. Petite roses or grape hyacinths are ideal varieties.

ROUND
Similar to a nosegay but generally larger and usually consisting of large, loosely arranged flowers.

That's a wrap

Although the most au naturel brides (particularly those seeking a single-flower style) may prefer the look of exposed stems, the majority of bouquets come elegantly wrapped. For a modern update of classic ribbon-wrapped stems, florists can layer ribbons in different colors or textures. To personalize your bunch, wrap the stems with an heirloom handkerchief (like the one your grandmother carried on her wedding day), adorn the stems with a locket bearing a photo of a deceased relative, or surround them in a ribbon embroidered with your monogram or signature motif.

Bridesmaid bouquets

Usually smaller than the bride's, bridesmaid bouquets don't have to be an exact match with the bouquet you carry, but they should play off your bouquet by complementing its color, shape, or types of flowers.

Keep your maids' dresses in mind too—their bouquets should complement the color of their dresses, so bring your florist a swatch. If they are all wearing the same dress (see chapter 15), consider varying their bouquets slightly (maybe with variations of one hue to create a spectrum from light to dark purple, for example, or change up the shapes but keep the hue the same). If, on the other hand, your bridesmaids are wearing different styles, keep their bunches consistent.

The no-thinking-involved option: Give your maids smaller versions of your bouquet. But if you want to do something different and keep things visually interesting, you may choose to have each bridesmaid carry a slightly different bouquet. Differentiate their flowers with ribbons, varying shapes, multiple shades, or completely different colors altogether (but ones that still relate to your wedding color scheme, of course).

FLOWERS FOR YOUR OTHER VIPS

Traditionally, the entire wedding party—and other special guests—carries or wears flowers on the wedding day. Here are your options for flowering the rest of your VIPs.

Grooms and groomsmen's boutonnieres

Boutonnieres typically consist of a single bloom or bud (or several small ones) attached at the left lapel of the jacket, worn by the groom, his attendants, the ushers, and the bride's and groom's fathers. While the men's buds were traditionally exactly the same as the bride's (in ancient Greece, they both wore strong-scented herbs to ward off evil spirits), the groom's boutonniere blooms don't have to exactly match the flowers in

---

CLEVER IDEAS
bouquet remix

Here are some ways to make your bunch stand out from your maids' bundles:

Carry the same arrangement but with a different bouquet wrap. Yours can match your gown color, and theirs can match their dress color.

Change the bouquet wrap accessory. Attach your grandma's cameo to yours and let them dress up their flowers with more modern brooches.

Carry the same flowers but in different colors. For you: lavender cymbidium orchids. For them: plum ones.

Hold a mix of different flowers, and have your bridesmaids each carry a different bunch of one of those flowers.

Walk down the aisle with a bouquet of many different flowers. Your bridesmaid bouquets can be identical to each other with just some of those flowers.

Choose one color and have each maid hold a bouquet of different flowers in that same hue.

attaching the boutonniere

Each boutonniere goes on the left lapel, the same side as the handkerchief pocket. The boutonniere can be pinned through the buttonhole; if there isn't one, you'll have to make a small hole in the jacket.

your bouquet, but they should share a common element, whether that's a bloom, greenery, or a nonfloral accent like feathers, felt cutouts, or small branches. The groomsmen's boutonnieres should coordinate with the groom's lapel décor, but his bout should stand out from those worn by the other men.

Corsages for the moms, grandmas, and special female guests

Made up of a single bloom (or a small cluster of blooms), arranged with lace, tulle, and/or ribbon, corsages come in pin-on, wrist, and handheld styles. Wrist and pin-on corsages are the most popular choices for Mom, Grandma, and that special aunt who helped fold all the programs during the ceremony. Orchids and gardenias are the most common flower picks. If you're going the corsage route, ask ahead of time which kind each woman would prefer—Mom might not want to put a hole in the lapel of her brand-new silk suit. Instead of a corsage, or in addition to one, you can have your mom and other relatives carry a small nosegay down the aisle or wear a flower in her hair. For other guests who deserve special recognition, a single orchid or rose is a nice alternative, too.

Flower child petals

A basket filled with rose petals is the flower girl's standard accessory. But she can also carry a pomander or garland instead. A floral wreath for her hair is a sweet touch, often seen at English weddings.

CEREMONY FLOWERS

Flowers are often the main décor element at the ceremony. Depending on where you'll wed, this can range from very simple to utterly lavish. Think like an interior designer when you're deciding on ceremony flowers. Is the ceremony site large or small? Ornate or plain? Also, check with your ceremony site before you start planning your flowers—there may be restrictions on décor, especially if you're getting married in a house of worship.

If you're getting married in an exquisite mosque, the architects have done you a favor by providing a built-in gorgeous backdrop—pare down the flowers so as not to distract from the building's beauty. If you're marrying in a church around a major holiday such as Easter or Christmas, the sanctuary may already be fully decorated for the season—lucky you!

If you're marrying outside, especially in a garden setting, you'll probably need little else to play up your lush surroundings, though lush arrangements can be used to define the altar and aisle. For a nondenominational ceremony in a loft, country club, or hotel, you may need some extra floral arrangements, such as a rose-petal–strewn aisle or trees brought indoors to flank either side of the aisle.

RECEPTION FLOWERS

Even more so than at the ceremony, flowers will be one of the key showpieces at your reception. There are a variety of options when it comes to reception blooms. Start by visiting the site with your florist, so she can get a feel for how you might want to decorate and can come up with ideas that will fit your style and your space. The type of flower, number of arrangements, time of year, location, size, and style will all play a role in how much your flowers will cost. (See "Budget Blooms," page 123, for flower savings tips.)

Reception arrangement considerations Like
bouquets, when it comes to centerpieces, think about scale. High ceilings are best complemented with tall floral centerpieces, such as angular glass vases holding sprays of long-stemmed roses or lush bunches placed on raised silver platforms (so guests can see each other). Small spaces need tight, bright arrangements that liven up the room without being distracting. Your tables aren't the only spots for flowers. You can also accent key reception areas—the entrance, the cake table, buffet stations—with floral bouquets, wreaths, or arrangements in vases.

A formal affair will call for different arrangements (think lush, towering blooms set atop tall candelabras or crystal vases) than a more casual reception would (such as low, loose, colorful bunches with a just-picked feel set in rustic wood vessels). If you're having an Asian-inspired event, arrange small clusters of orchids and other exotic flowers in architectural lacquered boxes; for décor with a vintage flair, mix all shapes and sizes of porcelain vases (or even silver ones) with pale shades of roses.

Finally, consider your personal taste: Are you and your fiancé sticklers for coordinated décor? If so, use the same centerpiece at every table, with a slightly more lavish arrangement for the head table (wherever you're sitting). Do you prefer a more modern or unique look? Ask your florist to play with three or four different arrangement types that will create a dynamic feel.

CLEVER IDEAS
flowers

Fun ways to decorate your ceremony and reception with flowers:

A central altar or two large pedestals topped with towering arrangements flanking where you two will stand

A flowering huppah (Jewish bridal canopy)

Blooms fastened onto pews or chairs

A lush wreath on the entrance door

Large potted plants or flower arrangements to delineate the ceremony area

A blooming arch for the wedding party to walk through

A floral arbor, trellis, or gazebo

Arrangements hung from shepherds' hooks dotting the aisle

Blooms as cake decorations

Edible flowers—such as hibiscus, roses, orange blossoms, pansies, marigolds, and geraniums—sprinkled in salads and drinks

Ivy interlaced with flowers draped from the ceiling

centerpiece shapes

It's not just about scale—shape matters, too. Here are the different
shape choices for your table arrangements.

breakaway
A few arrangements,
usually short in
height and containing
different flowers, are
grouped together to
make one.

globe
Flowers are
arranged in a
mounded
circular shape.

pedestal
This is based mostly
on the shape of the
vessel, which looks
like a trophy, but
the flowers tend
to cascade over
the sides.

trumpet
These arrangements
are narrower at the
top and wider at the

bottom, balancing
the shape of the
vase containing
them, which flares
at the top.

candelabra
For more formal
receptions, four to
six taper candles
stick out among the
flowers of this tall
arrangement.

tiered
This is when a taller
arrangement, like a
pedestal, trumpet,
or candelabra, is
surrounded by a ring
of flowers at the base.

The right-size centerpiece When choosing your
centerpieces, follow three guidelines: They should match the proportions
of the room. They should make sense for the size of the tables you're
using (long tables call for larger or multiple arrangements; shorter tables,
for smaller ones). And they should be the right height for conversation
(either tall enough or low enough that they don't block conversation and
guests' views).

LOW AND LOVELY Keeping the decorations close to the tables
works well in outdoor venues surrounded by natural scenery and
spaces with low or busy ceilings (think painted murals and tons of
chandeliers). The highest flower in the arrangement shouldn't go above
the shortest adult's chin. Since the arrangements won't be too tall,
you need some bold blooms—big-headed ones really pop in shorter
centerpieces, especially in bright colors like fuchsia and red. Peonies
and hydrangeas (which come in bunches) work, as do button mums for
modern arrangements.

HIGH AND MIGHTY Low centerpieces don't quite cut it when
you're in a venue with soaring ceilings. In this case, think big. The
lowest flower should hit above the tallest person's head. Two and a half

nonfloral centerpieces

If you want to do something other than flowers,
the options are endless.

a cluster of candles
A mix of pillars and votives in different heights can light up the night at an evening wedding.

a tray of candles
Hung from chains, this can transform your space into something resembling a medieval European castle.

candelabra
These regal candleholders are ideal because their bases are tall and thin. And you don't need to add anything extra to an ornate one.

feathers
A vase full of giant ostrich or peacock feathers guarantees glamour.

lamp shades
Set atop a tall cylinder vase, a patterned shade is retro and modern all at once.

fruit
Use fruit to brighten up your tablescape. Intersperse them with your centerpieces, or let them stand alone as the centerpieces themselves. Try apples, squash, or pumpkins in the fall, berries mixed with pinecones for a winter wedding, and citrus arranged in bowls for a bright modern affair.

lanterns
In a group or alone, these are ideal for a rustic indoor setting or an outdoor wedding.

branches
We love how they add height and a natural appeal in a cost-effective way, but even thin ones can get in the way of a cross-table chat.

crystal strands
So glamorous and so . . . distracting. If these aren't well above guests' heads, the light will reflect into their eyes!

wrought-iron chandeliers
To dress up a rustic space, try this elegant twist on the more opulent crystal chandelier.

BRIDE ON A BUDGET
budget blooms

Here are some savvy ways to save on your ceremony and reception flowers.

stay in season
Timing is everything. In-season, local blooms will be less expensive and look more vibrant. Marrying around Valentine's Day? Expect a significant increase in the price of a single stem.

reuse and recycle
Make your ceremony flowers do double duty. Instead of letting them go to waste, decorate the cake table or bar with the bridesmaid bouquets and altar arrangements.

simplify your centerpieces
Labor costs make florist bills bloom. Trim them by opting for less labor-intensive arrangements like simple centerpieces instead of wild topiaries. Also, nix any elaborate blooming structures.

go big
Large, full blossoms like cymbidium orchids and peonies cut down on the number of stems you need.

fresh flowers

Follow these tips to get the most photo-friendly blooms.

perfect timing

Be sure to coordinate the delivery time of your bouquets, corsages, and boutonnieres with your photographer's arrival, so they look as fresh as possible in pictures.

fresh direct

Have your flowers delivered boxed with cellophane and well misted—that way they'll look fresh throughout your ceremony and reception. Check out each bouquet first and remove any damaged blossoms. And don't leave the bouquets in the sun's path—direct sunlight will speed up the wilting process.

prep work

Your florist will need early access to your ceremony and reception site on your wedding day. Make the necessary arrangements—get written permission and a key, if need be—so she has ample time to set up.

water world

If you're keeping bouquets in vases of water to maintain freshness before the ceremony, don't forget to dry the stems thoroughly before handing them out to the attendants. You don't want big water stains on the front of all the dresses moments before they take the aisle.

to three feet up from the table is usually a safe bet. The height is the main attraction here, so the blooms don't need to be big—they just need to soar (think orchid sprays). Anything that distracts from what's going on up top won't work, so skip thick or colored vases and go with transparent vessels. Same with blooms submerged in water—keep the vase clear so guests can see (and sort of talk) through it. Another conversation blocker: cascading flowers. Bottom line: If it drapes down, it'll get between guests.

SUSPENDED If you can hang arrangements from the ceiling, a support beam, or a tree branch, you have a lot of control over where the centerpiece hits. Since the space between the table and the decorations is completely empty, this is the best choice for keeping conversation flowing. Just don't hang them too high—bare tables will look very empty if there's too much space between them and the hanging centerpieces. Arrangements with some overhang are ideal, like hanging amaranthus. Just avoid anything too heavy: If you're not sure it'll stay up above the tables the whole night, or if it requires chunky wires or thick cords to stay in place (which will compete with the beauty of the suspended centerpieces), don't bother. Crashing centerpieces will definitely interfere with conversation!

vessel varieties

You'll want to be able to picture exactly what your florist is talking about.

BUBBLE
A popular choice for casual receptions, this vase has a spherical shape. A line of them along a rectangular banquet table look gorgeous, no matter the formality of the occasion.

CUBE
This modern shape can hold its own in the middle of a table, but a few small ones around a tall, slim vase are ultrachic, too.

PILSNER
Named for the narrow-bottomed, wide-mouthed beer glass it resembles, this vase usually holds flowers loosely packed in a round shape.

PEDESTAL
Medium in height, this vase features a shape similar to a trophy's. It looks great with flowers and greenery dripping down its sides.

CYLINDER
The tubelike shape is ideal for showing off submerged blooms.

9

photography

TIMELINE

PLANNING

9–11 months before
Start researching
photographers

6–8 months before
Book your photographer

1–2 weeks before
Give photographer a
shot list, day-of timeline,
and seating chart

**1–2 hours before
the ceremony**
Take first-look photos (if
you want) and portraits
with your bridal party

during cocktail hour
Take formal portraits
with your bridal party
and each other

Your wedding is going to be gorgeous, memorable, and fabulously one-of-a-kind. It would be cruel to yourselves (and future generations) not to ensure you have mementoes from this spectacular affair—and nonfuzzy ones at that. Unlike the work of your other wedding vendors (music, flower arrangements, dress, cake), photographs aren't things you can hear, smell, taste, or even see at first—you don't really know what you're getting until after the fact. That means careful research and selectiveness regarding professional skills, artistic style, and personal demeanor are extra-important when choosing your photographer.

PHOTOGRAPHY BASICS

Photographs are quintessential wedding keepsakes. They speak volumes about the atmosphere, style, and emotions of the wedding day. Arranged artfully in an album, photos narrate the story of your event from the morning preparations—including the groom's contortions trying to knot his bow tie—to the last revelers getting cozy on the dance floor. For photos that will best reflect your personal sensibility—and help you relive those happy emotions for years to come—arm yourself with some basic information about what different photographic styles are available (and how to spot them), where to find a talented pro, and when (and how) to get the perfect shots.

Focusing on a Style

Top photographers can be booked up to two years in advance—some couples reserve in-demand image pros before they've even gotten engaged! Many photographers only shoot one wedding per weekend, so book early to be sure that wedding is yours. This means you need to start looking as far ahead as possible. But before you begin, you'll need to first decide what type of photography style you prefer as that will help determine which kind of photographer you'll want to shoot your wedding.

PHOTOJOURNALISTIC (OR DOCUMENTARY) PHOTOGRAPHY

Instead of a series of posed photos, these are candid or spontaneous pictures (read: not styled) of people, décor, and the action. Typical shots might include the lavish raw bar before guests start digging in, your motley crew of cousins dancing, and you and your bridesmaids laughing, champagne in hand. With a purely photojournalistic photographer, you won't ever see people staring at the camera—the photos capture the moments exactly as they happened and together they tell a story. There's also the middle-of-the-road option of more stylized candid shots. For example, your photographer might move a coat off a chair or straighten out the bedspread in the room before he begins shooting. (The shots are still candid but not purely photojournalistic.)

Advantages A collection of candid or stylized candid shots can tell the story of your whole day, from different angles and perspectives, without much manipulation of subjects. It's a fluid compilation that is fun, surprising, romantic, and true to life.

Disadvantages Sometimes the shots can be a little too real. You can't exactly choose your most flattering angle before the photographer snaps the shot. Another drawback: The photographer might capture

ASK CARLEY
PASS ON PORTRAITS?

We want all natural, candid shots. Can we skip the posed portraits?
Getting everyone together at one time (especially both of your families, looking their best, no less) is a special and rare occurrence, and the day will happen only once. Even if you think you don't want any portraits, you'll likely be glad to have them after the wedding's over (and your parents will be thrilled). If you want to minimize the portrait session, pare it down to just the must-take portraits: the bride and groom together, the entire wedding party, the bride and groom with their parents, the couple with the bride's immediate family, the couple with the groom's immediate family, and both immediate families all together.

your brother twirling Grandma across the dance floor but you may not get those posed shots of you with your college friends. For the best of both worlds, look for a photographer who does both posed shots and spontaneous, documentary-style shooting.

FORMAL AND CREATIVE PORTRAITURE PHOTOGRAPHY

These are posed shots of the two of you, friends, and family in front of various backdrops. That's not to say there isn't room for creativity in this category. While some photographers will pose subjects in a more traditional spot (like the ceremony altar or out on the lawn of the country club) and in more formal poses (standing as a group together), other photographers take portraiture farther into the creative realm with a more dramatic composition (the couple sitting on a lounge chair at their hip hotel reception venue, or the couple holding hands in the middle of a nearby dirt road with the mountains in the background).

Advantages It's a way to get the family portrait and a flawless shot of the two of you. This doesn't mean that the photos will be bland; it means that the composition and the subjects will be closer to "perfect."

Sami & Michael

NOVEMBER 8
PALM SPRINGS, CA

Inspired by their swanky venue, Sami and Michael replicated the famed pattern of the concrete block wall outside the Parker Palm Springs on the border of their invitations. To complement the bold, retro pattern and to pay tribute to the bride's interior-designer back-ground, the couple chose an orange-and-white palette and bold patterns mixed with chic details, like the Moroccan lanterns and colorful flower balls that dotted the grassy aisle during the ceremony.

color vs. black-and-white photos

Now that digital photos can be manipulated after the fact, you'll need to decide whether you want an album filled with color photos, black-and-white images, or a mix of both. No doubt, you'll want to capture the vibrant colors of the flowers you painstakingly selected and that brilliant sunset backdrop to your ceremony on color film. Flowers, food, favors—all the details you discussed and debated endlessly—will come through best in color. But when it comes to capturing the unscripted moments that will live on in your mind forever—the anxiety and joy of getting ready or the adoring glance your future husband casts your way—black-and-white images are often the way to go. The fewer colors your eyes have to process, the cleaner and easier an image is to absorb when viewing.

Unless your photographer is shooting on actual film, she'll be able to convert any of your images to black-and-white. If you love the look, though, let her know ahead of time so she can plan for it. Some photographers will switch between both mediums for the best of both worlds.

Disadvantages Posing for pictures is time-consuming, especially if you want to get every last combination of you, your families, the wedding party, and your friends. If you're taking them after the ceremony, you'll probably miss the entire cocktail hour. And if either of you has a tendency to freeze up in front of the camera, you may not want to spend forty-five minutes posing for pictures.

FINE-ART PHOTOGRAPHY Though it's similar to documentary photography, this style gives the shooter greater artistic license to infuse his particular point of view into your photographs. So while the shots reflect reality, it's the photographer's reality. The photos are dramatic and gorgeous, but look as though they were shot on film with a grainier, dreamier, more muted appearance. Usually the object (or couple) is in focus and the background appears to blur. Motion also looks very natural in this style of photography.

The few wedding photographers in the world who shoot only on film tend to fall into this category, and typically they shoot in black and white, though some will do a mix of both. That said, a photographer

photography styles

Here are some examples of what different photo styles might look like.

creative portraiture

stylized
wedding
photos

photojournalistic/
candid

fine art

using a digital camera can still get this style with the right gear and camera lens. And some photographers will alternate between digital and film. Not all photographers who take a fine-art approach shoot portraits, so if it's really important to your mom to have posed family shots, look for someone who does both or consider hiring a second shooter for the portrait sessions.

Advantages You get a compilation of wedding photographs that look as though they belong in a museum or coffee-table book. The results are more like works of art for your wall than typical couple portraits.

Disadvantages If the photographer is shooting on film, the production costs are usually higher. And the photos, while dreamy and nostalgic, may not look as sharp or realistic, so you may not want all your photos taken in that style. If your photographer is shooting with film, you won't get all the manipulation options you would with digital (however, some will switch back and forth between digital and film), and most of these photographers work in black and white only, though some will shoot in color, too. Some photographers may not be willing to work with a shot list and shoot formal portraits.

EDGY, BOLD PHOTOGRAPHY This style of photography is marked by outside-the-box, tilted angles (called "Dutch angles") and unconventional framing. So instead of a straight-on shot of the couple exchanging vows at the altar, the photo might look tilted, with an object, like an altar arrangement or candle, in the foreground. Or the photo of the bride having her makeup done might be shot from above with an emphasis on the eye shadow brush rather than the face. Even a single portrait of a bridesmaid might be shot so that her face takes over only the bottom right of the photo and the rest of the space is filled with the wall or whatever is behind her.

Advantages It's a unique style that stands out from the more popular classic wedding photography styles, perfect for couples who want more artistic images.

Disadvantages Those bold angles may distract from the subject. You might just want a straight-on shot of your first kiss without all the extra effects and angles.

FINDING A PHOTOGRAPHER

In addition to style, there are some key factors that will determine who you will choose to shoot your day. Your first step is to carefully review potential photographers' websites and blogs to check out photos of other weddings they've shot, which will give you an idea of their style. If you like what you see, book a time to meet with them and check out more of their work.

Looking through several weddings the photographer has shot will give you a sense of their quality over time as well as their natural style. Don't base your decision solely on what you see in their highlights gallery or album. For good reason, photographers show prospective clients a portfolio of their best pictures, all from different weddings, so you're seeing the best of the best. The problem with that is that you won't get a well-rounded idea of their work. Ask to see two or three full galleries from real weddings they've shot (not someone else at their company), so you can get a better idea of what your complete collection of photos might look like after the wedding. If you see that the full gallery and the photos are just about as good as the ones chosen in the highlight gallery (that is, they're all so good it's impossible to choose!), you're on the right track.

While you're flipping through the photographer's' portfolio, look for crispness of images, thoughtful compositions (does a shot look good the way it was framed, or is there too much clutter in the frame?), and good lighting (beware of washed-out pictures where small details are blurred—unless that's the style you're after). It's also very important that you detect sensitivity in capturing people's emotions; make sure the photographer's subjects look relaxed, not like deer caught in headlights.

If you see a particular photo you love, tell the photographer. Same goes if you don't like something you see: Let him know that you're not as in to that particular shot and why. Doing this helps your photographer start to gather clues as to how he'll approach your wedding.

This is not a decision that can be made on looks alone—you must meet your potential photographers in person, if at all possible. If you like what you see on their sites—and their fees are vaguely in your range— set up in-person meetings with two to five potential photographers to look at more of their work and assess whether your personalities mesh. Is the photographer excited by your vision when you describe it? When she makes suggestions, does she present them in a clear and respectful way? Is she timid? Are her mannerisms off-putting? In order to get the best photos, go with a pro who has a firm grasp of social graces but is assertive enough to go out hunting for great images and who, above all, puts you at ease and doesn't irritate you in any way. (Remember: She'll be shadowing your every move, and the more comfortable both of you are with her, the better the photos will turn out.) Likewise, you don't want the photographer to offend or annoy any guests, but to shoot them in their best light in an unobtrusive way.

PUTTING TOGETHER YOUR PACKAGE

You won't be able to nail down an exact dollar amount until you're sure of what you want, how many albums you need, and where your photographer is based, but in general, packages can range significantly, from $2,500 to $20,000-plus on the higher end of the spectrum. However, when interviewing candidates, you can ask for a general range based on the photographer's standard "shooting fee," plus their standard rates for the type of album you think you'll want and coverage you're hoping to book them for (day-of, full weekend, etc.). Some photographers will list general fees on their websites, so that's a good place to start comparing rates. You can also ask local brides in your area for photographer recommendations at TheKnot.com/local.

Coverage
Ideally, you want your photographer to be there for your full wedding day: from when you start getting ready until after you make your grand exit from the reception. While packages vary, most include about six to nine hours to cover everything from preceremony events (getting ready with your bridesmaids or first-look photos—see "First-Look Photos," page 137) to the end of the reception. Make sure everything you want photographed is included in your package and there is enough time for it all. It's generally better to pay for more coverage if there's a chance you'll run over, because overtime is usually charged at a high hourly rate.

Also consider whether you'll want the photographer at other events during your wedding weekend (the guys' golf outing, the bridesmaid lunch). By having him at the rehearsal dinner, you'll ensure he gets to know all of the key players, and family won't be meeting him for the first time on the wedding day, so they'll be more comfortable in front of the camera.

Shooter(s)
Many photo studios have more than one photographer, so don't just assume Bruce of Bruce Photographers will be taking

INSIDE SCOOP
what takes so long?

It usually takes at least a month to get all those photo proofs back from your photographer. Why? It's all postproduction work! Your photographer is shooting enormous raw files (way bigger than your typical JPG). Shooting raw files gives your photographer greater ability to correct the photo, but it also takes a longer time to process those files (in order to correct color levels and so on). It varies, but many photographers will spend about forty hours working on your images after the wedding, so it can take up to six to eight weeks (or longer, depending on the photographer) to get them.

questions to ask before booking a photographer

Flash these questions when interviewing potential shooters.

style

☐ What style(s) do you specialize in? Are you willing to do portraits [if that's not his or her typical style]?

☐ Do you shoot digital or film? Are you willing to do both?

☐ Do you shoot in color or black and white? Are you willing to do both and what percentage of each do you recommend?

☐ Will the photos be retouched and color-balanced? Is that done before I see the proofs? [These are some of the techniques magazines use to make models look flawless. Some photographers will polish all your photos, others will show you untouched proofs and work their magic only on the images you order.]

fees

☐ What exactly is included in the fee or package? [When comparing fees, check whether prints, albums, and proofs are included and factor them in—they can alter the costs significantly, with proofs running around $500-plus.]

☐ How many hours of coverage do we get? What is the charge for overtime?

☐ Does the fee include an engagement shoot or any other additional coverage?

☐ Does the fee include film costs and processing fees (if applicable)?

☐ Does the fee include an album? [Most packages don't include albums, which can run as high as $5,000 or more.] What is the price of your most popular album?

☐ Does the fee include prints and how many are included? Is there a minimum order for prints? How much do additional prints costs?

☐ How much extra would it be to have you cover the rehearsal dinner [or welcome party]? Are you available to cover mine [if you'd like the additional coverage]?

☐ Are proofs included in the fee? How will they be delivered to me? [Most photographers now post digital images to a website for your review. If your photographer shoots with film, he will send hard proofs.]

☐ What is the total fee? What is the deposit amount and when is it due?

☐ When is the final payment due?

shooters

☐ Will you be my photographer, or will it be one of your associates?

☐ Who will shoot the wedding if you are sick?

☐ Will there be a second shooter? Will you have an assistant with you? [Note: Some photographers call second shooters "assistants" or "associates"; other assistants serve more typical support duties like carrying equipment, so it's helpful to ask what the assistant will handle.] What is the fee for a second shooter?

logistics

☐ How long before we get to see the photos? [While some photographers turn them around as fast as a week after the wedding, most will get them to you anywhere from four to six weeks later. See "What takes So Long?" page 133.]

☐ How do you coordinate with my videographer? How do you envision working together? [Your photographer is a great source for videographer recommendations. If you go with a team that has worked together before, they'll be able to better complement each other's work to capture your day in the most complete way.]

☐ How many weddings do you do a weekend? [Most photographers do only one wedding per day, but it's a good idea to double check. If your photographer is shooting an afternoon wedding before yours, you'll want to work out a plan if the first event runs over and ensure that he'll have enough stamina to last as long as you want for your wedding. If you're considering having the photographer shoot your rehearsal dinner or other events as well, be sure to reserve his time in advance.]

☐ Will you check out the ceremony and reception venues beforehand? Will you work with our venue contacts regarding any photography restrictions they may have?

☐ Will you follow a shot list?

album

☐ What type of paper will the prints be on? [The answer should be acid-free archival-quality paper, which will stand the test of time, unlike the type of material drugstore photos are printed on, which deteriorates at a faster rate.]

☐ What are the restrictions for sharing photos online or for publication? Do you own the copyright to the photos? [See "Whose Photos Are They Anyway?" page 138.]

☐ Do you do photo booths? [Some photographers will rent them as part of their wedding packages.] Any other fun shoot ideas?

☐ Do you bring your own lighting? [Indoor shots call for extra lighting and different photography styles use different types of lighting. While most wedding photographers have mastered the art of lighting and will supply appropriate and subtle lighting if needed, double check that any equipment they bring won't be bulky or obtrusive.]

☐ What will you wear? Will you follow our dress code?

your wedding pictures. Unless you specify it in your contract, the lead photographer may not be the one shooting your day. Also, include specific stipulations in the contract about who will cover for them should something happen on the actual day.

If you have room in your budget, consider hiring a second shooter. Many top-notch photographers automatically bring a second shooter, but if this isn't included in your package, you may want to ask about the possibility. The main benefit is that your event can be covered from that many more angles. For example, during your formal photo session, one photographer can capture the formal photos, while the second one can

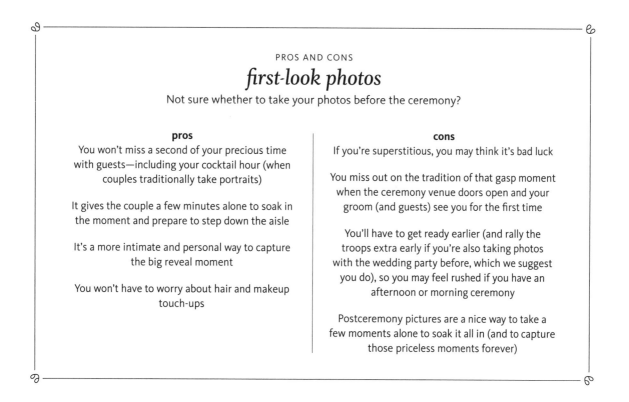

first-look photos

Not sure whether to take your photos before the ceremony?

pros	cons
You won't miss a second of your precious time with guests—including your cocktail hour (when couples traditionally take portraits)	If you're superstitious, you may think it's bad luck
It gives the couple a few minutes alone to soak in the moment and prepare to step down the aisle	You miss out on the tradition of that gasp moment when the ceremony venue doors open and your groom (and guests) see you for the first time
It's a more intimate and personal way to capture the big reveal moment	You'll have to get ready earlier (and rally the troops extra early if you're also taking photos with the wedding party before, which we suggest you do), so you may feel rushed if you have an afternoon or morning ceremony
You won't have to worry about hair and makeup touch-ups	Postceremony pictures are a nice way to take a few moments alone to soak it all in (and to capture those priceless moments forever)

get a behind-the-scenes, photojournalistic look (shots of guests while you two are posing for pictures alone, for example). If you're having a larger wedding (two hundred and fifty guests or more), you might even want to look into three shooters so that your photography team can be sure to capture the event from all angles.

Photo types and twists

You two look amazing. Your guests look delightful. The flowers look fantastic, the food delicious. Wouldn't it be a disaster if you didn't capture it all? Go over our list of traditional wedding shots and the rundown of some of the best images to snag. (All of these are wedding-video must-haves, too.) A professional photographer will probably suggest these on his own, but it's a good idea to incorporate them all into your day-of timeline, so you can let all relevant parties know when they'll need to be ready for their photo ops.

BRIDAL PORTRAIT Traditionally, the bride would go to a photographer's studio one to three months before the wedding to be photographed in her gown (perhaps even holding a replica of her bouquet). While this practice is becoming less and less common, some women still choose to pose for this formal shot so they can include it with their wedding announcement. The modern spin on this is the engagement photo—the two of you dressed in party clothes, or at some breathtaking or personally significant location.

HAPPY COUPLE A posed picture of the two of you on your big day is a must-have. More often, couples pose for this shot in the moments right after the ceremony. But we suggest you defy the superstition (that it's bad luck for the groom to see the bride's dress before the big moment!) and take this shot before the ceremony, when you're all dressed up and ready to go. Some photographers call this a first-look shot. Photographers can still stage these to capture the big reveal moment, so you won't miss the expression on your groom's face when he sees you for the first time in your dress.

WEDDING PARTY Group shots of your wedding party might include the girls and guys separately and then everyone together, either before or directly after the ceremony. (Or you can step out for a bit during the reception if you'd rather not miss the entire cocktail hour.) You also might want shots of you two and both honor attendants, and shots of each of you with your main attendant. If you're taking first-look photos, we suggest also taking pictures with the families and bridal party at the same time, so they can start enjoying cocktail hour as soon as their ceremony duties are over. If you decide to wait until the ceremony to see each other, take individual pictures with your families and attendants, so you have fewer shots to get through during the cocktail hour.

FAMILY Photos of each of you with your parents and siblings— taken before or after the ceremony—are a must (at least for Mom). Take a portrait of the two of you with each of your immediate family members, and you might also want to have one big photo of both families together.

GUESTS It's becoming increasingly popular to ask all your guests to pose for a portrait just after the ceremony or during the reception. It's a great way to get a visual record of everyone who attended your wedding, not just the people who walked down the aisle. Some couples choose to break it down into smaller groups (college friends, coworkers, cousins).

CEREMONY ACTION SHOTS Shots of your ceremony—beginning with your arrival and ending when you leave—are the cornerstone of your wedding album. Classic pictures include the groom waiting at

must-shoot list

There are some wedding moments you don't want to miss on photo.
Be sure to keep these in mind when talking to your photographer about which shots you want.

getting ready (before the ceremony)

The dress hanging (make sure you have a nice hanger)

Bride getting hair and makeup done (wear a simple white robe or button-down)

Full-length shot of bride with gown checking herself out in mirror (remember to keep all the underwear off the floor)

Groom getting ready with Dad and pals (tying the tie is a classic)

You two chatting with/crying with/hugging your parents and siblings preceremony

Mom helping bride with one last detail (give her veil duty)

Each of you ready to go (make sure you leave a moment for this)

Making your way to the ceremony (in the backseat of a limo, hailing a cab, walking down the road)

The bride holding her bouquet (manicure and moisturizer, please!)

the ceremony

Guests streaming into the site

Ushers escorting guests to their seats (you get to see if they did it right)

Close-up of the groom (adorably nervous) waiting for his other half

Flower girl and/or ring bearer walking in (how cute!)

Gorgeous bridesmaids going down the aisle

Bride waiting to make her entrance (stand somewhere pretty!)

Bride and her escort going down the aisle

Wide shot of audience during ceremony, from bride and groom's point of view (make sure your photographer is allowed behind the altar)

Close-up of your hands as you exchange the rings

The kiss! (Make it last)

You two coming up the aisle (look up so the photographer can see your face)

The getaway (classic cars make a classic shot)

the reception

Bride and groom arriving (make it dramatic—your faces through the dark glass of the limo, you two at the top of a staircase or pushing through a curtain)

Receiving-line moments (a good time to get shots with relatives)

Informal shots with your best friends

Your parents whispering during dinner

Kids playing with balloons and streamers (have cute props at the ready)

You two dancing (maybe with a slow shutter speed so the movement blurs the image a little)

The musicians or DJ doing their thing

The groom dancing with the maid of honor

The dance floor going nuts (again, slow shutter speed could be effective)

The bride and groom feeding each other cake (no smashing allowed!)

The bouquet toss

The glowing tent from a distance

TIP
portrait schedule

The timetable for your portraits depends on how many shots you want and your photographer, but a good rule of thumb is to figure it will take five minutes to assemble everyone and another five minutes to take each group shot. So figure it will take about an hour for all your family and wedding party portraits, and another thirty to forty-five minutes for the couple shots. To keep things moving so you can start greeting your guests, make sure everyone knows ahead of time where to be and when, so you aren't waiting while the troops gather, and allot time for travel if you're taking pictures in a few different locations.

CLEVER IDEAS
photography extras

photo booths
This popular cocktail hour and reception entertainment has gone mainstream, and now couples are finding ways to personalize their photo booths. Rent a retro photo booth that automatically prints photos right away for your guests or hire a company to come in and set up a backdrop (styled to your liking) and upload all the images to a site where guests can view and print them afterward. If you'd rather not rent one, make one. Create your own backdrop using a piece of patterned fabric, a simple curtain, or wallpaper.

themed engagement shoots
Couples are coming up with the most creative themed engagement photo shoots, from Breakfast at Tiffany's to more obscure 1950s backyard barbecue shoots. Not into the theme idea? Tone it down with a couple props, like colorful balloons, umbrellas, or a tandem bicycle.

day-of slideshows
Run a slideshow of images from the ceremony and cocktail hour from your photographer's laptop and project them on a screen during dinner. Guests will love looking at what they just experienced, and they'll have plenty to talk about at the tables.

style shoots
In addition to the engagement shoot and the wedding day, couples are opting for additional sessions before the wedding with more of a theme, like a "boudoir session" of just-for-him photos or a day-before fashion photo shoot with your photographer.

the altar, the wedding party, the bride and her escort going down the aisle, and ceremonial highlights (jumping the broom, exchanging rings, signing a marriage contract). You should also ask your photographer to get a shot of the entire crowd from your vantage point during the vows and several reaction shots of special guests crying/laughing/smiling— they tell the real story of the moment.

RECEPTION HIGHLIGHTS AND CANDIDS Apart from the spotlight dances, reception highlights like the cutting of the cake and dances with your moms and dads also should be memorialized. And the spontaneous shots of you and your guests mingling, munching, and moshing are often priceless.

Logistics
It's good to set up a time when your photographer can preview your site(s), if possible. That way, he'll have an idea of the lighting and layout, so it will be easier for him to get set up on your day. Verify and inform him of whether there are any restrictions about what photographers or videographers can use or where they can go at the ceremony site.

About two weeks or so before the wedding, set up a time to review your day-of timeline (see chapter 25), so your photographer can weigh in on the best times for photos based on the lighting. Bring a shot list to go over (see page 139), so he can give you a better idea of how long you'll need to allot for portrait sessions, too. You'll also want to give him the seating chart (so he knows where the VIPs will be) , as well as a list of key events (like the cake cutting) that you want to make sure he captures.

10
videography

TIMELINE
PLANNING

9–11 months before
Start researching
videographers

6–8 months before
Book your videographer

1–2 weeks before
Give videographer a video
list, timeline, and seating
chart

**1–3 hours before the
ceremony**
Take getting-ready videos
and scene-setting videos

during the reception
Show a highlight video

There's no doubt professional photos are the place to start when documenting your day, but there are many compelling reasons to have a wedding video, too: You'll get to see a lot of live action that you may have missed because you were off greeting guests/tending to those butterflies in your stomach/dancing with your grandfather. You'll also have a vivid record of the sounds of your wedding—your processional music, your best man's hilarious toast, the cacophony of guests chatting and laughing—as well as key moving images, such as your dance with your father, the bridesmaids' goofy moves, the bouquet-toss pileup.

VIDEOGRAPHY BASICS

A videographer combines the skills of a documentary filmmaker with the eyes of a movie director, and options abound when it comes to capturing the spirit or shaping the story of your wedding day. As the stars of your own made-for-TV movie, you have a few options in the style department. Before you begin shopping around for a videographer, figure out which directorial approach most appeals to you and how you want the video to feel. Your style choice will guide you in making all other video-related decisions, from whom you hire to how the day is filmed to how the footage is edited. But don't feel like you have to commit to one or the other—just like photographers, many videographers these days are capable of using a combination of styles.

Classic

Would you prefer it to be more cinematic—a movie telling the story of your romance and wedding day? Classic videos include photo montages, interviews with guests and even you two (though these are optional), and a linear progression of the day's events.

Documentary

Similar to photojournalistic style, this video style is closer to a raw documentary. It may contain a mix of color and black-and-white footage for contrast, and the result may feel more authentic and less contrived than classic wedding videos.

Cinematic

This blend of sweeping artistic angles and sound bites from your wedding day (your bridesmaids laughing while you're getting ready, the dad's toast) is one of the best ways to convey what it was like to actually be at your wedding. Formal without feeling stuffy, a cinematic-style wedding video captures every detail from virtually every angle.

Super 8

An increasing number of couples are opting for videos shot with Super 8 film using a retro-style camera that was popular in the sixties. Super 8 videos are grainy and the colors look muted and rich, with a romantic and nostalgic feel, which is what makes them so popular.

Sometimes one film style isn't enough. Ask your videographer about creating a combination of grainy Super 8, documentary, and cinematic-style videography. The best part is that most of the effects can be done postwedding during the edit.

the knot NOTE

videographer finder
You can watch
hundreds of wedding
videos from pros in
your area, plus find
their contact info.
**TheKnot.com/
videographers**

HIRING A VIDEOGRAPHER

Like your photographer, your videographer is someone you really need to trust and like, so it's extraimportant to check the person out carefully. Consult your wedding photographer (if you've already hired one) for a videographer he's worked with before, so the two can work together, complementing each other's efforts.

Videos

Check out potential videographers' websites—most post clips from videos they've done online, so you can get a feel for their work. When evaluating videos they've shot, be sure you're looking at footage shot by the videographer who will be shooting your wedding, not by other professionals who work at the same studio. Then if you like what you see, set up an appointment to meet with a videographer and to review an entire wedding he shot, as well as examples of different video options offered—most can send you a link to videos, so you can watch them on your own.

Technical skills

You'll also want to consider the videographer's technical skills: Are the images clear? Is the lighting too dim or harsh? How's the sound quality? Can you understand what everyone is saying? Does the music complement or overwhelm the visuals? Images should be bright and crisp, not dark and grainy. Faces should be natural looking, not shiny or washed out by too much light. Don't forget to listen for good, clear sound quality (no hissing or buzzing; sound levels should be steady from scene to scene).

To evaluate the videographer's editing capabilities, check if the transitions and special effects are smooth, as well as whether they enhance or clutter the story. Scenes should be put together in a coherent, logical fashion. Selected clips should be "best of" material (read: not boring).

If you want to include interviews in your video, make sure the videographer you pick is also a good interviewer who gets great quotes from friends and family. The people being interviewed on the tapes you're watching should seem happy and comfortable, not besieged or annoyed. And before you write them off, they don't have to be cheesy and obtrusive. The interviews can take place before the wedding, or your videographer can set up outside the reception or cocktail area for guests to stop by to record their well wishes for and memories of the happy couple. Voiceovers—taped interviews or statements—can then be recorded separately and used to enhance certain scenes. For example,

questions to ask before booking a videographer

- ☐ What's your style: cinematic, documentary, classic, or a mix?

- ☐ Do you shoot with a digital camera or use film?

- ☐ Have you done many weddings before? What's your storytelling approach when it comes to taping a wedding? [This clues you in to his or her experience and philosophy.]

- ☐ Can I see samples of other wedding videos you've done?

- ☐ Have you won any awards? Are you a member of any national or local videography associations?

- ☐ How do you coordinate with a wedding photographer? Have you ever worked with my photographer before? [It's a plus if you can find shooters who have worked together before. One way to guarantee a good tandem is to hire a studio that does both photo and video, or simply ask your photographer if he can recommend a videographer.]

- ☐ Have you ever shot a wedding at my ceremony or reception site? If so, can I see clips?

- ☐ Are there other weddings you're shooting on my wedding day or weekend? [Make sure there are no conflicts.]

- ☐ Will you be the one who will be shooting my wedding? [If not, make sure you speak to whomever will actually shoot and ask for clips of weddings the actual shooter has done.]

- ☐ What types of equipment (cameras, etc.) and editing techniques will you use? [Also, find out if the videographer is able to shoot in high definition to get an idea of the quality of the picture you'll get.]

- ☐ Tell me about the special effects you like to use for weddings, and how those effects are achieved and the benefit of using them. [You may not catch all the tech speak, but it helps to have a sense of what's what.]

- ☐ How will you ensure the sound quality is up to par? [In order to record the sounds from your wedding, you'll need to wear mics. A wireless mic is typically hidden discreetly just under the groom's boutonniere with a small pack that acts as the transmitter and clips onto the back of his waistband under his jacket. If placing the microphone on a boutonniere, it should be at least halfway down the lapel since if it is placed too high, it could easily pick up the sound of the groom breathing. At a Jewish wedding, your videographer can even try hiding the microphone in the huppah. If the church is large and full of echoes, or there are readings, a mic on the podium is advised as well. If your ceremony is outdoors, you'll need more mics, including for the groom, readers, and musicians. Some cameras can receive sounds from up to eight different mics at once, so for example, an on-camera mic can also record ambient noise and conversations, which can be blended with music.]

- ☐ Will you bring in your own lighting?

- ☐ Will a backup camera be on hand for the event?

- ☐ How do you charge for services? Are there packages? [Request a price list.]

- ☐ What types of videos (trailer, highlight reel, etc.) do you offer and which do you recommend?

- ☐ What is the editing process like and how involved will I be? [Think about what parts of the day you want (and don't want) to include, and don't be afraid to give your videographer as much direction as you'd like. Look for a videographer who will work with your vision, but stay open-minded and listen to his suggestions—that's why you're paying for a professional.]

a mother's well wishes for her son's marriage might be filtered in over scenes of the mother/son dance.

Personality

Once you've found two or three promising prospects, set up appointments to meet each of them face-to-face to see if your personalities mesh. Note your chemistry with the videographer: Does he make you feel at ease? Exceptional people skills are a must in this profession since videographers work very closely with you and your guests. Is he receptive to your specific vision for the video? Keep in mind that what you see is what you get; don't be swayed by a person's charm if his work isn't what you're looking for.

PUTTING TOGETHER THE PACKAGE

Videographers generally charge a flat fee that, as with photographers, ranges widely depending on the videographer, the location, the number of shooters, the package and medium, but packages can start at around $850 for four hours of coverage and run as high as $15,000-plus on the high end of the spectrum for a full day of coverage. Having a second shooter or extra coverage will raise the rate, but so will the type of video and editing you want included in your package.

Coverage

Beyond the ceremony and reception, there are many plot points in your love story that you may want to include in your video. The more coverage, the higher the fee generally, so consider which of the following elements you may want to have your videographer incorporate:

- Some video or snapshots of you two growing up or during your dating years
- Prewedding activities (a day of dress fitting and lunching with bridesmaids) and wedding weekend activities with guests (the rehearsal dinner, getting ready)
- Behind-the-scenes glimpses (getting your hair and makeup done, the groom nervously waiting for the ceremony to begin, final preparations at your site before the reception begins)
- Environmental elements like wildflowers or mountains that establish the setting
- Postwedding events such as the morning-after brunch and even honeymoon footage and snaps (that you provide, of course)

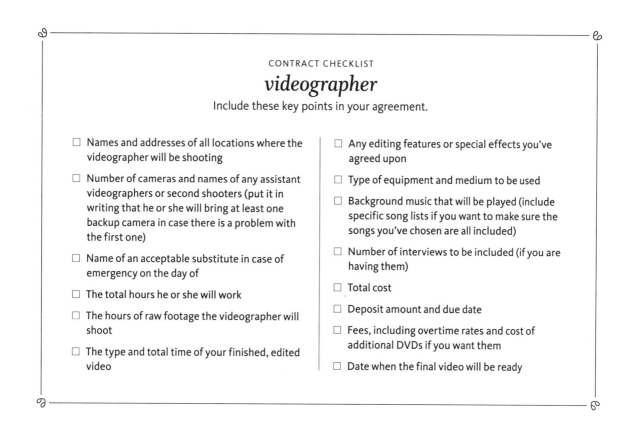

CONTRACT CHECKLIST

videographer

Include these key points in your agreement.

- ☐ Names and addresses of all locations where the videographer will be shooting
- ☐ Number of cameras and names of any assistant videographers or second shooters (put it in writing that he or she will bring at least one backup camera in case there is a problem with the first one)
- ☐ Name of an acceptable substitute in case of emergency on the day of
- ☐ The total hours he or she will work
- ☐ The hours of raw footage the videographer will shoot
- ☐ The type and total time of your finished, edited video

- ☐ Any editing features or special effects you've agreed upon
- ☐ Type of equipment and medium to be used
- ☐ Background music that will be played (include specific song lists if you want to make sure the songs you've chosen are all included)
- ☐ Number of interviews to be included (if you are having them)
- ☐ Total cost
- ☐ Deposit amount and due date
- ☐ Fees, including overtime rates and cost of additional DVDs if you want them
- ☐ Date when the final video will be ready

- Interviews with your wedding party, family, and guests (these have largely fallen out of favor, as they can interrupt conversation and put your guests on the spot, but you may want to set up a video confessional booth where guests can leave you messages and share some fun memories of the couple)

SHOOTER(S) Having two cameras is almost essential. At big moments, you'll get coverage from both perspectives—the father-daughter dance and the expression on Mom's face. You'll also have the equipment to film simultaneous activities—one camera covering the bride getting ready and one covering the groom. The cost of additional cameramen is either a flat fee or is prorated according to how long the extra coverage is needed: prewedding prep only, ceremony only, and so on. So if you want to keep the budget in check, ask to see if you can hire a second camera for just the ceremony and first part of the reception.

videography extras

same-day-edit videos

Videographers who offer this service will literally edit footage the day of the ceremony and/or wedding into a same-day-edit video to be shared at the reception (think footage of both of you getting ready and of the ceremony playing in the background during your first dance or dinner) or the day after at your good-bye brunch.

wedding music videos

You have to be brave to request this type of video. But you also have to admit that it doesn't get any more individual than this! Plus, it's a great way to make sure all your guests get some camera time on your wedding video.

engagement-shoot videos

The videographer accompanies your photographer on the engagement shoot to capture the real-time version of the day.

save-the-date videos

The stop-motion (when a chronological arrangement of photos is used to give the appearance of movie footage) wedding video trend is the perfect mix of modern and vintage. Talk to your photographer to see if they offer this service or collaborate with a videographer. Or, try a movie save-the-date: Base your save-the-date video off of your favorite movie style (in this case, Wes Anderson) for a totally personalized look. With a video camera and a little bit of editing know-how, you (or even better, your videographer) can create a short video to send to family and friends or to post on your wedding website.

love story videos

An interview-style setup of the two of you talking about how you met and got engaged and any other cute details from your dating days.

EDITS AND SPECIAL EFFECTS Once the filming is finished, some videographers will send you the raw footage (untouched, unedited) to preview before editing begins, so you can note scenes that you definitely want to keep or cut, like when your groom's voice cracked while reading his vows to you. (If you want to hold on to the raw footage for posterity, your videographer may offer it as part of your package.) During the editing stage, music and special effects (like grainy filters to make it look retro or lighting to make it look dreamy) can be added. Videographers often use filmic techniques (think flowing compositions, dramatic music, and wide-screen shots) to make the video even more dynamic. The results are wedding videos that feel more like feature films than ordinary home videos. Your videographer may be willing to do all the edits before sending the video your way. In that case, you will have worked out what you wanted to see in your video prior to the wedding day.

Video options

Wedding videographers are essentially filmmakers who want to capture the day and your personalities in order to tell your wedding story. Just as your photographer will Photoshop and retouch your photos to look magazine-worthy, so, too, will your videographer cut and edit your video to make scenes flow together like a real movie. Except, unlike Hollywood, this love story is real, and it's yours. Rather than your older cousin's four-hour video that you have to fast-forward through just to see the best moments (your grandma getting down on the dance floor, your cousin nearly falling off her chair during the hoorah), video pros are putting together viewer-friendly packages.

RAW (UNEDITED) FOOTAGE If you still want a record of every single minute just to have (even if you only watch it once), ask your videographer to include a video with all the raw footage (awkward toasts and all) separate from your wedding movie containing the highlights of the day.

CLASSIC WEDDING VIDEO This more old-school style of video is usually about two hours long and divided into chapters so, unlike raw footage, it's easy to skip around to your favorite parts. While it's edited for a polished look, many couples are finding they want to watch—and share—something that's even shorter.

HIGHLIGHT REEL Wedding videos have gotten shorter. As much as you'll want to relive your wedding day, trust us, even the two of you won't want to watch the entire five-hour play-by-play more than a few times (if that). Enter the highlight reel: a 15- to- 30-minute movie that includes highlights from your wedding day.

VIDEO TRAILERS For a version even your coworkers and little brother will sit through, there's the wedding trailer, a three- to five-minute-long mini motion picture that wraps up the entire day in one pretty (little) package . They're great keepsakes for your wedding party and families, and they're designed for sharing—instead of having everyone leaf through all five hundred ceremony photos that your photographer sent you, you can send everyone a link to your short but sweet trailer with all the day's highlights.

INSIDE SCOOP
must-record list

Give your videographer a copy of the must-shoot list you gave your photographer—see page 139. You'll also want to make sure you go over the timeline and key moments you want captured (like your spotlight dance) before the wedding (see chapter 25).

the food and drinks

11

TIMELINE

PLANNING

ASAP
Research caterers
(or inquire about in-house
ones at venue)

9–11+ months before
Book your caterer (if you're
not using an in-house chef)

6–8 months before
Start working on your menu

6–8 weeks before
Have a tasting and finalize
the menu

1–2 weeks before
Give your caterer the final
head count

Confirm the menu and
bar order

Your choice of food and cocktails not only fuels the party (literally), it also helps give your party personality. Truth is, most of your guests probably won't remember the flowers or linens the next week, but they'll definitely remember the food (and whether they had to wait in a long line to get their drinks). So how do you make your wedding meal memorable? First off, don't think your only choice is whether to have chicken or beef. And second, keep their glasses full. In this chapter, we'll let you in on a few of our top tips and tricks for creating a delicious, standout wedding-day feast.

COCKTAILS AND OTHER CONCOCTIONS

Weddings mean raising a glass, making a toast, and imbibing some bubbly. For most couples (and their guests), they also mean enjoying a few drinks along with the rest of the festivities, and naturally, at cocktail hour, the bar is the center of the affair.

Designing the bar
You don't have to serve top-shelf liquor and brand-name champagne for a great party, but you will want to make sure you have enough options to keep guests mixing and mingling until you're done taking pictures (or greeting all twenty of your mother-in-law's bridge partners) and to fuel the dance party after dinner. Start by deciding which type of bar you'll be offering.

THE OPEN BAR This is the most gracious approach. Guests can order any drink on the planet. You can choose top-shelf liquors, the brands of rum and vodka you love the most, or, as a more economical option, the generic versions. When you stock the bar, think about the brands that are most likely to satisfy the greatest number of guests. If your family is flying in from Scotland, you might want to substitute a single-malt for that Kentucky bourbon, but generally, standard bar fare will go over just fine. On the wine front, there is a greater opportunity to make choices based on your personal preferences and food selection.

Also, make sure you've got a few nonalcoholic options (especially if it's an outdoor summer wedding). For hotter months, try water infused with cucumber, melon, and mint over loads of crushed ice. During the winter, serve hot apple cider with cinnamon sticks.

There are two ways venues charge for bars: either by a set fee per person or by the amount of alcohol consumed. If your venue uses the latter method, at the end of the party, your bartender will count all the used and partially used bottles of wine and beer (and sometimes by the glass for mixed drinks) and charge you accordingly. The downside of an open bar is pretty obvious: Because there's no limit, people may drink like guppies, which can increase costs—and you may be concerned about a friend or uncle famous for imbibing (put a relative or member of the wedding party on babysitting duty so you don't have to worry). Note: It's best to decide ahead of time if you want to nix shots, which can up your bar bill considerably and lead to overimbibing if you have hard-partying friends.

signature cocktails

To add some personality to your cocktail hour, you could offer a specialty drink just for your wedding. Here are some ideas for totally-you cocktails.

make it your own
Whether it's a classic or totally new, you can match your signature cocktail to your color scheme or let it reflect your personality as a couple.

**pay tribute to
friends and family**
Name drinks after your bridal party, or serve favorite cocktails from both sets of parents.

rename a classic cocktail
Choose your favorite cocktail and work your married name into the title (Moore-tini).

**make a "something old,
something new" drink menu**
Choose four well-known cocktails, such as a dirty martini (old), a mango martini (new), a French martini (borrowed, say, from a friend's wedding or your parents' bar), and an electric lemonade (blue).

theme your drinks
If you're doing a *Great Gatsby* 1920s theme, serve Manhattans. For a Mexican destination wedding, serve margaritas.

set up a specialty bar
Instead of a specialty drink, you could have a cognac bar, a microbrew bar, a bubbly bar (with sparkling wines), or even a tequila bar. Ask your caterer about keeping an expert on hand during the cocktail hour to give suggestions and tasting tips.

THE LIMITED BAR Probably the most popular option, a limited bar offers—you guessed it—a limited selection of drinks (beer, wine, and mixed vodka drinks, for example). We like the idea of setting up a specialty bar with just your signature cocktail in addition to a beer and wine bar. During the cocktail hour, consider having waiters pass drinks on trays rather than having guests go up to the bar. You'll have to pay for those waiters, of course, but you'll probably save money on alcohol, and fewer guests will go overboard, since it will take everyone to get served. Or, instead of limiting the types of drinks served, you could limit the amount of time the bar is open, closing it after the cake cutting or during dinner. If you go with the latter option, have waiters circulate during dinner to refill glasses of water and soda.

THE CASH BAR A cash bar is a major faux pas—you don't invite people to your house for dinner and then charge them for butter, right? Trust us on this one. It's not a good cost-cutting solution. If you're on a tight budget, skip the liquor and just serve beer and wine and/or offer a signature drink and trim your budget in another area. You could also

signature mocktails

Offer a nonalcoholic signature drink so even guests who don't imbibe
can have something fun to drink.

sparkling spritzer
½ cup pinot noir
nonalcoholic sparkling
wine soda

½ cup ginger ale

Splash fresh lime juice

Pour into a wineglass and
add a piece of candied
ginger cut to fit over the rim
of the glass for garnish.

pink pomegranate passion
¾ cup pink sparkling
lemonade

¼ cup pomegranate juice

Pour into a wineglass and
add rock candy on a stick for
garnish.

apple cider mocktini
½ cup apple cider

¼ cup orange juice

Splash pomegranate juice

Pour into a martini glass and
add a cinnamon stick for
garnish.

virgin bellini
½ cup nonalcoholic white
sparkling wine

¼ cup peach nectar

Pour into a champagne
glass.

cran-raspberry mocktini
2 tablespoons fresh lime juice

granulated sugar

1 tablespoon crushed
raspberries

½ cup all natural cranberry
juice

Splash of raspberry-flavored
sparkling water

To prepare the martini glass,
wet the rim with lime juice
and dip it into sugar on a
plate. Shake the crushed
raspberries with the lime
juice and cracked ice. Add
the cranberry juice and
sparkling water and pour it
into a cup (straining out the
raspberry puree and ice).
Garnish with a thin stirrer
with raspberries on it.

switch the timing of your reception to, say, a brunch or afternoon tea,
which will naturally limit how much people drink or make the lack of
alcohol less of an issue for guests who like cocktails when they mingle.
Even offering no booze at all is better than charging your guests to
come to your party.

A DRY HOUSE If you, your families, and most of your guests don't
drink alcohol, it's fine to skip it altogether. Your bar can serve sparkling
water, sodas, and nonalcoholic mixed drinks instead. If you want some
bubbly to toast with, just serve glasses of champagne at toast time,
or opt for sparkling cider or sodas instead. An afternoon or brunch
reception fits particularly well with a dry house.

Staffing the bar   Want happy guests? Don't make them wait in line at the bar. To keep the bubbly flowing and the conversation going, follow these rules.

You'll need one bartender per fifty guests if you want everyone to be served in a timely manner. It's one of those little details that won't cost you much more in the end but will ensure the crowd stays happy. So if you're having a one-hundred-plus wedding, two bars is a must to avoid crowds and encourage mingling. It's also a good idea to have waiters walk around with trays of wine champagne and your signature cocktail during the cocktail hour.

Think about putting small drink stations around the room in addition to full bar(s). Pitchers of lemonade or your signature drink at one, tequila flights at another, and champagne at a third, for example, keep the lines at the bar short and let guests have fun exploring the room. Place a sign next to each station or tray with the name of the cocktail, as well as the ingredients and significance of your choice of drink.

BAR CHECKLIST

stocking the bar

Most venues (or catering companies) supply the bar and alcohol. But if yours doesn't, here's everything you'll need in order to offer a full bar during a four-hour evening reception for a hundred guests. (Note: Supplying the alcohol can save you money but check with your venue first—many charge a corkage fee for every bottle opened, which may negate any savings.)

ALCOHOL
Beer: 5 to 6 cases

Nonalcoholic beer: 2 cases

Whiskey: 1 liter

Bourbon: 1 liter

Gin: 2 to 3 liters

Scotch: 2 liters

Rum: 2 liters

Vodka: 6 liters

Tequila: 1 liter

Champagne: 1 to 1.5 cases

Red wine: 2 cases

White wine: 3.5 cases

Dry vermouth: 1 bottle

Sweet vermouth: 1 bottle

THE MIXERS
Tonic: 1 case

Club soda: 1 case

Cranberry juice: 2 gallons

Orange juice: 1 gallon

Grapefruit juice: 1 gallon

Ginger ale: 1 case

Triple sec: 1 bottle

Lime juice: 1 gallon

Sparkling water: 2 cases

Bottled water: 3 cases

Diet Coke: 2 cases

Coke: 2 cases

A CHAMPAGNE TOAST
18 bottles (assume 6 glasses per bottle, 1 glass per person)

MAKING A MEMORABLE MEAL

In every culture, an amazing meal is central to a celebration of marriage. In fact, the Chinese skip the ceremony altogether and consider the nine-course "wedding banquet" the formal sealing of the nuptial contract. Your options are truly endless—from the formal, seated six-course dinner, to a festive brunch of French toast and bacon, to nothing but your five-tiered fondant couture cake! We all have a passion for particular foods, and your wedding day is a perfect time to display the foodie side of your personality.

Cocktail hour fare
After the ceremony, and, potentially, the ride from the ceremony to the reception site, your guests are going to be hungry. So in addition to the bar, serve light hors d'oeuvres to tide guests over and prevent anyone from overimbibing before dinner.

If you are hosting a seated dinner, you'll need to find the perfect balance between satisfying their hunger and leaving room for dinner. Figure you'll need about six to eight hors d'oeuvres per person if a full meal is being served afterward (you'll need more like a dozen per person if you're throwing a cocktail-only reception). We love a mix of stations and passed appetizers, so if you're doing both, you can cut down to four appetizer options and two or three stations.

It's great to personalize your cocktail hour menu and even introduce something that may not have worked for the main meal, but make sure your offerings are diverse enough so that all of your guests will have at least one option they'll love. Try to hit all the bases with your spread: beef, seafood, poultry, vegetables. Tap into all the major tastes, too—serve something slightly salty, something sweet, something bitter, and something savory. And vary the genres—sushi, cheese puffs, short ribs. Remember: Your choices need to be easy to eat while standing and holding a drink. Think single bites served on mini spoons or in cones.

Reception meal options
Before you choose the menu, you need to know which meal you're serving, right? This depends mostly on when your reception will be: morning, afternoon, evening, late-night (cruise-ship style), or somewhere in between. (See page 37 for a timeline of reception meals.) Budget also influences what you serve, of course, and the price of your spread is set by a variety of factors. Generally, breakfast or brunch will cost less than dinner (because the foods involved take less effort to prepare and people won't drink as much). But other issues affect your bill, too—namely the day of the week your

cocktails by color

Have your bartender concoct something that plays off your palette.

red/pink
Cosmopolitan
Pink-grapefruit mojito
Pomegranate martini

orange/peach
Orange-slice martini
Tangerini
Tequila sunrise

yellow/gold
Honey sidecar
Lemongrass-ginger martini
Bellini

blue
Blue Hawaiian
Wild blueberry martini
Blue martini

green
Margarita
Mojito
Sour apple martini

party is held, how much food you actually serve, how formal the service is, how expensive (read: popular) the caterer is, and how costly your chosen ingredients are. There's also the issue of space, so talk to your reception site manager to make sure there is room for the style of meal you want—a seated dinner requires more space because of all the tables and a buffet will require extra space for the food and for guests to crowd around it.

You won't be able to finalize the menu until six to eight weeks before the wedding, when your caterer has a better idea of what's in season and available and what the market costs are for the ingredients, all of which fluctuate and, therefore, will impact what you serve. But you'll want to pick the type of meal you will serve much earlier, since it will affect the room layout, the centerpieces, any rentals you'll need, and of course, your budget.

Once you decide on a style, your caterer will draft an initial proposal to include in your contract. Schedule a tasting for a month or two before the wedding to finalize the menu with your chef. Afterward, make sure your caterer updates your contract with the menu details and both of you initial any additions or changes.

BREAKFAST, BRUNCH, OR LUNCH If you'd like to do more of a breakfast (say, after a sunrise ceremony), eight a.m. is the earliest start time to consider serving food. A brunch reception usually takes place between eleven a.m. and two p.m. Brunch can be served buffet-style or as a seated meal (or as a combination of the two). The other alternative is a cocktail brunch, where guests enjoy passed hors d'oeuvre–style delicacies (think scrambled-egg tartlets and mini French toast sticks in maple syrup shooters) and cocktails (such as mimosas, Bellinis, champagne, and punch) as they stand and chat and cheer, or celebrate and catch up on a mix of lounger furniture and at tables. Can you serve wedding cake in the morning? Of course! But you might opt for a lighter type, such as carrot, lemon, angel food, or even cheesecake.

Advantages

- A brunch is one of the most cost-effective receptions you can have. Your liquor costs will be much lower than they'd be for an evening affair, you won't have the expense of a band (although a classical guitarist or string quartet is a nice touch in the early hours), and often, reception sites are less expensive to rent in the daytime.
- Like sunset ceremonies, sunrise ceremonies up the romance factor.
- Brunch ceremonies are great for couples who expect a lot of children to attend the reception, as well as for second weddings.

- Brunch receptions are more conducive to dry houses (as well as limited bars), as the curtailed cocktail options (or lack thereof) won't be as noticeable during the daytime, when guests won't drink as much anyway (or even at all).
- You can leave in the afternoon or evening after the event and wake up in your honeymoon destination.

Disadvantages

- Very few people are truly in the mood to party at eleven a.m., let alone eight a.m., but if casual food is your focus, you may not care.
- Without all the dancing, talking, bouquet-tossing, and so on, your wedding may feel like less of a big deal (but then again, that may be exactly what you're after).
- You may wonder what to do with yourselves the rest of the day!

TEA Afternoon tea encompasses aspects of both a buffet and a seated meal. You can serve food on tiered stands on reception tables, where fancy scones, pots of jam, finger sandwiches, and pretty pastries will double as edible centerpieces. Or set up your spread buffet-style. Offer three or four kinds of tea, ice water, coffee, and sparkling sodas. Hire waiters to pour, or make it self-serve. Background music is a nice touch, too—anything from a string quartet to a bluegrass band can help create the right ambience.

Advantages

- Your guests will be floored by your taste and class.
- Older guests will adore your mellow sophistication—so much so that no one will realize that tea is far less expensive than a full meal.
- The reception will be shorter, which means you two get the entire evening alone together!

Disadvantages

- If you want hours of dancing, a tea reception is probably not the party for you.
- It may be a little too "precious" for some crowds.
- Anyone expecting a full meal may walk away hungry (or start nibbling on the doilies)—be sure to note "tea reception" on your invites so guests can plan ahead.
- Your reception may feel rushed or insufficiently monumental for the scope of the event.

COCKTAILS At a cocktail reception, you offer a slew of hors d'oeuvres instead of a full meal, and guests stand and chat while holding small, appetizer-laden plates in one hand and their wineglasses in the other.

The variety of treats depends on the length of the party. A good rule of thumb: For a two-hour party, serve at least six different kinds of hors d'oeuvres; for a four-hour affair, at least nine. Like a cocktail hour, hors d'oeuvres are either set up in stations or passed by waiters, but a mix of the two styles is a great way to keep everyone mingling and well fed.

Advantages

- The cocktail reception is a classy but typically lower-stress, more party-friendly option than a sit-down dinner.
- It can save you money depending on what you serve, how long it lasts, and the décor: You don't have to worry about setting up dozens of tables, complete with centerpieces, chairs, favors, and place cards—though you do need a few serving platforms and a smattering of small, nicely dressed tables and chairs (and perhaps a lounge area with couches) where guests can relax. You can skip the extensive breakdown crew, too.
- Cocktails tend to take less time than a full reception, meaning you're out the door and on your way to Tahiti sooner.
- You can still have a band and dancing.

Disadvantages

- The standing-and-chatting approach may be less comfortable for older guests than a seated-dinner soiree. If you go this route, make sure to provide plenty of seating options.
- Cocktail receptions aren't always a money saver. Guests may drink more than they would at a full meal, so liquor costs might be higher, and to ensure you have enough food, you may end up ordering more than you would for a plated dinner when portions are preset. And, of course, if you're serving gourmet appetizers or a variety of specialty stations (think wine and cheese or made-to-order crepe stations) at your cocktail hour, you'll likely end up spending more than you would for a plated dinner with chicken or family-style pasta dishes. So if you're going this route to save money, you'll want to carefully compare costs before deciding.

DINNER The most popular wedding meal is, of course, dinner, fitting in perfectly after a sunset ceremony, photos, and a festive cocktail hour. Guests will come hungry and expect a full meal. The options on setup—buffet, stations, or a formal seated dinner—are outlined below (see "Serving Styles, " page 160).

Advantages

- Dinner gives you an opportunity to truly treat your nearest and dearest, and you won't have to worry about anyone leaving hungry.

- A full meal lasts the longest (it typically includes a cocktail hour, too), so you have plenty of time to mingle.
- If you're a foodie, it's a great way to enjoy a variety of culinary delights.
- If your style is less formal, you may find dinner stuffy unless you choose to host a more low-key meal, like a buffet or family-style feast.

Disadvantages

- Dinner is generally the most expensive option unless you're having a super-fancy cocktail reception.
- The main downside: Dining time may cut into dancing time.
- There's more to plan and pay for: linens, centerpieces, chairs, china for every table, etc.

DESSERT The dessert-only party has its origins in the church-hall cake-and-punch soiree. Today, cake-and-champagne receptions take place in a variety of venues, from gorgeous backyards to elegant restaurants to sophisticated lofts. In addition to champagne and cake you might serve a dessert spread, but it's fine if you just want to let your cake be the star.

Advantages

- The dessert-only reception is the most economical, easiest, and fastest option.
- It's appropriate at any hour of the day. (When is it ever the wrong time to eat cake? Or drink champagne, for that matter?)
- You'll have less to prepare and coordinate.
- It's a great option for second marriages, when the couple wants to keep the celebration low-key.

Disadvantages

- Guests won't linger for long, so you'll be disappointed if you want everyone to make a fuss over you for hours.
- You and your guests may leave the party still hungry. (Again, make sure your reception invite says "dessert" so guests know what to expect.)
- There's less pomp and circumstance.

THE MIDNIGHT-SNACK WEDDING If you're only inviting locals and want something elegant and edgy but decidedly economical, have a nine p.m. ceremony followed by the world's best dessert bar!

Advantages

- It's a unique and festive way to celebrate your nuptials (and the midnight call time gives it a mysterious vibe).
- It's an affordable option on par with a cake-and-champagne reception.

Here are the four approaches to service, starting with the least formal. (As you'd expect, the more formal the service, the higher the price.)

family-style
Multiple dishes are delivered to strategic spots along long tables; guests pass them politely (or grab and hoard, depending on your family).

American service
Plates are prepared in the kitchen and waiters bring them out to the tables.

French service
Waiters prepare food on stands set up next to the tables and then serve individual plates.

Russian service
White-gloved waiters carry each course on a large tray and serve guests directly from it.

Disadvantages

- If you're inviting much younger or much older guests, it's not the best option. Grandma and Grandpa may not make it to nine p.m. to watch your ceremony, let alone midnight for the reception. Same goes for your four-year-old niece or even your ten-year-old nephew, so this type of setup is best for a kid-free reception.
- If you and your guests are not night owls, it may be hard to get the party going, and it could fizzle early.
- You'll have to start your ceremony fairly late in the evening, or have a break between the ceremony and reception, so you'll need to find a way to entertain guests who don't live nearby before and/or between events.

Serving styles

Choosing which type of meal you want is only the first of many decisions you'll need to make before you even get to the tastings. Next up: figuring out how you want to serve it. Even with a brunch or afternoon tea reception, you have options. Formality will be the biggest factor here—black-tie events call for sit-down dinners, but for more casual reception styles, like a cocktail or brunch reception, buffets and stations may work better.

BUFFET A buffet offers your guests a full meal and the chance to choose exactly which foods and how much of them they want. You might feature staff creating crepes or pasta dishes while guests watch or just have food set up in large serving dishes. (Table assignments aren't required, but we always suggest you give them—guests don't want to have to worry about finding an open seat.)

Advantages

- Guests can tailor the meal to suit their taste buds.
- Food stays hot (or cold) longer because it waits in heated containers (or on ice) until it's time to eat.
- Food preparation can double as entertainment (think sushi-rolling station).
- You can save on waitstaff since guests do much of their own legwork though we recommend having a few waiters on hand to serve guests at the buffets.

Disadvantages

- Elderly or physically challenged guests may have trouble maneuvering.
- Long lines may force your guests to wait awhile (but this can be avoided with multiple buffet lines and enough servers to keep the line moving).
- It's less formal and the food options may be more limited.

FOOD STATIONS This is like a wedding food festival. Guests are invited to sample foods from a wide array of stations in a buffetlike manner. Each station offers its own theme and a moderate assortment of cuisine—the food practically becomes the entertainment. Servers should be positioned at each station to help out. For the most part, guests are not assigned seats or even tables, so they're free to move around, and it will work for any-size wedding, as long as there are enough stops (and seating) for all. So this style works best for cocktail or dessert receptions, but couples often offer stations at their cocktail hour followed by a seated dinner.

Advantages

- The only limit to your food options is your imagination. Some favorite stations include sushi, Mexican, a high-class caviar-and-Bellini stop, or a Cuban sandwich bar.
- There's also major mingling at a party like this—people who love to schmooze will enjoy floating around the room. It's even better for you—the bride and groom get to visit with everyone!

Disadvantages

- Crowding around the stations can result when all your guests start heading for the food at the same time.
- Don't expect to have everyone seated and listening attentively when it's time for the best man's speech. It'll be difficult to get guests' eyes up and mouths closed all at once.

SEATED MEAL The traditional reception meal is a sit-down, four-course dinner consisting of appetizer, soup, entrée, and dessert—though a three-course dinner is perfectly acceptable. Additional courses may include hors d'oeuvres, salad, pasta, and fruit and cheese.

Advantages

- The seated meal is the most relaxing for your guests. They can sit comfortably without having to lug plates around, stand in line, or fret that the roast beef will be gone before they get their turn at the carving station.
- Less work for guests means more time to talk.
- You can have better control over how the party flows.

Disadvantages

- Many prefer buffets for their efficiency; seated dinners take more time, which means less of it for after-dinner mingling and dancing.
- Seated dinners typically are the most expensive, though it depends on what you serve and how you serve it.
- A traditional five-course dinner may feel stuffy to some.

Designing your menu

What's the one thing every wedding guest not-so-secretly hopes for? Amazing food. Luckily for you, creating a standout cocktail-hour spread and reception dinner is easier than you might think. We'll give you a hint: It's not all about the filet or the sea bass. The secret is making your guests notice the food (in a good way).

THINK SEASONAL Great cooks plan their menus around seasonal food—whatever's freshest that month or season. Your favorite summer tomato salad, for example, just won't be as juicy in January; pasta with a rich tomato sauce would be a better winter bet for tomato lovers. Ask your caterer and culinary pals what's fresh when, and see if you can incorporate those foods into your wedding meal vision.

STAY LOCAL Another great way to guarantee freshness (and authenticity) is to choose regionally grown or raised food. You've got a better shot at finding ocean-fresh lobster in Maine than in Minnesota, for example. Hometown food is also a great way to personalize your party and introduce your guests to the local cuisine, especially if you have a lot of out-of-towners or are hosting a destination wedding. Give them a taste of authentic Southern barbecue or a New England clambake.

CONSIDER TEMPERATURE One of the biggest problems with party food is the lag time between preparation and presentation. That creamy seafood in puff pastry looks great in the kitchen, but by the time it gets to table 23, the cream may have soaked through, creating a gooey, chewy mess. For a large reception, ask your caterer for dishes with a long shelf life.

CARE FOR THE KIDDIES If you're including a lot of little ones in the festivities, offer a kids' meal option. Many caterers provide special meals for children that cost half as much, and let's face it—chicken nuggets are going to be a bigger hit than chicken à l'orange with the under-twelve crowd. Talk to your reception site manager or wedding caterer about your options. If this isn't a common practice for them, perhaps they'll be willing to split a few adult meals in half for your smaller guests or make them otherwise kid-friendly—putting slices of steak between a couple of pieces of bread, for example.

PREPARE FOR PICKY EATERS It's impossible to foresee every single wedding guest's dietary needs and preferences. People with specialized food requirements don't usually expect to be served a special meal when they attend a large function such as a wedding. Your best bet is to choose one basic meat entrée (chicken is pretty universal) and one meat-free entrée for vegetarians. Also, consider having a buffet that includes a variety of palate-pleasing foods, so guests can choose what they'd like to—and are able to—eat.

FEED YOUR TALENT Don't forget: You'll also need to provide meals for your vendors, including your band or DJ, planner, and caterer. While you certainly don't need to serve them lobster tail and filet mignon, you do want to discuss what you'll serve with your caterer ahead of time so you can include the cost and amount to be served in your contract. Sandwiches or a basic chicken or pasta dish all work.

SERVE A LATE-NIGHT SURPRISE Bringing in a midnight snack to satisfy your guests' late-night munchies has become a popular part of reception menus. A food truck might be just the thing: waffles, grilled cheese, or spicy Thai treats handed down from a truck will hit the spot and add an unexpected touch of fun. For indoor weddings, rent mini food carts to be wheeled in at the end of the night with salty snacks like tacos, satay, sliders, and fries—or something sweet, such as kettle corn, gelato, or even cotton candy. You could also set up a dessert bar with your favorite childhood candy (Charleston Chews and Gobstoppers, anyone?) or a cupcake bar complete with a variety of frostings and toppings (see chapter 22 for how to turn dessert into a favor).

TIP
other treats

Talk to your caterer about all the locations where you'll need food on your wedding day. Consider getting snacks delivered to the bridal suite (like fruit and cheese and bubbly) or ordering boxed lunches for the wedding party on the day of. They'll also often pack up a wedding "good-bye" bag in case you were so busy posing and schmoozing that you didn't have time to eat. Just write it all into your contract.

CHOOSING A CATERER

Your caterer will do far more than prepare your food; he will help coordinate the evening and flow of events and, in most cases, supply the bar and cake. If you're getting married at a full-service venue, your package probably comes with the resident caterer, whom you're required to use. Some sites will only let you hire caterers on their approved list (or will charge you a fee if you don't), so your venue's list of preferred vendors can be a good place to start your search. Or you could go with an independent caterer or company. If you plan to bring in an outside caterer to your reception site, ask the site managers if they've worked with any of the caterers you're considering and what they think of them. Here's a rundown of where to find your wedding chef and what to expect from each option.

An on-site chef
If your venue comes with its own caterer, your choice may be limited—to that person. This isn't necessarily a bad thing—some of the most beautiful sites come with the region's best chefs. You'll be able to design your meal from set selections on their menu. If you have your heart set on a food they can't provide, ask if you

questions to ask before booking your chef

experience

☐ Do you have a license? [This means the caterer has met local health department standards and carries liability insurance.]

☐ Do you have liability insurance (if they are providing the alcohol)? What are the limits you foresee being imposed on the menu by my site?

☐ How many events will you work on during my wedding weekend?

packages

☐ Does the meal come full-service?

☐ Will you provide tables, chairs, plates, napkins, silverware, and salt and pepper shakers—and are they extra? Ask to see them to make sure they are up to par.]

☐ Will you provide waitstaff? How many are included in the package and what is the fee for additional waiters? [You'll want about three waiters for every six tables for a sit-down meal.]

☐ Do you also provide a bar and what sorts of packages are offered? How do you charge (by consumption or per person)?

☐ How many bartenders are included in the package? What is the fee to hire extra? [Aim to have four cocktail waiters for every one hundred guests and two bartenders for every seventy-five to one hundred guests.]

☐ Will you provide alcohol, or do we need to handle the bar separately?

☐ Can I provide my own alcohol and do you charge a fee for that?

☐ Do you provide wedding cakes as well and if so, can I see some past wedding cakes you've done? Is the cake included in the package?

☐ How many appetizer and entrée choices come with the package?

☐ Will you make special meals for children and vendors and what do you charge for each?

logistics

☐ When will the tasting take place? Do you offer tastings before we've hired you?

☐ How does delivery, setup, and breakdown work? What do you do and is there an additional fee?

☐ What will you and your staff wear?

☐ How much time will you need to set up? When will you need access to the site?

☐ Will you set out the place cards and menus we created?

☐ Who will oversee the event on the wedding day? What will happen if he is sick or otherwise unable to be there?

☐ Will you arrange the food attractively on the buffet or on plates? Can I see photos of previous presentations?

☐ Are there extra charges, such as a security deposit, sales tax, or service fees?

☐ What, if any, are the expected gratuities?

can augment the meal by bringing in a specialty caterer, such as a sushi chef. Also, feel free to inquire if the chef will prepare a family recipe (or just something you both adore) along with the customary spread.

A catering company
Professional caterers come in all different varieties, from those focused on classic weddings and corporate galas to those focused on a special ethnic cuisine. They handle everything from the actual food to hiring and managing the servers.

Some caterers will hold tastings for potential clients, so you can taste their wares before signing a contract. Ask to taste the offerings of every caterer you're considering. It's okay to attend a tasting with a caterer even if you're not sure you'll use them—the tastings are supposed to help you decide. Plus, every meal you sample may give you more reception-food ideas, whether you work with that caterer or not.

You will create a menu proposal with your caterer about a month or two before your wedding. Once your chef has a better idea of what is in season and the market prices for goods, you will have a tasting based on your vision and preferences and work with your caterer to tweak the menu based on your feedback. Any changes you make should be added to your contract accordingly and both you and your caterer should initial the changes.

The restaurant route
Many restaurants have catering departments or are willing to handle large affairs straight from their kitchens. A word of caution: Even if dinner for two at your favorite French bistro is divine, the same meal for two hundred may not be. It's easier for a kitchen to turn out small portions than huge ones. Ask how the restaurant handles big events: How many cooks are there? (The answer should be 10 to 15 guests per chef.) What's the lag time between preparation and presentation? How will your favorite dishes be affected? Have they done weddings or events of a similar size? If a favorite restaurant doesn't have experience with weddings or other similar events, consider hosting your rehearsal dinner or engagement party there instead.

the knot NOTE

finding a caterer
Your wedding chef is just a few clicks away. Search a curated list of top caterers by city. **TheKnot.com/local**

caterer

Make sure your written agreement includes the following key points.

☐ The date, location, start time, and length of your event. If your venue has several banquet rooms or ballrooms, refer to your venue room by its specific name.

☐ The number of guests you expect at your event. Even after you have your confirmed guest list, your actual number may go down because of a no-show or two. You are still expected to pay for the meal.

☐ The price per adult guest (ask whether or not the price includes taxes or other fees.)

☐ The price per child guest and vendor (most caterers charge less for kids and for meals for your DJ/band and other day-of vendors you're required to feed)

☐ If you're hosting a buffet-style or tray-passed event, the method by which prices are determined: by the guest or by the plate

☐ The maximum market price you agree to pay for specialty items (lobster, crab, and fine fish)

☐ Any rentals and supplies they'll provide, like linens, china, serving platters, etc.

☐ The total cost of rentals provided by your caterer (linens, dishes) or whether they are included in your package

☐ The ratio of waitstaff and bartenders to each guest. This is an important one. You want your guests to feel completely taken care of.

☐ The name of the person overseeing the staff and a suitable backup in case he is sick or otherwise unable to be there the day of

☐ The name of the party responsible for the event setup, cleanup, and breakdown, and her fee

☐ The type of service you want (sit-down, buffet, tray-passed, or some combination). Be specific, if you want a sit-down with French-style service, get that in writing.

☐ The attire for servers and bartenders

☐ The cost per hour or flat rate for servers/bartenders, including overtime costs

☐ The number of courses served, including the cocktail hour, if applicable

☐ The menu for each course, including acceptable substitutions, should ingredients be unavailable

☐ Any special arrangements needed for vegetarians, children, or guests with other dietary restrictions

☐ Where and when your to-go snack will be available (knowing they won't have much time to eat during the night because they'll be too busy greeting guests and dancing, some couples ask their caterers to package up the meal ahead of time so they can munch on it when they get to the wedding suite; optional)

☐ The wedding cake size, style, design, flavor, and cost, if applicable

- [ ] The groom's cake size, style, design, flavor, and cost (optional)
- [ ] Any additional cake-cutting and service fees
- [ ] The packaging of the wedding cake for guests to take home if applicable
- [ ] The preparation and freezing arrangement for the top tier of the wedding cake, if applicable
- [ ] The types of beverages that will be served, including brands, where applicable. If you're including some premium liquors, say Johnnie Walker Blue Label, specify the number of bottles and if there's a certain time or place you want them served.
- [ ] The times at which each type of alcohol should be served (that is, full bar for the cocktail hour, red and white wine during dinner, champagne for toasts and with dessert; optional)
- [ ] Mixers, nonalcoholic beverages, and condiments you want included at your bar, as well as equipment your caterer will provide (shakers, stirrers, ice, garnishes, etc.) and any fees for them
- [ ] Nonalcoholic beverages you want to serve during dinner, including coffee and tea

- [ ] If you're buying alcohol from your caterer, cost per bottle/drink breakdown
- [ ] Your caterer's buyback policy (for example, if you ordered seventy-five bottles of wine and opened only fifty, the price at which your caterer will "buy back" your unopened bottles)
- [ ] If you're supplying your own alcohol, when and where it should be delivered to the caterer
- [ ] Corkage fees, if applicable
- [ ] Overtime policy
- [ ] Proof of health license from the state
- [ ] Your caterer's proof of liability and insurance carrier information, including liquor liability insurance
- [ ] The latest date you can make changes to your menu
- [ ] The estimated total cost for the reception
- [ ] The deposit amount paid
- [ ] The balance due
- [ ] The payment schedule
- [ ] The refund and cancellation policy

SAMPLE
reception menus

PASSED HORS D'OEUVRES
Macaroni and Cheese Bites
Braised Kobe Beef Short Ribs
Mini Turkey Reuben Sandwiches

FIRST COURSE
Sautéed Maine Diver Scallops
Heirloom Tomato Salad

ENTRÉE SELECTIONS
French Roast Chicken, Whipped Potatoes, Sautéed Spinach
Seared Striped Bass, Braised Red Cabbage, Potato Mille-Feuille
Mushroom Risotto, Shaved Parmesan, Fines Herbes Salad

DESSERT SELECTIONS
Mini Ice Cream Sandwiches
Cappuccino Profiteroles
Homemade S'mores

LATE-NIGHT BITES
Beef Slider, Cone of French Fries,
Mini Grilled Cheese Sandwiches

sample seated dinner menu

CHICAGO NEIGHBORHOODS
Little Italy (Taylor Street)
Ricotta Gnocchi
Pan-Roasted Sea Scallops

Traditional Mexican (Pilsen Street)
Taco Station
Pulled Pork and Chicken Tamales

Greek Town (Halsted Street)
Grilled Baby Lamb Chops with Dijon-Herb Crust
Spanakopita Cup

sample themed stations

PASSED HORS D'OEUVRES
Shrimp and Grits
Prosciutto-Dusted Bay Scallops
Truffled Steak and Eggs
Quinoa Croquettes
Falafel Burger

PASSED SMALL PLATES
Lemon Sole Ceviche
Watermelon Salad
Sweet Pea Risotto
Pan-Seared Barramundi
Grilled Diver Scallop Sandwich

sample cocktail reception menu

12

wedding music

TIMELINE
PLANNING

12+ months before
Start searching for
reception DJs/bands

9–11 months before
Book reception DJ/band

6–8 months before
Research and book
ceremony musicians

6–8 weeks before
Go over the playlist and
day-of details

Just like the décor, food, and venue (perhaps even more so), the music will set the tone of your event. Music makes the mood, and it's the single most important factor that makes your wedding fun. You have so many options for your soundtrack: 1930s supper-club–style big band, 1960s-inspired rock band, hits of the nineties by a DJ, never mind your classic "wedding band." Think of the evening as a musical experience—starting out slow and ending in some spectacular dancing. The secret, of course, is hiring the right performers!

WEDDING MUSIC BASICS

Start searching for your music makers early—nine to eleven months in advance, or even earlier if you want to nail down a popular band or DJ during peak season. But before you can even start to think about who will provide the music for your wedding—whether it's a band, a DJ— you'll need to square away a few key things.

Budget

As with everything else, budget is your first consideration. About 10 percent of your overall budget should be allotted to entertainment—that includes cocktail-hour music and ceremony musicians. Reception-music fees are dictated by the talent, of course, but also the location, number of performers, day of the week, and time of day. But in general, a DJ costs less than a band unless you're hiring a celebrity DJ. A four-piece ensemble typically will charge between $3,000 and $10,000 for four hours of work, or easily five times that for a big-name band. Naturally, the more people in the band, the higher the expense. For a DJ, fees range from about $1,000 to $5,000 for a four-hour reception. You also will pay more for elaborate equipment (better speakers, for example).

Regardless of what kind of musicians you hire, ask whether there's a minimum number of hours you have to book them for (a two-to-four-hour minimum is not uncommon, which is a key consideration when hiring separate musical acts for the ceremony or cocktail hour) and how much they'll charge if you end up needing them to put in overtime. Since many couples decide in the moment to keep the party going, you will want to make sure you're aware of overtime fees, and you may want to see if it's possible to hire your musicians for the event, rather than for contracted hours, to avoid overtime charges altogether.

Site specifics

Check with your ceremony and reception sites to make sure there are no restrictions on the number of musicians or amount of equipment allowed, and find out whether there are any power-supply limitations, noise-level maximums, or time-of-day restrictions.

These are especially common if you're getting married in a public place, such as a city park or county beach. Consult the authorities in charge. You'll also want to make sure your space can accommodate the size of the band you want and their equipment—plus you and all your guests. An intimate space won't fit a twenty-two-piece orchestra, and a three-piece combo may not cut it for four hundred people. Make sure

---

your bandleader or DJ has a chance to familiarize himself with the space's layout, size, and acoustics. That way he can determine whether he'll need extra equipment (which typically involves extra costs) to get the best possible sound and performance on your wedding day. For an outdoor site, you'll need a flat stage area and electrical outlets for musicians to set up.

Think about what sounds you'll need to fill the space.. The sound of a harp will get lost in a grand cathedral, and a choir of bagpipes will be deafening in a friend's living room. You should also consider other competing sounds in that space: Crashing waves could easily drown out a string quartet or trio of flutes, and a windy mountain peak could render even the strongest voice silent.

SELECTING MUSIC FOR EVERY MOMENT

How do you decide who will handle the music—and therefore set the tone—for every moment of your wedding? Here's a guide to picking the best option for each part.

Ceremony music
You have a wide variety of ceremony musicians to choose between, from a solo guitarist to a large choir, but before you track down referrals for specific musicians, decide what it is you want—and whether you can have it.

CEREMONY MUSICIANS Most ensembles have a leader who works with clients to put together appropriate musical accompaniment from a single instrument (such as an organ or violin) to a ten-piece orchestra. The more instruments, the fuller the sound—but remember, the larger the combo, the higher the price tag. Also, while you may like the sound of a certain instrument, including it might not be as easy as just adding it to your ensemble. For example, you might want to add a trumpet, but then to balance it out you'll need three or four string instruments or else the horn will stand out awkwardly. Just ask the musicians what would work best. Here are some good basic combos to consider:

- String Duo (two violins or violin and cello)
- String Trio (two violins and cello)
- Flute Trio (flute, violin, and cello)
- String Quartet (two violins, viola, and cello)

ASK CARLEY

SELECTING A SPECIAL SONG

My fiancé and I don't have a song but we want something special. Any ideas?

Don't feel bad. Sit down together and think about some of the happiest times you've shared so far and whether or not there was a soundtrack. For example, what was in his iPod the day he realized he was in love with you? What song were you listening to on the day he proposed? Have the bandleader or DJ explain to guests before the dance why you chose that song, and it'll add even more meaning to an already emotion-filled moment.

ceremony musicians

Here are some options for ceremony musicians.

keyboardist
A classical pianist or organist can do it all, from soothing prelude tunes to a dignified processional to jazzy, upbeat postlude music.

trumpeter
A soloist or a horn combo can add either regal solemnity or peppy rhythm—or both—to your ceremony.

string quartet
Strings are pitch-perfect for classical compositions; they also add romantic elegance to contemporary selections.

flutist
Usually paired with either a pianist or string instrument, the flute is a romantic and calming way to start the festivities.

harpist
The ideal choice for a small, romantic ceremony or springtime vows in the garden. For larger affairs, hire two harpists—to sit and strum at either side of the altar—or an accompanying flutist for a baroque tinge. Just keep in mind: Harps are huge and you'll need to make sure one can fit through the door.

blues guitarist
The sound of a slide guitar is urban-romantic; it creates an all-American, down-to-earth, ultracool atmosphere. Hire one to play a mix of blues, jazz, and American classics at different stages of your ceremony.

vocalist/choir
Hymns, gospels, and even opera offer a wide array of feelings for the various stages of your ceremony.

jazz combo
Have a trio, quintet, or singer-and-standing-bass duet add some soul to your ceremony. Jazz standards create a sophisticated, glamorous atmosphere that's oh-so-romantic.

You might consider adding an organ, harp, or piano to any of the trios or the quartet, or jazzing things up with two trumpets. If you decide to add vocalists, it's a good idea to have the singing begin after everyone is seated for your ceremony. When a person steps up to a microphone to sing, guests may feel obliged to be quiet and pay attention, which creates awkwardness. It's also wise to make sure the vocalist is comfortable with your selections, because when a singer is nervous, it shows right away in his or her voice. Ask which songs the soloist knows well, and work together to build a song list that satisfies you both. If there's a song you want included that your vocalist isn't familiar with, have a violin, piano, or flute play an instrumental version of the selection.

CEREMONY PLAYLIST Many churches and temples have certain rules and regulations that will affect your choice of ceremony tunes. It's common for congregations not to allow secular songs (Catholic) or any music at all (Quaker). Speak to your wedding officiant or ceremony site's musical director before you have a classical version of Journey's "Don't Stop Believin'" composed for your walk down the aisle. Also, if your church or temple has in-house musicians, there may even be rules prohibiting outside performers.

The most basic wedding ceremony music setup involves a minimum of three types of songs: preludes, processionals, and recessionals. Prelude music is light, ambient music that sets the mood while guests are being seated and waiting for the ceremony to begin. It usually begins when the doors open, or as early as forty-five minutes prior to but no later than twenty minutes before the beginning of the ceremony.

Next is the processional, which accompanies the entry of the extended wedding party—family, bridal party, and bride. The same song can be used for each, but we love the idea of changing to another song when the bride enters to add drama and highlight her entrance. Many musical choices are appropriate, from distinguished concerto excerpts by Bach, Chopin, or Handel to mellow jazz standards to instrumental versions of more modern hits. Even if you're not incorporating music anywhere else in your ceremony, do it here—a solo flutist, violinist, or pianist is a low-key choice. Personalize your processional music by selecting an acoustic version of a song with sentimental value to you as a couple—your first dance, your parents' processional tune—or one that shows off your ethnic heritage.

At the conclusion of the ceremony, the recessional plays. As the name implies, this music accompanies you as you recess (that is, make your exit) and is traditionally bright and lively—a reflection of your joy. The music that plays while you're walking back up the aisle together should reflect the giddiness of your just-marriedness and get guests revved up for the celebration to follow. Again, classical music (like Widor's "Toccata" from Symphony No. 5 or Elgar's "Pomp and Circumstance") is a popular choice, as are upbeat contemporary songs.

ASK CARLEY
FRIENDLY OFFER

A friend of mine plays the guitar and has offered to perform at the reception. I love the idea of having him play, but will an acoustic interlude mess up the dance vibe of the party? Not if you have him play while guests are eating. The band or DJ will likely need a break anyway, so a good time for your friend's performance is during the main course while guests are happily sitting and will want a few minutes to digest before getting back up on the dance floor.

Many couples choose to add interludes or songs played during significant moments of the ceremony such as the unity candle lighting or the ketubah signing. Any tune is appropriate, from classic pieces such as Schubert's "Ave Maria," to hymns such as "Amazing Grace" and folk songs like "The Irish Wedding Song," to more current tunes. Have pieces performed by a vocalist or an instrumental soloist/ensemble.

You might also want to include a postlude, which is a selection played while guests exit the ceremony. Keep the good vibes going with more love-happy and spirited music playing as guests file out of the ceremony

CLEVER IDEAS

ceremony playlist

Options for the major musical numbers in your ceremony.

TRADITIONAL
processional: Bridal Chorus (Wagner)

recessional: Wedding March (Mendelssohn)

NEW TRADITIONAL
prelude: "Apotheosis" (Tchaikovsky's *The Sleeping Beauty*)

processional: "Spring" (Vivaldi's *The Four Seasons*)

bride's processional: "Jesu, Joy of Man's Desiring" (Bach)

recessional: "La Rejouissance" (Handel's Music for the Royal Fireworks)

GOSPEL/RELIGIOUS
prelude: "Amazing Grace" (John Newton)

processional: "In This Very Room" (Ron and Carol Harris)

bride's processional: "St. Anthony's Chorale" (Haydn)

recessional: "Blest Be the Tie That Binds" (Hans Georg Nageli)

MODERN
prelude: "You and I" (Stevie Wonder)

processional: "In My Life" (The Beatles)

bride's processional: "Can't Take My Eyes Off of You" (Lauryn Hill)

recessional: "Beautiful Day" (U2)

site. Have someone play a violin, or even a set of bagpipes, as guests head toward the exit. Some couples even ask the musician to lead guests out of the ceremony space in a paradelike fashion.

Cocktail hour music
The cocktail hour is a good time to get a festive vibe going, and music is key for setting the mood (mingling without some sort of background tunes can actually be surprisingly awkward). You can ask your ceremony musicians or a scaled-down version of your reception band to play. Or, if there's room in your budget, consider hiring a specialty music group to pep things up and add contrast. A mariachi band will energize your crowd after the ceremony and get guests in the mood to celebrate. Other ideas: a jazz trio, a bluegrass group, or even a barbershop quartet.

Most important, match your music to the mood you've set with food and décor. If you're having an outdoor affair that's casual and fun, why not hire a bluegrass band to serenade your guests? Serving spicy appetizers? Consider going with a Cuban soundtrack. Whether your cocktails are being served in a city loft (think jazz) or candlelit ballroom (classical), make sure your guests aren't noshing and sipping in silence.

Reception music
Good tunes create a party mood, get your guests loosened up, and even help bring together perfect strangers (just think of a group of girls from all different walks of life and generations belting out "R-E-S-P-E-C-T"). Your reception is your opportunity to play all your favorite songs that weren't appropriate for your ceremony, wow the crowd with any amazing dance moves you've patented, and celebrate with friends and family.

By now, you'll be able to use your reception style to help determine what music is best suited for your celebration. Daytime affairs like brunches and afternoon teas are generally better complemented by more low-key music (think string quartet, bluegrass band, or classical tunes). Cocktail or dessert receptions are all about mixing and mingling, so you'll want to follow the same musical notes as cocktail hours (see "Cocktail Hour Music," above). Play ambient music while the guests are eating, keeping the decibel level low enough that chatting is a breeze and guests can relax and enjoy the meal. Request instrumental music, whether classical or jazz. Or ask your DJ to play "lounge" or "ambient" music that's modern and laid-back. After dinner, of course, the party really begins.

TIMELINE
classic spotlight dance order

Bride and groom

Bride and her father; groom and his mother-in-law

Bride and her father-in-law; groom and his mother

Bride and best man; groom and honor attendant

Everyone else!

PLAYLIST IDEAS
classic first-dance songs

"At Last" (Etta James)

"Come Rain or Come Shine" (Ray Charles)

"As Time Goes By" (from *Casablanca;* try the Frank Sinatra version)

"Close to You" (The Carpenters)

"Dream a Little Dream of Me" (The Mamas and the Papas' version)

band vs. dj

In a perfect money-is-no-object world, you'd have your very own Weddingpalooza, with a variety of acts throughout the night—a big swing band, a house DJ, a jazz trio, and an indie band. But the reality is that you'll probably have to choose just one reception act. While we can't tell you which to choose—there are pros and cons to either option—we can give you the lowdown on each to help you decide.

BAND

pros

A fantastic band can't be beat in terms of getting the crowd stoked and moving.

A band really sets a sense of sophistication.

A charismatic bandleader also can be a great master of ceremonies.

A great band is more memorable and unique than a DJ spinning all the songs your guests are used to hearing.

cons

Bands are generally more expensive than DJs. Also, you have to feed all of your entertainers.

A band loses in the man vs. machine department—they'll peter out before a sound system ever does. Translation: They require breaks, which means a lull in the party (unless you pay extra for alternates to play during breaks). Most bands will play recorded music between sets, but that can sound canned in comparison.

Even the most open-minded of music ensembles does not have the repertoire that a DJ has at his fingertips. And no matter how good they are, covers of songs never match the sound of the real things.

Bands take up a lot of space: If you're hosting your reception in a romantic but cozy wine cellar or an intimate restaurant, you may not have room for even a trio.

DJ

pros

Sophisticated DJs offer a balanced and eclectic mix of musical styles conducive to parties of all ages and degrees of formality.

DJs are generally less expensive than bands.

You have more control over the sound of the songs with a DJ—whatever your favorite recordings are, you can probably have them played just the way you like.

Experienced DJs have enough tricks up their sleeve to last through a party that goes all night long; bands, understandably, can't play for much longer than five or six hours.

When DJs take breaks, they can play a great compilation mix to keep the party going without losing the energy of the room.

cons

DJs can seem a little less personal than bands. They can't time the song to match your dancing style during your first dance (and you worked so hard on that over-the-shoulder, through-the-legs move!) or improvise to accommodate sweet surprises (the flower girl and ring bearer joining in the dance with you, for example).

A bad DJ can spend way too much time on the microphone.

They don't have as large a presence as a band.

RECEPTION MUSICIANS: CHOOSING BETWEEN A BAND AND A DJ

To decide whom to hire, you will need to start by answering the core question: band or DJ? Live music is seen by many as the traditional, dignified uncle with good taste and DJs as the younger, hipper, less refined cousin. But the lines have really been blurred, and bands and DJs aren't what they used to be. Upscale DJs are offering sophisticated and polished presentations fit for elegant black-tie parties. Meanwhile, bands aren't just for fancy fetes anymore. They don't have to wear tuxes and can easily fit into a clublike venue or work a backyard bash.

THE SPOTLIGHT DANCES

You may have fallen in love to "Free Bird," but imagine how long nine minutes and eight seconds will feel alone on the dance floor. (And if you think it would drag for you, imagine how your guests will feel!) Pay careful attention to the length of your special song before committing to it for your first dance. Same goes for the mother-son and father-daughter dances. Time your song and practice dancing to it. Even four minutes can kill you if you're just rocking back and forth. If your heart is set on a certain ballad, look into having it cut down to a reasonable length (under three minutes is about right) with the help of your DJ or band.

The First Dance While, traditionally, the first dance is just for the newlyweds to share a sweet moment while dancing to a romantic song, many couples are choosing to mix it up—either by having family and friends join in or by working on a special routine to wow their guests. If you prefer to go this route, ask the bandleader to make it clear that "the happy couple wants everyone to dance the first dance with them!" And assign several members of the bridal party (and their dates) to head onto the dance floor, which will encourage other guests to join in.

Another option: After you've made a few laps around the floor as husband and wife, you could switch partners—the bride dances with her father while the groom dances with his mother-in-law. After another few turns, it's switch time again—the bride dances with her father-in-law, and the groom kicks it up with his mom. Then switch once more—the bride spins about with the best man, and the groom twirls the maid of honor. You'll probably want to ask your emcee to act as a guide so no one gets confused.

The Parent Spotlight Dances If you are dancing with multiple parents (perhaps a stepparent or grandfather will be cutting in, too), you may want to break up the dances over the course of dinner and dessert, or just keep the songs under two minutes each. And as important as it is

---

CLEVER IDEAS
go all out

You could sway to the entire song together while everyone watches or you might do a formal, choreographed first-dance sequence. Ambitious, dance-floor-confident couples are ditching the traditional waltzes and rumbas for elaborate, highly choreographed (and often very sexy) dance routines. Some couples take lessons for months in order to provide real entertainment for their guests. Just keep it under five minutes; even your awesome moves won't keep guests' attention any longer! Another popular move we're seeing at a lot of receptions: inviting the entire bridal party to join the couple on the dance floor to perform a choreographed dance.

making the band

Get the right size for your sound (and budget).

SIX-PIECE BAND: Perfect for anywhere low-key, such as a restaurant reception or smaller-size venue. This is one of the most budget-friendly options and includes the following:

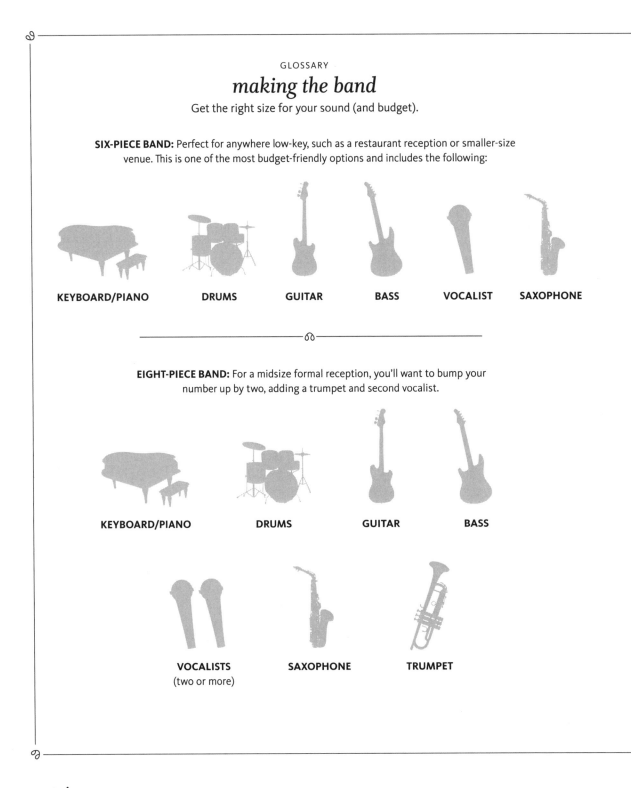

KEYBOARD/PIANO   DRUMS   GUITAR   BASS   VOCALIST   SAXOPHONE

EIGHT-PIECE BAND: For a midsize formal reception, you'll want to bump your number up by two, adding a trumpet and second vocalist.

KEYBOARD/PIANO   DRUMS   GUITAR   BASS

VOCALISTS
(two or more)   SAXOPHONE   TRUMPET

TWELVE-PIECE BAND: For a formal, black-tie affair, or an extra-large party at a huge venue, go with a twelve-piece band. This is the most costly option, but you'll get a trombone, third vocalist, second guitar, and additional percussion for your splurge.

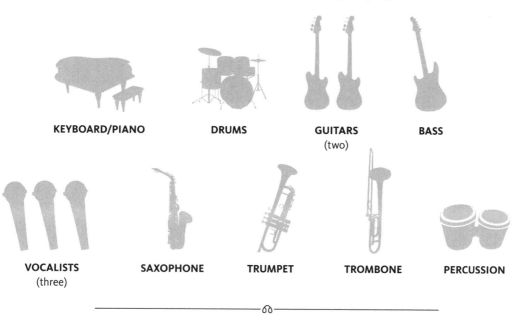

KEYBOARD/PIANO   **DRUMS**   **GUITARS**
(two)   **BASS**

VOCALISTS
(three)   **SAXOPHONE**   **TRUMPET**   **TROMBONE**   **PERCUSSION**

STRING QUARTET: Perfect for a ceremony, formal cocktail hour, or small, no-dancing reception, this type of band generally includes two violins, a viola, and a cello; this is your most budget-friendly option and can, in some cases, be rented by the hour instead of for a time block.

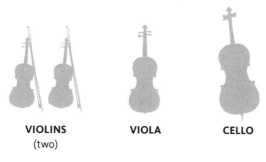

VIOLINS
(two)   **VIOLA**   **CELLO**

Here's a list of some quintessential hated tunes. (But we have to admit—we've had fun dancing to them at times!)

"Y.M.C.A."
(The Village People)

"Chicken Dance"

"Stayin' Alive"
(The Bee Gees)

"Every Breath You Take"
(The Police)

"Total Eclipse of the Heart" (Bonnie Tyler)

"Macarena" (Los Del Rio)

"My Heart Will Go On"
(Celine Dion)

"Mony Mony" (Billy Idol)

to perfect your couple's dance, don't forget to pick a song and practice your moves with Mom and Dad ahead of time, too.

Trying to come up with the perfect song to dance to? Start by deciding if you want a beautiful slow ballad and/or a song with meaningful lyrics. (Warning: If you choose a tearjerker, plan the dance for later on in the reception, when the party is beginning to wind down and most of the pictures have already been taken!) You can choose separate songs that have meaning for each of you and your respective parents, or you may want to choose one song and have both dances at the same time.

FILLING THE DANCE FLOOR We've all been to those weddings where the dance floor stays empty. That won't happen at yours—here's how you can be sure of it. Any good band or DJ knows that there's an art to playing music. Like a well-constructed story, a party has a beginning, middle, and end. Your reception playlist should manipulate the audience skillfully, building up momentum and excitement with crowd-pleasing hits, providing an ample crescendo of the wildest and most party-friendly of tunes, and then winding things down with smooth, soulful, sexy music.

Grooving with Your Guests Now, just because you should keep the first dance short and sweet doesn't mean you shouldn't spend some serious time on the dance floor over the course of the celebration. Translation: Get out there and enjoy yourself! Set an example for everyone, and when the dance floor opens up for the evening, be one of the first couples on it. Your guests will notice and be more likely to join you when they see how much fun you're having. It'll be a long, busy evening for you, so let your bridal party know how important it is that guests are up and dancing, and ask them to lead the movement to the dance floor. That way, they'll have your back if you get caught up talking with the grandparents.

Lay the Ground Rules Most DJs and bandleaders consider themselves to be artists, so if you're not specific about selection and style, you may get some completely unexpected sounds. Similar to the list of must-take shots you give your photographer, go over must-play and do-not-play lists with your bandleader or DJ. If you're afraid your musicians will play a hot-and-heavy dance track, thus offending Grandma and Grandpa, talk with your emcee beforehand. And don't forget to let the bandleader or DJ know ahead of time whether or not you want him to take requests from guests.

Just be careful not to micromanage. If your intention is to tell him

classic parent spotlight-dance songs

father-daughter dance songs

"Daddy's Little Girl"
(try the Al Martino version)

"Daddy's Hands" (Holly Dunn)

"If I Could" (Ray Charles)

"Isn't She Lovely?" (Stevie Wonder)

"Lean on Me" (Bill Withers)

"Lullabye" (Billy Joel)

"My Funny Valentine
" (try the Carly Simon version)

"My Girl" (The Temptations)

"Sunrise, Sunset" (from *Fiddler on the Roof*)

"Thank Heaven for Little Girls"
(try the Merle Haggard version)

"The Way You Look Tonight" (Frank Sinatra)

"Times of Your Life" (Paul Anka)

"Turn Around" (Harry Belafonte)

"You Are So Beautiful" (Joe Cocker)

"Your Smiling Face" (James Taylor)

mother-son dance songs

"Blessed" (Elton John)

"Could I Have This Dance" (Anne Murray)

"Have I Told You Lately"
(Rod Stewart or Van Morrison)

"Loves Me Like a Rock" (Paul Simon)

"I Can See Clearly Now" (Johnny Nash)

"I Wish You Love" (Gloria Lynne)

"In My Life" (The Beatles)

"Stand by Me" (Ben E. King)

"Through the Years" (Kenny Rogers)

"Unforgettable" (Nat King Cole/Natalie Cole)

"What a Wonderful World" (Louis Armstrong)

"You Are the Sunshine of My Life"
(Stevie Wonder)

"Do I Make You Proud" (Taylor Hicks)

"Forever Young" (Rod Stewart)

"Parent's Prayer" (Greg Davis)

exactly when to play what song, then you might as well have your brother-in-law create a playlist. Remember you're hiring a professional musician to make your party fun, so once you set the boundaries, allow some creativity. These guys are pros at reading crowds and tuning in to the right songs to play at the right moments to keep the energy high and everyone having a good time.

Make the Music Interactive Get guests in on the fun and let them request their favorite songs via RSVP card. You could even set up polling on your wedding website and ask everyone to vote on your first-dance song.

questions to ask
before booking a band or a dj

☐ What is your specialty? [Needless to say, asking a really great swing band to play seventies disco is asking for trouble.]

☐ How would you describe your style?

☐ Do you know our reception space and its acoustic, power, and amplification requirements? If not, will you check it out beforehand?

☐ [If you listen to/watch an audio or video recording of the band:] Is your recording live or produced in a studio? Is the sound technically enhanced? [You want to hear how they really sound.]

☐ No matter what your repertoire is, can you play the songs that are important to us, such as a hora or a favorite pop hit?

☐ If we have an original or esoteric piece we want played, will you learn it? How much lead time do you need? What will you charge to arrange it?

☐ How many musicians are in the band? How many vocalists? Are there different options as far as how many musicians/instruments we can hire?

☐ Would we need to rent any instruments (a piano, for example) or equipment (like extra speakers or a stage)?

☐ Will you bring your own sound system? How large a room can it accommodate? What does the equipment look like? Do you need a draped table to hide any equipment? What size are the speakers, and can they be camouflaged?

☐ Do you plan to use lighting or any other special effects?

☐ Who will do the setup, and how early will they do it?

☐ How do you ensure a comfortable sound level for everyone in attendance, from the seventeen-year-olds to the eighty-seven-year-olds?

☐ What do you typically wear? Are you open to following my dress code and are there fees for certain attire, like tuxedos?

☐ How many hours are included in the package? How many breaks will you need and for how long? What will happen during the breaks? Are you willing to split up the breaks so several musicians are always onstage?

☐ How do you handle requests?

☐ Can you act as master of ceremonies? If so, how do you view the role of emcee and what is your typical approach?

☐ How many weddings do you typically do a year? How long have you been doing weddings?

☐ Do you have another gig before or after ours? Are you prepared to play overtime, and if so, what are the overtime fees?

☐ What will happen if the bandleader or other key member of the group is sick the day of the wedding?

☐ What is your cancellation policy?

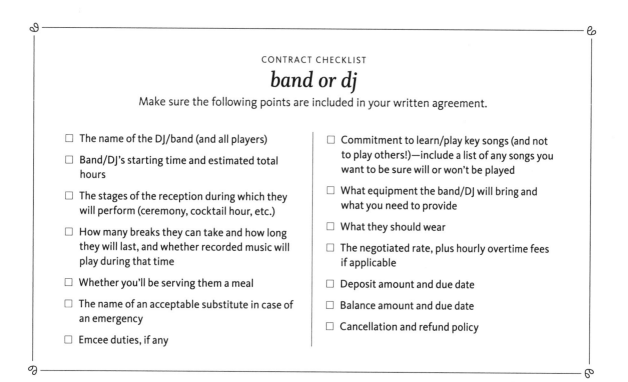

CONTRACT CHECKLIST

band or dj

Make sure the following points are included in your written agreement.

- ☐ The name of the DJ/band (and all players)
- ☐ Band/DJ's starting time and estimated total hours
- ☐ The stages of the reception during which they will perform (ceremony, cocktail hour, etc.)
- ☐ How many breaks they can take and how long they will last, and whether recorded music will play during that time
- ☐ Whether you'll be serving them a meal
- ☐ The name of an acceptable substitute in case of an emergency
- ☐ Emcee duties, if any

- ☐ Commitment to learn/play key songs (and not to play others!)—include a list of any songs you want to be sure will or won't be played
- ☐ What equipment the band/DJ will bring and what you need to provide
- ☐ What they should wear
- ☐ The negotiated rate, plus hourly overtime fees if applicable
- ☐ Deposit amount and due date
- ☐ Balance amount and due date
- ☐ Cancellation and refund policy

Give guests a treat they won't expect by throwing in a never-seen-that-before entertainment act. Think hip-hop dancers, break-dancers, or even flamenco dancers. Time it right and have them appear just as the toasts are wrapping up to get everyone out of their food coma and up on the dance floor.

The after-party playlist
If you have a lounge set up for your after-party, ask the band or DJ to stay for an extra hour or two (you'll also need to check with your location manager—some reception sites are more flexible than others). Make sure to bring this up during your contract negotiations with the performer—you'll want all price agreements in writing beforehand. If your reception is ending on the earlier side (any time before ten p.m.), you could hire a favorite local band to perform at the after-party. Or for the budget minded, plug in your own playlist or take the after-party to a local bar that has live music.

HIRING YOUR MUSICIANS

How do you choose one great-sounding band or DJ over another? Start by thinking about parties you've been to and what aspects of your friends' bands' or DJs' presentation and musical repertoire you did or didn't like. When it comes to finding a band or DJ that really can rock your (and your guests') world, hearing is believing. By listening to music samples online, you can literally search out the good bands without leaving your desk. Once you've found a few options you're interested in, schedule interviews and auditions.

If a band gives you a soundtrack or video to watch, be sure the musicians you hear or see are the same musicians who will play at your reception. Also, request a sample playlist, and look for songs you know and love. But a live show is the best way to gauge a band or DJ. Ask if you can pop your head in at one of their upcoming events or attend a dress rehearsal before you seal the deal, so you can gauge firsthand how they work the crowd and what their performance style is. Watch how the musicians interact with the audience: loudness, rudeness, and peacocklike strutting are bad; pleasantries, enthusiasm, and flexibility (playing audience requests, for example) are good. You also might want to look for an act that can play a wide variety of styles if it's important to you to get everyone up and hopping.

Interviewing potential players

Don't just catch a performance—sit down with potential bandleaders or DJs. You want to make sure there is chemistry and that his personality doesn't rub you the wrong way. In most cases, the band's front man (or woman) will serve as an emcee during the reception, encouraging guests to get on their feet and informing the audience of what's next. Look for a person or group who will mesh well with your friends and family and can keep the party going no matter what.

Make sure the band or DJ understands your vision and will execute it. Explain what musical selections you're leaning toward. See if they respond openly and get excited. If there's a song you really want to incorporate and the band doesn't know it, they should be willing to learn from sheet music if you provide it. If they're resistant to the idea, find out if it's because they think it won't work with their instruments (in which case ask them to come up with some doable alternatives of a similar style) or if it's just because they're unwilling to learn new songs (or charge a fee to do so).

13

standing on ceremony

TIMELINE
PLANNING

10–12 months before
Book your ceremony
venue and officiant(s)

Research your religion's
marriage requirements

Book ceremony musicians

3 months before
Nail down your
ceremony décor

Research your state's
marriage license
requirements

1–2 weeks before
Confirm setup time
and location with
ceremony venue

The ceremony is the wedding. It is about who the two of you are, together—and it's the whole reason you're planning this big, elaborate bash, after all. If anything from your wedding day is going to be permanently imprinted on your brains, it's bound to be the moment you look into each other's eyes and exchange vows. There's much more to this event than simply saying "I do": You need an officiant who understands you and your specific wishes and beliefs, a program that artfully guides your guests through the events (and lets them know the name of the girl three down from the bride who looks vaguely familiar), and, of course, a dose of décor and tradition to mark the occasion!

CEREMONY TYPES

Religious or civil? That's one of the most important decisions you'll face during the ceremony-planning process. The answer will help determine who officiates, where you exchange vows, and what elements you include in your ceremony. It may already be clear to you which way you'll go, but if not, read on.

Religious ceremonies
While a civil ceremony is all that you need to be legally married, many people want their church or congregation to recognize their marriage, too. A religious ceremony is officiated by a religious leader and incorporates the wedding customs, traditions, and rules of that faith, along with the state's legal requirements. The wedding can be short and sweet or long and lavish, although it generally follows a specific format prescribed by the religion. The precise elements may depend on the branch and, sometimes, the particular congregation.

A religious service can be held in a church, temple, mosque, or meeting room, and some clergy will officiate at nonreligious sites. You'll likely be required to have several sessions of prewedding counseling with your officiant as well (see "Prewedding Counseling," page 190).

Maybe you believe in God or some other spiritual force but not in organized religion and prefer to have an alternative clergy member (a Unitarian minister or an officiant from the American Humanist Association or Ethical Culture movement, for example) to do the honors.

Interfaith ceremonies
He's Jewish and you're Christian? Or your parents are Catholic, his are Muslim, and you two practice Buddhism? If one of you plans to convert to the other's religion, the ceremony can be a great time to begin involvement with the new faith. If you plan to keep your individual faiths, you may want to create an interfaith ceremony as the first of a lifetime of blending rituals.

Each religion has its own view on interfaith unions, from "Go for it!" to "No way." Some religions and sects leave the decision up to individual clergy members. If both of your religions are somewhat flexible, you may look for an officiant from each to preside over a joint ceremony. This is the most complicated plan but also the most popular because it guarantees that each side's beliefs are included. It also reflects the meaning of marriage: You're joining your lives. Your officiant(s) can help you identify which religious traditions won't conflict with the tenets of the other, and help you choose readings and musical selections, consult texts from both religions. Consider reading passages from each other's faith or asking family members to do so. Create as many opportunities for family to participate in as possible; it will make everyone feel included in this joining of two different backgrounds.

Civil ceremonies

A civil ceremony isn't necessarily a drive-through, Vegas-style affair. "Civil" merely means in accordance with the state's laws rather than in the eyes of a church, mosque, or temple. A civil ceremony is presided over by a legal official—a judge, magistrate, justice of the peace, county or court clerk, mayor, or notary public (not, despite what you may have heard, a ship captain—unless he also holds one of the above civil titles).

The exact requirements vary from state to state (and even from county to county) but generally include a charge to the couple ("Do you, Tracy, take Todd to be your lawfully wedded husband . . . ?"), a ring exchange, and the pronouncement of marriage by the officiant. Beyond the paperwork, it's pretty much up to you where you wed (providing that your officiant agrees to come). Call the county's marriage license bureau or visit their website for details on the civil process and requirements in your wedding location.

Same-sex ceremonies

As laws are changing across the country (and world) with regard to who can legally wed, more and more states are recognizing gay marriages as legal unions just like any other. Others still do not allow same-sex marriages to be performed but will recognize unions performed in other states that do recognize gay marriages.

LEGAL CEREMONIES If you live in a state that recognizes same-sex marriage, you can ask a judge or justice of the peace to sanction your union, or you can contact an Ethical Humanist officiant. You can also ask a dear friend or relative to get ordained and do you the honor. If you'd like to have a religious ceremony, speak with a minister or rabbi from the congregation to which you or your partner belongs. Or contact a Unitarian Universalist, Universal Life, or Metropolitan Community church, all of which support same-sex unions. You can also look for an officiant from a religion that leaves the decision to individual clergy (Buddhist, some Protestant, Reform Jewish).

Your ceremony can follow the same timeline and traditions that we outline in this chapter—save for a few changes in the wording—but it's up to you. If you choose a religious officiant or another person affiliated

the knot NOTE

gay weddings
Find an up-to-date list of same-sex laws in every state, plus gay wedding etiquette, fashion advice, and ceremony advice and ideas.
TheKnot.com/ gayweddings

second weddings and family ceremonies

A second wedding is just like a first wedding, except one (or both) of you has a bit
more experience. And you'll probably feel a little less tied to tradition. Brides, you
can walk down the aisle in whatever dress you want—white, purple, or leopard print!—no
matter how many times you've tied the knot.

including the kids

If you have kids, include them in the ceremony.
Even if they're thrilled about their new stepparent
and your wedding, they'll probably need
reassurance about their continued importance in
your life (particularly if they don't live with you).
Don't expect them to do more at your wedding
than they usually can; if your five-year-old refuses
to stand still for ten minutes on an ordinary
Saturday afternoon, he won't suddenly do so at
your wedding. You can ask children to:

Take vows accepting their new siblings or family

Be a flower girl, ring bearer, or usher

Be a junior bridesmaid or groomsman
(this one's for the teens)

Escort you down the aisle and "give you away"

Do a reading

Sing a song; play the guitar; accompany a singer
on the banjo, guitar, violin, or tap shoes

Create the program

Pass out candles, flower petals, or birdseed

dealing with the past

If you're still friendly with your ex-spouse and your
ex-family-in-law, go ahead and invite them, if you
want to. If your ex is the father of your children,
including him shows your kids that they don't have
to "take sides"; your new spouse doesn't mean
they get a replacement parent. But consider the
feelings of your partner, too. If he or she will be
uncomfortable with your ex at the wedding,
you might want to withhold that invite or just
have him attend the ceremony.

with a group (such as an Ethical Humanist), he or she may give you
"sample" ceremony wording from which to work. Like any wedding, the
more secular the officiant, the more creative license you will likely have
over what is said, read, sung, or played during the ceremony.

COMMITMENT CEREMONIES If you live in a state that does not
legally recognize same-sex marriages (including marriages performed
in other states), you can opt for a civil union, performed by judges,
justices of the peace, or clergy. Having a commitment ceremony or Holy
Union serves the same purposes as a traditional wedding: It makes a
public proclamation of your love and intent to remain together; joins
your family and friends to support your union; gives you a sense of
permanence, stability, and security; and helps you to gain domestic
partner status (in some states).

A commitment ceremony can incorporate any or all of the traditional wedding customs, or you can do something completely different. Pretty much anything goes here, as you're not bound by religious or legal restrictions. A civil servant is somewhat gratuitous, since his or her primary role is normally to legalize the event, but you can ask a judge or justice of the peace or a member of your clergy to symbolically sanction your ceremony. Since it's not legally sanctioned, you can also ask a layperson to conduct your ceremony.

FINDING YOUR OFFICIANT

Your choice of officiant is crucial. He or she will help set the tone of your ceremony and can also help you select the perfect words for the day. You need someone whose beliefs coincide with yours and who is as modern or traditional as you desire.

Where to look
You might already have an officiant in mind—the pastor at your church, a rabbi from the temple you attended as a child, or whichever county judge is available on your wedding date. If your ideal officiant is booked, or if you need help finding one, here are some sources to check out.

RELIGIOUS OFFICIANT Start with your house of worship, a childhood or college church, or the church or synagogue your parents belong to, and ask if someone is available for your wedding date or if there is someone you're required to use (some congregations won't allow you to bring in an outside officiant, so if you're set on getting married in a certain church or temple, you may have to stick with an officiant from their clergy). Another option: Call that beautiful church or temple you love to drive by and ask to make an appointment with a clergy member. Note: Some churches may require you to join before hosting your wedding, while others will marry nonmembers or even rent their spaces.

INTERFAITH OFFICIANT In some cities, you'll find Christian/Jewish "clergy teams." These ministers and rabbis have performed many interfaith ceremonies and will work together to help you plan yours. If your religion is in the "No way" camp (such as Orthodox Jewish), a clergy member who won't officially oversee your wedding may be willing to bless it in a smaller, more private setting. Your other options include going with just one of your religions, finding a third, neutral religion, or taking the civil route. You could also hold two

the knot NOTE

officiant finder
Find a list of reputable interfaith and nondenominational officiants in your area, as well as sample wording for your ceremony and unique ceremony rituals.
TheKnot.com/local

separate ceremonies instead. Only one is legally binding; the other serves as a blessing over your union.

CIVIL OFFICIANT For a civil service master of ceremonies, call up city hall, ask for recommendations from friends and family, and search online. You can check out the websites of potential officiants for hire to get an idea of fees, style, and whether they might be right for you. Another increasingly popular choice: A friend or family member of your choosing can get ordained—online, no less—and marry you. But not all states recognize this certification, and even if yours does, it may require additional paperwork. Many states will also allow residents to obtain a one-time license to perform a marriage, which may require standing before a judge. You should note that some religious denominations will not recognize a marriage performed by someone ordained outside the faith. So, although you may be legally married, your congregation may not acknowledge it. Contact the Universal Life Church for details on how to get ordained.

Interviewing officiants If you know whom you'd like to have officiate, make a preliminary phone call to confirm whether he or she is available on your planned date. Get a general understanding of any requirements and restrictions and how much flexibility you will have to personalize the ceremony to make sure it's a good fit.

Also, inquire about officiant fees or required donations. These range from nonexistent to upward of $1,000, depending on the congregation and/or individual officiant.

If all sounds good, set up an initial meeting to discuss details. When you meet with an officiant for the first time, you'll discuss your wedding plans, find out if the officiant is open to your ideas, ask about any requirements or restrictions (like religious rituals or music or décor restrictions), and decide if, ultimately, the three of you want to work on this wedding together.

The officiant plays a huge part in shaping the ceremony. Take the time to get to know a potential officiant during your initial one or two conversations, and make sure he or she is open to any plans you have for writing your own vows or incorporating unique elements and ethnic traditions. Look for an officiant who understands you, your relationship, and your ceremony priorities. If a potential officiant is inflexible or dismisses your ideas, keep searching.

auditioning officiants

Ask any potential officiants the following questions to get a feel
for whether they're right for you.

- ☐ Will you perform an interfaith ceremony, if applicable?

- ☐ How long are your ceremonies typically?

- ☐ Will you perform another wedding on the same day as mine?

- ☐ Are there any special rules or restrictions?

- ☐ Are you open to personalized vows, readings, poems, or music?

- ☐ Will you give a sermon or speech?

- ☐ What kind of prewedding counseling is required, if any?

- ☐ What is the ceremony fee or required donation?

- ☐ Will you give us input on our vows?

- ☐ Will I have input on your sermon and/or hear it beforehand?

- ☐ Can I tour the sanctuary/ceremony room? [Check seating capacity, number of aisles, general layout, and wheelchair accessibility, if that's a concern.]

- ☐ What does the site provide and what would we need to provide ourselves in terms of décor (pew ribbons, runner, flowers, candles)?

- ☐ Are there any restrictions on the type or amount of décor I can bring in?

- ☐ Are there any specific restrictions on the type of music I can play or on the content of the readings?

- ☐ Is there a dress code?

- ☐ Can I include my pet in the ceremony?

- ☐ Can you help me deal with family conflicts connected to the ceremony?

- ☐ Do we bring our marriage license to the ceremony, or will we all sign it together before the wedding?

- ☐ Can I have a videographer and/or photographer in the sanctuary/ceremony room?

- ☐ When would the rehearsal be?

- ☐ Would you (and your spouse) like to come to the reception and/or rehearsal dinner?

- ☐ Would you play a role there (give a blessing, etc.)?

Once you've found the right person, seal the deal and make sure you have the officiant and ceremony site reserved for your wedding date and time—and rehearsal. While you probably won't need a formal contract, it's important to have something in writing confirming the date of service, contact information, and fees, as well as a backup plan in place in case there is an emergency and your officiant can't do it.

CEREMONY BASICS

Before you begin cooking up the ceremony of the century, take a look at the ingredients. If you're having a religious ceremony, that ceremony will be shaped by the rituals and requirements of your faith. Since most ceremonies in the United States today are either Christian or Jewish, we've highlighted some of the traditions of each faith in this chapter. Head to TheKnot.com/ceremony for a look at what other major religions require for weddings, plus a rundown of religious traditions.

Whether your service is civil or religious, it will likely follow the same general structure—a civil officiant will simply omit the religious rituals. You'll probably start with your officiant's basic structure and then add custom details. And don't worry, your officiant will likely schedule a rehearsal with you and your bridal party to go over all of this.

Ceremony seating
Traditionally, an usher offers his right arm to a female guest, while her male escort follows them down the aisle. If that seems too formal, you can always let everyone seat himself with the ushers just directing. Here's a breakdown on seating:

ACCORDING TO RELATION As a rule, the closer the person is to you emotionally, the nearer he or she sits to the action, and the later he or she takes a seat. Typically, the first and second rows are reserved for immediate family—parents, siblings, and grandparents; the third through fifth rows are for aunts, uncles, cousins, godparents, stepfamily, and other special guests. The rest of the seats are fair game for everyone else.

ACCORDING TO YOUR RELIGIOUS TRADITION In Christian ceremonies, the bride's mother is always the last person to be seated (right after the groom's mother), signifying that the ceremony is about to begin. (The bride's father is usually not seated until after he walks his daughter down the aisle.) Generally, in Christian ceremonies, the bride's family and guests sit on the left (when entering from the back). For Jewish services, it's reversed.

ACCORDING TO YOUR OWN SYSTEM You certainly don't have to separate the bride's and groom's sides. In fact, some couples like to mix it up and make it a free-for-all to symbolize the joining of families and friends. If you've invited a hundred and twenty people and your partner just has, well . . . Mom and Dad; if your divorced mom and dad must have an aisle between them to stay civil; or if you want everyone to be there in support of both of you (symbolically at least), don't divide

ceremony setups

traditional

Chairs or benches are arranged in straight rows, like you would see at a church, facing the altar. There is a main aisle dividing the rows into two groups, and a smaller aisle on the far side of each group of rows. In many houses of worship, this is really your only option. With this seating arrangement, guests stuck in the back rows may have trouble seeing—and therefore connecting to—the ceremony. The other drawback: Unless you choose to face your guests with your officiant's back turned toward the audience, your backs are to your guests for the majority of the ceremony. The upside, though, is you have your perfect center aisle.

amphitheater

Guests are seated in semicircles, resembling arcs, around the altar. The rows are traditionally staggered like stadium seats, and typically, there is a larger center aisle and smaller aisles on each side breaking up the rows. This arrangement affords guests, even those sitting in the back, a better view of the ceremony and lends a grand, momentous feeling to the event. But it's hard to create if your site doesn't already have the seating for it built in, and you'll have to figure out a place for your attendants to stand, either in the aisles or on the stage, depending on the size of your bridal party.

in the round

Guests are seated in a circle around the altar, keeping you front and center. The benefits of a circular seating arrangement are that all of your guests have a great view of the action, and it gives your ceremony a more intimate feel. Your bridal party may line up along two of the four smaller aisles used to break up the rows. The issue here: You will inevitably have your backs to a row of guests, making them feel more shut out than they might if your backs were to everyone, so you may want to switch your placement throughout the ceremony.

by family. Just have your ushers direct people to the best seats available to create a balance.

The processional
You each make your way to the altar separately, symbolizing the fact that you're coming from different backgrounds and families. You meet at the altar or stage and move closer to each other throughout the ceremony (holding hands, exchanging rings and vows, planting the kiss).

Who heads down the aisle when? If you're having a civil ceremony, you can improvise, or you might choose to follow the order of religious processionals: The doors of the church, temple, or grand ballroom are thrown open, and your wedding party marches down the aisle. Then it's your turn: In a traditional Christian processional, the bride is escorted by her father, while the groom waits for her up front. In a traditional Jewish processional, both the groom's parents escort him down the aisle and the bride's parents both walk with her as well. Or you can choose your escort based on your situation (see "Walking Down the Aisle," left).

ALTAR ARRANGEMENTS Where should everyone stand once you get to the altar? There isn't one correct altar arrangement; you have several options. Or you could design your own with your officiant. Here are the details on the traditional lineup.

Bride and Groom In a traditional Christian ceremony, the bride stands on the left (with her back to the congregation), with her groom to the right. In a Jewish ceremony, this is reversed.

Attendants Attendants generally divide up by gender (groomsmen to the groom's side, bridesmaids to the bride's), or walk and stand in pairs (one groomsman-bridesmaid pair to the right, the next to the left, etc.). They either line up behind the spot where you'll stand to form a V or form a big semicircle around you. If you take the couples approach, each groomsman-bridesmaid pair remains together in the line, or the bridesmaids stand on a step behind their escorts. In a Jewish wedding, your attendants stand next to the huppah with you, with your honor attendants one diagonal step behind you, other attendants behind them.

Parents Your parents' places depend on how much you want to include them in your ceremony. If both your parents walk both of you down the aisle, all four might remain standing with you for the entire service (as in a Jewish ceremony, where the parents remain under the huppah, one pair on either side of the rabbi). Traditionally, if the bride's father walks her down the aisle, he either leaves her at the altar with her groom or

ASK CARLEY
WALKING DOWN THE AISLE

Does the bride's father have to walk her down the aisle?
Not at all. While in Christian processionals, the father typically walks the bride down the aisle (in Jewish ceremonies, both parents walk the bride down the aisle), that's certainly not your only option. If you're close to both your parents, it's fine to make the march a *pas de trois* (one that includes both parents); if your mother and stepfather raised you, you could walk with both of them (or just your stepdad); or if your aunt raised you, ask her. If you feel you've arrived at this moment on your own, you may want to go it alone. Or the two of you can enter the ceremony together.

remains standing between them until the officiant asks, "Who supports this woman in marriage?" at which time he and her mother give their blessing and take their seats in the front pew (the mother is seated right before the bride walks down the aisle—see "The Processional," following). The groom's parents traditionally sit in the front pew throughout a Christian ceremony.

The Rest of Your Party Include pint-size attendants in the altar lineup only if they're old enough to stand still comfortably for the duration

---

sample ceremony schedule

To get an idea of how long your ceremony will run, we put together a sample ceremony timeline for a five p.m. wedding ceremony.

4:40 p.m. Ushers begin seating guests (start seating early-bird guests about twenty minutes before the call time on your invites, at five p.m. in this case)

5:10 p.m. Prelude music begins (guests will inevitably run late, so set the call time for twenty to thirty minutes before you actually want guests to arrive)

5:30 p.m. Processional begins

Groom and officiant enter

Groomsmen enter with bridesmaids

Ring bearer and flower girl enter

Bride's mother stands, guests follow

Bride walks down the aisle with her father

5:40 p.m. Ceremony begins (yes, forty minutes after the call time! This is to give everyone plenty of time to take their seats or places and prevents any stragglers from interrupting the ceremony. This extra time is especially important if there is another ceremony or event after yours and starting late isn't an option)

6:00 p.m. Recessional begins with bride and groom leaving first, followed by children attendants, wedding party, and parents

---

THE ORDER OF THINGS
the processional

Christian processional
The officiant, groom, and best man wait at the altar for the:

Groom's grandparents

Bride's grandparents

Groom's parents

Bride's parents

Groomsmen (who walk in from the side, single file, in pairs, or accompanying bridesmaids; alternatively, they may file in from the side and wait at the altar with the groom)

Bridesmaids (starting with the attendant who will stand farthest from the bride at the altar)

Ring bearer and/or flower girl (child attendants can be seated with their parents once they reach the front)

Honor attendant(s)

The bride, walking to the left of her escort

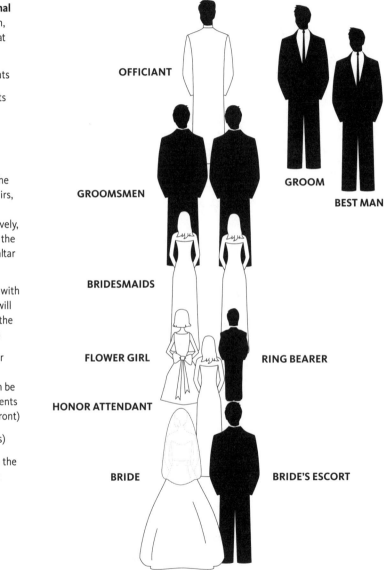

OFFICIANT

GROOM

BEST MAN

GROOMSMEN

BRIDESMAIDS

FLOWER GIRL

RING BEARER

HONOR ATTENDANT

BRIDE

BRIDE'S ESCORT

Jewish processional

Unlike in a Christian ceremony, everyone walks down the aisle, and they go in the following order:

Rabbi and/or cantor

Grandparents of the groom

Grandparents of the bride (the grandparents are seated in the first rows; with the groom's grandparents on the left, bride's on the right)

Groomsmen (typically in pairs)

Best man

The groom and his parents (Dad on his left, Mom on his right)

The bridesmaids (starting with the one who will stand farthest from the bride)

Honor attendant(s)

Ring bearer and/or flower girl

The bride and her parents (Dad on left, Mom on right)

CANTOR

RABBI

GROOM'S GRANDFATHER

GROOM'S GRANDMOTHER

BRIDE'S GRANDFATHER

BRIDE'S GRANDMOTHER

GROOMSMEN

BEST MAN

GROOM'S FATHER

GROOM
GROOM'S MOTHER

BRIDESMAIDS

HONOR ATTENDANT

BRIDE'S FATHER

BRIDE'S MOTHER

BRIDE

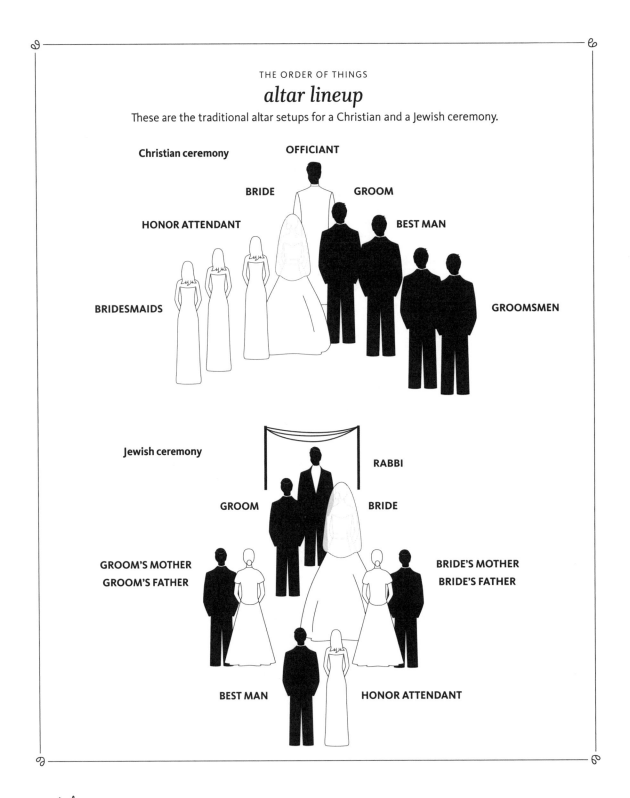

THE ORDER OF THINGS

altar lineup

These are the traditional altar setups for a Christian and a Jewish ceremony.

Christian ceremony

OFFICIANT

BRIDE GROOM

HONOR ATTENDANT BEST MAN

BRIDESMAIDS GROOMSMEN

Jewish ceremony

RABBI

GROOM BRIDE

GROOM'S MOTHER BRIDE'S MOTHER
GROOM'S FATHER BRIDE'S FATHER

BEST MAN HONOR ATTENDANT

of your ceremony. Otherwise, stand them behind you, in front of your older attendants, or have them sit with their parents. Readers and special performers rise to do their bit, then retake their seat.

The officiant's opening remarks

Once you're up at the altar, the officiant calls things to order, welcoming the guests (and acknowledging God, if it's a religious ceremony). You've heard it a hundred times in the movies and probably also in real life: "Dearly beloved, we are gathered here today . . ." By including your guests, the introduction reminds them that they are sharing in this important event with you, acting as witnesses to it, and agreeing to support your marriage.

Charge to the couple

This is the "Do you, Mary, take John to be your lawfully wedded husband?" part, to which you each respond "I do" or "I will," verifying that you're marrying of your own free will. (This charge isn't an official part of a Jewish ceremony, though some rabbis will include it.)

The exchange of vows

Your vows are your promises to each other—a statement of your intentions and expectations for your marriage. If you wish, you may choose the familiar "To have and to hold, for better or for worse" vows. Repeating words that have been used for centuries gives some couples a sense of permanence, a bigger-than-both-of-us feeling.

Alternatively, you might decide to write your own vows. If you take the personalized approach, you'll probably need to run your plans by your officiant. He or she may want to check to make sure your vows clearly define your views on marriage and address the commitment seriously. (See "Vows That Wow," page 201, for tips on writing your own vows.)

The ring ceremony

As you exchange rings, you generally say, "With this ring, I thee wed." You may add something a bit more personal about what the ring (and your to-be-wed) mean to you, as well.

The pronouncement of marriage

The officiant makes it official ("I now pronounce you husband and wife").

The kiss

And now the moment everyone has been waiting for: your first kiss as husband and wife. While of course you should be mindful of your audience, don't just give each other a quick peck—go ahead and show some emotion. Make it last as long as you like.

CLEVER IDEAS
about-face

Consider facing your guests, with your officiant's back to the congregation instead of yours, while you say your vows. This will allow everyone a good view of the exchange and make them feel more a part of the moment.

the ceremony kiss

The final ceremony kiss is an ancient Roman tradition; even contracts were sealed with a kiss. It was also believed that when you kissed, you exchanged a bit of your soul through your breath.

INSIDE SCOOP
well received

Here's the lowdown on the traditional guest-greeting method—the receiving line.

what it is

A receiving line allows you to welcome every guest in an organized, directed manner and guarantees your guests at least a minute of face time with you.

how it works

Directly after the ceremony or at the beginning of the reception, the bride and groom, along with the bridal party (if you want) and their families, line up outside the ceremony site's doors (in the vestibule, in the hallway, or on the front porch). You can also line up somewhere near the reception party entrance (by the doors, in the cocktail lounge, or in the lobby) and welcome guests as they arrive instead.

the lineup

Traditionally, the bride's parents head the receiving line and are the first to greet guests. The couple stands next to them, with the groom's parents filing in after. If you choose to include the honor attendant and the bridesmaids, they should line up after the groom's parents. If most of the guests are your friends (not your parents'), you can head the line yourselves and be the first greeters.

what you do

Say hello, give hugs and kisses, thank well-wishers for coming, and make introductions as guests exit the ceremony (or in some cases, enter the reception).

why do it

The receiving line is no longer as popular as it once was, in part because it can feel trite after a while, and the quality of the time you spend with each guest may not be all that high as they shuffle by. The more casual greet-them-as-you-see-them approach, where you mingle with guests throughout the cocktail hour and reception, is your other option these days. But the downside of that approach is you may spend the whole party ducking out in the middle of conversations to say hello to people you haven't greeted yet or miss dinner because you're too busy greeting each table. If there are fewer than fifty guests (and you take your pictures ahead of time), though, you could make the entire cocktail hour a meet-and-greet instead of doing a formal receiving line. Otherwise, as outdated as this custom may seem, we still recommend it!

Closing remarks

Your officiant wraps up the wedding with a few words to you and a blessing, if it's a religious ceremony. If it's a Jewish wedding, the groom—and sometimes the bride too—will step on a glass wrapped in a napkin. When the glass shatters, the crowd shouts, "Mazel tov!" meaning "Good luck!" to congratulate the couple and wish them well.

The recessional

You're done—it's time to party! All you have to do is exit the ceremony—together, this time. You two should be the first to exit after the ceremony, followed by your wedding party and parents. The order is basically the processional in reverse.

If you plan to take photos at the ceremony site, you could just walk out the front door after the ceremony ends and then circle back around through a back door for the pictures. That should give guests enough time to file out. Or, if you plan to have a receiving line (see "Well Received," opposite), you would want to exit and wait just outside the door to greet guests as they go. Once all the guests have been through the receiving line, that's your signal to go ahead and make your grand exit.

CEREMONIES WITH PERSONAL STYLE

While there are certain things that are the same in most ceremonies, there are still ways to put your personal twist on things. From the words you recite to the background music you select and the readings or performances, even if you're having a more traditional ceremony, you can add some of you into this special part of your day.

Music-worthy moments

Music can be used throughout this monumental event, from the time your early-bird guests arrive to the moment you walk out of the ceremony as husband and wife. Flip back to chapter 13 for the basic components of ceremony music. For creative ways to give your ceremony playlist a unique spin, see "Personalizing Your Ceremony Playlist," page 204.

Vows that wow

This is the most important promise you'll make, so it should reflect your hearts, minds, and voices. You may prefer to stick with the traditional vows that you might already know by heart. Or you might want to pen your own sentiments.

Before you get carried away and start spilling your heart on the page,

---

CLEVER IDEAS
it's a toss

Historically, cultures around the world have showered different things on couples as they left their weddings. In Italy, guests threw coins, dried fruit, and little pieces of candy (the original confetti). Today, your guests may throw birdseed or flower petals, blow bubbles, ring miniature bells, or even release birds to symbolize a life of plenty.

military weddings

If you and/or your fiancé is on active duty or retired from service, you can have a military wedding. Not all military members choose to do so, but holding such a service can be a wonderful way to demonstrate national loyalty and pride. For each branch of the armed forces, specific time-honored customs and rituals accompany brides and grooms as they embark on their journey into marriage. Here are some of the standard ones.

the setting

Military weddings are usually held at base chapels and synagogues. However, you may hold your military ceremony at a host of other locations on or off base, and it can be performed by the officiant of your choice.

special seating

All high-ranking officials (lieutenant colonel and above) must be seated in positions of honor at both the ceremony and reception. Additionally, a special place should be reserved for the commanding officer(s) of the bride and/or groom.

official attire

If the groom is a member of the military, he must wear his appropriate military dress uniform. Depending on his branch of service and whether or not he's a commissioned officer, the groom may decide to wear a saber or cutlass. If he does, the bride stands to his right at the altar (instead of to his left, as traditionally done in nonmilitary weddings) in order to avoid the blade.

If the bride is in the service, she has her choice of wearing either her military dress uniform or a traditional wedding gown. If some wedding-party members are in the military and others are not, service members may be asked to wear civilian clothes.

the arch of sabers

Reserved only for commissioned officers, the forming of the arch is a symbolic act that ensures the newlywed couple safe passage into their new life together. As soon as the ceremony is over, the ushers line up on either side of the aisle to the chapel steps. At the head usher's command—"Draw sabers [or cutlasses]"—the ushers raise their blades, edge up, into the air, carefully forming an archway. The newlyweds pass under the archway, and at the command "Return sabers [or cutlasses]" the ushers return their weapons to their sides. They then turn and escort the bridesmaids down the aisle.

the cake cutting

On command, the saber or cutlass bearers enter the reception room in formation in front of the wedding cake, facing each other. The bride and groom pass beneath the sword arch again and approach the cake. The groom hands his new bride his unsheathed sword, and with his hands over hers, they cut the first piece of cake together.

check with your officiant to make sure that it's okay to pen your own vows; some religions do not allow for variations on traditional vows. Even if you've gotten the go-ahead, it is imperative that you run the vows by your officiant once you've finished. He or she may raise faith-based questions or objections to your wording, or contribute a thought or a quote that might make your vows even more emotive.

Once you're cleared to create your own vows, set aside one to two months to work on them and have the final version ready at least a week before the wedding. Here's how to nail down the right words to express how you feel.

GET ON THE SAME PAGE Decide whether you will write your vows together or alone. If you go solo, you may want to take turns running them by each other before the big day—or not. Just make sure that both have approximately the same amount of text so that one person isn't rambling on for five minutes while the other says ten words.

Make your vows funny and warm but not cryptic or embarrassing. Don't let them drag on and on. Be concise (a minute each, max) and

the knot NOTE

vow helper
Set the tone for your ceremony, be it playful or tearful. Not sure where to start? We've collected some great passages to help with your quest for the perfect ceremony readings, to reflect your feelings, tastes, and personalities. **TheKnot.com/vows**

Katie & John
MAY 5
YORKTOWN, VA

A rustic garden theme fit perfectly with the outdoor setting of Katie and John's springtime nuptials. Instead of a strict color scheme, the pair incorporated a variety of colors that complemented the season. To play up the whimsical vibe, the couple used a vintage desk topped with two tall arrangements for their altar. The mood of the day was elegant yet low-key, just like the bride's look—a simple fit-and-flare gown paired with a long lace veil.

the ceremony program

Wedding programs make great souvenirs, but they're also a gracious gesture. They help guests understand all of the details of the ceremony and introduce attendees to the major players in your wedding. (Skip ahead to chapter 19 for more information on designing your ceremony programs; you can also go to TheKnot.com/ programs for DIY program ideas.)

Guests should receive programs as they arrive for the ceremony. Ask a special cousin or usher or two to man the ceremony entrance and distribute them. You can also put them on a table or in decorated baskets near the entrance and let guests pick them up themselves. If they are pretty, and it isn't windy, place one on each seat (or hang them from chair backs), where they can serve as a decorative detail.

CLEVER IDEAS
personalizing your ceremony playlist

One way to express your personalities is to choose songs that are meaningful to you or that speak to your religious, ethnic, or cultural backgrounds. Incorporate one or more of these elements into your ceremony music to make it your own.

ethnicity
Use traditional musical instruments, such as a sitar (India), bouzouki (Greece), fiddle (Ireland), or didgeridoo (Australia). Play national folk songs during the prelude.

religion
Have a choir lead everyone in a hymn or religious tune; hire a gospel group or klezmer band (a traditional Jewish wedding band); incorporate a Buddhist chant.

wedding style
Match the musicians to your wedding theme (read: a jazz trio for a 1920s-themed wedding; a steel-drum band for a Caribbean beachside ceremony).

site characteristics
Take musical cues from your site. Dramatic organ music goes well with a large Gothic church; a folksinger is perfect for your grandparents' living room; a string quartet goes hand-in-glove with a formal garden.

"your" songs
Choose tunes that have one of your names in them (Elton John's "Daniel"; the Beatles' "Michelle"), bear special meaning for both of you (a song from your parents' wedding, for example), or are significant to you as a couple, such as a song that was played at the concert where you met.

get to the core of what marrying that person means to you. Save some words for the toast, and the honeymoon, of course.

If you choose to make it a joint task, pen a mutual vow that you'll both take. A vow-writing "date" is a great way to get started. Over dinner or breakfast in bed, discuss what marriage means to you.

GET INSPIRED With your notepad or laptop in hand, dish (with your fiancé or solo) about important events and turning points in your relationship: how you met, when you fell in love, when and how you said "I love you." List the qualities you most admire in your fiancé and the characteristics that he brings out in you.

Don't feel like you have to come up with a brilliant piece of prose all on your own. Incorporate quotes from love letters (or your own

vow wording ideas

Here is an example from a real couple who penned their own promises.

ALEX & MICHELLE

groom

I promise to encourage your compassion,
Because that is what makes you unique and
wonderful.
I promise to nurture your dreams,
Because through them your soul shines.
I promise to help shoulder our challenges,
For there is nothing we cannot face if we stand
together.
I promise to be your partner in all things,
Not possessing you, but working with you as a
part of the whole.
Lastly, I promise to you perfect love and perfect
trust,
For one lifetime with you could never be enough.
This is my sacred vow to you, my equal in all
things.

bride

I promise to encourage your individuality,
Because that is what makes you unique and
wonderful.
I promise to nurture your dreams,
Because through them your soul shines.
I promise to help shoulder our challenges,
Because through them we'll emerge stronger.
I promise to be your partner in all things,
Not possessing you, but working with you as a
part of the whole.
I promise to share with you the joys of life,
Because with you they will be that much sweeter.
Lastly, I promise to you perfect love and
perfect trust,
For one lifetime with you could never be enough.
This is my sacred vow to you, my equal in all
things.

BRADLEY AND JENNIFER

groom

I pledge to actually use the GPS, to not leave
loose change and receipts everywhere, and to
take my dirty hockey gear out of the backseat of
the car after the game.

bride

I pledge to actually learn how to use the remote,
to not to eat off your plate at restaurants (as long
as I can still do it at home), and to watch at least
one Red Sox game.

DAVE AND STEPHANIE

groom

I, Dave, take you Stephanie to be my wife, my
partner in life, and my one true love.

I promise to be there with you through the
toughest of the trials in our life and to cry with
you. These trials do not include things like the
first ten minutes of the movie *Up* or YouTube
footage of soldiers being reunited with their
daughters. You're crying on your own with those.

bride

I promise with all my heart to love you when
times are good and bad. When you're sore on
Monday from sitting in the same position all day
during Sunday football.

When I'm scared you make me feel safe. When
I'm sad you make me smile. There has yet to be
a day where we haven't laughed together. I never
want there to be one.

I take you to be my husband, the father of my
children, and best friend until death do us
part. Just stay away for one week per month!

The Apache mix colored sands in a crystal bowl as a symbol of unity.

At Japanese weddings, 1,001 white paper cranes are used to symbolize good luck—times 1,000.

For Hindus, red, not white, is the color of marriage. The bride might wear a red sari or veil and sport orange-red henna designs.

The sake-sharing ritual is the main bonding rite of a Shinto ceremony (an ancient religion practiced primarily in Japan).

In an Eastern Orthodox wedding (Russian and Greek), the bride and groom exchange their rings three times to represent marriage under the Holy Trinity.

romantic e-mail exchanges), poems, "your" songs, romantic literature, spiritual texts, your favorite authors' works, a sentimental or favorite movie, or childhood favorites like *The Little Prince,* Dr. Seuss, or even Winnie-the-Pooh (his musings may be simple, but they are always sentimental: "If you live to be a hundred, I want to live to be a hundred minus one day, so I never have to live without you"). Borrow freely from what you've gathered, and have fun picking and choosing exactly the right words. Just try to avoid sappy clichés.

PRACTICE Yes, your vows are for the man (or woman) you're about to marry, but they are also for an audience. Practice out loud, alone, or with a trusted friend. Also, watch out for tongue twisters and unruly sentences (you may run out of breath—you'll be nervous enough as it is).

If you think you can memorize your vows, go for it. If you're likely to draw a blank, we are giving you permission to cheat: Have a copy ready to read from or have the officiant read them for you to repeat. You probably won't want to pull them out from the corset of your gown, so assign your maid of honor and/or best man the duty of holding the vows until the moment arrives. Copy your words onto stationery or a beautiful card, so your guests aren't distracted by a crumpled piece of paper (plus, it ensures you'll have them in print for years to come).

Readings to remember
A reading can be traditional, biblical, poetic, humorous, or serious—anything that elaborates on your ideas of marriage and your relationship. Religious texts are, of course, a great source for tried-and-true wedding readings. You can find your readings in similar places where you might find inspiration for your vows: song lyrics, love poems, stories, essays, fables, books, movies . . . you get the picture.

Ask friends, relatives, stepparents, or mentors to read at your wedding. Or do readings yourselves, alternating verses or paragraphs.

Unity symbols
Incorporate visual representations of the marriage bond and include your families in the ritual to symbolize a broader blending.

UNITY CANDLE The bride and groom, each holding a candle, light a third, centrally located candle together. You may blow out the individual flames, or all three candles may remain lit throughout the rest of the ceremony.

UNITY CUP Each family fills its own cup with wine. The bride and groom each pour half of their "family" cup into one shared cup. Then they each take a sip.

wedding rings

If you're like most couples, you'll have a basic idea of what you want before you head out to the jewelry stores. Keep cost in mind: We recommend setting aside about 3 percent of your budget for both wedding rings. Platinum is the most expensive material for bands (even more than gold), and diamonds can add considerably to the cost.

time it right
Give yourselves at least two months to browse, research, price, and revisit rings that catch your eye. Allow even more time if you're interested in a custom piece.

consider your lifestyles
You'll be wearing your bands every day so comfort is key. If you play sports or an instrument, opt for a slimmer ring with rounded edges (appropriately called a "comfort fit"). Those who work with their hands will want a simple, solid metal ring, as stones can come loose and carvings will trap dirt. And if you are highly allergic to certain metal alloys, you will want to choose titanium or palladium, or invest in platinum, which is hypoallergenic for most people.

incorporate your styles
Select a style that you'll still love in twenty years. Keep in mind, some religions or cultures have certain restrictions that may affect your choice of ring. Traditional Jewish bands don't have stones, which break the circle.

take a close look
Wedding bands should have two marks inside the band: the first is the manufacturer's trademark (which proves that the company stands behind its work), and the second is the quality mark (*24K* or *PLAT,* for example, which proves that it's what they say it is). If the ring consists of two or more metals, make sure there is a quality mark for each.

mix or match
Just because you and your fiancé are a perfect match doesn't mean your rings need to be. To support the meaning behind the rings (symbolizing the joining of two lives), some aspect should match, which can be as simple as the metal or the inscriptions.

honoring the deceased

Here are some ways to pay a tribute to a special someone who's passed away.

Write something about him and read it aloud.

Read her favorite poem or a selection from her favorite author.

Have everyone sing his favorite song, or have your musicians play it. Wear something belonging to her.

Make a donation to a charity in his honor and list the information and significance in the programs.

Display a memory photo album or framed picture.

After the wedding, leave your bouquet on his grave.

OTHER OPTIONS Create your own unity symbol, drawing on an ethnic custom or just using your own vision. Your symbol might be a tree you plant together. Or it could be religious—such as the figure-eight-style rosary that's draped over both partners' shoulders.

registry

> **TIMELINE**
> ## PLANNING
>
> **1 month before the engagement party**
> Start your registry
>
> **6–8+ months before the wedding**
> Register for (more) gifts
>
> **1 month before the shower**
> Update your registry
>
> **2–3 months before the wedding**
> Attend your shower; write thank-you notes within 2 weeks after your shower
>
> **1–3 months after the wedding**
> Send all remaining thank-yous

From your engagement party to beyond your big day, you'll be showered with parties in your honor and an almost obscene number of gifts. It's officially time to shift your focus from all the wedding planning to planning your life postwedding—what gifts you need and want to help you "set up" a home. Daydreaming about, registering for, and unwrapping the downpour of gadgets, housewares, and honeymoon extras is one of the perkiest perks of engagement. So get going, because your engagement party—and shower—are right around the corner and guests will be curious about what you want.

REGISTRY BASICS

Creating a wedding gift registry is kind of like an adult version of creating a list for Santa, except you don't have to be good to get everything you want. Lest you (or your mom) think, however, that registering is a tacky fishing-for-presents tactic, remember that the most compelling reason for doing it is to help your guests in the daunting process of choosing gifts that you'll love and actually use. Most of your (busy) guests—particularly those who aren't familiar with your board game obsession or your love of African art—will appreciate the direction. It's not as though you're dictating exactly what a guest should purchase; rather, you're offering a variety of suggestions guaranteed to please. The registry system also helps you avoid (or at least minimizes) the number of duplicate gifts you get. Stand mixers are essential, but one is probably enough!

It's a good idea to set up a registry soon after your engagement, particularly if your parents are hosting an engagement party. You can always update your list and add more items at any time. Just keep in mind: If you have more than a year to go before your wedding, you may want to hold off on seasonal items that could go out of stock or even be discontinued by wedding time.

DECIDING WHAT GOES ON YOUR LIST

Now that you can register for almost anything, where do you even begin? It's hard to know exactly what to add—a Japanese Shun Elite knife or a German chef's knife? The nonstick saucepan or the stainless steel one? Begin by asking yourselves these essential questions—the answers will help you determine where to register and what exactly to include on your wish list. In the appendix you'll find a complete registry checklist (page 412) with all the items you'll need to build your newlywed nest (and if you've been building your nest for years already, check out the "Alterna-Registry" checklist on page 211).

WHAT'S OUR DESIGN STYLE?   This may seem like a loaded question if you already know that you're midcentury modern and he's American classic. But it's good to get a handle on your individual tastes and consider how you can combine them before you register. Need help coming to a compromise? Try this: Sit down together with a few design magazines and home catalogs, and tear out items you both like. Find your common ground in colors, accessories, and furniture

---

GLOSSARY
what is crystal?

plain crystal
Is just that: smooth glass with no decoration. If you're a minimalist, you'll probably choose this simply elegant crystal pattern.

cut crystal
Features a pattern that can range from relatively simple to extravagantly ornate. Your preference depends on your taste. If you're an entertainer extraordinaire or long for the days of Edith Wharton, ornate cut crystal is for you.

banded crystal
Has a gold or platinum rim. If you already have (or are registering for) metal-rimmed china, you may choose this type of crystal, which needs extra care.

GLOSSARY
china vs. porcelain

bone
Bone china is known for being the best in fine china. It's made of bone ash, which gives it a higher translucency and creates a warm, ivory color.

porcelain
Porcelain china is made with kaolin, which is the clay that makes the china a stunning bright white.

the knot NOTE

registry checklist
Get the scoop on the latest technology to help manage your registry.
TheKnot.com/registry

styles. Keep in mind: Mixing and matching different styles can look modern and chic.

DO WE LIKE TO COOK? If the answer is "occasionally," then it's okay to register for just the kitchen basics. We always recommend getting at least a starter set of pots and pans, basic bakeware, a standard tool set, classic cooking gadgets (mixer, food processor, and blender), and fine knives, all of which are expensive, because you never know if down the road (perhaps when you have a nice, big kitchen and/or kids) you'll decide to get into cooking. If you both love to cook already, you'll probably want to upgrade to nicer equipment or add specialty items like mandolines and sauciers.

DO WE LIKE TO ENTERTAIN? (AND IF SO, WHAT'S OUR ENTERTAINING STYLE?) If you're cocktail-party people, then you'll definitely need large serving pieces and lots of barware. If you like dinner parties or you plan to host family for holidays, you're going to want lots of place settings (at least twelve) and you may want to own formal china and crystal, or at least dishes and glassware that can work for more formal occasions. If the backyard barbecue reigns supreme, you'll also need grill gear and some plastic serveware.

WHAT WILL WE BE LIKE TEN YEARS FROM NOW? You can't just register based on who you are today—the tiny urban apartment dwellers who eat out every night would end up with nothing! Gift occasions like this only come around once in a lifetime, so make the most of it. Think of your future holiday dinners for twenty or your ultimate desire to learn how to bake or the extra set of towels and sheets for when you have a guest room (or kids). You can always keep items in storage at your parents' houses for a couple of years.

WHAT HOUSEHOLD ITEMS DO WE NEED? If you'll be Mr. and Mrs. Fix-It, then you should consider including a lawn mower or premium power tools. Do you need a new vacuum or a grill for your backyard? Or maybe you're dying for an "adult" couch, new lamps for your home office, or a nice piece of art for your living room? These big-ticket items are perfect for your friends who want to go in on a group gift.

WHAT ARE OUR HOBBIES? If you both love movies, think about signing up for a state-of-the-art TV. Enjoy skiing? Maybe it's time for some new equipment (yep, sports equipment is absolutely fair game for your registry). Wine lovers? Register for a wine-of-the-month club so you can try new varietals.

alterna-registry

Whether you choose gifts that are strictly for fun or prefer more practical household items, consider some of these nontraditional registry picks.

- ☐ Honeymoon items (many resorts, as well as third-party sites, offer registry programs, where you can register for room upgrades, dinners, spa treatments, and excursions)
- ☐ Home down payment
- ☐ Furniture
- ☐ Electronics
- ☐ Camping gear
- ☐ Art

- ☐ Club or museum membership
- ☐ Donations to a favorite charity
- ☐ Delivery clubs (cheese of the month, weekly flower arrangements)
- ☐ Backyard games (badminton, croquet set)
- ☐ Sports equipment (skis, tennis rackets)

cookware 411

aluminum
A lightweight material and a great heat conductor, but it scratches and stains easily.

stainless steel
Durable and easy to maintain, but it's a poor heat conductor.

cast iron
Inexpensive but heavy and corrodes easily.

copper
Expensive, scratches easily, but is a great heat conductor.

enameled steel and glass
The most stylish options because they're colorful, but they chip easily.

nonstick surfaces
Nonstick pans like Teflon make cooking and cleanup a breeze.

CHOOSING THE RIGHT RETAILERS

Once you've inventoried your personal life, start auditioning stores. In general, two or three stores is the perfect amount, allowing you to register for a variety of items without making it difficult to keep track. There are several key areas to investigate before choosing where to set up your registry.

SELECTION What range of products and brands do they carry? Make sure the store you pick has the brands you want, a variety of price points, and a large selection of different products.

SHIPPING Will they ship to the address you designate? Can they send gifts in a batch? The best retailers will send your gifts to any address you specify.

CONVENIENCE Is the process hassle-free for buyers? Does the store have a toll-free number or live help available on their site? For smaller boutiques, will your registry be available online? Can guests purchase gifts online? (Surprisingly, there are still some that have no e-commerce capabilities.)

TRACKING How will the retailer keep track of your registry? How fast after a gift is bought will the purchase be reflected on the list? Big retailers should have a computerized system that's updated instantly. Also, how long will your registry list be kept active after the wedding? Guests think they have up to one year from your wedding day to buy you your gift, so your registry should be kept active for at least that long. But we like stores that keep it active indefinitely; after you put all that work into making selections, why have your wish list disappear?

EXCHANGES How long is the exchange/return period? What are the terms? The exchange and return policy is crucial. You don't want to end up with any duplicates or get back from your honeymoon and find out that you only have ten days left to exchange or return any items you don't want.

PERKS Retailers offer different benefits. For example, some places have what's called a completion program that allows you to purchase whatever you don't receive from your registry at a discount. Some stores offer you rewards on their store brand or a credit card for every gift your guests purchase in your name.

CREATING YOUR LIST

Once you pick a registry program, ask for a registry form or scanner (or sign up online) with which to indicate your desired objects. Either with the help of a store consultant or on your own, tour the store or website, recording the items you want.

While online registries are convenient, we always recommend at least one in-store visit to get better acquainted with the merchandise, especially for the things you are choosing for a lifetime. Do touch tests of bedlinens, feel your flatware, confirm you love the china pattern—as anyone who's ever shopped online knows, sometimes things look very different onscreen than they do in person.

THINK BEFORE YOU SCAN Avoid filling your list with things you're never going to use. If you two aren't the formal-party types, you probably won't need a crystal punch bowl, as compelling as it may seem when you walk by with that registry scanner. Before you register for anything monogrammed, be extra-sure of your choice. Once your name is on it, you probably won't be able to return it.

PICK A RANGE OF PRICE POINTS As much as you may be hankering for that gorgeous $350-per-place-setting silver, you should

---

ASK CARLEY
CASH GIFTS

We're saving for a new home and would prefer cash over cookware. Is there a polite way to ask for money?
Many couples would prefer money to material gifts, but be very careful because it can be considered crass. The first thing to remember is not to put your wish for moolah in writing anywhere—neither your invites nor your wedding website. Instead, tell close friends and family that cash is your gift preference; they'll spread the word when guests ask them where you're registered. There are also innovative gifts registries where you can specify cash requests for things like contributions to a down payment on a home or a honeymoon fund. Many stores allow you to register for gift cards, too, and you can use them to buy the things you want and need . . . later. Register for some traditional items though, to accommodate guests who would prefer not to give you a specific dollar amount. (Even though you may be fine with a check for $35, the $35 gift-giver may feel much more comfortable giving you candlesticks!) Very few stores let you return gifts for cash, but credit can be helpful too.

TIP
saying thanks

Let your guests know their gifts have arrived—promptly. Thank-you notes for gifts received before the wedding should be sent within two weeks of their arrival. Notes for gifts received on or after the wedding day should be sent within a month of receipt. To help, add a designated gift column to your guest list manager tool or spreadsheet (see chapter 4) and record every present as you receive it. The extra step will help you write thank-you notes that are accurate, descriptive, and personal. Plus, you'll have your guests' addresses at your fingertips when you go to send them.

register for items in a wide range of price points: under $50, under $75, under $100, under $200, and beyond. That way, all of your guests can choose gifts they can afford. You don't want your college friend feeling overwhelmed by the fact that he can't find a single gift in his price range, and on the opposite end of the spending spectrum, you don't want your parents' closest friends to have to scramble to buy you a multitude of unrelated smaller items to give you a generous gift.

CHECK IT TWICE When you're done, ask for a master list and read it carefully to make sure there are no mistakes. Most important, double-check the mailing address for where gifts will be sent (unless, of course, you don't mind if all your gifts go to your old roommate). If you don't have room at your place for everything you're choosing, be sure you're svending the right stuff to Mom and Dad's basement and the stuff you want now to your residence. Get the contact info of your point person at the store, should you have any questions or problems.

MANAGING YOUR LIST Throughout your engagement, periodically check out and update your registry, especially after each wave of gifts arrives (engagement party, shower, and during the wedding-gift wave). Delete purchased gifts the store didn't catch. Add more items to your list if you find that your generous loved ones are cleaning out your registry.

looking the part

15

the dress and all the rest

TIMELINE

PLANNING

❧

8–10+ months before
Start shopping

6 months before
Order dress

Select a veil or headpiece

3 months before
Select your shoe height

Buy undergarments

2 months before
Have first fitting

1 month before
Have second fitting

6 weeks before
Choose the rest of
your accessories

2–3 weeks before
Have final fitting

As *what-to-wear occasions go,* your wedding tops the list. Not to make you nervous or anything, but this is pretty much the one time you can be certain all eyes will be on you. And, you'll probably spend more on whatever it is you decide to wear than you have on any outfit you own. Maybe you've imagined a big ball gown since the age of six. Or maybe you've studied fashion and are enamored with the couture shapes of Alexander McQueen. Maybe you'd never be caught dead in one of those confections they call bridal gowns and you have a chic white suit (or big black dress) in mind instead. What you wear on your wedding day is completely up to you. The only requirement is that you feel fantastic.

WEDDING DRESS BASICS

Shopping for a wedding gown is a bit more complicated than shopping for any other dress you've probably ever purchased. Wedding-dress shopping comes with its own language, and the more you know about what types of silhouettes, necklines, and shades of white might flatter you, the easier finding your dream dress will be.

Practical considerations
Before we get into the nitty-gritty of silk tulle versus AlenÁon lace, consider these more practical parameters for choosing the perfect dress. Obviously, your body type and personal style will shape what you wear, but there are other factors you'll want to keep in mind, too.

WEATHER For beachside nuptials, you'll want to opt out of a heavy satin ball gown and slip into a sheath or slim A-line in a lighter fabric that won't have you sweating on the sand. Generally speaking, silk satin and mikado work well in all types of weather, while brocades and velvets work better in cold climates, and chiffons and crepes in warmer ones. As a rule of thumb: Consider the typical temperature on your wedding day when selecting a material (keep reading for more on your options), and save the shiny stuff for evening.

YOUR VENUE Clearly an ornate ballroom calls for a different dress code than, say, a rustic ranch or even an urban loft. If you're getting married at a house of worship, check with your ceremony officiant to find out whether there are any attire guidelines, such as covering your shoulders.

BUDGET Some brides clearly consider the dress a top priority, but that doesn't mean you shouldn't take a money-is-no-object approach to dress shopping. Trust us—you're better off not trying on gowns outside your price range. You'll either end up falling in love and being disappointed by every other dress you see (even if they're just as beautiful) or you'll blow your budget.

Finding Your Bridal Style
Both your personal style and your wedding style will play a role in what you decide to wear for your Oscar moment. Consider what look you're going for ahead of time, so you can give store consultants some direction. There are some key style categories used in the bridal fashion industry that you'll want to get familiar with so you can give the consultant at the salon a clear idea of what you have in mind. Here are descriptions of some of the most popular bridal styles to help you home in on the right look.

the wedding dress

Here are some sneaky ways to save on "the one."

simplify or substitute
If your dream gown is highly embellished, ask if the designer can limit the beading (which increases the price) to the bodice and skip it entirely on the skirt or train. Or ask if the dress comes in an alternative fabric that is less expensive.

try other brides
You'd be surprised at how many brides change their mind after their dress arrives and choose to get a new one at the last minute. (Note: That's why, even if you think you've found "the one" at the first salon you visit, it's important to shop around and take your time to choose the right gown. Trust us—there are a lot of dream-worthy gowns out there.) Peruse online postings for dresses that have never been worn before.

buy ready-to-wear
If you're looking for something straight and simple, shop the resort collection at your favorite department store. Many designers have white or cream dresses that will fit a more formal setting but may come with a more budget-friendly price tag.

hit up sample sales
A few times a year, bridal designers and some retailers like Kleinfeld will host mega sales to make room for the next season's merchandise. (For more on sample sales, see "Where to Shop," page 233.)

CLASSIC New England prep sums up your style, and for your wedding day, you are going for simple yet elegant by channeling your style icon, Audrey Hepburn. Your timeless look starts with your neckline—jewel or bateau—and a skirt with straight lines. Also on your checklist: your mother's pearls, a clutch, and proper pumps.

ROMANTIC You're all about the big lace ball gown. Pretty is your operative word. You'll clothe yourself in a formal princess gown with traditional embellishment like intricate embroidery, gauzy ruffles, or layers of lace.

GLAMOROUS You'll look to the red carpet to inspire your aisle style. Get screen-starlet perfection with a curve-hugging mermaid dress with ruching and decadent beading.

CASUAL ELEGANCE To translate your unfussy yet chic style, you want a look that is elegant but doesn't seem like you tried too hard. An airy, ethereal gown will appear understated, perfect for an outdoor or low-key indoor setting. Go beach chic with a Grecian-inspired gown, or take on a more vintage goddess style with a lace sheath.

EDGY Off-beat and unique are how you would describe your day-of vision. A tea-length or short dress in a non-traditional color (blush, blue, even black) and cut (one-shoulder, perhaps) will fit your one-of-a-kind style.

Designs for the Day Different silhouettes, necklines, hemlines, and cuts flatter different body types. The silhouette and neckline determine if a dress flatters your shape. The skirt is where the gown's personality really shines. In order to find the right gowns for your shape, there's some lingo you'll need to master.

SILHOUETTES *Silhouette* refers to the overall shape of a gown. And not all are equally flattering to every bride's figure. Here are some suggestions as to which wedding-dress shape will look best on you. As with most things in life, it's all about proportion.

A-line As its name implies, the A-line cut is narrow at the top, close to the rib cage, and extends out along the body in the shape of a triangle (or "A") in a smooth, elongated line. It's the most popular skirt option, flattering a variety of body types.

Modified A-line Somewhere between a mermaid silhouette and an A-line, this shape is roomier in the hips than a mermaid style and slightly flared at the bottom, giving the gown movement as you walk. It's a flattering fit for someone who wants more shape than a simple A-line and more mobility than a mermaid style.

Ball Gown The classic ball gown has a fitted bodice, a natural waist, and a full skirt. It's truly feminine (think *Cinderella*) and looks particularly good on women with boyish figures (narrow hips), because it will make you look curvier. When paired with a fitted bodice, it's great for pear shapes, too, because it defines your waist, while billowy tiers will hide your hips. And tall brides will appear statuesque in voluminous silhouettes.

Mermaid A slim, tapered, curve-hugging skirt that follows the line of the hips and thighs and flares out below the knee. Go this route if you want to show off your curves.

Trumpet Often confused with a mermaid-style silhouette, the big difference is that the straight-lined skirt subtly flares toward the hem in a trumpet shape starting at the knee. Again, it's a popular option for showing off your curves that is slightly easier to move in.

Sheath If you're petite or just have a sleek figure, consider this formfitting style, which follows the body's natural line. A slim

silhouettes

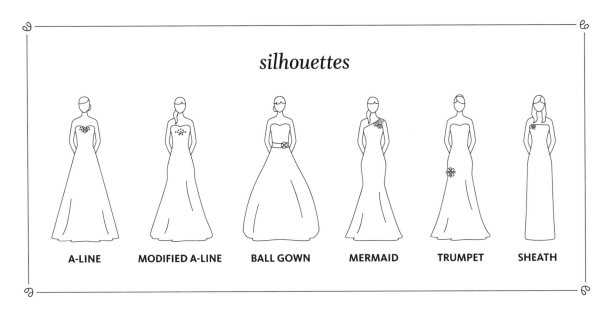

A-LINE **MODIFIED A-LINE** **BALL GOWN** **MERMAID** **TRUMPET** **SHEATH**

silhouette adds length, and it won't overwhelm a small woman like a big, elaborate gown could.

WAISTLINES Technically, the waistline of the wedding dress is the horizontal seam that joins the bodice and skirt. Along with the neckline and sleeves, the waistline brings shape and balance to the gown and dictates how a dress works on your figure.

Asymmetrical Features a change in waist height from one side to the other; has a slimming effect, especially if you're thick-waisted.

Basque Forms an elongated triangle below the natural waistline. It also has a slimming effect on your waist and deemphasizes hips.

Empire Also a high waistline, this seam just below the bustline is great for deemphasizing the waistline and hips, while making you look longer and leaner. Because this style really has no waistline, it's great for apple shapes. If you have a large chest or full hips, you probably want to stay away from this one.

Natural The seam of the waistline lies, obviously, at the natural waist; flatters hourglass figures.

Dropped Falls several inches below the natural waistline and elongates the torso.

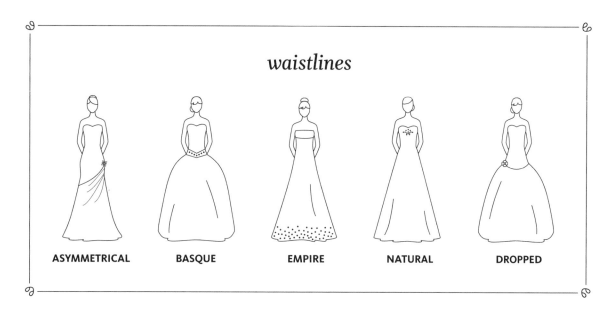

waistlines

ASYMMETRICAL **BASQUE** **EMPIRE** **NATURAL** **DROPPED**

NECKLINES The right neckline can add character to a gown, show off an accessory, or highlight your favorite feature—be it a long, graceful neck; a daring décolletage; or toned shoulders. Keep in mind: The lower the neckline, the longer your neck will look; the higher the neckline, the shorter it will seem.

Asymmetrical This neckline appears different on either side of the center front; one example is a one-shoulder design. It's great for showing off your arms, but it's not the best option for bustier brides.

Bateau This wide-necked shape gently follows the curve of the collarbone, almost to the tip of the shoulders. The Sabrina version—made popular by actress Audrey Hepburn—is always sleeveless; the front and back panels of fabric just touch at the shoulders. This style does wonders for brides with smaller chests.

Halter Often backless, this shape features straps that wrap around the neck or a high neck with deep armholes. It works perfectly for someone with great, broad shoulders but doesn't allow for much bra support and isn't the best option if you have narrow shoulders.

High Neck A band collar that extends up the neck. The mandarin version of this style is taken from traditional Asian dress and doesn't quite meet at the center front. Higher necklines have an elongating effect and work best on smaller chests and broad shoulders. Conversely, they are not the best option if you're curvier on top or have narrow shoulders.

necklines

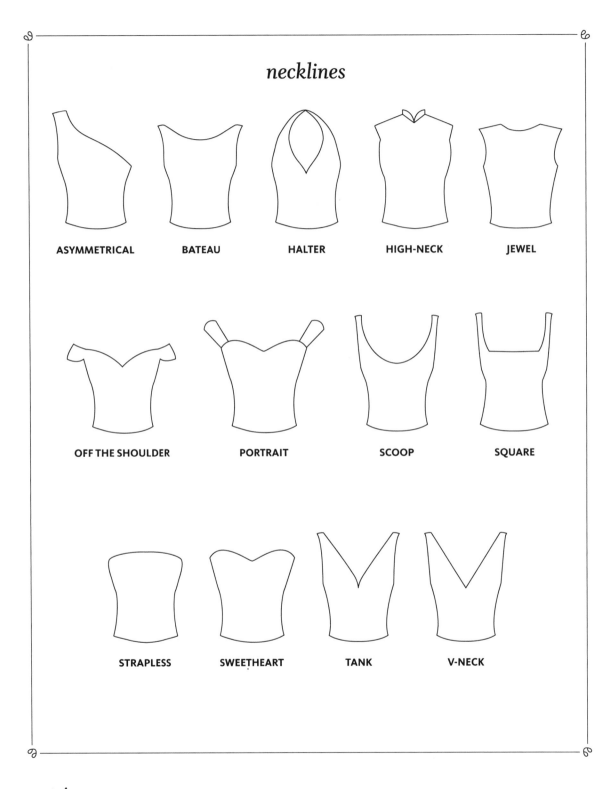

ASYMMETRICAL   BATEAU   HALTER   HIGH-NECK   JEWEL

OFF THE SHOULDER   PORTRAIT   SCOOP   SQUARE

STRAPLESS   SWEETHEART   TANK   V-NECK

Jewel Also known as the "T-shirt neckline," this is a round neckline that sits at the base of the throat. If you're full-chested, this may not be the best choice for you—it will just make you look bustier. But for petite or smaller-chested women, this neckline can enhance your décolletage.

Off-the-Shoulder This one is self-explanatory—the neckline sits below the shoulders, with sleeves that cover part of the upper arm. If you have broad shoulders or fuller arms, skip this look; this neckline is super-flattering to medium- or full-chested women and pear-shaped brides.

Portrait Characterized by a wide, soft scoop from the tip of one shoulder to the tip of the other, it flatters brides with fuller arms and prominent collarbones. If you have undefined or very bony collarbones though, steer clear.

Scoop A square neckline with rounded edges (or a variation on that shape). Often the scoop continues on the back of the dress. Just about everyone can wear this one, too.

Square Cut straight across the front, this universally flattering cut is especially great for busty brides, as it cuts low but isn't revealing.

Strapless One of the most popular necklines for brides, this bodice is usually cut straight across, but it can also peak on the sides or have a slight dip in the center. It especially flatters broad or thick shoulders, as it's a great way to show off your shoulders and collarbone, but bustier brides may want to think twice, as it does not allow for much support up top.

Sweetheart This neckline is shaped like the top half of a heart and really accentuates the bust, so it's great for brides who are curvier up top and want to go with a strapless style. For a more modest look, the sweetheart often is done with an overlay of lace or sheer material that rises higher than the heart shape.

Tank Similar to a men's undershirt, with deep armholes under the shoulders and narrow straps. It accentuates a great pair of arms and is a nice sleeveless option for brides who want the added support of a bra with straps.

V-Neck The neckline dips down in the front in a flattering V-shape, elongating the neckline and deemphasizing the bustline, so it's a solid choice for bustier brides.

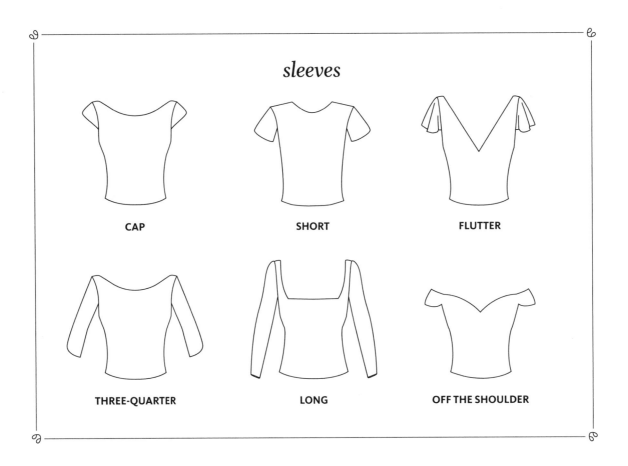

sleeves

CAP

SHORT

FLUTTER

THREE-QUARTER

LONG

OFF THE SHOULDER

SLEEVES Wedding-dress sleeves can add extra interest to a bodice and provide balance for a skirt. While sleeveless styles remain the most popular, with strapless being number one, sleeves have made a comeback thanks in large part to the Duchess of Cambridge's lace-sleeved wedding gown.

Cap Sleeve Little sleeves that pretty much just cover your shoulders. Shorter than a T-shirt sleeve, and more rounded and elegant.

Short Sleeve Longer than cap, this style is about as long as your average T-shirt (naturally) and looks best on women with fairly slender or well-toned upper arms. A good option for brides who want to cover their upper arms but don't want to go all the way (long sleeves). If you're self-conscious about baring your triceps/biceps, this style may be for you.

Off-the-Shoulder Sleeves These sleeves cover the upper part of the arms while leaving the tops of the shoulders and décolletage exposed. This style flatters both big- and small-busted brides, and the sleeves cover enough of the upper arm to make almost anyone comfortable.

Flutter Sleeves A loose, tapered short sleeve that falls in folds over the upper arm for a romantic, ethereal look. This style is best for lithe arms.

Three-Quarter Straight sleeves that end midway between your elbow and wrist, this style has a classic, ladylike feel. It's an elegant look in bridal—cool yet covered.

Long Sleeves that come all the way to your wrist, often with cuffs banded in lace, satin, even velvet are a great choice for a winter wedding or a wedding that requires more modest attire. Long sleeves made of sheer tulle (see "Illusion Sleeves," right) or lace look elegant without feeling buttoned-up. Also in this category is the unfortunately named "leg-of-mutton" sleeve, which is full at the armhole and gradually tapers to the wrist in a bell-shaped formation (like a leg of mutton) to further deemphasize full upper arms. This Victorian-era sleeve is rarely seen anymore.

HEMLINE HEIGHTS The hemline of a wedding gown refers to its length. Generally speaking, the longer the dress, the more formal the affair—though these days, anything goes.

Floor-Length As the name implies, the skirt falls to the floor.

Ballerina A full skirt that reaches just above the ankles.

Hi-Lo Has a shorter hem in the front and a floor-length hem in back.

Tea-Length Hemmed to a few inches below the knee.

Cocktail-Length Hemmed above or at the knee.

SKIRT CONSTRUCTION A few well-placed details can make the difference between a gown that's average and one that's out of this world, adding length and volume, style and depth.

Draping Swaths of fabric pleated or gathered to a side or back seam of a skirt, adding fullness.

Flounce A wide ruffle around the bottom of a skirt.

Overskirt A second skirt that partially covers the skirt beneath it.

Petal An overskirt of a different fabric that falls in rounded sections.

GLOSSARY
illusion sleeves

Sometimes sleeves are simply a style of embellishment. Made out of see-through tulle, lace, or netting, this type of sleeve can make it look like the embroidery and beading is floating on your body. These magical sleeves are a great way to make you feel covered up, though you won't necessarily look it.

---

skirt construction

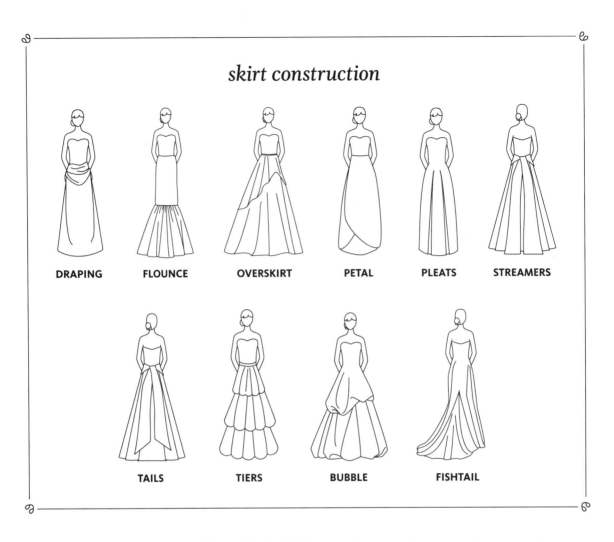

DRAPING **FLOUNCE** **OVERSKIRT** **PETAL** **PLEATS** **STREAMERS**

TAILS **TIERS** **BUBBLE** **FISHTAIL**

Pleats Folds of fabric pressed on top of each other like an accordion or box shape.

Streamers Strings or ties that trail down the gown's back.

Tails Panels of the same or contrasting fabric, which trail behind the gown like a train.

Tiers Fabric layers of various lengths.

Bubble Balloons out and then tapers at the hem.

Fishtail Has an additional, stitched-on panel in the back, like a, well, fishtail.

TRAINS More than any other element of the wedding dress, the bridal train has the ability to transform. It's an extension of your gown that trails out behind you, and requires your maid of honor to readjust it so it fans out perfectly at the altar. Generally, the more formal the wedding, the longer the train, but some dresses—like a tulle ball gown—will have no train at all.

When choosing a train, consider your ceremony venue; a cathedral-length veil that drags behind you isn't ideal for a grassy (or potentially muddy) outdoor setting. And unless you are walking down the long aisle of a grand venue, like Westminster Abbey, a twelve-foot train (or veil for that matter) will look silly taking up the whole aisle. Your train should also be in proportion to your body. A few feet of extra fabric can overwhelm a petite frame.

Here are the types of trains you'll see when dress shopping.

Watteau Attaches to the gown at the shoulders and falls loosely to the hem.

Sweep Also called a "brush," this is the second shortest train, extending back one foot or less after the fabric hits the floor.

Court Extends one foot beyond the sweep train.

Chapel A popular option that extends three and a half to four and a half feet from the waist.

Semi-Cathedral Extends four and a half to five and a half feet from the waist.

Cathedral A formal option that extends six and a half to seven and a half feet from the waist.

Extended Cathedral/Monarch Also known as "royal"; flows to twelve feet (or more) from the waist.

Fabrics Style, cut, texture, drapery, season, and budget are all important factors in determining the best fabric for a wedding gown. The same dress style can look and feel quite different in another fabric, since every fabric will hang a certain way on your body. And, of course, there are price differences, too—pure silk being the most luxurious material.

All the things we think of as "fabric" are actually "fibers" woven together, like cotton, for example. The type of fibers woven into a fabric define its weight, luster, luxuriousness, texture, and cost.

GLOSSARY
hot- vs. cold-weather fabrics

hot-weather fabrics
Chiffon
Charmeuse
Organza

cold-weather fabrics
Brocade
Faux fur
Velvet

all-weather fabrics
Satin
Silk
Tulle
Crepe
Taffeta

trains

WATTEAU

SWEEP

COURT

CHAPEL

SEMI-CATHEDRAL

CATHEDRAL

EXTENDED CATHEDRAL/MONARCH

train types

If your dress doesn't have a detachable train, you'll want to bustle it (gather the train fabric at the back of your dress and secure it with buttons or hooks) after the ceremony so you can move around freely at the reception. As with every other element of your gown, there are different pickup options to choose from.

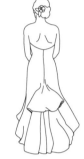

AMERICAN BUSTLE
This style of bustle is made by raising and securing pieces of the outside of the train to the waistline of the gown.

PICKUP BUSTLE
This simple style of bustle requires the least amount of buttons (sometimes just one) and matching eyelets to create a little lift to your gown's train.

FRENCH BUSTLE
This unique bustle is created by tying a series of numbered or coordinated ribbons underneath the gown's train. On the outside, it looks like an understated fold.

TUFTED BUSTLE
This type is ideal for a gown that already has a series of pickups or tufts on the train. A seamstress can easily create more tufts to blend and shorten the train to floor-length.

SYNTHETICS Synthetics are man-made fibers that are typically stronger, more budget-friendly, and less wrinkle-prone than natural fibers. Because it's a more durable fiber, many wedding gowns are made of silk woven with synthetics. Synthetics like polyester, rayon, nylon, and acetate can come in stark white, whereas natural fibers like pure silk cannot be bleached that white.

BLENDS Don't be turned off by the words "polyester" and "nylon"—even the top dress designers will use a blend of natural and synthetic fibers to help strengthen the fabric without sacrificing the look. Blends often look and feel just like pure silk—so much so that most people can't tell the difference. In fact, a high-quality blend will look more luxurious than a low-quality silk. That said, quality also counts when it comes to synthetics. Cheap synthetics will be obvious. It's the types of fibers that make up a fabric that affect its price. For example, duchesse satin is made of a blend of silk and rayon fibers, so it's less expensive than a satin dress made of 100 percent pure silk.

POPULAR WEDDING-GOWN FABRICS

Brocade Jacquard-woven fabric with raised designs, typically a floral pattern. A popular fall and winter fabric.

Charmeuse Lightweight, semi-lustrous, satinlike fabric. Often used in slinky gowns.

Chiffon Delicate, sheer, and transparent, with a soft finish. Popular for overskirts, sheer sleeves, and wraps. Works well with goddesslike gowns, too.

Duchesse Satin A heavy fabric with a gorgeous sheen, duchesse satin holds weight well because of its density, so it's often used for formal classic ball gowns with full skirts, as well as structured bodices.

Organza Crisp and sheer like chiffon, but with a stiffer texture. It has an effect similar to tulle but is more flowy. It's popular for skirts, sleeves, and bodice or back overlays.

Gazar A loosely woven fabric with a low luster that looks like a thicker version of organza; often blended with silk to soften it, so you may hear the term "silk gazar."

Satin A smooth fabric with a lustrous face and a dull back that is typically heavy but can come in different weights. There's some satin on just about every wedding dress, and popular types include silk-faced satin and duchesse satin.

Shantung This lightweight fabric has a rough, slubbed texture running through it; it is semilustrous and gets its name from the area in China where it was originally woven.

Dupioni A heavier version of shantung.

Taffeta Crisp and smooth, with a slight rib. You probably remember it best from high school prom dresses and for the sound it makes when you walk. It's not used as often on wedding dresses as it once was but it's a good lightweight material for ball gowns.

Tulle Delicate netting of silk, nylon, or rayon. It's used primarily for skirts (think ballerina tutus), overlays, illusion sleeves and necklines, veils, and more.

Velvet Thick fabric with a soft finish that's sometimes used for details at sleeve cuffs, on bodices, even occasionally for the dress itself; primarily used for winter wedding dresses.

Crepe Medium-weight, light fabric with a crinkled look; has a similar drape to charmeuse.

Faille Raised ribbing and low shine with a stiffer, middle-of-the-road weight.

Mikado A heavier fabric with medium shine; it's commonly used to make gowns with lots of pleating and layers.

EMBELLISHMENTS Silks and satins are just, well, silks and satins without the intricate embellishments that turn them into works of art. Here are a few of the most popular kinds of accents that can be a part of your masterpiece.

Appliqués Fabric elements like flowers, ribbons, or cutouts stitched or embroidered onto a gown; sometimes raised

Beading Pieces of glass, crystal, gems, or other material sewn onto lace or fabric

Border Trim Braided, ribboned, ruffled, or scalloped edging that provides a decorative effect

Bows Used in various lengths and sizes, from one giant butterfly bow to a tiny shoestring tie

Edging A narrow, decorative border of lace, embroidery, braid, or ribbon used as trim; can also be braided, ribboned, ruffled, or scalloped

Embroidery Fancy needlework patterns of various fine threads done by hand or machine

Fringe Ornamental trim consisting of loose strands of thread or beads fastened to a band

Insert A piece of fabric, usually of contrasting texture, inserted between pieces of the gown's main fabric

Keyhole A wedge- or keyhole-shaped cutout in the center of a high, round neckline

Laser Cutouts Clean-edged, intricate patterns cut into fabric via a laser

Overlay A piece of fabric, usually sheer, layered on top of the main fabric of a garment

Quilting A sandwich of two layers of fabric and batting, which is then stitched in a pattern; offers subtle surface interest

INSIDE SCOOP
additional dress considerations

Factor an extra $200–500 for the following into your dress budget, depending on the scope of the alterations you need and whether your salon or seamstress includes cleaning and pressing and if you need the gown shipped.

Alterations

Shipping/delivery

Pressing/steaming

Cleaning

If you need to ship your gown, ask the bridal salon to do it—it's worth the extra expense to ensure it arrives safely and wrinkle- and stain-free. If you are traveling with your gown, we always recommend keeping it with you (and avoid the risk of having it end up in a different part of the world than you). Place your dress into a hanging garment bag, then put it into the dress box (the salon or your seamstress can give you one). As soon as you arrive at your destination, hang your dress in an area where there's lots of space and it won't touch the floor, and use a portable steamer to get out any wrinkles.

Ruching Fabric that is gathered and pleated

Sequins Tiny, shiny, iridescent plastic disks sewn into place on a gown to add twinkle

Paillettes Larger versions of sequins, these shiny or matte plastic disks are sewn at one end to the gown to provide movement

COLOR There's no other tradition as synonymous with marriage as the white wedding gown. But white is never just white—there are varying shades to choose from. What's important is choosing the shade of white that looks best on you. The easiest formula to follow: The darker your skin tone, the brighter the white you can wear well.

Stark white The brightest, crispest white you can get. This whitest white is best achieved with synthetic fabrics (satins, taffetas, polyester blends). Looks stunning against dark skin. Fair-skinned beauties should stay far away—it'll wash you out.

Natural white Also called "silk white" or "diamond white," this is the whitest white for natural fibers—a shade off stark white. It looks pretty much the same in photos but is much more flattering to most skin tones (especially skin with yellow undertones).

Ivory Also referred to as "eggshell" or "candlelight"; some ivory dresses have yellow undertones, making them look creamy, while others are just a "quiet" white. Fairer skin tones and women with pink undertones in their skin look best in yellow-ivories.

Champagne Has golden undertones but looks nearly white in photos, so it's great for dark complexions or yellow/olive undertones.

Other colors There's no rule that says you must wear white at all. In recent seasons, designers have created dresses in soft shades of lavender, rose, even blue, or with color in the details: embroidery, lace, bands of satin. If your complexion gets totally washed out by white—no matter what shade—send up the white flag and try a color.

THE SEARCH

Now that you're so well-versed in bridalspeak, you're ready to go out and use it. Be prepared to shop early—nine to twelve months before the wedding. Most wedding dresses are custom-made, which means they need to be ordered well in advance so the manufacturer or designer has time to create the dress (it can take six to eight months, though some designers can do it in less) and you have time for multiple fittings.

Where to shop Get a feel for what's out there by asking married friends where they had luck and finding the local stores that carry the dresses you loved online and in magazines. Then, call the salons to make appointments—you can't always just walk in.

Make appointments for evenings or weekdays, when the salon won't be as crowded, so you'll get more one-on-one attention. Also, ask the price range of the dresses in the store (most won't post them on their websites) so you aren't surprised. Where to start shopping? The following are your options for acquiring the dress of all dresses.

BRIDAL SALONS These independent stores sell made-to-order, designer wedding dresses and are the most traditional places to shop. They'll carry the collections of anywhere from ten to seventy different designers. You can expect full service (a salesperson well versed in the world of wedding gowns helping you), and your dress is going to be custom-ordered and altered to fit you. You also can buy bridal accessories such as veils and headpieces at most salons, too. A salon is a good place to try on a lot of dresses and get some expert feedback on what looks best on you.

TRUNK SHOWS Trunk shows are special events at bridal salons when a specific designer (or a representative of a bridal line) brings his

---

INSIDE SCOOP

twice as nice

Sometimes finding the right wedding dress can be double the trouble.

dressing for two

If you're expecting, try to find a bridal salon that will be able to work with you and your timeline. Luckily, there are tons of maternity options available these days. But if you don't find something you like, wait until the date gets closer and then find a dress off the rack. (Since you won't know what your exact measurements will be by the time the wedding rolls around, a custom-order gown is a risky bet.) If you don't like any of the maternity styles you see, opt for an Empire-waist dress.

dressing for dancing

Dying to wear a big frothy ball gown, but still want to be able to tear up the dance floor at your reception? Lots of brides are choosing to wear two wedding dresses—first, a more elaborate gown for their ceremony, pictures, and first dance, and then a shorter, more low-key frock for the dance-party portion of the reception. Others just can't decide between two (or more!) dresses and want to show off a few different looks throughout the evening. If you're into the idea of wearing more than one wedding dress, just factor that into your dress budget.

or her entire latest collection for brides to try on. The advantages: You get to see every dress in the line of a designer you really like, not just the styles that one store has chosen to sell. And you may get the thrill of style or fit advice from the designers themselves!

DESIGNER BOUTIQUES Small, elegant stores that show the collection of a single designer—their own! They're mostly found in top cities and are generally on the highest end price-wise.

BRIDAL CHAINS These stores manufacture, import, and sell their own private-label gowns in many stores across the country. The style selection may be more limited than in stores that carry a wide range of different designers and their visions. Due to the mass manufacturing, prices will most likely be lower. But the quality of service for the bride may be somewhat lower, as well, meaning you may not get as much individual attention.

FASHION RETAILERS   A few nontraditional bridal brands like J.Crew and Ann Taylor sell small bridal collections in stores, catalogs, or online. Their prices can be very reasonable, and some even sell accessories like veils and shoes, as well as having on-site experts to help you select your dress and handle all fittings. But your customization options are typically very limited. While gowns fit true to size and you can get a gown within a week and make quick exchanges and returns, make sure to purchase it at least three months in advance, so you have time for alterations—a process that is a lot harder than it sounds, particularly with beading, embroidery, and lace.

CUSTOM COUTURE Can't seem to find the dream dress you see in your head in any store, anywhere? Get yourself a couture designer or highly skilled seamstress and have her create your vision. Show her pictures of dresses with features you like (sleeves, waistline, etc.). She'll probably create a "test" dress in muslin first, so you'll be able to see what it will look like. You pay for the material, which you can pick out yourself or have her buy for you. The design and fabric fee can vary—a simpler design will obviously cost you less than a complicated one.

SAMPLE SALES Sample sales are events at stores, online, or in warehouses where the "sample" inventory—the dresses used for brides to try on—is sold. Some stores have sample dresses in an array of sizes, but the typical sample sizes are 6, 8, and 10. (Remember: Wedding dresses run small, so if your regular dress size is between a 2 and an 8, you may be in luck.) The dresses may not be perfect, but you can get a great price and then put some of the savings toward a good dry-cleaning and alterations.

VINTAGE Whether you're wearing your mom's dress or you've found a gorgeous fifties ball gown in a consignment store, wearing an old dress often means restoration is in order. Maybe the dress needs updating or a little brightening and mending. Take it to someone who specializes in restoring old wedding gowns. If the fabric is torn or weakened from moisture or mildew, you might be out of luck. If the dress is made of polyester, though, you're probably okay—it's the easiest material to restore. (Silk is one of the most difficult.) You can also update the dress by getting it altered to fit differently, putting on new sleeves, cutting it short, or adding beading or other appliqués.

E-COMMERCE SITES There are hundreds of websites selling wedding dresses, many professing to be direct from the same manufacturers of the big brand names. Beware: Many of these businesses are counterfeit. If you do find a dress you're dying to buy online, check the actual designer's website for a list of authorized retailers (or call the 800 number of the designer) to be sure that the website is, in fact, an authorized seller.

Also, keep in mind that what you see online may not be what you get—in person, fabric may feel cheap, quality may be poor (check the stitching), and color can be off by more than several shades.

INSIDE SCOOP

salon speak

Here are some of the odd things you might hear while trying on dresses—and what they mean.

"Let's get your hollow-to-hem measurement"
She wants to see how long your dress should be. The "hollow" is the little divot, or dimple, at the base of the front of your neck. She's planning to measure from just below that to where you want the finished hem of your dress to fall.

"This can probably be let out"
If the dress is a bit snug, the idea here is to make it bigger by using the fabric from the seams. Get it? You "let" the fabric "out" of the seams.

"Let's add a modesty panel"
A modesty panel is a swatch of fabric (usually made from the same fabric as the bodice of your gown) that's sewn into the bustline of a particularly revealing gown. It's a nice way for the salesperson or seamstress to let you know that you're showing a bit too much cleavage.

WAREHOUSES Inside these sometimes huge, more often cramped, outlets are row upon row of racks of wedding gowns you buy "as is" and take elsewhere for alterations. Some are top designers' past designs or samples that have had their run in the salons; others are designed by lesser-known companies whose names you may not recognize. We must warn you: Dream dresses are sometimes few and far between, and prices aren't always as heavily discounted as you might expect.

RENTAL SHOPS Maybe the logic of buying a multi-thousand-dollar dress to wear for one day is lost on you. In that case, it may make more sense to rent. Some shops may even be willing to order a brand-new dress for you to rent. You won't have to worry about dry-cleaning or storing the dress after the wedding. But keep in mind: You will be limited in terms of alterations—while you can have it fitted, you're typically limited to temporary alterations that can be undone (in other words, no cutting away extra fabric), so you won't be able to alter it to fit perfectly or make any other changes to the dress design, like removing sleeves or embellishments.

The shopping trip
At some salons and shops, you'll be able to look through the sample dresses and choose what you like. At others, it's "closed stock"—you don't get to see all the dresses, only the ones the salesperson brings you. So bring all your favorite dress photos with you to help guide the store in making selections for you.

At a bridal salon, a specific salesperson (sometimes called a "bridal consultant") will be assigned to help you. You will work with this person every time you come into the store and after you buy the dress (for alterations, etc.). A good salesperson will ask you questions about the

CHECKLIST

dress shopping

- ☐ When you're trying on dresses, you want to get an idea of how the entire package will look on you. This means bringing along some accessories.

- ☐ A strapless bra or bustier (for trying on strapless gowns or those with corset-style bodices)

- ☐ Heels (the same height as the pair you want to wear on your wedding day)

- ☐ Control-top pantyhose or a slimmer like Spanx (particularly if you'll be trying on sheaths)

CHECKLIST

the right fit

Here are some things to consider during your dress fittings.

☐ Do I like the way the material falls?

☐ Do I like the way it fits in the bust? Does it feel like I'll fall out?

☐ Is there any obvious puckering, bunching, or bulging?

☐ Does everything seem well sewn?

☐ Can I move comfortably? [Walk around the salon to make sure.]

☐ Does everything stay in place? Does it feel like it will stay up? Even when I dance?

☐ Is there anything poking into me?

☐ Is it the right length for my shoes?

type of wedding you're having (that is, style and formality), how you envision yourself looking, and what kinds of dresses you're drawn to. She also will check you out and decide for herself what kinds of dresses will flatter your body type, height, and weight. Then she'll bring you dresses to try on.

EXPLORING YOUR OPTIONS Though it's essential to have a vision of your dream dress, keep an open mind. Try on all different kinds of dresses—and then decide what shape and style you look best in. If the salesperson brings you something she says you must try, just try it, even if you detest the way it looks on the hanger. We know many brides who ended up falling in love with and walking down the aisle in a dress the salesperson persuaded them to try on.

No matter how much you love a dress, always sleep on it before you place your order. (And be sure to check off the points outlined in "Questions to Ask Before Buying a Dress," page 239.) Since dresses are custom-made, most salons put a no-return policy into their contracts. Even if you can get some money back, it probably won't be more than 50 percent of the total cost. So you should be absolutely sure that this is the one for you before taking the plunge and handing over your credit card.

The perfect fit When you're ready to order your dress, the store

will take your measurements—bust, waist, and hips, as well as some odder measurements, like hollow-to-hem (collarbone to the lowest part of the dress's hem). They use these measurements to calculate your size for that particular dress, or they send them to the couture designer if each piece is custom-assembled.

JUST YOUR (WEDDING-DRESS) SIZE For some insane reason, wedding dresses run small—which means you'll probably need to order a size or two larger than your regular dress size. Resist the urge to order a smaller size than the salesperson recommends because you plan to lose weight before the wedding. If you do lose weight, it's much easier to tailor the dress to your slimmer shape than it is to add fabric because you didn't reach your weight-loss goals—not to mention easier on your ego.

DRESS FITTINGS Every wedding dress needs alterations. Alterations can be as simple as taking in the waist a bit and hemming the dress, shortening the sleeves, taking in the bodice, or even adding beading or lace. Most bridal salons do alterations in-house, but if the store doesn't do its own alterations, chances are the salesperson you've been working with can recommend a good seamstress. Bring your wedding-day undergarments and shoes to all your fittings—a simple bra switch or change in heel height can cause your dress to fit very differently.

You'll probably have at least two or three fittings, though more may be necessary. You'll want to do your first fitting six weeks before the wedding and your second one a month before. The third and final fitting typically takes place one or two weeks before the wedding day

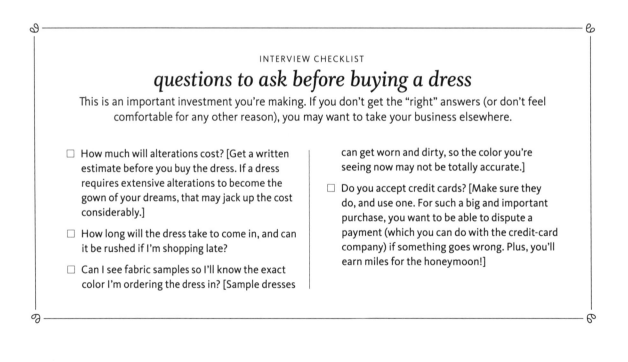

INTERVIEW CHECKLIST
questions to ask before buying a dress
This is an important investment you're making. If you don't get the "right" answers (or don't feel comfortable for any other reason), you may want to take your business elsewhere.

☐ How much will alterations cost? [Get a written estimate before you buy the dress. If a dress requires extensive alterations to become the gown of your dreams, that may jack up the cost considerably.]

☐ How long will the dress take to come in, and can it be rushed if I'm shopping late?

☐ Can I see fabric samples so I'll know the exact color I'm ordering the dress in? [Sample dresses can get worn and dirty, so the color you're seeing now may not be totally accurate.]

☐ Do you accept credit cards? [Make sure they do, and use one. For such a big and important purchase, you want to be able to dispute a payment (which you can do with the credit-card company) if something goes wrong. Plus, you'll earn miles for the honeymoon!]

INSIDE SCOOP
quality considerations

SIGNS OF A HIGH-QUALITY DRESS

Seams: even, level, straight, and invisible

Beading, appliqués, and other add-ons: sewn on, not glued

Lining: completely lined underneath with no unfinished seams

Zippers (if any): hidden

Fabric: not too shiny; comfortable; not itchy or coarse; feels substantial

Hem: scalloped, not stitched across; ball gown hems should be lined with horsehair

Buttons: buttonholes are finished and hand-bound; buttons are discreet

Corset: built-in and boned

when you pick up your gown and try it on one final time to adjust for any last-minute weight fluctuations.

During the fittings, speak up if you see something you don't like. Now is your chance. If there's a problem, continue to schedule fittings until you're completely satisfied. When the day of your final fitting arrives, ask your mom and maid of honor to come along so they can learn how to bustle your dress and help you get dressed. Also, ask how to banish last-minute wrinkles (can you use an iron, and on what setting? What about a steamer?) and what to do if you spill (any product you should or shouldn't use?).

THE FINISHING TOUCHES

A wedding dress by its very nature is special, but that doesn't mean you shouldn't accessorize. From the top of your head to the tips of your toes, there are plenty of extras that will take your look to the next level: your jewelry, veil, and headpiece; the right lingerie; and the perfect shoes.

veils

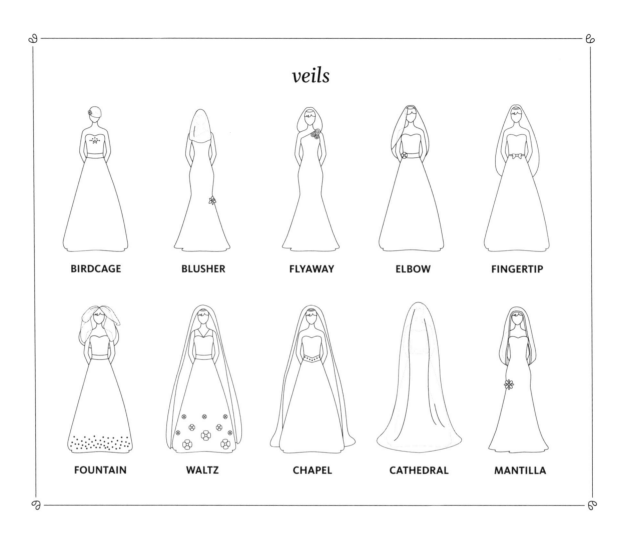

BIRDCAGE   BLUSHER   FLYAWAY   ELBOW   FINGERTIP

FOUNTAIN   WALTZ   CHAPEL   CATHEDRAL   MANTILLA

Veils and headpieces
Whether you wear your hair down and flowing or in a formal updo, you'll want a final detail to tie your whole look together. Some dresses are made with matching headpieces, which can make it easy for you—your bridal salon may even alter a headpiece if it doesn't sit quite right on you. If you've already found a headpiece or are wearing your mom's veil, bring it with you to your fittings.

VEIL VARIETIES Veils are typically worn for the ceremony and sometimes the first dance but are taken off before dinner and dancing (though if you want to keep it on the whole time, feel free). Veils are usually made of tulle or organza and can be plain, embellished with lace, sprinkled with crystals, or bordered with satin. There are quite a few styles to choose from, too.

Birdcage A short style that delicately covers and frames the face and is most often seen in a wide net.

Blusher If you're planning to wear a veil over your face when you walk down the aisle, this shorter veil is the piece that the groom typically turns back over the headpiece when he kisses the bride. Often it's attached to a longer veil or a hat.

Flyaway Multiple layers of veiling that brush the shoulders. Considered less formal.

Elbow Extends twenty-five inches in length to your elbow.

Fingertip Several layers of veiling that extend to the fingertips. This is probably the most popular veil length and works great with ball gowns.

Fountain A veil gathered at the crown of the head that cascades over the shoulders to form a "fountain" shape. Usually shoulder or elbow length.

Waltz A veil that falls somewhere between the knee and the ankle.

Chapel A formal style that extends to the floor; it falls two and a half yards from the headpiece.

Cathedral One of the most formal veils available, it falls three and a half yards from the headpiece.

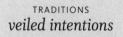

EXPERT ADVICE
framing your face
As with your dress, choosing a veil that will complement your (face) shape is key.

a diamond- or oval-shaped face
Congratulations! You're perfectly symmetrical, so any style will flatter.

a round, full face
Opt for a veil that falls along the sides of the face to help narrow it.

a square jawline
A longer veil will work better than a short, wide one.

an oblong face
Complement a long, oval face with a bit of width. Opt for a fountain veil paired with a wide tiara, wreath, or bun wrap.

a heart-shaped or triangular face
You'll want to add width at the jawline. Since most veils will be too full for you, the best choice is a backpiece (see "Other Headpieces," left), where the width shows up behind the neckline.

a rectangular face
Don't be afraid to try more voluminous veils—the poufy quality will make your face look more symmetrical.

ASK CARLEY
**RING
PLACEMENT**

**Should I take off my
engagement ring for the
ceremony or should my
fiancé put the band on
top of my ring?**
Traditionally, your
wedding band should be
placed first on your ring
finger, "closest to your
heart." So rather than
fumbling at the altar to
make the switch, stow
your engagement ring in
a safe place or switch it
over to your right hand
before you walk down
the aisle. On the way to
the reception, move it
back to its rightful place,
above the wedding band
on your left ring finger.

Mantilla A Spanish-inspired lace veil that's worn without a headpiece; it's draped right over the head with a pretty lace border around the face.

OTHER HEADPIECES Hair ornaments come in a variety of styles and bring anything from a little sparkle to a dramatic focal point to your outfit. Some headpieces look better with long hair, while some work better with short hair.

Headbands These look great with any hairstyle and are perfect for prettily pulling your hair away from your face so everyone can see that bridal glow.

Tiaras Though associated with royalty, today's tiaras are more like 3-D headbands than queenly crowns. Crystals or rhinestones are always popular, but beads, jewel-toned stones, or even metal fashioned into different shapes can give a tiara a more modern look.

Combs Perfect for embellishing an updo, combs can be decorated with rhinestones, lace, embroidered appliqués, pearls, crystals, silk flowers, even sequins.

Backpieces These embellished clips or combs sit at the back or crown of the head, where they can be attached to a veil. Backpieces work best for those with shoulder-length hair or longer.

Jeweled Barrettes Pull long hair back to one side with a pretty barrette just over the ear.

Fascinators Made famous in 2011 during the royal wedding of Kate Middleton and Prince William, a small hat embellished with feathers or ribbons can be a dramatic finishing touch.

Hairpins Hairpins are great for the bride who just wants a touch of sparkle in her hair. These jewels are attached to bobby pins. The pins are then either dotted throughout the hair in an updo, placed along the crown of the head, or nestled behind the ear.

Floral Headpiece Fresh blossoms or silk flowers on a comb—tucked behind the ear, into a chignon, or into a formal updo—is a great look that can go from the ballroom to the backyard. If you opt for fresh blooms, check with your florist before choosing a flower, as some will hold up better than others during a long day out of water.

Wreaths No longer just for brides channeling their inner hippies, wreaths made of flowers and greenery have a romantic vibe.

Jewelry

Your wedding ring isn't the only piece of jewelry you'll need to worry about on your wedding day. From earrings and a bracelet to a gorgeous necklace, a few well-placed baubles can make all the difference in the world and complete your look. The great thing about wedding-day jewelry: You don't need to wear a lot to make a big impression.

Choose pieces that complement the embellishments and color of your gown for a pulled-together look. First, let the dress's embroidery and beading dictate your jewelry choices. Silver details look best with silver-tone jewelry, gold with gold, and so on. If your gown is unembellished, match your jewels to its hue. For bright-white gowns, choose pearl or platinum jewelry—gold may clash with this shade. For natural-white gowns, gold and silver and rose gold and pearl . . . pretty much anything works. For ivory gowns, gold jewelry is the way to go— it's the best way to highlight the creamy tint of the fabric.

EARRINGS Your earring decision will be largely based on your hairstyle. If you're planning on leaving your hair down and over your

Erin & Rahim
MAY 28
NEW YORK, NY

Erin and Rahim took a page out of an Edith Wharton novel to create an elegant Old New York affair using creams, whites, and blush for their palette. In keeping with the day's vibe and the formal private club setting, the bride wore a dramatic ivory silk organza ball gown covered with sculpted silk flowers and finished it off with a cathedral-length veil and a large bouquet of white roses. The groom and his groomsmen kept it classic in black tuxes.

ASK CARLEY
GLOVE HANDLING

I want to wear gloves during the ceremony, but I'm not sure what I'm supposed to do when we exchange rings. Here's what you do: Carefully unstitch the seam of the ring finger on the left glove so you have a small opening. During the ring swap, slip your finger out, and once the wedding band is in place, slip it back in—no need to take the gloves on and off! You could take the glove off and hand it to your honor attendant during the exchange, too, but if the gloves are long, that solution could leave you fumbling at the altar, so practice beforehand. (And since it would probably be too much trouble to put it back on again at that point, prepare to be asymmetrical for the rest of the ceremony.) Also, take gloves off while shaking hands in the receiving line and while eating and drinking during the reception (you'll end up wearing them mostly for the ceremony and formal photographs).

ears, there's no reason to go for the big earrings—elegant studs or small drops will do. If you intend to wear your hair up, putting your neck center stage, you'll need something with a little more zing, like a gorgeous pair of drop or chandelier earrings.

While you can certainly invest in a special pair for your wedding, you can also borrow some heirloom stunners from Mom or Grandma (bonus: That takes care of your something borrowed), or go with costume jewelry. Above all, choose earrings that are comfortable—the last thing you want to deal with on your wedding day is that nagging pulling feeling and sore earlobes.

NECKLACE If your dress is already very ornate, adding a necklace might look too busy. Avoid designs that too closely mimic the shape or embellishments of your gown; instead, choose a necklace that complements them. Here are some guidelines to help you match your necklace to your dress.

Halter Dress Your best bet is a princess-length necklace, which should fall just below the throat. Keep it simple so your bustline doesn't look cluttered. A pendant charm also works nicely with halter necklines.

Sweetheart or Strapless Dress Choose a piece that falls higher than the dip in your neckline so your gorgeous necklace doesn't get stuck in your cleavage. A simple choker is always a safe choice. One with ornate details will really stand out, while something more streamlined will show off your décolletage with minimal decoration. Or show off your style with a statement piece.

Bateau Neck If the neckline is higher, either choose a piece that's smaller, like a single stone or a thin chain, or skip the necklace altogether. Another good choice: A matinee-length necklace (which falls at the top of the bust) will add flair to a gown that shows less skin.

Scoop Neck Try an elegant two-strand necklace and add a pair of cluster earrings for a hint of shine that won't look too busy or too simple.

One-Shoulder Gown Choose an equally modern necklace like an opera-length or solid chain.

BRACELETS A fabulous bracelet can tie your whole look together with just a flick of the wrist (pun intended). If you're wearing a statement necklace, slip on only a small bracelet or a simple chain. Or for a bolder look, a thicker cuff or a set of delicate bangles is the perfect touch. (Just remove any jingly wrist wear for the ceremony.)

Shoes

Of course you want a gorgeous pair of wedding-day shoes, but you also want them to feel good on your feet. You'll be standing for long periods of time, and the last thing you want while saying your vows or performing your first dance is to be in excruciating pain. Lots of shoes feel comfortable when you try them on in the store, but remember that you'll be wearing them for hours on your actual wedding day. We highly recommend investing in high-quality shoes for this occasion.

For maximum comfort, consider the height of the heel, the type of straps, and the material. If you opt for heels, don't go too high; two inches is enough. You should also give yourself plenty of time to break in your shoes. Wear them around the house for a couple of weeks before the wedding. Be sure to note areas that are prone to blisters, and wear cushions or moleskin there on your wedding day. You can also provide extra padding under the ball of your foot by buying insoles made specifically for high heels.

Undergarments

What you wear under the dress is just as important to looking good and feeling great as the gown itself. Even when you're just going in for your fittings, you want to make sure you have the right foundation.

THE BRA The bras and bustiers sold at bridal boutiques, while sometimes pricey, have wedding-dress-specific details that are worth investing in, such as boning, illusion backs, and extra shapers built in. Make comfort—not looks—your priority in this department. It's smart to begin by looking at the brand you usually wear for the correct style and type of support—you're already used to how that brand fits you. Take home a handful of styles and try them on when you attend your first fitting. Move around a bit, do some dance moves—test the bra for comfort and to make sure it stays hidden.

If your dress has a low- or wide-cut neckline or skinny little straps, you'll want a strapless bra. The most versatile style is one with removable straps, which will also let you create a crisscross or halter back on other occasions. For a completely backless dress, there's something called a "backless bra" that hooks at the waist. Or consider stickies—flesh-colored tape—or supports that you stick right to your skin. While they don't offer the same lift as a bra (which means they're probably not a good choice if you're full chested), you can dance assured that you have no nipples or straps showing.

SLIMMERS While old-fashioned girdles went out of style after your mother's wedding, a number of contemporary slimming undergarments

ASK CARLEY
SAME-SEX WEDDING WEAR

My fiancée and I couldn't be more excited about our wedding, but we both want to wear a wedding dress. Will it look weird or like we're matching?

Just as we say to any bride or groom, wear whatever you like! Some lesbian couples walk down the aisle in traditional wedding gowns and veils, complete with bridal bouquets, and some choose "tuxedas" (tuxedos designed for women). Men might choose traditional formalwear or nice suits purchased especially for the occasion. You can wear identical ensembles or choose separate outfits that complement your individual styles. The bottom line: Whatever style you choose, make it your own.

そ

that use Lycra or spandex rather than stiff stays or ancient whalebone are available. If you plan to use a slimmer, make sure to take it with you to your fittings—a body-support garment will give a slightly different shape than just sucking in your gut. And consider wearing it before your wedding day for practice. You want to make sure this is a type of support garment that you can wear for the duration.

UNDERWEAR Choose panties or a thong that offers comfort over sex appeal. (There's just no way to discreetly rearrange a wedgie through a wedding dress!) If your dress has an unusually slinky cut, you may want to go with a pantyhose-underwear combo so you don't see any panty lines.

HOSE These days, hose are certainly not required, and in some circles, they're considered dated. If you're wearing peep toes or sandals, or you just don't want to deal with pantyhose runs, skip them. If you do wear hose, buy extra in case yours run. Also, make sure there are no lines visible through your dress and that the color matches your skin tone. And if you think you might kick off your heels as the evening progresses, you might want to go with knee-highs that you can slide off along with your shoes.

The rest of the gear You're not done quite yet! Don't forget these final finishing touches.

CLUTCH A purse is certainly not a necessity, but it's a great way to store emergency items like mints, lipstick, tissues, and your cell. A simple evening clutch in a metallic, jeweled, or neutral hue will work best.

GLOVES Gloves are a Victorian artifact that had a resurgence in the thirties and forties, when they were worn for just about every formal occasion. Gloves add a vintage vibe to your outfit, and they come in all kinds of fabrics: silk, satin, lace, eyelet, knit, even kid leather. Wear wrist-length gloves with short-sleeved gowns, elbow-length with cap-sleeve gowns, and over-the-elbow gloves with strapless gowns. If you're wearing a long-sleeved dress, skip them.

WRAPS If you're getting married in fall or winter, or at a house of worship that requires covered shoulders, that still doesn't mean you have to wear a dress with sleeves (though we do love the look of illusion sleeves). A simple shrug or bolero can help keep you warm and covered. A bolero (a cropped jacket) is a great option for a fall wedding, while a shrug will cover the top of your shoulders without overshadowing your dress. For a wintertime affair, a fur stole adds a glamorous touch.

TRADITIONS

something old, something new . . .

This wedding tradition (old, new, borrowed, blue) is from an old English rhyme. Here's what it means and how to incorporate it all into your look.

something old

The idea is to carry a token of the past into this new phase of your life. Go for: a locket with a childhood photo or your parents' wedding portrait; an antique necklace, bracelet, or pair of heirloom earrings; an inherited book of prayers or poems (read from it during the ceremony); a piece of your security blanket or a family quilt sewn into the hem of your dress.

something new

You are being reborn as a married woman—the idea is to celebrate the novelty. Go for: brand-new lingerie; a sparkly tiara or pair of barrettes; a daring haircut or color (one that you've tested out, of course).

something borrowed

Marriage is about community, both your tight family unit and your wide support circle. Give your community a nod by wearing something that belongs to a loved one. Go for: your mom's or sister's veil; your best friend's earrings; your niece's charm bracelet; gloves borrowed from your grandma.

something blue

The color of fidelity, of course! Go for: blue toenail polish; baby-blue heels; bluebells scattered in your bouquet or tresses; a navy satin purse; sapphire earrings; your new name monogrammed in blue on the inside of your dress.

16

dressing the groom and the guys

TIMELINE

PLANNING

3 months before
Decide: tux, suit, or tails?

Make appointments for you
and your posse to get fitted

1 month before
If you're buying a tux,
go in for a final fitting

Settle on every accessory

1 week before
Buy undergarments
and socks

3–5 days before
Pick up your tux and try
it on to make sure it fits,
and make sure the
groomsmen do, too

The groom's look should complement the bride's dress and reflect the wedding location, time of day, and degree of formality. Still, it's the groom's day to shine, too, so even if he's sporting a classic tuxedo, he should still stand out. Start firming up the groom's look at least three months before the wedding, since his outfit will dictate the groomsmen's attire. To help you figure out what the men will wear, we have included a head-to-toe guide, from what to wear when to how to tie a bow tie to grooming tips.

MEN'S FORMALWEAR 101

Like wedding dresses, formalwear has its own lingo that you and your fiancé will want to get up to speed on. There are also some etiquette rules that will help to inform the groom's day-of attire as well—though the rules are far looser than when your parents got married. The land of men's formalwear is confusing territory for pretty much anyone who's never been a maître d' for a living. To help you make sense of all your wedding fashion choices—and the cryptic tux jargon—here are the key elements you need to know.

Jackets and coats
If you're renting a tux, you'll choose it based on the jacket and wear whichever pants come with it, though you may get to make basic choices (pleated or flat front). But if you're investing in a new tux or suit, you have a lot more options to choose from when it comes to the jacket.

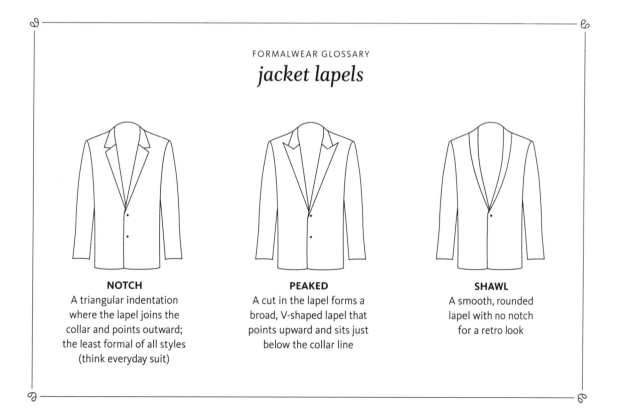

FORMALWEAR GLOSSARY

jacket lapels

NOTCH
A triangular indentation where the lapel joins the collar and points outward; the least formal of all styles (think everyday suit)

PEAKED
A cut in the lapel forms a broad, V-shaped lapel that points upward and sits just below the collar line

SHAWL
A smooth, rounded lapel with no notch for a retro look

jacket styles

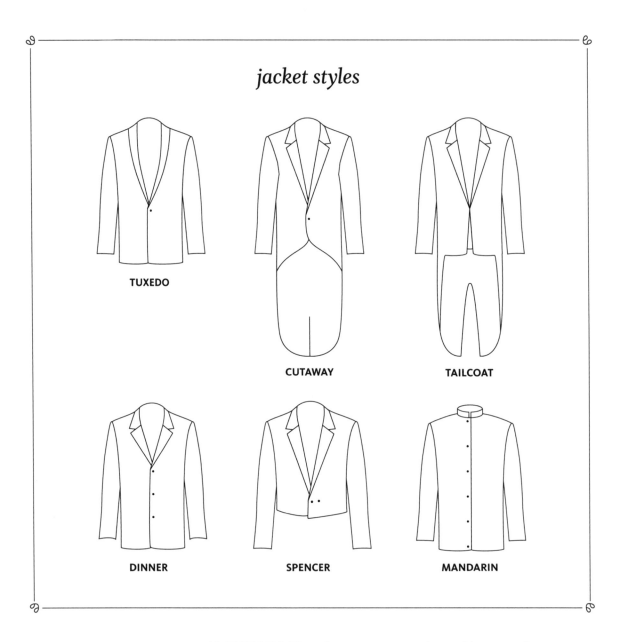

TUXEDO

CUTAWAY

TAILCOAT

DINNER

SPENCER

MANDARIN

JACKET STYLES Jackets are pretty much a wedding must, but you have many styles and colors (white or black, dark gray or light gray) to choose from.

Tuxedo Jacket The basic tux coat can be single-breasted (with a one-to-four-button front) or double-breasted (with a two-to-six-button front), with your choice of three lapels: peaked or shawl (see "Jacket Lapels," page 249).

Stroller Coat A semiformal jacket cut like a tuxedo. It can be black or gray and often has pinstripes.

Cutaway/Morning Coat Also short in front and long in back, it tapers from the waistline button to one broad tail in the back, with a vent. Usually it comes in pinstriped charcoal gray, solid gray, or black and is paired with matching pants.

Tailcoat Short in front and long in back, it tapers from the waist into one or two tails down the back and has a two-to-six-button front. Usually black, but sometimes you see it in white.

Dinner Jacket Tuxedo-cut jacket in white or ivory (think James Bond). You also can get it in other colors or funky fabrics. It's worn with black satin-striped trousers.

Spencer Coat An open coat without buttons, cut right at the waistline. Worn in the evening or daytime, depending on color (black for evening).

Mandarin The Nehru jacket, or Mao, has a stand-up collar with no lapel and must be worn with a mandarin-collar shirt. This combo does not require a tie.

JACKET CUTS Whether you are wearing a suit, tux, or sport coat, you'll want to consider the cut.

Single-Breasted Coat A one-to-four-button-front jacket that can be part of a suit or worn on its own and typically comes in gray or navy blue. This is the most popular style thanks to its slimming effect.

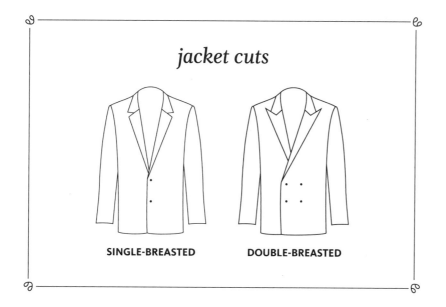

jacket cuts

SINGLE-BREASTED   **DOUBLE-BREASTED**

Double-Breasted Coat A less forgiving cut, this two-to-six-button-front jacket can be part of a suit or worn on its own and typically comes in gray or navy blue. It's worn without a vest or a cummerbund when paired with a tuxedo jacket.

Shirts

White is the traditional shirt color for tuxes and formal suits, but you have more options for a more low-key event. When choosing a shirt, pay special attention to the quality of the cotton. Fine cotton will look dressier than cotton weaves and other fabrics and will also feel more comfortable against your skin. When it comes to shirt styles, there are actually quite a few options to choose from. Start with the front view; then choose the cuffs (see "Shirt Cuffs," below).

The standard stiff-fronted shirt, the aptly named piqué shirt, has a central front panel made of piqué—a thick cotton fabric with a dimpled surface. A dress shirt with pleats, on the other hand, is called, no surprise here, a pleated-front shirt. While these two styles are the traditional formal options, their popularity has waned in favor of plain-front shirts, dress shirts without pleats in the front, which usually come with buttons or holes for studs.

SHIRT COLLARS

At the end of the day, what really matters is the part you see: the collar. This is what separates a good shirt from a basic button-down. The collar should flatter the shape of your face and coordinate with the jacket lapels and any neckwear.

Wing Collar A stand-up collar with downward points. This is the most formal style and the one most often worn with a tuxedo jacket and works well with a bow tie.

Turndown, Lay-Down, or Point Collar Similar to a business-shirt collar, but in a more formal fabric, this collar is a more modern option that works well with a tie.

Spread Similar to a turndown collar but less pointy, it resembles the standard button-front shirt but folds over and around the neck, with a wide division between points in front. The wider collar is a good choice with a Euro tie or a standard necktie with a Windsor knot and is often paired with a morning coat.

Banded or Mandarin Collar Narrow banded stand-up collar without points that is held closed with a button cover (or stud), but not a tie. Stands up around the neck, above the tux buttons.

Crosswick Crosses in front and is fastened with a shiny button.

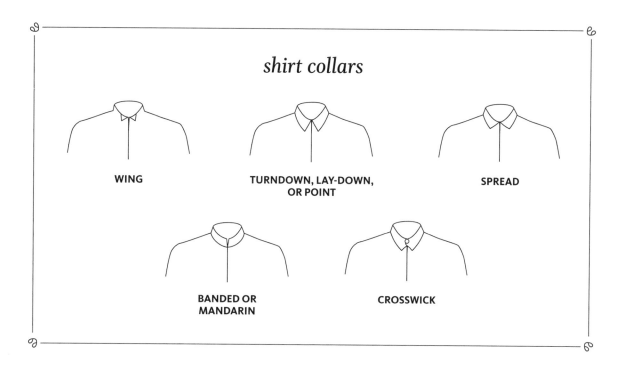

shirt collars

WING

TURNDOWN, LAY-DOWN, OR POINT

SPREAD

BANDED OR MANDARIN

CROSSWICK

Formalwear accessories

The type of formalwear will dictate the type of accessories he'll need. But this is also a place to show some individual style. Whether he's wearing a tux or suit or something more low-key, the accessories are key when it comes to the groom's appearance. Add some personality to the equation by helping your guy choose accessories and shoes that set him apart.

ASCOT A wide, formal, usually patterned scarf looped under the chin and fastened with a tie tack or a stick pin (very British). Generally reserved for ultraformal daytime weddings and worn with a wing collar, a cutaway/morning coat, and striped gray trousers.

NECKTIE A standard tie in formal black or dark gray silk or in a subtle pattern.

EURO TIE A long tie with a square bottom and a thin strap so that it can be worn with both spread-collar and wing-collar shirts.

BOW TIE The traditional neckwear of tuxes, bow ties come in multiple colors (black is the classic pairing with a tux). Wear it with any collar.

BOLO If you're having a Western-themed wedding, live in Santa Fe,

formalwear accessories

ASCOT

NECKTIE

EURO TIE

BOW TIE

BOLO

CUMBERBUND

VEST

WAISTCOAT

or really love John Wayne, try a bolo tie, which usually has a silver or turquoise design at the throat.

CUMMERBUND A pleated sash made of brocade, silk, or satin worn to cover the trouser waistline, with pleats facing up. The color may or may not match your jacket, but it usually matches your tie.

VEST Worn instead of a cummerbund or suspenders under the coat. In black, white, or any other color or pattern, vests are great under a tuxedo or dinner jacket and come in full or backless versions.

WAISTCOAT Like a vest except usually cut lower in front; a more formal look, especially appropriate with a cutaway/morning coat or tailcoat.

CUFF LINKS These hold the sleeves of a dress shirt together at the wrists. Personalize your links—with scrabble letters, rainbow trout (to

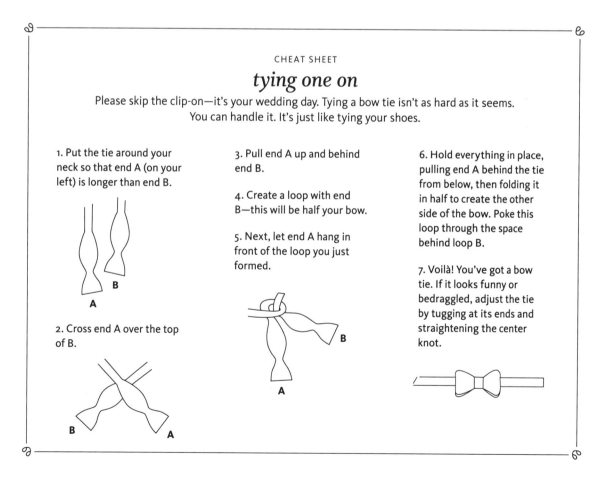

tying one on

Please skip the clip-on—it's your wedding day. Tying a bow tie isn't as hard as it seems.
You can handle it. It's just like tying your shoes.

1. Put the tie around your neck so that end A (on your left) is longer than end B.

2. Cross end A over the top of B.

3. Pull end A up and behind end B.

4. Create a loop with end B—this will be half your bow.

5. Next, let end A hang in front of the loop you just formed.

6. Hold everything in place, pulling end A behind the tie from below, then folding it in half to create the other side of the bow. Poke this loop through the space behind loop B.

7. Voilà! You've got a bow tie. If it looks funny or bedraggled, adjust the tie by tugging at its ends and straightening the center knot.

Depending on the event, here are some ways grooms can stand out:

Wear a different jacket—a tailcoat if the groomsmen are in tuxes, or a white dinner jacket if they're in black.

Switch up the vest/ cummerbund and bow tie color to stand out, while his men match with the bridesmaids.

Wear a different tie that complements your gown.

Sport a military uniform (when applicable).

Switch out the boutonniere for a pocket square or wear a boutonniere different from those of your groomsmen.

Wear colored or striped socks, bright suspenders, or even sneakers instead of dress shoes to stand out from the sea of suits.

---

play up his fly-fishing passion), or a monogram—so that they always remind you of your special day.

OTHER FINISHING TOUCHES Studs, tie tacks, pocket squares, suspenders (note: belts are not worn with tuxes).

SHOES The traditional look is formal black patent-leather shoes, but if you're just not down with the shine, look for matte-finish formal leather shoes or wingtip shoes. If you don't own your own patent pair, you can rent black shoes to go with your tux. The biggest fashion faux pas grooms make? Wearing brown shoes with a black tux or suit. And remember to match your socks to your pants (which should match your shoes).

What to wear when

The groom's attire needs to reflect the occasion. For example, a tux wouldn't be appropriate at a wedding taking place on the sweltering sand in Jamaica. Most of the rules about what kind of formalwear is appropriate have to do with whether you're getting married before or after the sun goes down and how formal or casual the festivities are going to be, as well as the location of your event.

FORMAL DAYTIME Choose gray strollers with ties and vests, cummerbunds, or waistcoats, or formal suits (again, in white or light colors for the summer, darker shades in the winter).

FORMAL EVENING In the evening, formal usually means black tie: The groom and groomsmen wear black tuxedos with white or ivory shirts and black ties (or white or ivory dinner jackets and black tuxedo pants), with cummerbunds or vests.

ULTRAFORMAL DAYTIME The groom and groomsmen traditionally wear cutaway coats with charcoal-colored striped trousers, gray waistcoats (sometimes available with a print), wing-collared shirts, and ascots or striped ties. It's a very dapper look that you're not going to get away with on any other occasion—and your bride (and mom!) will love it, trust us.

ULTRAFORMAL EVENING White tie (also known as "tails full dress") is reserved for the most elaborate evening weddings. The groom and groomsmen wear black tailcoats with white waistcoats or vests, wing-collared shirts, and white bow ties. They also may wear fancy studs and cuff links, and their shoes are black patent leather. (You can skip the top hats and canes.)

SEMIFORMAL DAYTIME The groom and groomsmen wear suits (navy or charcoal are great year-round; reserve khaki or white linen for the warmer seasons) with nice shirts and ties.

SEMIFORMAL EVENING Opt for black tuxedos with bow ties and cummerbunds or vests (or nice dark suits work, too). Their shirts may have wing-tipped or turned-down collars and are either white or ivory to match the bride's gown.

DRESSY CASUAL DAYTIME White or khaki pants and a blue blazer are perfectly acceptable for more laid-back affairs—especially if you're getting married near the water. Or kick it up a notch and opt for a full khaki or linen suit with a light-colored shirt and optional tie. You can also wear a light gray or navy blue suit, but if you do anything dressier, the casual tone of the affair is lost.

DRESSY CASUAL EVENING Skip the tux. Choose a solid-colored suit, maybe navy or charcoal; a white shirt; and a tie.

SHOPPING FOR HIS ATTIRE

The best resource for picking the right style and size of formalwear to match your occasion and personal style? The salesperson who helps you at the formalwear store. Let him in on the time of day you're getting married and how formal the wedding will be (describing where it is and what's in store will tell him all he needs to know). Wherever the groom buys or rents his attire is also the place where the rest of the men in your party will likely order their formalwear and where all the men will get fitted, so you want to choose right.

Where to shop (or rent) Choose a formalwear store that
has updated their inventory regularly since 1986. (If you see powder blue and ruffles, run.) A good formalwear dealer will know how to measure you properly (inseam, waist, jacket size) and give you a fitting in advance of the wedding. The store also can supply you with all the accessories you'll need: bow tie, cummerbund, cuff links, suspenders, even shoes. Finally, all the groomsmen should get their clothing at the same shop, to ensure color and style coordination. If you've got faraway groomsmen, get them to go for a fitting at a store near them (they can try on the tux you've chosen to check out how it fits them) and then send their measurements to you.

the knot NOTE

groom guide
Need help finding a tux or a suitable alternative he'll wear? Find all the latest styles for grooms, plus top retailers and rental shops near you.
TheKnot.com/groom

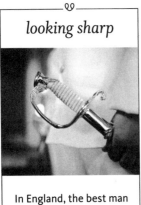
Renting vs. buying

For most grooms, renting a tuxedo will probably suffice. But if you think you'll have reason to wear a tux in the future, it may be worth buying one. Look at it this way: Renting costs about 25 to 30 percent of the price of a new tuxedo and you won't necessarily get the most stylish cut or the style you want. Buying a decent tux will cost you, but if you get invited to a lot of functions (work or play) a tux is a good investment—it will pay for itself after three or four events. And as long as it's a classic style with a notched or shawl collar—and you don't grow a gut—you'll be able to wear it for quite a few years. But if you don't attend many formal events or your weight is constantly in flux, renting is probably the way to go.

Finding the perfect fit

Even the most expensive tux on the rack will look and feel awful if it doesn't fit you right. Comfort is key, especially in a wedding tux—you'll be wearing it for four to eight emotional, fun-filled hours. You should be able to move around easily—do lots of twists, turns, and arm raises when you're trying one on.

Before you sign the rental contract, find out about deposits, alteration fees, and return deadlines. Getting this information ahead of time and distributing it to all your groomsmen will make it easier for them to keep track of their responsibilities.

If you're renting, your tuxedo should be ready for pickup three days before the wedding. Try it on right away to check the fit and make sure it's the right tux (you don't want to surprise your bride with a navy-blue ensemble while your groomsmen show up in black). Because most rentals must be returned to the store the day after the event, make a plan with your best man for him to take your tux back for you.

DRESSING THE REST

The groom's look sets the tone for his side of the aisle. Wait to decide what the rest of the men will wear until after you nail down the groom's look.

The groomsmen

Traditionally, the groomsmen wear attire that's the same or similar to the groom's, but it's up to you. If all or most of the men in your group own tuxes or suits in your chosen color, let them wear what they have, but be specific about the shirts and accessories you'd like them to sport. You may want to consider gifting them matching ties or shirts. Unlike with bridesmaid dresses, these presents can be considered groomsman gifts because they can be worn again.

If you're all renting tuxes, get fitted together about three months in advance. Get the measurements of any groomsmen who can't be there—just make sure they get them done by a professional tailor (no DIY with the tape measure at home). Then reserve all the tuxes and pick a time for you and your men to go and try them on and pick them up at least a few days before the wedding, so no one finds out the morning of the event that his pants are too short or jacket is too small.

The dads

Have both dads join the fitting party if they're up for it and don't have their own tuxes (or haven't bought a new tux since their own wedding). They don't have to exactly match the groomsmen by any means but they should fit the formality of the event. Here's the drill: If the groom and groomsmen are wearing tuxedos, cutaway coats, or tailcoats, the dads should, too—especially if you're asking guests to dress way up. Even if the groomsmen are not going black tie, the dads should feel free to don a tux for the big day (though they shouldn't wear a tuxedo if the groom is in a suit so they don't outshine their son or son-in-law at the wedding). That said, formal suits in appropriate colors (black, navy, or charcoal for evening or winter; navy, brown, or beige for summer or daytime) are appropriate, too. And remember to give each dad a boutonniere to tip guests off as to his special status.

CONTRACT CHECKLIST

formalwear rental shop

If your groom (and the rest of the guys) are renting their attire, make sure they request a letter of agreement that includes the following points.

☐ Name and contact info

☐ The salesperson's name and contact info and company name and address

☐ Your wedding date

☐ A detailed description of the formalwear, including any accessories he's renting like shoes and studs

☐ Size and specific measurements

☐ Alterations list and estimate for each

☐ Number of fittings included in the price (if any)

☐ Total amount

☐ Amount of deposit and date paid

☐ Balance and due date

☐ Details of what will happen if formalwear is damaged

☐ Cancellation and refund policy

tailoring tips

When you're sizing up a tux and getting fitted, here's what to look for.

the jacket

Should fit comfortably at the neck and shoulders and fasten easily. Try standing and sitting with it buttoned. The jacket-sleeve hem should fall at your wrist bone, the bottom hem of your jacket should cover your butt, and the vent shouldn't pull open. If it does, it's too tight. Make sure it hugs your shoulders perfectly—if it's too big, it could create a fold of fabric down your spine.

the shirt

Should fit comfortably at the neck, shoulders, and waist. About one-quarter to one-half inch of cuff should show below the jacket sleeve. The collar should lie flat on the back and sides of your neck without and gaps or bulges.

the vest

Should fit comfortably across your chest with the buttons lining up to the front of your jacket. The bottom should fall slightly over your trouser waistband. Usually, you can adjust the waist with a slide strap for a good fit. Or consider a vest with a full back, so when you take your jacket off during the evening, you're not flashing a strap and the back of your shirt.

the trousers

Should button comfortably and feel good when you sit down. Many styles have adjustable waistbands, or you can opt for suspenders. The hem should break just over the tops of your shoes. Flat-front pants are generally more slimming than their pleated counterparts—less fabric gives the illusion of less weight. Pants should break (or crease horizontally) across the top of the shoes.

The ring bearer's outfit When you ask a potential ring bearer's parents if he can be in the party, you're operating under the assumption that they'll pay for his attire, so bring it up at the beginning. Look for a tiny tux or suit if you're having a black-tie affair. If your style is more casual, there are tons of cute options for the little ones: A lightweight cotton or linen suit, short-alls in a matching hue, or a sailor suit would all work well.

The ring bearer doesn't have to match the groom or groomsmen perfectly—though he can if you can find the mini suit or tux to match. Just give him a bit more color and flair than you would his older counterparts. The most important accessory for this mini party member is the ring pillow—choose one that complements your theme without clashing with his outfit.

17

dressing the girls

TIMELINE

PLANNING

8 months before
Start thinking about
what you want for your
bridesmaids' look

6–8 months before
Decide on your
bridesmaids' dresses and
let them know so they
can order them

2–3 months before
Choose the bridesmaids'
accessories

1–2 months before
Make sure your girls get
their dresses fitted
(if need be)

Bridesmaid dresses these days are nothing like the teal taffeta monstrosities of weddings past. In fact, we think you'll be hard-pressed to find a dress your bridesmaids truly hate. That doesn't mean, however, that we are going to tell you to choose "something they can wear again." Why? Because unless you pick a simple black dress or let them pick their own dresses, they probably won't. Even if they adore the dress you choose, it's still a bridesmaid dress, and trying to find a dress that a group of women, with all different shapes and tastes, will all love to wear again is like trying to find that season's "it" pumps in a size 7 at a sample sale—next to impossible. The point is: Try to choose dresses that make your girls happy and comfortable—and that you like, too—and let that be enough.

DRESSING YOUR MAIDS

You may be shocked to see just how many styles of bridesmaid dresses are available. And no longer do your maids all have to wear the same exact thing if you (and/or they) don't want to. But all those options can make outfitting your girls feel overwhelming, especially if you're trying to keep them all happy (or at least not unhappy).

Key considerations

The quickest way to get labeled a bridezilla? Invite your best friends to be in your bridal party and then turn them into fashion victims by asking them to wear dresses that are less than flattering. Here are the factors to think about before you even start shopping to ensure that they look their best on your wedding day, too.

YOUR DRESS Take your time and decide how you want the bridesmaid dresses to complement your wedding gown. Find a style that evokes the same feel as your dress but still allows you to stand out.

WEARABILITY Be kind—don't ask your friends to purchase a bridesmaid dress they absolutely wouldn't be caught dead in. Think about what your maids will do with the dresses after the wedding. (Little black dresses and classic styles in neutral tones are more likely to be worn again. Pink taffeta gowns? Not so much.)

LENGTH Typically, formal and semiformal weddings call for floor-length, ballerina-length, or tea-length dresses. At an informal or daytime wedding, bridesmaid dresses can be short or long, like the bride's dress. In general, tea- and ballerina-length dresses tend to be the most flattering and party-friendly. The one major rule: Steer clear of thigh-baring minidresses. Not every girl loves her thighs, and conservative members of the audience may gasp.

STYLE From fitted sheaths, A-line styles, and Empire-waist numbers to halter, strapless, and sweetheart necklines, you've got pretty much as many choices when it comes to bridesmaid dress silhouettes as you do for wedding dresses. The key to choosing one for your party: Search for a style that flatters the different sizes and shapes of your bridesmaids. Cramming a tall, voluptuous bridesmaid into the exact same style as a petite, skinny girl would be totally unfair to one or both. A-line skirts and Empire waists tend to look good on all body types, and chiffon and taffeta are the most flattering fabrics. If you're considering strapless dresses or bridesmaid gowns that don't accommodate bras, ask your bridal party if they would be comfortable in such a style before you

---

ASK CARLEY
PAYING FOR WEDDING ATTIRE

Are my bridesmaids supposed to pay for their dresses? What about the groomsmen—do they pay for their tux rentals?
Wedding party members usually pay their own way when it comes to clothing—the women buy their dresses and the men rent their formalwear. (And you should let everyone know about this financial responsibility before they accept the invitation to be in your wedding.) While it would be very generous and obviously appreciated if you two offered to pay for the attendants' dresses and tuxes, it's certainly not mandatory or expected. Just keep your attendants' budgets in mind when choosing their attire and they should be happy.

decide. If you want all your maids to wear the same style, start with the one who is toughest to fit (though you probably shouldn't put it in those terms to her), and work from there. Or for a very popular approach, you can choose the fabric and color and let them decide on the style they feel best in.

COLORS Look for colors you like and think would look good on all of your maids (consider their complexions and hair colors). Brighter colors are generally more universally flattering. Pastel hues might look lovely on girls with fair complexions but can be unbecoming on friends with a darker complexion. Cool palettes like blush and blue work with most skin tones. If you want something more vibrant, jewel tones like raspberry are good options. Just be careful if you're going with green— some shades, like sea green, are really difficult to pull off. Also, think reusable. Dark-colored dresses like navy and black look great on almost every maid and can be worn to formal events later.

BUDGET Remember to think about everyone's financial situation. (A typical price range for bridesmaid dresses is $150 to $400.) If you fall in love with a dress that is a bit over their budgets, consider covering the difference yourself.

MIXING AND MATCHING Traditionally, all the bride's attendants wear the same dress. This works best when all the women have similar body types and coloring—which doesn't happen all that often. If you want to retire the matchy-matchy maids look for a more dynamic lineup, here are some options that will still allow you to keep the overall look cohesive.

Standout Honor Attendants Some brides choose to put their maid of honor in a dress that's slightly different from that of the rest of the bridesmaids, to emphasize her place of honor.

Same Style, Different Colors You might decide to ask your maids to all wear the same style dress but each in a different color—of your choosing or the shade each woman feels she looks best in. You can create a rainbow of jewel tones or pastels this way, or put the attendants in different shades of the same color (purple, lavender, lilac, etc.).

Same Color, Different Styles Most of your attendants are tall and thin, and one is shorter and rounder? Keep in mind that she may need a lot of alterations for her gown to fit her well, so you might want to let her wear a slightly different style that's more flattering to her instead. One designer may have several dresses you like that flatter different body types, all available in the same color and fabric. If you go this

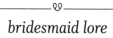

bridesmaid lore

These days, the bride is supposed to stand out, but did you know that back in the day, bridesmaid dresses all used to be identical to the bride's? They dressed just like her to confuse and stave off evil spirits on her wedding day.

route, your maids will match in shade, but each woman can choose the style that looks best on her.

Free-form If you have no control-freak genes whatsoever, consider putting this decision into your bridesmaids' hands completely. They'll probably be grateful (this way, they can control how much they spend, too). Some attendants get thrown for a loop if they don't receive any guidance from the bride, however, so be sure to give them something to go on. Maybe you want everyone to wear a sheath, or something in a shade of pink or black, but beyond that you're comfortable with leaving it up to your maids to choose.

Going shopping

Ideally, you want to start looking for bridesmaid dresses about eight months before the wedding so you can settle on a look and your girls can order their dresses around six months before. It may take a few months for the dresses to come in if they're custom ordered, and you want to be sure your maids have time for alterations and to deal with any problems (wrong color, wrong style) when the dresses arrive.

WHERE TO LOOK Start your search online and by flipping through magazines. Jot down style numbers, save images to your inspiration board, and tear out pages with dresses you like to zero in on three to five of your favorites, so you have an idea of what you want before you start shopping.

Bridal salons almost always carry bridesmaid dresses, as well. Some have separate rooms or even stores solely devoted to bridesmaids. You also can find maids' dresses at bridal warehouses and in special-occasion dress departments at big department stores. Many mass retailers are also getting in on the bridesmaid-dress brigade and are making it easier for your bridesmaids with online ordering.

WHO TO BRING Consider what kind of shopping trip suits the different personalities in your party. You might want to go alone first to see what's out there or take along your honor attendant so she can test-drive dresses you like. Another option: Take the whole gang to the salon and make a group decision—just narrow down your top picks first. Too many opinions will only stress you out.

If not all of your maids live in the same city, or you want to make them feel involved but don't want to spend four hours at the bridal salon debating the options, go to TheKnot.com/bridesmaid dresses to search through thousands of dresses and e-mail the ones you like to all your maids so they can each choose their top picks.

ASK CARLEY
TABOO COLORS

I love the idea of navy bridesmaid dresses, but my groom and his groomsmen will be wearing black tuxes. Will they clash?

Just as you can now wear white after Labor Day if you style it right, wearing black and navy together is one of those fashion rules that's become chic to break. There are a few ways to pull off the look so that your girls and guys walk down the aisle together in style. For the girls: Choose a shade of navy that's closer to black than it is to blue. To do this, hold up a fabric swatch next to both true black and cobalt blue to see which hue looks better. Also, make sure the dress fabric and style match the formality of the tuxedos.

bridesmaid dress shop

Yes, there's typically a contract for the bridesmaid dresses, too. If they are being custom made (which most bridal salon styles are), your maids will not be able to see the dresses before they order them and will be required to pay for the dresses before they are made, so it's really to protect them (and your altar style). Before they order their dresses, make sure the following is included in a written agreement.

- ☐ Designer, style, and style number(s)
- ☐ Color of the dress
- ☐ Delivery date
- ☐ Total cost
- ☐ Date and amount of deposit paid

- ☐ Balance due date and amount
- ☐ Additional fees (alterations, ironing, shipping)
- ☐ Address where the dress will be shipped [if applicable]
- ☐ Refund and cancellation policy

Measuring your maids

Since it's unlikely that all your maids live in the same place, you might be the one collecting their measurements and money for the salon to place the order, or your maid of honor might offer to take care of it for you.

Like your gown, most bridesmaid dresses are made to order, so your attendants will have to get measured. Make sure this is done by a professional seamstress or a good-natured tailor at a favorite department store. As simple as it sounds, you actually need a pro to measure properly. Otherwise, the dresses may require extensive (read: more expensive) alterations. Warn your maids that, like gown sizes, bridesmaid dress sizes run a little small and they're typically ordered using a person's biggest measurements as a guide, so they shouldn't stress out if they end up having to order a gown a size or two larger than normal. Don't let a friend pick a size that's too small. If she plans on losing weight before the wedding, alterations on a dress that is too big shouldn't be a problem. But if she selects a size that ends up being too small, it's likely that she will need to order an entirely new dress or pay for pricey alterations to add fabric. Either way, not fun.

It's best to order all gowns at the same time so that they come from the same dye lot. Otherwise, the hues could vary slightly, even if one person orders from Sally's Dresses in Chicago and the rest order from Sally's Dresses in Miami. The good news: If the bride and bridesmaid dresses are ordered at the same store, you (and/or they) may receive a discount or free alterations, so ask before you order.

Once the gowns arrive in the shop, it's likely that every bridesmaid will need to have a fitting. As with the bride's gown, the shop can probably handle any alterations—taking in the waist, bringing in the shoulders, hemming the skirt. But a professional seamstress can also do the job, so you don't have to ask all your out-of-town maids to fly in for fittings (sorry—doing so, veers into 'zilla territory). To save you some stress, put your maid of honor in charge of making sure all the ladies get their dresses altered and pick them up in time for the wedding.

Accessorizing your maids
It's up to you whether you want head-to-toe wardrobe control, but we should warn you: By demanding that your friends buy specific footwear and jewelry to match their dresses and wear their hair in matching styles, you're officially entering bridezilla territory. That said, there are specific occasions where the right shoes or jewels can make the outfit. Your best bet: Give guidelines

Callie & Kris
OCTOBER 23
ELGIN, TX

Embracing the rustic charm of the bride's parents' ranch, Callie and Kris created an elegant but relaxed vibe for their fall nuptials. Subtle nods to the ranch setting, like fabric-covered hay bales for ceremony seats and old wooden signs directing guests, complemented the feel of the venue. Even the bridesmaids' dresses—brown satin paired with cowboy boots—reflected this juxtaposition of elegance and down-home Texas style.

(gold jewelry and nude sandals) but don't insist they buy additional accessories. If you really want all your maids to have the same exact shoes or necklace, consider covering the costs.

THE UNDERGARMENTS Remind your girls to get the right undergarments. While we're not suggesting you advise one of your maids to invest in some Spanx (though they might want certain undergarments to avoid lines or bulges under their dresses), depending on the type of dress (strapless, one-shoulder, halter), your maids may need some special support or hidden straps. When you're choosing the dresses, you may want to ask what the consultant or seamstress at the store suggests and just fill your maids in on her recommendations.

THE JEWELS If you have a specific look in mind, you could give them a necklace or pair of earrings you want them to wear as bridesmaid gifts. (Just make sure it's something they might want to wear again.) If they'll be supplying their own jewels, the easiest way to set guidelines is by size and color. Small and subtle is a fail-proof combo for maids' jewelry (think studs and a pendant necklace). Then let the color of their dresses determine which metal will look best: Gold jewelry flatters warm tones, silver complements cool shades, and diamonds and pearls go with pretty much everything.

THE SHOES If you want to score big points with your maids, let them sport a style they can truly use again. Consider picking a neutral color that goes with everything, like a metallic, nude, or black sandal or pump. The next best thing? Pick a color and heel, and let them choose the style. When picking the heel type and height, consider whether the wedding will be indoors on solid ground (where any heel can work as long as it's comfortable enough to stand in for the entire ceremony and beyond) or on the grass or sand outside, where you'll want to opt for platforms or flats that, unlike stilettos, won't get stuck in the grass or sink in the sand.

THE FLAIR Give matching maids a unique look by choosing accessories that complement their personalities and dresses. You can choose coordinating accessories or mix it up a bit to show their individuality (just stick with the same general style like all statement necklaces or all pendants). Try bright satin belts or statement necklaces. If it will be chilly, cashmere or chiffon wraps are elegant add-ons, while faux fur stoles look breathtaking at an extravagant winter wedding. For a final touch, pretty beaded clutches make great gifts that they can use for storing phones and lipstick during your wedding—and after.

the knot NOTE

bridesmaid looks
There's a new hot bridesmaid dress designer on the scene every minute. Find out the latest looks.
TheKnot.com/ bridesmaids

DRESSING THE OTHER WOMEN IN YOUR PARTY

The styling portion of your job isn't done quite yet, though you've definitely got the hardest part out of the way. If you're including any younger cousins or nieces in the wedding, you'll need to choose their dresses too, and you may need to give your moms (yours, his, or both) some guidance as well. From the little girls to the moms and the ladies in between, here's how to dress them in style.

Junior attendants
Preteen maids can often wear the same dress or formalwear as their older counterparts. If your bridesmaids are wearing something that might not be as suitable for a twelve-year-old girl (a strapless neckline, for example), put her in a more age-appropriate style in the same color or a complementary shade.

Flower girls
The flower girl's parents traditionally pay for her attire, so unless you're planning on making a gift of it, be sure to be up-front about this when you ask permission to include her in your wedding. A general rule of thumb: A flower girl's dress should echo the styling of the bridesmaid dresses or the bride's dress. Flower-girl dresses are nearly always high-necked and tea- or floor-length. If she'll be coming down the aisle with the ring bearer, go the mini-bride-and-groom route, with her in white. If you're having multiple flower girls, choose dresses that coordinate in style and color with your bridesmaids. Another option is to meet in the middle and choose a white dress with an embellishment or a sash that matches the bridesmaid dresses. Many bridal retailers sell flower-girl dresses, but you can also check out department stores, mass retailers like J.Crew, and specialty children's boutiques.

Consider your flower girl's age and maturity level (what is she really going to be able to wear or carry?) and keep the accessories simple. If you know that the adorable floral crown you picked is going to be off her head within minutes, you may want to reconsider having her wear it at all. A basket of petals or a pomander is probably plenty for her to handle.

The moms
This is a big day for moms, too; they probably haven't shopped for a dress this important since their own weddings. Each mom should choose and pay for her own attire, but more likely than not, they're going to ask for your help, and it doesn't hurt to give some guidelines. The moms don't have to match each other—they just shouldn't clash. Tradition says the mother-of-the-bride gets first pick and

then fills the mother-of-the-groom in on her pick, so she can then select something in the same "family"—meaning that the choices complement each other in terms of formality and style. But now that the bride's parents aren't necessarily footing the entire bill for the wedding (and therefore, not the sole hosts of the evening), who buys first doesn't matter as much, as long as both women are comfortable and feel great in what they decide to wear. If possible, you may want to go shopping all together or plan a separate shopping trip with each mom (that way, you can also communicate guidelines to each mom to ensure their outfits coordinate).

Anything from a classic suit to a cocktail dress or formal gown can work, depending on the formality of your wedding. Use the bride and bridal party as a guide for the formality of the moms' ensembles—you want everyone to go together, so consistent skirt and sleeve lengths are helpful. Ultimately, though, it does need to be their decision: Comfort is key since both moms will be circulating at the party and posing for countless pictures throughout the day. So don't force your mom to wear something you think is modern but she thinks is "too old" or "too conservative" to wear.

The moms' outfits shouldn't clash with the wedding colors, but the dresses don't have to match those of the bridesmaids—or each other. Steer the moms clear of whites, creams, and ivories—unless you really want to match with your mom (or future mother-in-law). Good colors include navy, gold, and jewel tones but, traditionally, moms are supposed to avoid black because it's considered the color of mourning. If both moms want to wear the same color, they should choose different shades for an easy compromise. If you don't go shopping together, find out the colors of their dresses so you can give them coordinating corsages, pomanders, or small bouquets to help them further stand out as mothers of the bride and groom.

ASK CARLEY
DRESS CODES

We're planning a casual wedding. How can we let guests know this on our invitations?
Spell it out for them, the same way you might see "black tie optional" printed on an invite. How you word it depends on just how casual you want guests to dress. If you're thinking summer sundresses and khaki suits, you can stick with "casual cocktail attire." If you're planning a more laid-back celebration and flip-flops or going barefoot is okay, try saying something like "beach chic" or "summer casual, please." Since those terms (and even guidelines like "cocktail attire") are open to interpretation, your wedding website is a good place to elaborate on the appropriate attire for your wedding—and all the other related events.

18

looking your best

TIMELINE
PLANNING

ASAP
Get a manicure—your hands will be getting a lot of attention now, thanks to that sparkler!

5–6 months before
Start a skin-care routine

Begin a diet and fitness regimen

3–4 months before
Book makeup artist and hairstylist for the wedding

1–2 months before
Do hair and makeup trial runs

2 weeks before
Get final haircut and color touch-up, if applicable

Grooms get final trim

1 week before
Get final eyebrow shaping

1 day before
Get mani-pedi

We know you're crazy-busy choosing invitations, florists, bridesmaid dresses, and a honeymoon spot, but don't neglect one of the most important tasks of all—getting yourself looking and feeling great. There will be more pictures taken of you on your wedding day than any other day of your life.

So how do you ensure you'll be at your absolute best? First, keep in mind that how you look on your wedding day begins well before that morning. Start a beauty and fitness regimen as early as possible. Trust us, the results will be well worth it—plus taking a break from all those to-dos for a workout or some prewedding pampering will help keep you sane. In this chapter, we'll show you how to prep your skin, hair, nails, and body for your big white-carpet moment. (And don't think we're not talking to you, too, grooms—there are guy-approved tips in this chapter as well.)

ENLISTING BEAUTY EXPERTS

If you're not much of a makeup person—and even if you are—and no matter how good you are at makeup or hair, if you can fit it into your budget, you should hire a professional makeup artist and hairstylist for your wedding day. An expert can give you picture-appropriate makeup and hair that will last the entire wedding and look just as good in-person as in photos (no easy feat!).

To find a makeup artist and hairstylist, begin by asking for recommendations from recent brides whose wedding looks you liked. Talk to your photographer, too—most have worked with reputable hair and makeup pros and can recommend ones who will give you a photo-friendly result. Start looking three to four months in advance, or even earlier if you are hoping to book a top makeup artist or hairstylist in a major city like New York or Los Angeles. If you have room in your budget, you may want to test out a few different pros, so you can see whose work you like best.

Hair Pros
One of the most reputable ways to hire a hairstylist is through a salon. The plus side: reliability. The salon will ensure that the stylist is where they're supposed to be when they're supposed to be there—because the salon's reputation is on the line. The downside: price. If the wedding will require the stylist to be out of the salon for a whole working day, you may be asked to pay what they'd normally bring in if they were in the salon. You can also find a good person through a salon but hire him privately. If your wedding is on a day when the salon is closed, the stylist may cost less because he wouldn't be earning any money on that day, anyway. As with everything else, just be sure to get a signed contract. If you already have a reliable salon where you get your hair cut or colored, see if they offer hairstyling services or can recommend someone who does. If you're having a destination wedding, you may consider flying your stylist out if you have room in your budget, or ask your stylist for recommendations.

MAKEUP GURUS Many salons provide makeup application services, too, and may offer a discount if you book both professionals there. Some may even have professionals who do both hair and makeup, so you can just hire one person and be done. You can also head to your favorite makeup counter at a local department store for a free makeover (or visit five different counters and pick your favorite). If you like what you see, ask the salesperson if she does any outside makeup work. She may be willing to come to you on your wedding day or recommend an experienced makeup artist who will.

the knot NOTE

beauty pros finder
The top bridal hair and makeup gurus book months in advance. Start researching now the most in-demand beauty pros.
TheKnot.com/ makeupartists

beauty pros

Questions to ask before booking beauty pros

☐ How long have you been styling hair for weddings?

☐ Do you have pictures of other brides you've styled for their weddings that I can see?

☐ Can you provide references from past brides?

☐ How many weddings will you be working on the day of my wedding? [You want to make sure there is plenty of time for your hair and/or makeup and you won't be waiting for the pro on your wedding day.]

☐ Do you have suggestions for my hair and skin type? What style(s) would you recommend given my dress description, personal style, and wedding style?

☐ Are you open to input and can you emulate styles I show you from magazines and pictures?

☐ Will you come to my home/getting-ready spot? Will it cost extra and am I expected to pay for your travel expenses?

☐ What will happen if you can't be there on the day of my wedding? Will you arrange for someone else to do the job or am I on my own?

☐ Will you do the bridal party's hair and/or makeup, as well, or do you have an assistant or another pro at your salon or agency who can do the bridal party's hair and/or makeup (optional)? What is the additional charge?

☐ Will you stay with me throughout the day to do touch-ups before the ceremony and photo session? What is the additional fee?

☐ Can we do a trial run? How much do you charge for a trial run? How many do you recommend?

☐ Do you charge a per-person fee or a daily rate? Is there an agent fee?

☐ Will you help me set up a timeline to make sure everyone is ready on time? How early will you arrive to set up? [Thirty minutes is standard.]

☐ What kind of products do you use? Do you have specific types of products for my particular skin and/or hair type? Can I bring my own for you to use (optional)?

Trial runs

Once you've booked your beauty professionals, schedule at least one trial run for wedding-day hair and/or makeup to test out different possibilities. Many salons or professionals will charge a trial-run fee and then a separate wedding-day fee (day-of fees can run anywhere from $150 to $1,000). Others will charge one price up front and include a free trial run as part of the package.

During your trial session, the stylists will create versions of your actual wedding-day look. You will probably experiment with a few different hairstyles in one afternoon so you can choose the one you like best. Same goes for makeup: Your artist might do the left eye with one color combination and the right with another, so you can compare and decide which works better for you.

For your trial, collect pictures from magazines to show the makeup artist. Keep in mind that your wedding is not the time to start experimenting—stick to an enhanced version of your everyday self. Your hairstylist will also need a snapshot of your dress so he knows what kind of neckline he's dealing with. A swatch of your dress fabric will help your makeup artist pick shades that will go best with your shade of white (or nonwhite). Wear a top with a color and neckline that are similar to your gown, so you get the full effect. Bring your wedding-day musts, too: You'll need your veil, earrings, and headpiece to figure out how they'll fit in with your hairdo.

Also, bring a camera so you can get a photo of each finished look from four different angles—front, back, and both sides. If there's one particular style you like, ask her to write down exactly which products and techniques were used. Since a wedding consultation can take place months before your actual event, it's important to keep notes and take pictures so you can both remember what worked.

Don't forgo the trial run just because you're using a favorite hairstylist to whom you have been going for years—having your hair done for a big event is very different from getting a great cut or color. Don't skip this step just because you're doing your hair and makeup yourself, either. Try different hairstyles and looks to see what you can pull off. Then practice, practice, practice.

Scheduling your beauty pros

Ensuring a great hair day on your wedding day will all come down to timing—which means you'll need to schedule your hair appointment at precisely the right moment. Do it too early and your coif could start to look stale just as the festivities are getting started, but if you start the hairstyling too late you'll feel rushed. During your hair trial run, time how long it takes to get your mane perfect, then allow that amount of time plus a half an hour of leeway, and schedule your hair appointment for as late as possible. For example, if photos are scheduled to begin at four, and your hair takes an hour, schedule it for two thirty.

Always start with hair, so if you need to sit with rollers in your hair, you can have your makeup done while your curls cook. If you and your maids are getting your hair and makeup done together and sharing one or a few pros, you'll want to get yours done in the middle to ensure

TIP
trial timing

Schedule your trials before your prewedding parties and other special events. Most stylists charge for these practice runs, so you might as well get some use out of them.

you'll be ready on time but still look fresh for the ceremony (and any preceremony pictures). For example, if you have six bridesmaids, you should go fourth.

Allot one hour for each person's hair, including your own (add an extra fifteen minutes if you need a veil applied), then tack on an additional forty-five to sixty minutes for each person's makeup, so about two hours per person is a safe bet. Time your hair and makeup trials to get a more realistic picture of how long you'll need for each. Then tack on an extra twenty minutes so you don't feel rushed or in case you want to redo an eye or a curl, and if you are heading to a salon to meet your pros, pad in additional time for travel (and potential traffic!) as well.

EXPERT ADVICE
beauty blunders—and fixes
Issues that might arise on your wedding day, and the best ways to save face if they do.

chipped nail polish
Don't try to pull off those magic nail fixes they do at the salon with just a drop of nail polish remover and a light touch. Simply apply a dab of polish on just the chipped area and wait two minutes for it to dry. Then apply one coat of polish over the entire nail area and add some quick-dry topcoat.

puffy eyes
The tried-and-true beauty trick is tea bags—green tea works best (the caffeine is a natural shrinker). Dip the tea bags in water, lie down, and place them over your eyes for ten to twenty minutes. Another DIY cure: a frozen spoon on each of your eyelids. Combine these two tricks for double the depuffing power.

a monster zit
If you wake up the day before with a new neighbor on your face, a dermatologist can give your face a quick injection of cortisone, which will bring down any blemish swelling and make it practically disappear by the following morning. But on the day of, you'll have to banish it with a touch of a zit-zapping cream that contains benzoyl peroxide or a drop of Visine (seriously), which will take any redness out of the area. The more you try to hide it, the more prominent it will become—so go easy on the cover-up.

day-of beauty timeline

To help you figure out what time your beauty pros should arrive, here
is a chart of what your day-of beauty schedule might look like.

time	hair	makeup
1st hour	Bridesmaid 1	Bridesmaid 2
2nd hour	Bridesmaid 2	Bridesmaid 3
3rd hour	Bride	MOB
4th hour	MOB	Bride
4th hour	Bridesmaid 3	Bridesmaid 1

If you can, have them come to you, so you don't have to worry about
running around on the morning of your wedding. And ask one of your
maids to keep an eye on the clock, so everyone stays on schedule, or
even set a timer so that everyone's ready by go-time.

Once your hair and makeup are finished, factor in enough time to get
dressed—it takes longer than you might think. You'll need at least forty-
five minutes to get dressed and ready once your hair is done, and figure
each of your maids will need thirty minutes to dress.

CHOOSING YOUR BRIDAL LOOK

When you envision yourself on your wedding day, what do you see? Sexy
screen siren? Royal-wedding material? Modern-day Greek goddess?
Browse magazines and websites for hair and makeup styles that
represent what you want your appearance to be like on your wedding
day (find tons of hair and makeup ideas on TheKnot.com/beauty).
Other great places to find inspiration: celebrity red-carpet pictures and
pictures of other real brides. Pick a variety of options though—even if
your favorite celebrity or another bride looked fabulous with red lips
and romantic waves, the key question is, will it look good on you? Go
to TheKnot.com/hair to try out different styles and hone in on your top
picks to test during your hair trials

ASK CARLEY
MAIDS' MAKEUP

**Who pays for the
bridesmaids to get their
hair and makeup done?**
The attendants are
already paying for their
dresses and—if they
don't live in the wedding
city—for travel and
accommodations. So
they shouldn't be
expected to pay for
professional hair and
makeup as well, unless
you make the service
available for everyone. If
you want to make sure
everyone gets done up
by a pro, consider gifting
day-of hairstyling and
makeup application to
your maids. If covering
your maids' styling isn't
in your budget, trust
them to do a good job
on their own.

Photographs

Scrutinize favorite pictures of yourself and figure out what you like about how you look in them. Maybe it's your smoky eyes, or perhaps you love the rosy glow you had in your cheeks that day. This will help you zero in on the features you want to highlight (and those you want to disguise) so that your photographs come out well. This is your red-carpet moment, and you don't just want to think about what will wow your guy when you stand on the altar; think about what you want to see in those photos you'll be gazing at for years to come.

The wedding style

Your hair and makeup are just as much a part of the day as your centerpiece and the cake, so you want them to tie in with the overarching theme of your wedding. Loose locks and a bronzed, dewy glow are perfect for a beach wedding but not as fitting for a grand ballroom affair. Leave your hair loose or down to fit a romantic mood or more laid-back affair. Do the opposite for a formal affair.

Your dress

Think of your makeup and hair as accessories: You want to make sure your appearance above the neck coordinates with your appearance below the neck. In other words, if your gown and your details evoke all-American preppy, dramatic smoky eyes won't work. And if you want to show off your dress's neckline, you will want your hair pulled back.

YOUR WEDDING-DAY HAIRSTYLE

Wedding-day hair is, for many brides, as important a decision as the dress. Though stylists today often seem like they can spin straw into gold—just look at how quickly celebs change up their locks—it's more sensible to try to work with the hair you've got.

Curly hair

It's best not to fight what nature gave you. If you have super-curly hair and it's August, you can flat-iron it straight, but within an hour those curls will come back. Instead of ditching the curls, play them up—and whether it's summer or winter, look for styling products with humidity-fighting ingredients to help keep frizz at bay.

Straight hair

Similar to curly hair, you can't fight your natural texture—tight curls may fall by the end of the ceremony. Either keep curls big and loose, or go for an updated sleek style like a low bun to one side or a bowlike French twist to show off your hair's fabulously smooth texture.

diy hair and makeup

If a hair and/or makeup expert isn't in your budget or you just don't trust someone else, here are some tips to help you create your wedding-day look.

take a lesson
Take advantage of the makeup counters at your local department store to get free tips—and stock up on any supplies you need to pull off your look. Or schedule a makeup lesson for you and your maids with a licensed professional.

pick the right products
The right shade of foundation is essential to get your skin camera-ready: Never make a decision about foundation unless you've applied it to your jawline first and looked at it in daylight. The color should blend and essentially disappear. Use waterproof foundation, primer, eyeliner, and mascara. You don't want makeup running down your face, either from tears or too many dances.

keep shine in check
Although it looks beautiful in person, mineral-based makeup shows up oily in photographs. Use a primer under your foundation to help keep foundation in place and oil away. Powder and oil-blotting sheets are a must for your day-of beauty kit.

Fine hair If your hair is very fine or thin, keep the look simple. Go for an updo—if you wear your hair up, you don't have to worry about it going limp on you. Fine hair should be slightly dirty for updos—just-washed hair is too soft to hold pins.

Thick hair Show off lush locks with a twisted half-updo, which is more formal than simply wearing your hair down. If you do want to wear it down, plan for extra time at the salon to first straighten your thick hair and then curl for extra control.

CLASSIC BRIDAL MAKEUP LOOKS

You may hate makeup or love wearing your hair down, but remember: This is not any old party. This is your wedding. Yes, you want your groom to recognize you, and you want you to recognize you, but you don't want to look like you do every other day either (no matter how beautiful you are). So don't be afraid to try something new—as long as you test-drive it before the wedding. You may find that colors or combinations you normally shy away from actually look great on you. Whether you're getting glam on your own or enlisting the help of a pro, follow these tips to pull off the prettiest (and most popular) bridal looks.

Ethereal
This earthy look is ideal for outdoor events, whether you get married on a ranch, vineyard, or in a garden. It's also the best way to go if you don't usually wear makeup.

To brighten your eyes, make a tiny "C" around the inner corners with a gold highlighter pen and then blend with your fingers. Apply an ultrathin line of brown liner to the top lash line and line the lower inner lash line with a nude pencil. Lastly, add two coats of lengthening mascara. When it comes to your lips, less is more. A swipe of sheer peach or clear gloss should do the trick. If your lips are redder or pinker than the average gal's, try a frosty nude color for that angelic appeal. Keep the face natural, too: Use an oil-free moisturizer and translucent powder. Lightly dust peach-colored blush on the apples of your cheeks using an outward motion toward your hairline.

TELL YOUR MAKEUP ARTIST: "I want a completely natural look: nude lips, soft, porcelain skin, and just a little bit of brightening eye makeup."

Romantic
Halfway between made-up and natural, a subtle, rosy-pink flush flatters almost any bride in any kind of environment. Focus on rosy cheeks to create a natural glow. Start by applying a tinted moisturizer that matches your skin tone. Choose a pink blush with cool undertones and dust on the apples of your cheeks with a big powder brush. Keep your look understated by dusting a nude shadow on your lids from the lash line to the crease and applying two coats of mascara. Next, use a dab of highlighter in the inner corners of your eyes. Try going with a pink stain, instead of traditional lipstick, for color that won't rub off. Let the stain set for about ten seconds and then complete the look with a clear, neutral gloss.

TELL YOUR MAKEUP ARTIST: "I'd like a fresh face with a pink glow, with extra emphasis on the cheeks and lips."

getting in bridal shape

Will you ever have better fitness motivation than your wedding day? Take advantage
of this rare window of opportunity to look your absolute best. Whether you want to drop
a dress size or get in killer shape, here are some tips and tricks to get you started.

be realistic

Not every bride must be a size
2 on her wedding day. Create
reachable goals based on your
body type and current size.
Remember: He loves you the
way you are, and if you need a
reminder, just look down at
that ring on your finger.

start early

A healthy weight-loss goal is
one to two pounds per week,
for a total of four to eight
pounds per month. Need to
lose twenty pounds? Start at
least six months before your
wedding. But we say get going
right away so you're not under
the gun during the weeks
leading up to the wedding
(you'll have enough to
stress over).

take your routine to the next level

If you continue to do what
you've always done, you'll
continue to get the results
you've always gotten. Want to
make more progress? Then
you'll need to push yourself a
little harder, increasing the
intensity of your workouts
each week.

stay well-rounded

For the best results, put it
all together. That means
combining a sensible diet with
a proper exercise regimen.
And don't just focus on your
upper body because that's
what will show in your gown.
Remember, the dress and tux
eventually come off (it's
called your honeymoon).

nix the crash diets

Dropping key food groups
from your diet, such as
carbohydrates, may help you
shed water weight in the short
term, but it also deprives the
body of energy and nutrients,
which can cause breakouts,
hair loss, and mood swings.
Your best bet: Eat a balanced
diet and watch your
portion sizes.

Hollywood glamour
Channel a classic starlet (think Greta
Garbo) with a perfectly polished face and red pucker that's ready for
a close-up. Apply brown liquid liner on your upper lash line and then
switch to a pencil for the lower inner lash line. Blend a golden-brown
shadow from the lash line to the crease, and use off-white shadow right
under your brow for even more definition. Finish with two coats of
volumizing mascara. Crimson lips are classic glam glam, so test different
shades of red at a makeup counter until you find the right one for you. A
long-wearing formula is your best bet. Oil-free foundation nixes shine.
Then use a light, neutral blush to keep the focus on your lips.

TELL YOUR MAKEUP ARTIST: "I want a matte complexion along
with strong, red lips and sultry, defined eyes."

timing it right

The average engagement is just over a year, which gives you plenty of time to feel "perfect," whatever that means to you. To look your best on your wedding day, start well in advance and keep in mind these extra beauty to-dos.

If you . . . plan to show off your engagement ring from now until your wedding day, get manicures every two weeks starting right away to keep your nails in good shape.

If you . . . are planning to honeymoon somewhere that's flip-flop friendly? Start getting monthly pedicures three to four months before your wedding day. Pop in for a final prewedding mani-pedi the day before your wedding. Purchase the exact color that the manicurist uses on your nails for your wedding-day emergency kit.

If you . . . are getting professional help for any major skin concerns, book a dermatologist appointment as soon as possible to talk about treatments and get started on a regimen (many can take six-plus months to kick in).

If you . . . want to lose weight or tone up for your wedding, consult a trainer to develop a workout plan at least six-plus months in advance (go to TheKnot.com/workout for workout tips, toning moves, and nutrition tips).

If you . . . want a brighter smile for your wedding pictures, choose a teeth-whitening plan—whitening strips, professional bleaching, or just a whitening toothpaste—five to seven months in advance.

If you . . . plan to get your eyebrows professionally shaped, book an appointment three to four months before your wedding and have your final waxing, tweezing, or threading one week before your special day.

If you . . . color your hair, schedule a trim and color touch-up if necessary two weeks before.

If you . . . want to get that "bridal glow," book regular facials every six weeks, starting four months before your wedding. Pop in for one last facial, this time without extractions (they could irritate your skin), a week before your wedding.

If you . . . will be wearing a bikini on your honeymoon, get a bikini wax the week before the wedding.

Modern sophisticate

Whether your wedding is on a rooftop or in a loft, play up your eyes with a sexy look fit for a Saturday night on the town. Your eyes are the main attraction for this look, so go for sheer coverage with a lightweight foundation and keep your blush minimal. A subtle smoky eye will give you a sexy look that still feels bridal. Start with light gold shadow in your eyes' inner corners; then graduate to a deeper golden hue in the middle. Use plum or bronze shadow at the outer corner and under the lash line as well. Apply three coats (yes, three!) of black thickening mascara to give your eyes maximum definition. Finish off with subtle lips: Line with a nude pencil and fill in with a pale mauve lipstick or sheer gloss. Keep it simple so your eyes get all the attention.

TELL YOUR MAKEUP ARTIST: "I'd like to focus on my eyes—dark and smoky, using brown and purple tones—and nude lips."

GROOM GROOMING

Now, grooms, we know what you're thinking: Real men don't do spas. But all rules have exceptions, and as you're probably starting to figure out, a big exception to just about every rule is your wedding. On this day you're expected to look better than your best.

Personal trainer
Even if you're not up to a total groom session, there's one thing you could (and should) do to look your best for your wedding: Get your butt into the best shape of your life. Start six months in advance, and splurge on a trainer.

Professional shave
Let's ease you guys into this pampering thing with a totally acceptable "treatment" for a man to get: a straight-edge shave from an old-school barber. Try it before the engagement party (or shoot) or your next dinner with the in-laws to make sure you don't have a reaction to the chemicals in the shaving cream or lotions. Then schedule one a day before the wedding.

"Man"-icure
We know, we know. But here's the deal: On your wedding day, people will focus more on your hands (and fingernails) than in every other moment of your life—combined. Don't worry—no one needs to know. They'll just file down the ragged nails and buff (and you can even tell them to skip the shiny clear stuff). Get one at least one or two days before the event.

Facial-hair trim
Pluck the unibrow. Nothing will distract your guests, ruin a wedding video, and spoil every photograph like these two little words: nose hair. Attend to these during your day-before shave.

Haircut
Warning: Don't experiment on the day of your wedding. Your fiancée already likes the hair that you have (or don't have). The last thing you want is to be showing off a goofy new style for the ceremony. Schedule a cut two weeks before the wedding so it has time to grow out a bit and you look like a man ready to get married, not a kid who's ready for the first day of school.

the details and the big day

the invitation suite

TIMELINE
PLANNING

9–11 months before
Research styles and
stationers

6–8 months before
Order and send
save-the-dates

Order thank-you notes

4–6 months before
Order and finalize
invitations, reply cards,
and any other enclosures

Reserve a calligrapher
(if using one)

4 months before
Drop off envelopes with
calligrapher or address and
stuff invitations on
your own

6–8 weeks before
Send invitations

Order table numbers,
escort cards, place cards,
and menus (or start
working on them if you're
going the DIY route)

Finalize and order
ceremony programs (or
start working on them)

1 month before
Send invitations for
any peripheral parties
you're hosting

Drop escort cards and place
cards off with calligrapher
or print yourselves

As the first sign of your wedding that guests receive, the save-the-dates and invitations you select can go a long way in setting the tone. Besides just letting guests know when and where the festivities will take place, they provide clues as to the formality of the affair and give guests the first taste of your wedding vision.

From paper types and printing techniques to fonts, motifs and monograms, envelopes, and etiquette, wedding invitations are a bit more complicated than your typical thank-you card. This chapter will walk you through everything you need to make the perfect first impression.

SELECTING A STATIONER

When you first start looking for wedding paper, there are a few factors to consider. Chief among them: where you will order from. Options abound, from small boutique stationers who create custom invitations for each wedding to large-scale operations that offer many different stationery lines. The entire range of stationers is well represented online, so whether you are thinking boutique or big-name printing house, they're all a click away.

Boutique stationers

If you're looking for a high level of customization—especially if you want a design created just for you—a small, local stationery designer is the right option. Choosing a boutique stationer means you're generally working directly with the designer and, in some cases, directly with the printer, too. You'll have more stylistic leeway and choices when it comes to the design compared to mass retailers. If you are the type of couple who is going to want tons of tweaks with multiple proofs (a preview of your invitation), the flexibility and hands-on approach of a smaller vendor is probably best for you. You'll typically pay more for the higher level of customization and it may take longer for a smaller operation to fill your order.

Stationery store

If you want to see myriad options in many different (predesigned) styles, from a big range of designers, visit a stationery store. At these larger retailers, you'll browse through catalogs and samples by various designers. While you may not be able to go as crazy with customization, with so many options, you almost certainly will be able to find a style that suits your wedding to a T. Even though the options are large in scale, there will be someone on hand to help you with the wording and any customized elements like maps or monograms. You'll also find competitive pricing.

Ordering online

Stationers have gone paperless too, with online stores that let you play with styles, colors, layouts, and more so you can see your designs come to life virtually before your eyes. In some cases, you can enter all of your information and view a proof instantly online. Others will mail you a physical proof within twenty-four hours, and many companies will gladly send you samples of paper types and styles as well, usually for a nominal fee (often this cost is credited back toward your order), so there won't be any surprises when you get your actual invites. You'll find some of the most competitive prices online.

the knot NOTE

invitation galleries
Browse the widest selection of invitations imaginable and find out where to purchase them. **TheKnot.com/ invitations**

Hiring a designer

A graphic designer will create a one-of-a-kind design for you based on your vision and wedding style and may hook you up with a trustworthy print shop. But the process can take a while, so start looking for a talented pro early (eight or more months in advance). And be aware that this option can be costly and time-consuming, as you'll have to source and pay two people—the graphic artist and the printer—which could wind up being more expensive than a one-stop shop.

Doing it yourselves

For those on a budget, most craft stores have do-it-yourself kits called "printables." The design is done, the paper is cut, and all you need to do is put in your details and print them out using a home computer. Some online stationers also allow you to purchase their templates to design and print from (prices can run from $20 to $100 for the template, but don't forget to factor high-quality paper and printer ink into the equation). The designer selection is much more limited than you'll see at a stationery store, and making two hundred invitations is far more time-consuming than making twenty birthday party invites.

SAVE-THE-DATES

The day is chosen and the planning is under way—time to get your guests in the loop with a save-the-date. This preinvitation mailing officially announces your wedding date and lets guests know that they will, in fact, be invited to the celebration. This extra element has become fairly standard, and it's a must if you are hosting a destination wedding. Between travel arrangements and busy schedules, sending a save-the-date will increase the chances that your invitees will attend the celebration.

The timeline

It's best to start spreading the news about six months prior to the ceremony, or about eight months prior if it's a destination wedding or during a particularly busy time of year or a holiday weekend. This gives wedding guests plenty of time to block their calendars, book their travel, and ask for days off from work. Any earlier, and they may toss the notice aside and forget. Any later, and it might as well be an invitation.

The number

Only send save-the-dates to the people whom you definitely plan to invite to your wedding. Once these are in the mail, there's no changing your mind or altering the guest list. That's why it is best to have your guest list finalized before you send your save-the-dates. And even if you've already received confirmations from certain guests (bridesmaids, siblings, parents), you still need to send them a save-the-date (and invitation for that matter).

The wording

Unlike invitations, you don't need to include nearly as many details. Rather than crowd the card with too much information, just print the basics—your names, wedding date, and location. Then include the address of your wedding website, where more in-depth information (like a schedule of events and hotel and flight information) can be featured. Or opt for a booklet with multiple pages to provide the lodging information (hotel names, phone numbers, rates, websites, and booking information for any blocks you reserved); transportation, including airlines and rental car information; and even an itinerary of weekend events (if you have it settled) and activities in the area for guests to check out during downtime.

Don't include an RSVP on the save-the-date. The excess cushion time could cause some guests to put off replying, and they might wind up forgetting altogether. If someone receives a save-the-date, however, and will be unable to attend, he or she may let you know in advance. In that case, you'll still need to send a wedding invitation as a common courtesy, but it's a plus to have the heads-up that you can invite someone in that person's stead.

While your guests will likely want to know where you are registered, it's inappropriate to print this information on your save-the-dates or invitations. Gifts, of course, are not required—and guests know that they can ask around or call you or your parents to get this sort of scoop. The only acceptable vehicle for registry information? Your wedding website (flip back to chapter 4 to find out how to set that up).

The design

While coordinating stationery helps clarify your wedding style, your save-the-dates don't have to match your invitations, so don't feel pressure to have your invitation design nailed down. The goal is to create an item that gets a bit of attention and sets the tone for the rest of your wedding. If classic elegance is more your scene, you can never go wrong with engraved script on a pretty card. But save-the-dates can be more informal than the invitations, so feel free to have fun with the design, too. Getting hitched in Italy? Send postcard-style

save-the-date wording ideas

You can announce your day in a more traditional way, or feel free to get
a little more playful with your save-the-date wording.

Paige Breeden
&
Jason Reed
WILL BE MARRIED ON
MAY 3, 2014
IN PHILADELPHIA, PA

Formal invitation to follow
paigeandjason.com

classic couples

Paige & Jason
ARE
[insert silly phrase—
"Gettin' Hitched," "Going
to the Chapel," etc.]

MAY 3, 2014
PHILADELPHIA

Invitation Coming Soon
paigeandjasongethitched.com

quirky/casual couples

TWO HEARTS, ONE LOVE
Paige Breeden
AND
Jason Reed
MAY 3, 20014
PHILADELPHIA, PA

Invitation will follow
paigeandjasonforever.com

sentimental couples

PLEASE JOIN US
IN PARADISE
AS
Paige & Jason
EXCHANGE VOWS

MAY 3, 2014
CAPE TOWN,
SOUTH AFRICA

Invitation and
details to follow
paigeandjasonweddingsafari.com

destination weddings

save-the-dates. Planning to walk down an aisle of sand? Think about using message-in-a-bottle save-the-dates. Or, use those engagement shoot pictures to create photo save-the-dates.

WEDDING INVITATIONS

Not just another design element used to express your wedding style, your invitations also serve a function, spelling out the essential information. So it's important that they are not only attractive but also easy to read and understand.

The timeline
Once you know what you want and have connected with a specific vendor, work backward from your wedding date to figure out when you need to order your invitations. You'll want to mail them out six to eight weeks before the wedding, allowing more time if most of your guests are from out of town or if you're skipping save-the-date cards. Add to that the estimate of how long printing will take, which can be anywhere from one to eight weeks. And if you're having a calligrapher do the envelopes, tack an extra two weeks onto that. Plus, you'll want to give yourself time to assemble and stuff all the envelopes. Altogether, that means you'll want to order invitations approximately six to eight months before your wedding date—so you should start looking for a stationer eight to ten months out.

The number
Stationers tend to sell invitations in batches of twenty-five, but you should always round up when ordering. A good rule of thumb: Order enough invitations for your guest list, plus twenty-five extra in case of any addressing mistakes, or if you need to resend an invitation, want to have a few keepsakes for you and your families, or hope to send invitations to a "B-list." It will cost you more if you have to order extra invitations after the fact than if you buy them in bulk. If you have a lengthy B-list, consider ordering another fifty or, better yet, a second set of invitations with a different RSVP date.

The wording
The invitations should tell guests who's getting married; who's hosting the wedding; and where, when, and what time the festivities will take place. Keep the text simple and concise to avoid crowding the card. Save your wedding website details and information about peripheral events for the enclosure cards.

The wording of the invitation should reflect who's hosting the party.

custom invitation timeline

Planning to have a bespoke invitation or tweak a standard design extensively to suit your style? Invitation designers recommend budgeting about an extra month for your invitations to make sure they're designed and printed on time.

invitation wording ideas

The way you phrase your invitations will depend on the formality of the event and the hosts.

when the bride's parents are hosting the wedding
Reverse the order—groom's parents and groom's name first—if the groom's parents are sponsoring.

MR. AND MRS. PETER JOHNSON
(or "Peter and Miranda Johnson" for a casual affair)
REQUEST THE HONOR OF YOUR PRESENCE
AT THE MARRIAGE OF THEIR DAUGHTER
Heather Amanda
AND
Jeffrey Michael Harris
SON OF
MR. AND MRS. BRADLEY HARRIS
(OR BRADLEY AND WENDY HARRIS)
THURSDAY, THE THIRTEENTH OF MAY
AT SIX O'CLOCK ("in the evening" is optional but
typically used for formal weddings)
CHIP OF HEAVEN CHURCH
111 YUMA AVENUE
KIRKWOOD, MISSOURI

Ms. Heather Amanda Johnson
AND
Mr. Jeffrey Michael Harris
REQUEST THE HONOR OF YOUR PRESENCE
AT THEIR MARRIAGE
THURSDAY, THE THIRTEENTH OF MAY
AT SIX O'CLOCK
CHIP OF HEAVEN CHURCH
111 YUMA AVENUE
KIRKWOOD, MISSOURI

when the couple is hosting their own wedding

when both sets of parents are hosting Note that the bride's parents are listed first even if both parents are hosting.

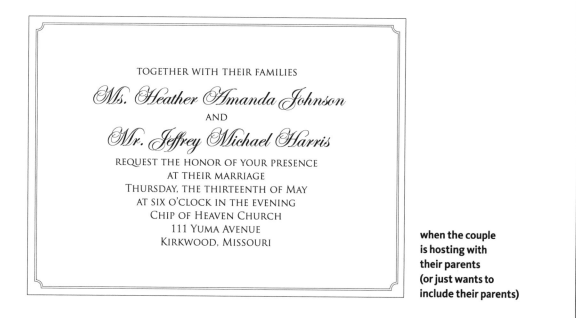

MR. AND MRS. PETER JOHNSON
AND
MR. AND MRS. BRADLEY HARRIS
REQUEST THE PLEASURE OF YOUR COMPANY
AT THE MARRIAGE OF THEIR CHILDREN

Heather Amanda
AND
Jeffrey Michael

THURSDAY, THE THIRTEENTH OF MAY
AT SIX O'CLOCK IN THE EVENING
CHIP OF HEAVEN CHURCH
111 YUMA AVENUE
KIRKWOOD, MISSOURI

TOGETHER WITH THEIR FAMILIES

Ms. Heather Amanda Johnson
AND
Mr. Jeffrey Michael Harris

REQUEST THE HONOR OF YOUR PRESENCE
AT THEIR MARRIAGE
THURSDAY, THE THIRTEENTH OF MAY
AT SIX O'CLOCK IN THE EVENING
CHIP OF HEAVEN CHURCH
111 YUMA AVENUE
KIRKWOOD, MISSOURI

when the couple is hosting with their parents (or just wants to include their parents)

invitation wording ideas (continued)

when divorced parents are hosting jointly (without their spouses)
Divorced parents should never be put on the same line on an invite; it may confuse guests as to their relationship. Only the names of couples who are married should go on the same line.

MR. PETER JOHNSON
AND
MRS. MIRANDA PECK
REQUEST THE PLEASURE OF YOUR COMPANY
AT THE MARRIAGE OF THEIR DAUGHTER
Heather Amanda Johnson
TO
Jeffrey Michael Harris
SON OF
MR. AND MRS. BRADLEY HARRIS
THURSDAY, THE THIRTEENTH OF MAY
AT SIX O'CLOCK IN THE EVENING
CHIP OF HEAVEN CHURCH
111 YUMA AVENUE
KIRKWOOD, MISSOURI

MRS. MIRANDA PECK AND MR. JOHN PECK
AND
PETER JOHNSON
REQUEST THE PLEASURE OF YOUR COMPANY
AT THE MARRIAGE OF THEIR DAUGHTER
Heather Amanda Johnson
TO
Jeffrey Michael Harris
SON OF
MR. AND MRS. BRADLEY HARRIS
THURSDAY, THE THIRTEENTH OF MAY
AT SIX O'CLOCK IN THE EVENING
CHIP OF HEAVEN CHURCH
111 YUMA AVENUE
KIRKWOOD, MISSOURI

divorced and remarried parents hosting with their spouses
Stepparents can be included on the same line as their spouses if everyone agrees to it.

Traditionally, the bride's parents host, so their names would be at the top of the invitation on the host line. If the bride's parents are paying for all or most of the wedding, the names of the groom's parents traditionally are left off the invite, but we like adding the "son of" line as a way of acknowledging the groom's parents, too (see "Invitation Wording Ideas," opposite). Typically, the phrase "request the honor of your presence" is used formally and for ceremonies taking place in a house of worship; "request the pleasure of your company" is a bit more familiar and used for secular settings. The bride's name is traditionally listed first (without her last name since her parents' last name already appears).

If you have a strict dress code, it may be best to include the information on your invitation in the bottom right-hand corner ("black tie," "black tie optional," "jackets required," and "beach chic"). But if there aren't any strict guidelines, you may rely on the formality of the invite and your wedding website to guide guests' wardrobe choices. RSVP information should only be printed on the bottom-left corner of the invitation if you're not including separate response cards. It can be phrased like this: "The favor of a reply is requested before the thirteenth of May" or "RSVP before the thirteenth of May." Set the deadline no more than three or four weeks after guests receive the invitation. Any more than that and they may forget to respond.

Invitation etiquette

Along with the right wording, there is proper punctuation that must be followed for formal wedding invitations.

- Spell out numbers for the date, year, and time, but not in addresses
- Abbreviations are a no-go—spell everything out. So instead of a.m. or p.m., a formal invitation should say "in the evening" or "in the morning." Rather than using *Dr.*, you should spell out *doctor*. The exceptions: *Mr., Mrs., and Ms.*
- The first word and all proper nouns get capitalized, as well as any line that stands alone and would be the first word of a sentence (like "Reception to follow" or "Cocktail attire").
- Leave out commas and periods at the end of each line. They're only used after a title or in the middle of a line.
- The third person is used for formal invitations, so it would say "Mr. and Mrs. John Doe invite you to celebrate . . . ," but some couples are choosing to break with tradition and use the first person ("We invite you to celebrate . . ."). See "Invitation Wording Ideas" for different host wording.

the knot NOTE

invitation wording tool
Figuring out the perfect combination of words and proper titles for your invitations can be tricky. Our wording wizard will do the hard work for you. Just choose your particular family situation and get an example of how to properly word it. **TheKnot.com/ wording**

Before you officially order your invitations, your stationer will send you a proof to look over. This invitation mock-up will be your last chance to make any changes to the wording, so read it carefully. Also, ask both sets of parents and a grammatically inclined friend or coworker to look over the invitation proof. Take a note from proofreaders and read from right to left; it will help you see each word separately so you don't automatically read over something that's wrong.

Enclosure Cards

Some of the more traditional enclosure cards have fallen out of favor with most couples and you're not expected to include any enclosures with your invitations—provided you can fit all the necessary information on your invitations. Response cards are still a must and will make your lives easier. You might also choose to include map cards (with illustrations or directions indicating where the main events are for the weekend), which are an ultraconsiderate touch that is making a comeback.

RECEPTION CARDS If your ceremony and reception will be at two different places, you'll need a small card to add to your invitation with the reception information printed on it.

The Number The number of guests at the event—plus twenty-five extra. Like your invitations, you always want to order extra in case of any lost invitations and last-minute add-ons, and to have for keepsakes.

The Wording Reception cards should include the location, address, and start time of the reception (if there is a break after the ceremony and reception).

RESPONSE CARDS We are big believers in spontaneity—but not when it comes to how many people are going to show up at your wedding. That's where the response card comes in. Unless you're

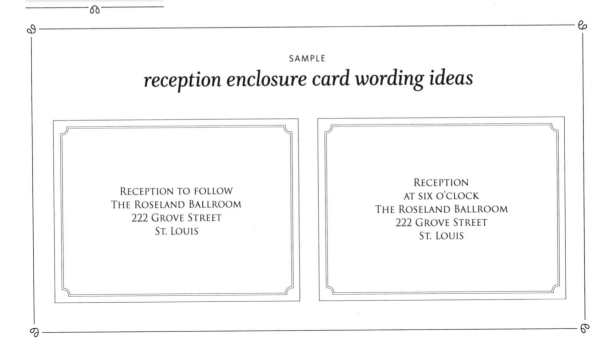

SAMPLE
reception enclosure card wording ideas

RECEPTION TO FOLLOW
THE ROSELAND BALLROOM
222 GROVE STREET
ST. LOUIS

RECEPTION
AT SIX O'CLOCK
THE ROSELAND BALLROOM
222 GROVE STREET
ST. LOUIS

including an e-mail address or the URL to your wedding website for guests to RSVP on your invites, this is an essential bit of wedding stationery.

Couples having plated dinners with a few entrée options may choose to ask guests to mark on their reply cards what they would like to have, giving their caterer a better idea ahead of time, so he doesn't have to order two of everything.

Timeline If your caterer needs a head count two weeks before the wedding, set the reply date at least three weeks before the wedding. (If you're planning to have a B-list, set it even earlier—about four to six weeks before the wedding, and send the invites out around eight to twelve weeks before the wedding.)

The Number Print enough for all your guests—plus twenty-five extras.

The Wording Include the deadline for RSVPs is a must-include. If you prefer to track responses electronically, use the invite to send guests to your wedding website or an e-mail address where they can send their RSVPs.

The Envelopes Include a stamped (don't forget the stamps!) response-card envelope addressed to the person in charge of the guest list (you, Mom and Dad, your planner).

TRANSPORTATION CARDS These let guests know details about transportation you may be providing to and from the wedding or between the ceremony and reception. Though you can include this information on your wedding website, it's a nice reminder if you have room in your budget (and your invitation envelopes).

The Number Number of guests—plus twenty-five (same as invitations).

The Wording Traditionally, they just have something as simple as "Transportation will be provided from the ceremony or reception" or "Transportation will be provided from suggested hotels to the wedding ceremony and home from the reception at the end of the night." You may also want to include the URL to your wedding website for guests to get more details, like the pickup and drop-off times and addresses of pickup spots, as the wedding date approaches. As an alternative, some couples choose to have a separate enclosure card with just their wedding website information.

TIP

tracking rsvps

It will make your life so much easier that it bears repeating: In your spreadsheet of guests' names and addresses, assign each guest a number. Write that number on the back of guests' response cards in pencil. That way, if they return the card to you and their name is illegible, or they've forgotten to write it altogether (it will happen—trust us), you'll be able to identify who replied.

response card wording ideas

KINDLY RESPOND BY MARCH 1
or
THE FAVOR OF YOUR REPLY
IS REQUESTED
BY THE FIRST OF MARCH

blank cards

M_____
___ACCEPTS
___REGRETS
FOR SATURDAY, THE 21ST OF SEPTEMBER
or
KINDLY REPLY BY THE 21ST OF SEPTEMBER
M_____
WILL ____ ATTEND THE WEDDING

fill-in-the-blank response cards

THE FAVOR OF A REPLY IS REQUESTED.
M_____
WILL ____ ATTEND THE WELCOME
BARBECUE ON FRIDAY, SEPTEMBER 20

WILL ____ ATTEND THE WEDDING ON
SATURDAY, SEPTEMBER 21

WILL ____ ATTEND THE BRUNCH ON
SUNDAY, SEPTEMBER 22

checklist

TOGETHER WITH THEIR FAMILIES
Ms. Heather Amanda Johnson
AND
Mr. Jeffrey Michael Harris

REQUEST THE PLEASURE OF YOUR
COMPANY AT THEIR MARRIAGE
SATURDAY, THE FIFTEENTH OF MAY
AT SIX O'CLOCK IN THE EVENING
THE INN ON THE GREEN
MARLBOROUGH, MASSACHUSETTS
RECEPTION TO FOLLOW

THE FAVOR OF A REPLY IS
REQUESTED BY THE 25TH OF APRIL
JEFFREYANDHEATHERGETMARRIED.COM
OR
JEFFREY@
JEFFREYANDHEATHERGETMARRIED.COM

**invitation with
response information
included (no separate
response card needed)**

ACCOMMODATION CARDS If you've also reserved a block of rooms at local hotels for far-flung guests, include that info on the same or a separate card.

The Number Enough for your out-of-town guests (or all guests for a destination wedding)—plus ten to fifteen extras (to be safe).

The Wording Accommodation cards should include the name and contact information for nearby hotels, as well as any information guests will need in order to take advantage of room blocks you may have reserved.

MAP CARDS If you're inviting a lot of out-of-town guests to your wedding or are getting hitched in an out-of-the-way place, you might consider ordering map cards to insert in your initial invitation mailing.

The Number Number of guests (it's a fun touch even for those who live in the area)—plus twenty-five extras (again, just in case).

The Design Sometimes you can get a map from the venue itself, which you can have printed onto your cards. Or you can do a hand-drawn map—a graphic designer, calligrapher, or your stationer can help you with the design. It should clearly spell out road names and major orientation points, and you may want to point out favorite restaurants or sites for guests to check out.

REHEARSAL DINNER AND PERIPHERAL-EVENT CARDS Though the traditional etiquette holds that the groom's family should send out a separate invitation if they're hosting, if you're throwing the rehearsal dinner yourselves or planning to invite everyone to the rehearsal dinner, you can print the details on an enclosure card with the rest of the invitation to save money and to make your lives easier. Or, if you're hosting a next-day brunch or welcome party, you may want to put the details on separate enclosure cards and include them with your invitations. If not everyone is invited to every event or someone else is hosting, it's best to keep the invitations separate to avoid confusing guest lists.

The Number Number of guests invited to the event—plus ten to fifteen extras.

The Wording All relevant details, like the date and time and venue, as well as the RSVP information. You should also identify the type of party (cocktails and dessert, bagels and bloodies) and the attire, since guests may not know.

CHEAT SHEET
common titles

Here's how titles should appear on the outer and inner envelopes, respectively.

Lawyer: Ms. Ingrid Innsbruck, Esq.; Ms. Innsbruck

Physician: Jill Jamal, M.D., or Doctor Jill Jamal; Dr. Jamal

Professor: Professor Kirk Kant or Kirk Kant, Ph.D.; Prof. Kant

Judge: The Honorable Lucy Lindqvist; Judge Lindqvist

Mayor: The Honorable Marion Myrtle Missioni, Mayor of Grand Forks; Mayor Missioni

Captain: Captain Neville North, U.S. Army; Captain North

Minister: The Reverend Olivia Orton; The Reverend Orton [Roman Catholics use *Father*]

Rabbi: Rabbi Pinkus Pressman; Rabbi Pressman

---

wording ideas for other party enclosure cards

PLEASE JOIN US FOR A REHEARSAL
DINNER IN HONOR OF

Becky and Steve

FRIDAY, FEBRUARY 2
EIGHT O'CLOCK IN THE EVENING
THE SMITHS' HOME
333 MICHIGAN AVENUE
LAKE FOREST

rehearsal dinner enclosure card

PLEASE JOIN US IN SENDING
THE NEWLYWEDS
OFF ON THEIR HONEYMOON
SUNDAY, FEBRUARY 5
TEN THIRTY IN THE MORNING
THE SMITHS' HOME
333 MICHIGAN AVENUE
LAKE FOREST
KINDLY RESPOND TO
KIM@KIMSMITH.COM

brunch enclosure card

SIGNED, SEALED, DELIVERED

The envelope is the first thing guests will see, so make a good impression by addressing them properly and adding a little flair. You might opt for a colored envelope, add a design element from the invitations to the outside of the envelope, choose a colorful liner, or just have the addresses written in beautiful calligraphy.

When you order your invitations, see if you can take the envelopes home immediately—or at least as soon as they are ready (if you're having your return address printed on them). That way, you can start addressing them while your invitations are being printed or get your calligrapher going early. Once they come in, here's how to address them.

The inner envelope

Formal invitations are always slipped into an unsealed inner envelope that is placed inside the outer envelope. The tradition dates back to the Victorian period, when envelopes would get dirty en route to the recipient, and the outer envelope was used to keep the letter and envelope inside clean (the outer envelope was removed before it was handed to the recipient). Now they are mostly decorative, with just the names on the outside. If you'd prefer to skip the extra envelope, that's perfectly okay.

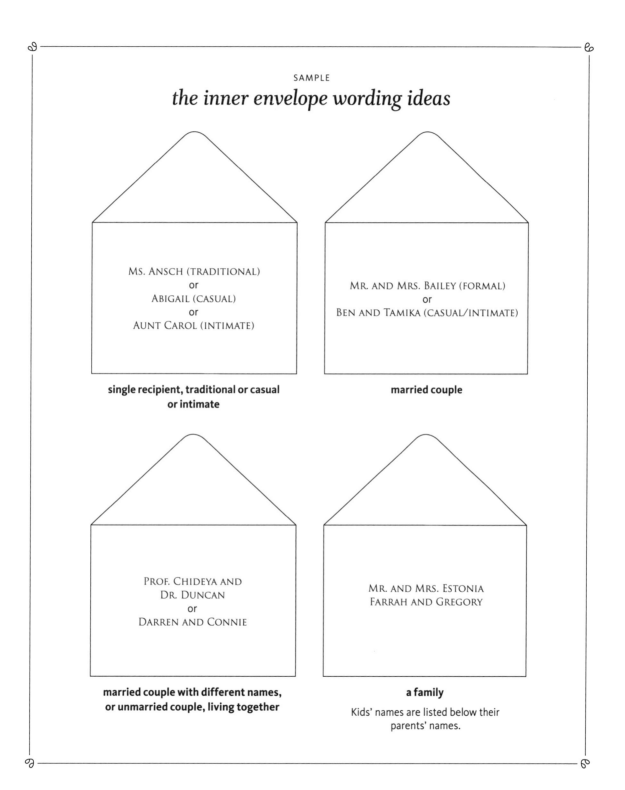

the inner envelope wording ideas

MS. ANSCH (TRADITIONAL)
or
ABIGAIL (CASUAL)
or
AUNT CAROL (INTIMATE)

**single recipient, traditional or casual
or intimate**

MR. AND MRS. BAILEY (FORMAL)
or
BEN AND TAMIKA (CASUAL/INTIMATE)

married couple

PROF. CHIDEYA AND
DR. DUNCAN
or
DARREN AND CONNIE

**married couple with different names,
or unmarried couple, living together**

MR. AND MRS. ESTONIA
FARRAH AND GREGORY

a family

Kids' names are listed below their
parents' names.

outer envelope wording ideas

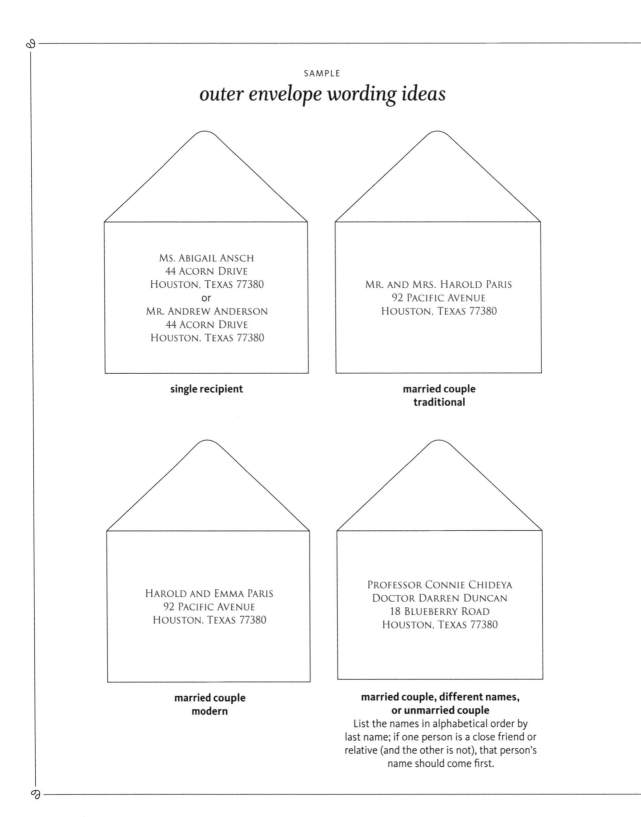

MS. ABIGAIL ANSCH
44 ACORN DRIVE
HOUSTON, TEXAS 77380
or
MR. ANDREW ANDERSON
44 ACORN DRIVE
HOUSTON, TEXAS 77380

single recipient

MR. AND MRS. HAROLD PARIS
92 PACIFIC AVENUE
HOUSTON, TEXAS 77380

**married couple
traditional**

HAROLD AND EMMA PARIS
92 PACIFIC AVENUE
HOUSTON, TEXAS 77380

**married couple
modern**

PROFESSOR CONNIE CHIDEYA
DOCTOR DARREN DUNCAN
18 BLUEBERRY ROAD
HOUSTON, TEXAS 77380

**married couple, different names,
or unmarried couple**
List the names in alphabetical order by
last name; if one person is a close friend or
relative (and the other is not), that person's
name should come first.

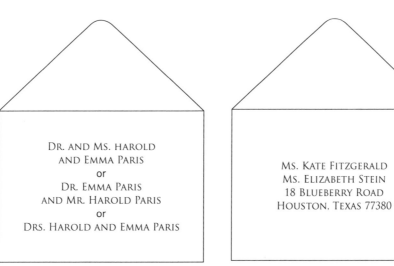

DR. AND MS. HAROLD
AND EMMA PARIS
or
DR. EMMA PARIS
AND MR. HAROLD PARIS
or
DRS. HAROLD AND EMMA PARIS

MS. KATE FITZGERALD
MS. ELIZABETH STEIN
18 BLUEBERRY ROAD
HOUSTON, TEXAS 77380

couples with doctor titles

same-sex couple
List in alphabetical order by last name.

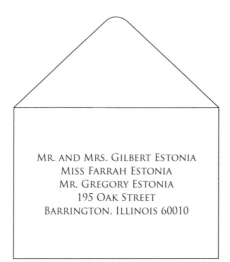

MR. AND MRS. GILBERT ESTONIA
MISS FARRAH ESTONIA
MR. GREGORY ESTONIA
195 OAK STREET
BARRINGTON, ILLINOIS 60010

family with kids under age eighteen
List any children after the parents'
names in order of age. (Note: A child over
eighteen who still lives at home should
receive a separate invite.)

Go to the post office and weigh a complete invitation so you know exactly how much postage each one requires. This step may sound tedious, but the alternative may be having your invites returned for insufficient postage, which could throw your wedding-planning schedule for quite a loop. Also, to avoid damaging your invitation envelopes, ask the post office to hand-stamp your envelopes rather than running them through the machine.

THE WORDING Include the names of all invitees at the address, including children under eighteen, and the names of any dates (writing "and Guest" on an inner envelope is too impersonal and should be avoided if at all possible). The formal way is with titles only: "Mr. and Mrs. Smith" (or "Ms. Jones and Mr. Smith," alphabetically, if a couple has different last names). They are addressed in a more informal fashion though—typically only title abbreviations and last name. But if your wedding is more casual and intimate, you can use just first names or familiar titles ("Aunt Zoe").

The outer envelope

The outer envelope is where you write the recipients' full names—official titles, first names, and all. It's where tradition is upheld and decorum celebrated; that means no cutting corners with abbreviations such as *Dr.*, *NY*, or *St.* (*Mrs.*, *Mr.*, *Ms.*, and *Jr.* are the only acceptable shorthands).

Names of children under eighteen need not appear on the outer envelope, but over-eighteens who live at home should either appear on their parents' envelope or, preferably, be sent their own invitation. For a single recipient bringing a date, get the other individual's address and send a separate invitation. As with the inner envelope, writing "and Guest" on an outer envelope is too impersonal. Roommates who aren't dating should also each receive their own invites.

THE RETURN ADDRESS Traditionally, the bride's parents' return address would be blind-embossed on the back flap of the outer envelope (as well as the response card envelope). But it's perfectly okay to have it printed, too. Today, most couples put their own return address on the outer envelope if they are keeping track of the guest list; it also indicates to guests where gifts from the registry should be sent.

DESIGNING YOUR WEDDING PAPER

If you're a newbie to the world of wedding stationery, this section will get you up to speed. While you can trust the experts to guide you, it helps to have a sense of direction, to understand a bit of the vocabulary, and to know your options before you start flipping through catalogs of invitation samples.

assembling the invitations

1. Depending on the style of your invite, it will be left flat, folded in half, or folded into fourths, with the text on the front of the "booklet," the fold on the left, and all other "pages" blank.

2. Tuck any enclosures inside, or set them on top of the card.

3. Place all the paperwork in an unsealed inner envelope, if you have one, with the print facing the back so that it's immediately visible upon opening. (Note: A high-end printer will probably place a piece of tissue paper on your invites to prevent smudging. You don't need to keep it, as the ink will have dried by the time you send them, but if you have a delicate overlay or other design you want to protect, feel free to leave the extra layer of tissue there. Leave the inner envelope unsealed.)

4. Handwrite the guests' names on the inner envelopes.

5. Place the inner envelope inside the outer envelope, with the guest's name facing the back.

6. Handwrite or have a calligrapher write guests' full names and mailing addresses on the outer envelope, or have a calligrapher do it. See "Outer Envelope Wording Ideas," page 300, for guidelines. Your stationer will probably be able to advise on any questions you have about how to address your invites to people with different titles.

7. Go to the post office and have the finished products weighed. If your budget allows, opt for specialty stamps—they're a nice touch.

8. Presto! Let the U.S. Postal Service do its magic.

Picking your paper
When it comes to designing your invitations, order matters: Start with the most basic layer—the paper—as that in turn will dictate the type of printing technique, font colors, and flourishes you can use.

PAPER WEIGHT When you start shopping for invitations, you'll hear terms like two-ply cardstock regularly. Paper weight is measured by ply, and the heavier and thicker the paper, the higher the ply. The thicker and heavier the paper, the fancier and more luxurious the invitation will feel. In general, you want an event of this magnitude to be on substantial paper (and have some weight) so it stands out from the rest of the mail. After all, you don't want guests to mistake it with any old piece of mail or party invitation.

PAPER TYPES The type of paper you use is as important as the actual design in establishing the mood of your wedding. Most formal wedding invitations use heavy card stock with squares of delicate stocks like tissue or parchment tucked into the envelope. The texture of the paper will determine how well ink will take to its surface (and therefore, which printing techniques you can use—keep reading for more on that), while the finish is another element that will help bring out your wedding style. Here is the lingo you'll need to know when deciding what materials you want for your wedding stationery.

100 Percent Cotton Elegant, understated, and pure; makes great keepsakes because it won't discolor over time.

Linen Another classic choice, linen papers are grainier than pure cotton stocks for a more textured appearance.

Wood Fiber Paper An increasingly popular choice that can be made in a variety of weights and colors.

Vellum A thin cotton blend (and thus, somewhat less expensive) with an opaque, nonreflective finish; often layered on top of card stock. When used alone, it's often paired with flat printing, as vellum is too thin for some printing techniques, including letterpress and engraving.

Glassine A very thin, waxy paper. Thinner than vellum, its surface is slick and shiny, whereas vellum is more translucent. Glassine is best suited for envelope use, while vellum is sturdy enough to be printed on and is therefore better for invitation use.

Handmade Made from natural materials, including cotton, rag, hemp, and plant fibers, so it's considered a more eco-friendly choice; uneven or rough in texture.

Industrial Made from chipboard or newsprint, often from recycled fibers, industrial papers have a rugged, edgy look about them. Corrugated cardboard and brown kraft paper (think brown grocery bags) are examples.

Jacquard Screen-printed paper that creates an illusion of layering; for example, paper that looks like it's overlaid with a swatch of lace.

Laid Like vellum except with a rougher, textured finish.

Marbled Decorative paper marked by swirling, abstract patterns that resemble the surface of marble.

Matte Paper with an opaque, nonreflective finish.

Moiré Named after the fabric, this stock bears subtle watermarks.

Mylar Foil-like, noncrinkling paper with a shiny, mirrorlike finish. It's best for envelopes and not appropriate for the invitation (ink doesn't take to it well).

Parchment Cloudy, translucent paper that creates an airy, dreamy effect.

Rice Paper A thin, soft paper that is actually not made from rice but from other fibers, including mulberry and hemp. It's nontraditional but beautiful and elegant. It can only accept the letterpress printing mode; cream and ivory are the most common colors used in invitations.

Corrugated Thick, folded stock with wrinkles, ridges, and grooves that says "urban chic."

Deckle Edge The irregular, feathered, torn-looking edge of handmade paper that can have a whimsical or vintage look.

Printing techniques

An important factor in an invitation's character—and price tag—is the way it's printed. There are a handful of printing techniques, each with its own distinct charms, challenges, and costs.

ENGRAVING When most people think of wedding invitations, engraving is what they envision. The printer uses a metal plate engraved with the text you've provided to stamp the words onto the paper from behind. The final product is textured, with raised letters in the front and "cavities" in the back that can give invites a formal air—though depending on the colors and motifs you choose, engraving can also look festive and fun. Choose engraving if you:

- Have a generous invitation budget (this is one of the most expensive print methods, used for ultraformal wedding invites)
- Can find a retailer that does this (mass-market shops sometimes don't)—your best bet is a boutique stationer
- Are willing to wait up to eight weeks for the job to be completed (high style hurries for no one)
- Are having a very formal affair with a huge guest list (the engraving will tip guests off that you mean formal business, and ironically, the larger the order, the more cost-effective engraving is)

THERMOGRAPHY This is the most popular method of printing, used by most large stationery manufacturers. A heat-based process fuses ink and resinous powder to create raised lettering. It's virtually indistinguishable from engraving unless you feel the back of the invitation, which remains smooth, but it's more cost-effective than engraving. Thermography is a great option if you:

- Have a less-than-gigantic budget but still want formal invitations
- Want a unique (think: nonblack) ink color (often not available with engraving)
- Don't have the two months you'd need to wait for an engraved order (thermography takes anywhere from two weeks to a month)

LETTERPRESS Letterpress—in which the text and patterns are impressed into the paper—is a beautiful printing alternative to engraving, but more expensive. Dating back to the fifteenth century, the method involves inking an image to produce an impression. The impression is then transferred by placing paper against the image and manually applying pressure. The images and typeface appear precise—individually "stamped into" the paper—and very rich in color. Letterpress requires heavy paper, and the printing process itself is relatively labor-intensive, so it tends to be pricey. However, many stationers offer lower-priced letterpress lines, too. Letterpress is a great option if you:

- Are using unusual paper, motifs, or typefaces, or want to play around with pigments, as engraving and thermography restrict these possibilities (with both thermography and engraving, you're pretty much limited to one color, for example)
- Have room in your budget (it's one of the most expensive printing types)
- Are having a traditional, more formal affair
- Want to impress your guests
- Have room in your timeline for the three-to-four-week turnaround

DIGITAL Digital printing is similar to what you'd get from a home laser printer, but professional printers offer higher quality, so you won't wind up with fading or smudging that you might get from printing them yourself at home. It is the least expensive printing option and can be done very quickly (in five to ten business days once the proof is approved). Digital printing can only be done on lighter weights of paper (heavier card stock won't work), but you can play with a greater variety of colors. Go digital if you:

- Have a limited stationery budget or just don't see the point in spending a ton on fancy printing techniques
- Are having a less formal affair
- Want to play with a variety of colors
- Are tight on time

OFFSET In terms of appearance, offset printing is similar to digital, but the quality is higher. Again, the printing itself is flat—the only texture you will have is whatever is in the paper itself. You'll have more paper options with offset printing, though it is slightly more expensive than digital printing. It also has a relatively fast turnaround time—the norm is about five to ten business days from proof approval. Offset is perfect for couples who:

calligraphy 101

Most couples use hand calligraphy for addressing their envelopes, though the use of spot-calligraphy (using the fancy technique just to call out important details like your names or the wedding date) is becoming popular for invitations. For a smaller wedding, some couples choose to do the entire invitation in calligraphy, but as you would expect, this is a special service that can be expensive.

finding a calligrapher

Your stationer may offer the service or be able to recommend someone. The key to good calligraphy is consistency: Shape, stroke, weight, spacing, and rhythm are all factors in letter perfection, so request font samples from potential calligraphers.

budget

Calligraphy can range anywhere from three dollars to eight-plus dollars an envelope. Computerized calligraphy is a cost-effective alternative to handwritten script and is also much faster if you're tight on time. While nothing compares to the look of handcrafted cursive, you might be surprised at the elegance of digital calligraphy.

style

While classic calligraphy has a very ornate look, many calligraphers can do a range of fonts to achieve more modern looks. Many will also create custom monograms, designs and maps that you can then use as a template to send to your stationer for your invitation suite.

envelopes

If you're using a calligrapher to address your invitations, you'll need to give her a typed guest address list. To make it easy to follow, leaving little room for error, lay out your list in an orderly, three-line format (most calligraphers don't like to work off of spreadsheets):

Mr. and Mrs. John Davidson
123 Main Street
Merrytown, MA 12345

When you receive the finished product from your calligrapher, check and then double-check each invite and envelope to make sure all names and addresses are correct. In addition to addressing the envelopes, some calligraphers, for a nominal fee, will stuff, seal, and stamp the invitations, which is a simple way to save some time.

timeline

Calligraphers require roughly ten to fourteen days to address one hundred invitations. If you are getting married during a popular month (May through October), more time may be needed, especially if you are looking for something elaborate (designs, scrolls, and so on). So plan your invitation order accordingly.

- Want to play with different colors of ink or want complicated invitation art (think intricate motifs)
- Are looking for a cost-effective technique
- Don't have the luxury of time

EMBOSSING A raised printing method usually used for large initials or borders, embossing comes with a hefty price tag. Hence, hardly anyone has an entire invitation embossed. The technique is most commonly used for the return address on envelopes. Blind embossing is a printing process that employs a die (a tool used to cut various paper shapes, commonly employed with envelopes) to yield colorless letters and images with a raised "relief" surface. Choose embossing if you:

- Want a spectacular-looking monogram on your thank-you notes or formal stationery
- Are having a formal wedding and want a border or other raised detail on your posh invites
- Are a sucker when it comes to "extra" touches
- Have ample room in your stationery budget
- Want to give your envelopes a luxe look

Typefaces

Choosing a unique font is one of the easiest ways to express your individual style. Some typefaces feel formal; others feel festive. Some seem like an ode to the past and others seem futuristic.

All-script invitations are becoming a thing of the past. Instead, many couples opt for a mix of fonts (block capital letters and script, for example). Couples hosting casual celebrations are also starting to choose more informal-looking fonts, like all-lowercase—even for the names. Just remember: Your guests still need to be able to read it.

Design options

Figure out what sort of style (modern, traditional, retro) you want your wedding to have and how you want your invitations to convey that feeling. If you wouldn't think of sending anything other than the classic ecru card with black script, you can skip ahead to printing considerations. But if you want the invitation to express a less traditional style or foreshadow your theme, read on.

COLOR Decide if and how you'll incorporate your wedding-day hues—perhaps with colored paper, colored envelopes, or colored text and graphics on white paper. Paper and ink options go far beyond traditional black and white. Depending on your wedding style, anything from bold hues (fuchsia, coral, and lime) to shades of gray can work. Always balance bright colors with neutral, and make sure the

type types

Here's a rundown of some of the most common fonts—some of which you probably already know.

serif Serif fonts feature little "flags" on the tops and bottoms of letters. Though they don't have to be, serif styles tend to look formal but not overly so—lots of everyday typefaces (think Times New Roman or Courier) are serif fonts.

sans serif Sans serif fonts don't have those flags—and again, you probably use sans serif fonts all the time without even thinking about it (fonts such as Arial and Helvetica are sans serif). These kinds of type tend to look stylish and modern, a good choice for a loft or rooftop party.

script The typeface equivalent of cursive, letters are (or have the appearance of being) connected to each other. Like handwritten calligraphy, script fonts are often slanted, usually to the right. The more curves at the tips of the letters, the fancier the font. The especially ornate scripts are best for black-tie ballroom and country club weddings.

italic By far the most popular, this simple "hand" style looks good on any paper. Italic letters slant upward to the right and are based on an oval shape, with the width of the letters usually half the height. The lines are clean and crisp, making italic fonts especially good for semiformal weddings.

copperplate A close second to calligraphy, this font feels formal and old-fashioned.

gothic Also called "Old English" or "blackhand," Gothic is a very formal, heavy handwritten font with a broad-tipped pen. It works well for theme or period weddings.

text is readable. Bold ink hues like navy and fuchsia are all easy to read, but lighter shades should be avoided.

PATTERN Patterns are particularly popular with letterpress invites because of the printing style's lush, textured look. You can echo designs from the invitations in the programs, the menus, and even the china pattern, cocktail napkins, and favor packaging.

MOTIFS You may want to include a dingbat, which is stationery speak for a decorative motif. From monograms and family crests to a design element that echoes your wedding locale (like a city skyline or palm tree) or theme (like a lobster or a maple leaf), include a design element that can easily be carried through from the invitations to the other wedding details, like the menus and even the cake.

SHAPE Circles, triangles, or ovals are a great alternative to the classic square or rectangular invite. Keep in mind that oddly shaped mailings can cost extra to send.

OTHER WEDDING STATIONERY

If you have room in your budget and you're not the DIY type, you may want to have your guest book, menus, and ceremony programs printed by your stationer so they all coordinate.

Ceremony programs Printed programs are a wonderful way to make your guests feel like a part of ceremony, especially if you're incorporating readings or ethnic traditions. It's also a nice place to list your VIPs, and to include notes of remembrance and thanks.

THE NUMBER Number of guests—plus twenty-five. (Trust us—you'll want to keep a few as keepsakes and so will your parents.)

THE WORDING Include the names of everyone in your wedding party and their relationship to you. There should also be a ceremony itinerary so guests know what's coming next. Explain any special rituals, and include any original texts or literary passages that will be read. This not only helps guests to follow along, it also elevates the program from simple schedule to true wedding keepsake.

THE DESIGN Some couples include pictures of the couple. You can also incorporate your invitation motif or logo. For an outdoor ceremony during the summer, you can create fan-shaped programs to keep guests

clever ways to save on stationery

stick with plain envelopes
While colored, textured, and lined envelopes are pretty, no one will notice if you go plain on the envelopes. Think about it: It's the one part of the suite you know will be thrown out.

keep it light
The more enclosure cards and extras you include, the heavier—and more expensive to send—your invitations will be.

utilize your wedding website
Instead of tons of enclosure cards, print any extra information about hotel blocks, transportation, and peripheral events on your wedding

don't leave a paper trail
While we strongly recommend sending paper invitations for your wedding invitations, Evites are perfectly acceptable for the surrounding events, like the next-day brunch and welcome party.

go simple
The more personalized and fancy you go, the more room you'll need in your budget. Choose less expensive printing methods, paper, and designs. In other words, skip the letterpress, vellum overlays, and embossed designs.

diy
From computerized calligraphy software to invitation-printing kits, you can print your own programs, menus, save-the-dates, envelopes, and even invitations.

---

cool. Ceremony programs are typically placed in a basket near the entrance of the ceremony venue or set on guests' seats.

Escort cards and place cards
Both are small cards that help guests find their dinner tables and seats. Usually escort cards are laid out alphabetically on a table outside the dining space and include each guest's name and their table number or name. Place cards, on the other hand, are set on the actual tables at each place setting and indicate where each guest should sit. If you are only assigning tables, not seats, you will only need escort cards.

THE TIMELINE You can order both escort and place cards with your invitations, but you won't be able to have guests' names printed (you won't have your guest list or seating chart finalized until about two or three weeks before).

THE NUMBER Number of guests—plus twenty-five for last-minute changes or mistakes.

THE WORDING The point of these cards is to direct guests to the proper tables and seats. On the escort cards, print the name of each guest and the table number or table name. For place cards, print the name of each guest (they'll be placed at each guest's respective table setting in advance).

THE DESIGN Add a fun motif to carry out a theme on your reception cards. If you're marrying on the shore and naming your tables after islands or beaches, navy blue lighthouses would be appropriate. Or stamp the cards with a red rose if that's a primary bloom in your bouquet. See left for more creative escort ideas.

Menu cards As reception menus take on personal significance, more and more couples are providing menu cards: Guests appreciate knowing what they will be served or what a waiter will be coming around to ask them to choose between when they sit down.

THE TIMELINE Obviously, you'll have to define your menu and wine offerings before you get these printed. So start your tastings early (six to eight months or more before the wedding) and order your menu cards no later than six to eight weeks before the wedding.

THE NUMBER One for each guest, two to three per table, one for each station, or one in front of each dish on the buffet table.

THE WORDING List each course and what will be served along with drink options. If at a buffet line, identify and explain the dish in a bit more detail. If you've created a menu to reflect your heritage, explain why you are serving *limoncello* as a dessert drink. If you are offering special wines to fit with each course, explain why each wine has been paired with each dish.

THE DESIGN If you are putting menus at each place setting, medium-to-heavy card stock works best. You don't want a piece of paper covering your plate. If there are a few at each table, you can use a size like four by six or five by seven—these fit nicely into a frame for everyone to see. Buffet menu cards will need larger type, and eight by ten would even be appropriate here—again, framing the cards is always a nice touch. You can carry your wedding motif through the menu cards or add your new couple monogram (if you're following a traditional timeline, you'll be married by the time guests see your menus, so it's okay to use your married monogram or initials on the paper at the reception). You might also choose to print each guest's name at the top of the menu and let your menu cards double as place

wedding announcement wording ideas

MR. AND MRS. PETER JOHNSON
AND
MR. AND MRS. BRADLEY HARRIS
HAVE THE HONOR OF ANNOUNCING
THE MARRIAGE OF THEIR CHILDREN

Heather Amanda

AND

Jeffrey Michael

ON THURSDAY, THE THIRTEENTH OF MAY
TWO THOUSAND FOURTEEN
KIRKWOOD, MISSOURI

from the parents

*Heather Amanda
Johnson*

AND

*Jeffrey Michael
Harris*

(or "Jeffrey and Heather Harris")
ANNOUNCE THEIR MARRIAGE
(etc.)

from the couple

cards for a personalized touch. (See chapter 11, page 162, for creative menu ideas.)

Wedding announcements
Traditionally, wedding announcements are a formal way to announce your marriage to anyone whom you weren't able to invite to the wedding but whom you want to update. Like formal engagement announcements, wedding announcements have largely fallen out of favor. Still, some couples choose to send a formal wedding announcement, especially if one person's name is changing. It's also okay to send a more casual announcement via e-mail to let your guests know about your new status—and update them on your new name and/or contact information if it's changing.

THE TIMELINE Wedding announcements are mailed immediately after your ceremony—traditionally, the couple is supposed to mail them on the way to the reception. But it's perfectly acceptable to have your moms send them out while you are on your honeymoon or to do it yourselves right after you return.

THE NUMBER This will vary depending on the number of people who did not receive an invitation but with whom you would still like to share the news. You may want to order ten to fifteen extra too, as you may realize there are more people you forgot to fill in than you realized in the excitement of everything.

Thank-you notes
Rules of etiquette dictate that every gift deserves a thank-you note. This means that between the gifts you'll receive before, on the day of, and after your wedding, you two will be doing a lot of writing.

THE TIMELINE Even though it's hard to find time to squeeze them in prewedding, it's better than having to sit down and do them all at once posthoneymoon. You should send them no more than two weeks after receiving prewedding presents and six weeks after returning from your honeymoon.

THE NUMBER Lots and lots. Many people will be giving you more than one gift (for your engagement, your shower, etc.). And yes, you need to write them a separate note after each event, for each gift. You're going to get a lot of stuff, and thank-you notes never go bad. Stock up.

THE WORDING Personalize each note to reflect your relationship to the addressee and the specific gift they gave. For example: "Dear Aunt Joan, thank you so much for the barbecue grill. We can't wait to throw our first July Fourth party and hope you'll be able to join us." It doesn't have to be a work of genius; a dash of humor and a sprinkle of loving sentiment are the essential ingredients.

THE DESIGN A thank-you note is traditionally a simple ecru sheet or folded card. You might add a monogram, choose ready-made cards, or design something original with your stationer. This is your opportunity to continue your wedding theme or to create a new one for yourselves as a couple. We love the idea of using postcards from your honeymoon destination or including a video trailer from the wedding with the note as a small thank-you gift.

20

a rousing reception

TIMELINE

PLANNING

12+ months before
Book your reception
location

5–6 months before
Finalize your cocktail-hour
details

Plan your reception
timeline, complete with
surprises

1–2 weeks before
Call the location manager
and make sure your vendors
will have access to the site
when they need it

Your wedding reception will likely be the biggest and best party you ever get to throw—but half the fun should be planning it. There are many components that go into an amazing celebration—music, food, cocktails, décor—but the real secret to planning a memorable event is creating an experience for your guests. You are taking them on an entertaining journey over the course of four hours, and your goal should be to make it a really great one. What will they see first? When will they ooh and aah? What are the moments of surprise? Don't worry, we've outlined all the basic rituals—the standard framework for the classic reception—so you know what to expect (and what's expected of you). But this chapter is really about figuring out some uniquely personal ideas for making it a night neither you nor your guests will ever forget.

RECEPTION TIMETABLES

What you do at your reception depends largely on the type of party you're throwing. The more elaborate and traditional the reception, the more elements you may want to include.

Don't even consider running your own reception—you cannot be both stage manager and star of the show. If you aren't using a wedding planner, we strongly suggest you hire a day-of coordinator, a professional to manage all of the details in the days leading up to the main event as well as the timing and final calls the day of. If this isn't an option, appoint a reception master (this person can be a friend, a relative, even the banquet manager), and ask him or her to monitor the party and make sure everything happens on schedule. Your bandleader or DJ can serve as public "master of ceremonies" during your reception, but someone needs to tell him what to announce when and how much to say. In fact, a script with a minute-by-minute timeline is important guidance that everyone involved in your event needs.

Five hours—cocktails, dinner, and dancing

If you are having the classic wedding—hors d'oeuvres and cocktails followed by a sit-down dinner and dancing—the party will run four to five hours. The most common start time is six o'clock, except in the summer, when the days are long and couples want to wait for a sunset ceremony. The standard order of events looks something like this:

- **7 p.m.** Cocktail hour begins.
- **8 p.m.** Guests head from the cocktail hour into the reception and find their seats.
- **8:15 p.m.** Your emcee begins introducing the wedding party, starting with your parents and ending with you. (Note: Some couples choose to skip the wedding party introductions and just do their big entrance.)
- **8:20 p.m.** The first dance, during which waiters start serving the first course.
- **8:25 p.m.** A welcome speech or a blessing. If you're not having either, begin the toasts now—the parents of the bride followed by the honor attendants.
- **8:30 p.m.** The main course is served. The emcee asks guests to take their seats. Music should be low enough so guests can talk at their tables.
- **9:15 p.m.** The music starts to get a little more upbeat to get guests who are finished with their meals out onto the dance floor.
- **9:30 p.m.** The father-daughter dance, which is followed by the mother-son dance.

TIP
speak up

If your bandleader or DJ is going to be the talent hosting your personal Oscars, give her specific instructions as to how much you want her to say and what the tone should be. If, on the other hand, you don't want this person making announcements at all, then make that very clear. Be aware, however, that someone will need to quiet the crowds when the first dance is supposed to begin or the father of the bride is ready to toast.

- **9:35 p.m.** A dance set begins with more upbeat songs to entice guests out of their seats.
- **9:45 p.m.** A couple of slow songs play.
- **9:50 p.m.** Back to the more upbeat songs.
- **10:30 p.m.** The cake cutting.
- **10:35 p.m.** Some midpaced songs play as cake is served so guests can dance if they want.
- **10:45 p.m.** Guests are seated for cake.
- **11 p.m.** The bouquet toss, followed by the garter toss, if you're doing these.
- **11:10 p.m.** The final dance set. Time to cue up those songs you couldn't play while all the elder guests were still there!
- **11:55 p.m.** The last dance, followed by your grand exit, if you're making one.

Three hours—lunch or brunch

Lunch receptions tend to be on the shorter side, running three to three and a half hours. They should start sometime between eleven and one. Instead of a full cocktail hour you can have a quick champagne toast or mimosas and a simple passed hors d'oeuvre. Once guests move into the reception, the events unfold pretty quickly according to this schedule:

- **11 a.m.** Guests head into the reception area and make their way to their seats.
- **11:10 a.m.** The emcee introduces the newlyweds; you do your first dance right away.
- **11:15 a.m.** A welcome speech, a blessing, or just the toasts, starting with the best man.
- **11:20 a.m.** Lunch/brunch is served.
- **11:55 a.m.** As guests are finishing their food, have your father-daughter dance, followed by the mother-son dance. Keep the songs short!
- **12 p.m.** A forty-minute power dance set (or mingling and maybe a few games if you're skipping the dance party altogether).
- **12:40 p.m.** The cake cutting.
- **12:45 p.m.** Some slow songs play while the staff plates and serves the cake.
- **1 p.m.** Guests are seated for cake.
- **1:15 p.m.** The bouquet toss, if you're going to do one. (We recommend skipping the garter toss—it's a little early in the day for that!)
- **1:20 p.m.** The final dance set begins. The most upbeat music plays now (or more mingling).
- **1:55 p.m.** The last dance.

You want to minimize the time between your wedding ceremony and reception to make it easy on your guests, but sometimes circumstances don't make that practical or possible. Huge time gaps between the ceremony and the reception (you know, the ones where the ceremony starts at noon, but the party isn't until seven P.M.) aren't a great idea, because you're often leaving guests in the middle of nowhere with absolutely nothing to do. With that said, it's okay to have some time between your wedding ceremony and reception—as long as you keep it under three hours and make sure guests are entertained or have the option of being entertained. You may want to plan an outing—a sightseeing tour or a casual lunchtime barbecue at the home of a friend or relative—or set up a hospitality lounge, with drinks and snacks, at the hotel where your guests will be staying. Your main goal is to make sure nobody's left with nowhere to go and nothing to do.

Two hours—cocktail-and-cake reception

The two-hour wedding reception is perfect if you want a less formal gathering in the late afternoon (say a three P.M. ceremony followed by champagne and light snacks or cake from four to six) or late evening (an eight P.M. ceremony followed by cocktails, food stations, and a dessert bar). Since there is no seated meal, no time is devoted to serving and clearing and the reception rituals take center stage. Here is a suggested order of events:

- **9 p.m.** Guests head into the reception area.
- **9:05 p.m.** The emcee introduces you and your groom. Once you're in, start greeting guests!
- **9:10 p.m.** Food stations open, and passed hors d'oeuvres start rolling out.
- **9:30 p.m.** The first dance. Food service pauses.
- **9:35 p.m.** The father-daughter and mother-son dances. (Food service is still paused.)
- **9:40 p.m.** Food service resumes. If there will be more dancing, an upbeat set would start now.
- **10:10 p.m.** The toasts.
- **10:15 p.m.** The cake cutting.
- **10:20 p.m.** A couple of slow songs play as the staff cuts and plates the cake.
- **10:25 p.m.** Cake is passed around.
- **10:40 p.m.** The final dance set plays (or mingling continues if you're skipping the dancing).
- **10:55 p.m.** The last dance.

RECEPTION RITUALS

The ceremony is over and you've officially sealed the deal; time to celebrate with some cocktails and carousing! Every classic ritual at a wedding reception—from the best man's toast to the cutting of the cake—serves a purpose. Every one of the activities is optional, and you should choose to include only those that excite you. But be forewarned: If you don't cut the cake, Grandma is going to wonder—as well as worry about—when she can leave the event, as the cake cutting is the signal that it's acceptable to leave.

Feel free to blow out a few traditions—performing an ultrachoreographed first dance, for example—and downplay others. If you are choosing a nontraditional order of events or are replacing expected rituals with something more creative, explain your decisions to your wedding party, banquet manager, and bandleader so they can help guests understand what comes (and not worry that a mistake is being made by their staff!).

Cocktail hour

The cocktail hour is when you finally get to kick up your heels and kick off your party. It's your chance to charm your guests (as well as refresh them) once the pomp and circumstance of the ceremony are over. While these sixty minutes are easy to overlook when you're busy planning the ceremony and reception, they will help set the tone for the rest of the night. The reality is that you may miss most of the cocktail hour if you're off taking photos. So you really want your loved ones to feel taken care of: These sixty to ninety minutes are mostly intended as an opportunity for guests to mingle, to nibble, to toast, and most of all, to relax. We cover everything you need to keep the bar stocked and whet guests' palates with amazing hors d'oeuvres on page 155.

As for how to keep your guests entertained during your happy hour, think of your cocktail hour as a souped-up version of your favorite happy hour with your top drinks, fun appetizers, great music, and comfortable seating.

If your cocktail hour lasts longer than an hour, or many of your guests do not know each other, it is a good idea to have some activities of some kind. Food stations where guests can watch a chef prepare sushi can double as entertainment, or set up a cigar bar or bring in a caricaturist or fortune-teller. Flip to chapter 12 for musical ideas for your cocktail hour. This is also a great time and place for the photo booth and guest book. For help decorating your cocktail-hour space, turn to chapter 7, page 102.

Transitioning from cocktails to dinner

About ten minutes before the cocktail hour ends, your musicians and waitstaff should encourage guests to make their way to the reception area. Of course, an announcement is the simple way to do this, but subtle cues, like having your musicians play softer songs and ending the hors d'oeuvres service, will also help send guests the message. A surefire way to get guests into the reception space is to close the bar. This transition is harder than you may imagine; guests are having fun and hate to move. Often your planner's staff will have to walk through the space physically encouraging people to move into the reception room. Some hotel banquet managers also have a soft, almost Buddhist-sounding bell they

---

CLEVER IDEAS
the new sit-down

Many foodie couples don't want the meal interrupted by dancing and prefer to have a full, formal dinner party followed by a transition to another space set up as a club where partying can truly be the focus. Play very light music during the meal so that conversations are actually possible.

Make sure the youngest wedding guests are taken care of.

Hire a babysitter to keep an eye on little guests.

Turn the kids' table kid-friendly. Use smaller plates, utensils, and glasses. Covering the table with white paper and crayons or markers will keep them contentedly busy. (Provide washable markers and you'll win over the parents, too.) You can also put out bubbles and small games.

Hire an entertainer just for them, like a clown, musician, or face painter.

Create a children's menu with fun choices like peanut butter and jelly, grilled cheese sandwiches, fries, or pizza.

Create an activity center by turning an unused room into a play area. Rent or borrow Ping-Pong tables, air-hockey tables, hula hoops, and jump ropes.

CLEVER IDEAS
the wow factor

Add extra oomph to your cocktail hour or reception with some specialty entertainment.

wine tastings
Bring in an expert sommelier for your cocktail hour. Near the bar, set up a small wine-tasting area where guests can learn more about the evening's selections (this will also help them decide on what to order during dinner).

professional dancers
From ballroom to belly dancing to salsa, book professional dancers for your reception. This visual display will entertain your guests while they eat, and hey, they might even learn some moves.

silhouette artists
Hire artists to create trendy black hand-cut silhouettes of guests during the cocktail hour and throughout the reception. Bonus: They double as a great personalized take-home favor. A cartoonist doing caricatures works, too.

a painter
Hire an artist to capture the reception scene in oil or acrylic on canvas. Guests will love checking in on her progress, and you'll have an incredible keepsake for your wall.

fireworks display
For the ultimate wow factor, give guests a lasting impression with a fabulous send-off. Your display can be individually crafted for your wedding to match your wedding colors or motif.

ring to send guests the signal. Warn your bridal party if this is an activity you will need their help with so they don't let down their hair too much during those sixty minutes.

The big entrance
Once the guests are seated in the reception, many couples choose to be "announced," along with their wedding party and sometimes their parents. You assemble outside the reception room with your wedding party and then the bandleader, DJ, or your highly entertaining uncle takes the mic and announces everyone by name as they enter ("Please welcome the bride's parents, Jane and John Smith"). After the bride and groom's parents usually comes the wedding party, walking with the partners they had at the ceremony. Finally, you two: "And now, for the first time as husband and wife, Mr. and Mrs. . . ." enter

the room. This ritual works well if you are literally seeing people for the first time at the reception because you spent the entire cocktail hour taking pictures. If you have been at the cocktail hour or it just seems too contrived, try instead to have the "announcement" of you as a couple lead directly into the first dance instead. Your introduction onto the dance floor will feel more like an official kickoff to the party.

The spotlight dances
The first dance physically reiterates what the ceremony just stated: You are a unit now. The first dance is a way of sharing an intimate and romantic moment together as newlyweds with two hundred of your friends and family watching before you're pulled in a hundred different directions the rest of the night.

Your first dance can happen right with the band's first song, after the toasts, after the first course has been served, or even after everyone finishes eating. The point is that it's not necessarily the first dance of the evening, just the first time you hit the dance floor (alone) as newlyweds. (Flip to chapter 12 for more spotlight dance song ideas.)

Our preference is for your dance to literally be the first dance of the night. People often feel awkward heading out onto the dance floor during the first number that the band plays. The bandleader has to try too hard to get people dancing, which adds to the discomfort all around. If everyone is literally standing and watching the hosts dance, it is a much easier transition for them to start filling the dance floor. As your song ends, typically the father of the bride steps in for the father-daughter dance and the mother-son dance comes next. If you'd rather space them out, you can have the parent spotlight dances during the main course. In that case, just ask the bandleader to invite guests to join you on the dance floor after the first dance, you wave everyone in, the next number starts, and the party is in full swing!

The feast
Time to eat! Depending on what type of reception you're having, this is when guests sit down and are served, head to the buffet, or mix and mingle while sampling from the food stations you've selected. The food-service portion of the evening takes time. Speak with your banquet manager to get exact details, because the number of guests, amount of waitstaff, and level of service all factor into the time allotment. A three-course dinner typically takes about an hour and a half (not including dessert), while a family-style dinner will last about 45 minutes. For a buffet, you can loosely do the math yourself: Figure for every foot of buffet food, it will take guests 3 seconds to file through. So if you have 5 feet of food, that's 15 seconds of buffet time per guest. For 150 guests, multiply 150 by 15 and you get 2,250 seconds, or 37.5

TIP
assigned seating

Guests should pick up their escort cards during the cocktail hour or in the transition into the reception area. Displayed creatively, escort cards can double as dramatic décor. Just make sure your display can be approached by many people at the same time and is not placed too close to the door of your space or else you will end up with a traffic jam—and less time for your reception.

minutes, on average, for all your guests to put food on their plate, plus another 20 minutes for them to eat.

The arrival of the entree can be entertaining, too. If an army of well-dressed waitstaff comes out of the kitchen in a dramatic way, it can inspire oohs and aahs among guests. A good rule of thumb to follow when timing out your meal: Budget about twenty minutes for everyone to be seated (smaller parties of under a hundred may only need ten minutes); then allow ten minutes for each course to be served, ten minutes for everyone to eat, and ten minutes for the course to be cleared. So at thirty minutes per course total, you would need to allot one and a half hours for a three-course meal and two hours for a four-course meal. But there is simply no way for clearing the plates to be pretty. Quiet and unobtrusive are all you can hope for, so guests can continue to talk!

Reception blessings
Your officiant or an honored family member might say a blessing or prayer before you eat. At a Jewish reception, the rabbi, the couple's parents or grandparents, or another honored guest gives a formal blessing, called the *hamotzi*, over a loaf of challah. Pieces of the bread are then passed around to all the guests.

Couples of other faiths may also choose to have their officiant or an honored family member say a blessing or prayer, or perform other traditional rituals, before the meal begins. If you plan to include a prefeast blessing or other ritual in your reception, let your emcee and caterer know, so the food doesn't get served during the middle of your spiritual moment.

The welcome toast
Toasts usually begin after everyone has found a seat and been served the first course. You could also toast during cocktails, after everyone has been served champagne. Traditionally, the father of the bride, along with his wife (if they choose to do it together), makes the first toast, particularly if this is "their" party (read: they paid for it). If the parents of the groom are contributing to the wedding fund, they might follow next. Otherwise, their toasts take place at the rehearsal dinner. Next up: the best man and then the maid of honor. During the speeches, everyone else remains seated, including the toastees (you). Just raise your glass at the end of each toast and smile and mouth the words *thank you*.

To finish off, the groom typically takes the floor, with—or followed by—the bride, to welcome guests and thank the parents and members of the wedding party; the bride and groom also thank each other. Toasting is a way of stopping in the middle of a fabulous moment to acknowledge your good fortune and is not meant to be another painful rite of passage. If you'd rather ski the North Pole in a bikini than speak in public, just say a quick "Thanks for coming, everyone!"

Some toasting sessions can turn into marathons where both sets of parents speak, as do other relatives, childhood best friends, and other members of the wedding party. If this is the kind of reception entertainment you and your guests would enjoy—and you have the wordsmiths in your midst to keep it lively—then by all means let everyone know before the wedding that their words will be welcome. If you would personally rather skip ahead to the dancing portion of the evening (which your guests will probably appreciate—marathon toasts can get tedious), you may want to assign the groom's family and your bridal party to speak at the rehearsal dinner and leave the reception toasting to just your parents and you two.

The tosses
The bouquet and garter tosses are modern takes on old superstitions. Some couples wouldn't dream of omitting these entertaining traditions, while others wouldn't dream of including them. If the mere thought of these traditions makes you cringe, it's okay to skip them. Or do one and not the other. Both take place toward the end of the party, usually before the cake cutting, but you can have them right before the last dance if you'd rather your grandparents not witness the silliness.

THE BOUQUET TOSS The single female guests gather on the dance floor. The bride either faces them or turns her back and lobs her bouquet over her head. According to tradition, whoever catches it will be next to marry. If you want to save your bridal bouquet but still do the flower toss, ask your florist to create a smaller "tossing bouquet."

THE GARTER TOSS This is the guys' turn to be embarrassed: The single men gather in the same area. The bride sits on a chair while the groom lifts her skirt up to remove her garter, slipping it off her leg with his hands (please, gentlemen, do us a favor and don't use your teeth and keep it clean!), and then whips it at the crowd of single men. Whoever catches the garter poses for a photo, dances with the winner of the bouquet toss, and, of course, will be the next to get married!

Cutting the cake
Wedding cake serves two purposes: It taps into the ancient ritual of sharing a bite of food to seal the marriage bond, and it's dessert, of course! Cutting the cake typically happens near the end of the reception. For a champagne-and-cake-only affair, you might do it after the receiving line.

TIMELINE
traditional toasting order

Parents of the bride

Parents of the groom (if cohosting, can stand up with the bride's parents)

Best man

Maid of honor

Other guests (optional)

Bride and/or groom

TRADITIONS
ancient tales of tossing

The garter toss comes from an old English tradition: After the wedding, friends crowded into the honeymoon suite, the women to throw the groom's stockings backward over their heads at him, the men to do the same with the bride's. Whoever hit the mark was believed to be the next to marry. The bouquet toss comes from an ancient belief that certain herbs are lucky. A bride would give her bouquet to a friend for luck.

Fun ways for guests to celebrate your getaway from the ceremony or reception.

Confetti.

Sparklers! Light up the night as you make your escape.

Paper airplanes. Give your exit a retro spin!

Ribbon streamers. These DIY beauties can also double as décor.

Silly String. Dash to your limo as your guests fire off a colorful storm.

Banner flags. Have miniature flags printed with a fun phrase (like "Yay!") for guests to wave you off with.

Bubbles. Perfect for a spring or summer wedding.

Pinwheels. Go on, give 'em a spin!

Petal toss. Set out paper cones of flower petals for guests to shower you with as you dash out.

Glow sticks. Rave style.

Candles. Make sure they have hand guards (and it's not windy!).

Wish lanterns

Fireworks

Present your bouquet to a close friend or relative as a way to honor that person. You can do so privately or make an announcement about the meaning of your handoff during the reception.

Have both women and men try to catch the bouquet.

Instead of calling out the single guests, celebrate marriage by asking all married couples to come to the dance floor. Then ask couples who have been married one year, five years, ten years, and so on to sit down until you are left with just one couple standing. Ask them how long they have been married and present them with the bouquet.

Toss rose petals so everyone can get a piece of the bridal bouquet, rather than just one "lucky" single guest.

Toss wedding favors—just make sure to choose favors that won't hurt anyone as they land. Gift cards or soft candies are a good option. Have your child attendants or relatives help out.

Start your own tradition and explain it to your guests. To honor your Mexican heritage (or wedding theme), have single girls hit a wedding cake piñata instead of the bouquet toss. The girl who broke the piñata got the candy and the bouquet!

Here's how it works: The groom puts his hand over the bride's and they slice through the bottom layer of their cake together, feeding each other from the slice. Cameras flash, and then the couple may each serve slices to their in-laws. Some fun-loving couples choose to smash the piece in each other's face. Please reconsider! Do you really want to ruin your dress with blue frosting? Keep it classy.

The getaway

While not all couples leave their receptions in a blaze of glory, it certainly makes for a nice ending to a spectacular event. We love the idea of a "last dance" song to cap the night on a high note. Then, once everyone stumbles outside to line up for a fond farewell, the glamorous couple makes their way through the applauding crowd and into the back of their getaway car. Your photographer will want to catch this special moment, so be sure to give him the heads-up.

the cake

TIMELINE

PLANNING

6–8 months before
Research cake bakers and
schedule tastings

Book your cake baker

4–5 months before
Determine cake design
and flavors

Order cake and groom's
cake (if having one)

Determine cake display
and accessories

2 weeks before
Give cake baker final head
count and confirm cake
delivery details

1–2 weeks before
Check with your venue
to make sure they have
all the delivery info

Of all the wedding food you choose, your cake takes the . . . well, cake. The tradition dates back to ancient Greece, where newlywed couples would share crushed sesame cakes to ensure fertility. In the Middle Ages, guests crumbled wheat cakes over the couple's heads, again to wish them good fortune and children. The wheat-cake concept slowly evolved into a sweet dessert cake in sixteenth-century England. The French then one-upped the English, introducing the tiered, sugar-covered cake that we know and love today. This next chapter is all about achieving confection perfection.

FINDING YOUR CAKE DESIGNER

Ideally, you should start shopping for a baker at least six to eight months before the wedding, but take note: Some of the best wedding cake designers can be booked over a year in advance, so you may want to get going even earlier if you have one in mind. Before beginning your search, check whether your wedding venue has certain regulations regarding wedding cakes—some require you to use particular bakers, while others may charge you a fee for bringing in your own.

Before you decide on a type, it's important to have an idea of what you want in terms of design and flavor. If you have a specific style in mind, you'll want to meet with cake bakers who can pull off that particular construction and ask to see at least a few cakes in their portfolio that are similar to what you want. When you meet with the candidates, bring swatches of your wedding colors, other cake designs you like, pictures of your dress, and anything else that inspires you. Visuals are also key because your idea of something as small as sugar flowers can be very different from what each potential baker envisions.

Bakers by the dozen
As with florists and planners, you've got a few options when it comes to cake pros. Your choice will depend first and foremost on your venue, and then on your caterer and budget, as well as on the design you have in mind. Here's the rundown of your options when it comes to cake creators.

YOUR CATERER Nine times out of ten, these folks can produce a delicious wedding cake. But just because you trust their take on poached salmon and herb-roasted chicken doesn't mean they're wedding cake wizards. Our advice? Be specific about your desires. During your meeting, show your caterer visual examples of what you like and ask to see pictures of past wedding cakes he's done. Then sample the wares. You want to make sure he can create your dream wedding cake design—and taste.

COMMERCIAL OR BOUTIQUE BAKERY If you have a cherished bakery, find out whether they make wedding cakes. While you may have to work with limited, simpler designs, commercial and boutique bakeries often cost less. They also often make up for it in the taste department, with a focus on ingredients and flavor.

CUSTOM WEDDING CAKE BAKERY Seek out an independent wedding cake master for the ultimate in design, ingredients, flavor, and decoration. You'll get great taste, too. Naturally, this route will cost you more—sometimes much more. Wedding cake designers are passionate about their work and treat each confection like a piece of art. This approach allows for personalization and imaginative constructions, so if you have a complicated idea in mind, a gifted cake designer is often the only one who can turn that vision into a reality.

Vetting cake bakers
Many reception sites have in-house bakers or a list of preferred cake bakers (vendors they have relationships with) that they require you to use, so start by checking with your site. You'll also want to see what your caterer offers. If you're planning to go with an independent baker, ask your caterer, site manager, and planner for recommendations.

Meet with your top three favorite bakers in person to look at photos and actual cakes they've done, if possible. If you have a custom style in mind, talk to the baker about it to make sure they can do it. It's also a good idea to ask candidates to create sketches of the cake based on your discussion to give you an idea of what you can expect and how well they can interpret your vision. If you like what you see, sample a few varieties they have on hand and talk about flavors and filling options.

Taste test

As you start setting up appointments, find out when each baker's next tasting is scheduled. At tastings, clients are invited into the bakery to sample exemplary cakes, ask questions, and review portfolios. This is an excellent opportunity to meet bakers and fully understand the range of their abilities.

While some bakers will host individual tastings, a group tasting is more the norm. If your baker is hosting a group tasting, the rest of the audience will likely contain other to-be-weds and planners, so he'll probably have a couple different wedding cake slices to impress you. Otherwise, you might get bites of different flavors and just have a portfolio of his past creations to flip through.

When choosing a filling, taste your wedding-cake-to-be at room temperature—not just out of the fridge—so you can make sure it will hold up after it's been sitting out for a while. For example, cannoli cream is a fantastic filling, but it's not so tasty after five hours on a counter. Keep in mind: Some bakers excel at taste but not at construction, while others create masterpieces that aren't so palatable. Really good bakers can do both. Sample a real wedding cake—one with icing and other decorations—to ensure you'll be getting a cake that tastes as good as it looks.

Locking down the logistics

Make sure your baker has a solid way to transport your cake to the reception site (appropriate boxes, packing materials, and even a refrigerated vehicle) and that it will be sufficiently insured in case of any mishaps. To make sure that this happens, you need to include all the transportation and travel details in your contract.

Always have the cake baker deliver the cake—it's not as easy as it sounds. Not only do they have the equipment to keep it perfectly refrigerated and to prevent the decorations from smearing, but once it's in your hands, you are responsible for it, so you can't expect your cake baker to come running if you had to slam on the brakes and smushed the cake. Cake delivery takes coordination. For example, complex cakes may not necessarily be delivered in final form, so allow time and space for your cake baker to assemble it on-site, if needed. And if you're using fresh flowers to decorate the cake, you will need to put your cake baker

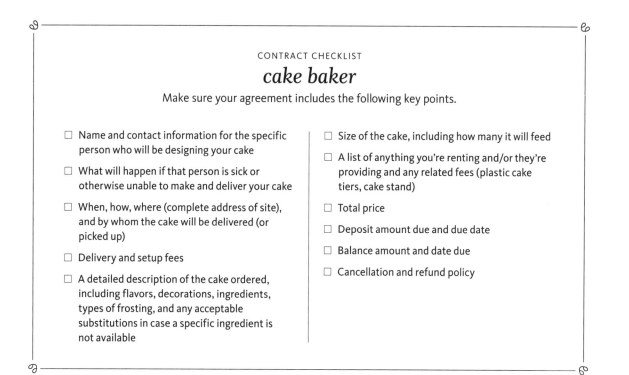

cake baker

Make sure your agreement includes the following key points.

- ☐ Name and contact information for the specific person who will be designing your cake
- ☐ What will happen if that person is sick or otherwise unable to make and deliver your cake
- ☐ When, how, where (complete address of site), and by whom the cake will be delivered (or picked up)
- ☐ Delivery and setup fees
- ☐ A detailed description of the cake ordered, including flavors, decorations, ingredients, types of frosting, and any acceptable substitutions in case a specific ingredient is not available

- ☐ Size of the cake, including how many it will feed
- ☐ A list of anything you're renting and/or they're providing and any related fees (plastic cake tiers, cake stand)
- ☐ Total price
- ☐ Deposit amount due and due date
- ☐ Balance amount and date due
- ☐ Cancellation and refund policy

and florist in touch so they can coordinate who will be adding the flowers and when so they still look fresh for the reception.

Designate a place to put the cake once it arrives at your reception site. It should arrive at least a few hours before the reception, so make sure you will have refrigerator space at the venue. You should also have someone on hand, like a planner, site manager, or caterer, who can transport the cake to the cake table right before the reception is scheduled to begin so the cake is in top form. Put the catering manager in touch with your cake baker, so they can coordinate delivery and fridge accommodations.

CREATING YOUR CAKE

Work with your baker to determine the design, flavors, and fillings that you want. Since the wedding cake is a centerpiece for the whole reception, make sure yours represents your wedding, from the inside (fillings) to the outside (icing and topper). Your choice of color, flavor, shape, size, and motif will come together to create a showstopping focal point of your reception.

Cake considerations
Before you start working on your cake design or flavors, take into account the following factors that may affect what you choose.

GUEST LIST SIZE Generally, three tiers will serve fifty to a hundred guests; you'll likely need five for two hundred guests or more. If the reception is in a grand room with high ceilings, consider increasing the cake's stature with columns between the tiers. (This is opposed to a "stacked" cake, one with its layers sitting directly atop each other, with no separators.)

BUDGET The price of a wedding cake is usually calculated by the slice and based on how labor-intensive the design is. The bigger the cake, the more it will cost as well. The type of frosting (fondant tends to be pricier than buttercream) and the intricacy of the design will also affect the cost. All add-ons, including marzipan fruits, chocolate molded flowers, and lace points, will also raise the rate. If you don't use an in-house baker, some venues will also charge a cutting fee (which can run up to $8 a slice). Check with your reception manager or caterer before finalizing your cake budget. The price the cake baker quotes you is usually just the cake cost. Ask about transporting fees and tax, and factor in a cake-cutting fee if your cake baker is not working at your reception site.

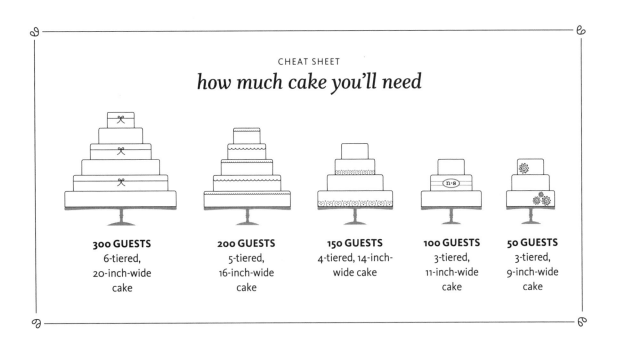

CHEAT SHEET
how much cake you'll need

300 GUESTS
6-tiered,
20-inch-wide
cake

200 GUESTS
5-tiered,
16-inch-wide
cake

150 GUESTS
4-tiered, 14-inch-
wide cake

100 GUESTS
3-tiered,
11-inch-wide
cake

50 GUESTS
3-tiered,
9-inch-wide
cake

WEDDING STYLE Deal with the cake after all decisions about dress style and reception décor have been made. These elements can serve as a blueprint for the design and structure of your wedding cake. Choose a cake that's compatible with the style of the venue, the season, your gown, the flower arrangements, or the menu. If you want colorful accents (such as sugar flowers or icing ribbons), give your baker fabric swatches so she can match the color. Choose a detail that reflects your personality, the time of year, or a recurring theme throughout your wedding. If you're a "less is more" kind of couple who still wants to make an impression, try an understated yet whimsical design, such as a cake covered in blush-colored frosting and festooned with tiny, silver-dusted polka dots or monograms.

COLOR You want your wedding cake to coordinate with your wedding-day colors, but remember that your guests will still be eating it. In general, the less food coloring used, the better the taste will be, particularly when it comes to red, green, or blue food coloring, which are notorious for their less-than-stellar flavors. Instead of a bold red

TIP
don't forget the accessories!

Give some thought to what kind of cake stand you'll use to display your cake. Make sure your venue or rental company can also provide a stand and a cake knife, or better yet, borrow one (or both!) from your mother or grandmother for your "something borrowed."

Jessica & Peter
SEPTEMBER 5
MONTECITO, CA

Though the summer temperatures were still lingering, signs of autumn could be seen everywhere at Jessica and Peter's early September nuptials—including on their cake. Figs, berries, grapes, pinecones, and flowers gave the buttercream confection a decidedly seasonal look that coordinated with their fall theme. Low, jewel-toned centerpieces set in vintage tins brought out their wedding's rustic-chic style and complemented the courtyard venue.

sneaky ways to save on your wedding cake

compare prices
When you're shopping around for a cake designer, always ask potential candidates to break it down by cost per slice instead of just giving an overall price. That way, you can compare each candidate's prices. Expect to pay about $2.50 to $3 a slice, but know that slices can run as high as $25 or $30 if you're using a celebrity baker.

use the sheet cake trick
One way to save is by purchasing a smaller-size wedding cake or even a fake cake made of inedible tiers that you can still slice into (seriously!), plus several sheet cakes of the same flavor that you can serve.

go simple
Skip the fancy designs, shapes, and add-ons, which take more manpower and therefore cost more. A simple buttercream cake topped with fresh flowers (which typically cost less than handmade sugar flowers) will look just as elegant but won't make as big of a dent in your budget.

cake with gold accents, go for a white or chocolate cake with a few red and gold accents. If you're having a blue and green wedding, for the best flavor, get a white cake with blue ribbon trim, or ask your baker for green-frosted accents or flowers. Consider your frosting options when choosing a color. Both buttercream and fondant can be dyed just about any basic shade, but you'll get a wider color spectrum with fondant.

Cake shapes
Though round tiers are a classic, oval, square, octagonal, and hexagonal confections are fun, too. Your options are as limited as your baker's imagination—and your budget, of course. As with so many other elements of your celebration, the right cake shape should reflect your wedding style. Also remember: Some wedding cake shapes, like those with uneven tiers, are tough to pull off, and while they look amazing, there's always the chance that they'll topple over if they're unbalanced.

ROUND While some might think the shape is a little plain, the simplicity of a classic round cake provides the perfect backdrop for interesting textures and colors. There's no need to hold back on décor with a round cake.

SQUARE A square cake is the modern alternative to a round cake— perfect for couples looking for something different but not over-the-top. Play up the shape as little or as much as you want.

PETAL Often referred to as "scalloped," this shape has a flowerlike appearance. To keep the result from looking too bold, go light with the add-ons so that they complement and draw attention to the unique shape.

HEXAGONAL This six-sided wonder is the modern answer to the same old square cake, with hexagonal tiers. The result is striking, so you'll want to keep the adornment clean and simple—the shape itself brings a lot to the table even without decoration.

TOPSY-TURVY This unique design is sure to make a bold statement at your wedding, so consider the overall style of the day—it's perfect for a funky loft or restaurant but won't work as well in an elegant ballroom or country club. Stray from anything traditional, such as flowers; instead play up the whimsical shape with funky add-ons and bold colors, like diamond fondant cutouts in a mix of hues.

Decorations and designs
When it comes to dressing up your cake, the options are endless. Cakes featuring sugar or buttercream interpretations of feathers, draping, flowers, monograms, and embroidery

cake décor

beading
A border along the edge of tiers that resembles beading or tiny pearls.

basket-weave
A piping (see below) technique that features interwoven vertical and horizontal lines (like a wicker basket).

cornelli
An elaborate piping technique that yields a 3-D lacelike pattern.

dotted swiss
A piping technique that forms tiny dots in random patterns that resemble a fine Swiss-dot fabric.

dragées
Round, edible sugar balls coated with silver or gold and used for decorative purposes.

gum paste
This paste of sugar, cornstarch, and gelatin is used to mold realistic-looking fruits and flowers to garnish a cake. Gum paste decorations are edible and will last for years as keepsakes, but some say they don't taste as yummy as marzipan. So you'll have to decide whether you'd rather have a piece of the cake to save for years to come or the instant gratification of the best-tasting cake on your wedding day.

latticework
A piping detail that crisscrosses with an open pattern.

petal dust
Adds sparkle to a cake.

pillars
Separators used in a tiered cake. They can be made of plastic or wood in several lengths to achieve the desired look.

piping
Decorating technique created using a pastry bag and various metal tips to create 3-D designs. Piping details include leaves, borders, basket-weave patterns, and flowers.

pulled sugar
A technique in which boiled sugar is manipulated and pulled into thin strips to produce 3-D flowers and bows, as well as cotton candy–like decorations around cake tiers. Also known as "spun sugar."

royal icing
Made of egg whites and confectioner's sugar, this icing starts life as a soft paste piped from a pastry bag to create latticework, beading, bows, and flowers. When dry, its texture is hard and brittle—it should not be refrigerated.

are a popular way to add texture and interest. You can also incorporate ribbons, 3-D add-ons, intricate patterns and designs, and even a jeweled brooch or other accent. The major factor in choosing your cake decorations will be your budget, as these extras can really add up when it comes to the cost of your cake. Gum paste accents are the most expensive embellishment, as they're formed meticulously by hand. Fresh or sugar flowers are another popular and gorgeous option for wedding cakes.

No matter what you choose, don't overdo it: Flowers and other additions like polka dots and stripes are great, but use them in moderation. Whether you're going for large sugar flowers like tulips or small ones like stephanotis, you don't want to overwhelm the cake. Make sure your design allows for breathing room (read: white space) on at least the top or bottom tiers.

SELECTING YOUR FLAVORS

Don't forget about the taste when choosing your cake. The three F's all impact what you and your guests will taste. In addition to your taste buds, the season and weather may impact your selection of flavors, fillings, and frosting.

Flavors and fillings

Remember: What's inside counts equally as much as what's outside. Finding the right combo of cake flavor and filling is one of the best parts of choosing your cake. You'll taste lots of samples along the way (forget the diet—this is "research"), and you might be surprised to find that this isn't your average chocolate cake because of the . . . fillings! Yes, interspersed between layers of moist cake, you could find fresh fruit, custard, or ganache (a fancy word for a concoction made of chocolate and heavy cream). And once cut, each piece—with horizontal layers of different-hued flavors and fillings—makes a dramatic statement on the plate as well as on the palate.

You could go safe with chocolate or vanilla, or opt for more exotic flavors such as passion-fruit buttercream or Grand Marnier Bavarian cream. If you have your heart set on an unusual flavor that your baker doesn't offer, ask whether she would be willing to find a recipe. Moist chocolate cake is always a favorite, especially when the rich layers are spread with fillings like mocha-espresso mousse or amaretto. Lemon cake, a strong summer choice, can be filled with tart lemon curd, as well as white chocolate or light lemon mousse. Other fabulous, fruity cake flavors to try (and try again if they'll let you) include pineapple, marionberry, and wild cherry, along with passion fruit, mango, and

fresh vs. sugar flowers

FRESH FLOWERS	SUGAR FLOWERS
pros	**pros**
Can be all the décor a plain cake needs	Edible
More budget-friendly	Less coordination required: Your cake baker can make them
cons	More flexibility: Sugar flowers can be beautiful, whether molded into something small and dainty or large and lush
Not all flowers are edible	**cons**
Takes an extra step to coordinate with your florist *and* cake baker	More expensive than real flowers
Limited options: Some flowers can wilt over the course of the day or evening (stick with the heartier blooms like roses, dahlias, and calla lilies)	Take longer to create than real flowers
	Not all food coloring tastes the same, so if you want your guests to enjoy the cake, you'll want to avoid reds, greens, and blues

blood orange mousses. Note that mousses such as mango, white chocolate, pistachio, and ricotta provide a lighter consistency without sacrificing richness of flavor. For more on every flavor choice, see "Cake Flavors," page 336.

Heavier combinations like chocolate cake with mocha-praline filling are perfect for a winter wedding, and lighter sponge cakes with fruits, curds, and preserves are more ideal for a summer affair. Some flavorful combinations we especially like: chocolate-banana cake layered with custard and brushed with banana liqueur, white cake with raspberries and cream, and almond cake with apricot preserves, brushed with rum.

Frosting factors

When it comes to icing your cake, you have a number of delicious and gorgeous choices. Buttercream, made from butter and sugar, is smooth and creamy. Fondant, another popular option, is made of sugar, corn syrup, water, and gelatin, and is rolled out with a rolling pin before it's draped over the cake to make a smooth, firm base for decorative details. For the best of both worlds, ask your baker to add a thin layer of fondant over buttercream frosting, so you get the taste of buttercream and the look of draped fondant. Other icing

cake flavors

Every cake has its flavor, and some are better than others.
Here's what works well—and not so well—together.

chocolate cake

Fruits like raspberry (Chambord), cherry, orange (Grand Marnier, Cointreau), banana, strawberry

Nuts like almond (including marzipan), pistachio, hazelnut, peanut butter, praline

Mousses and creams like mocha, coffee (Kahlúa, espresso, cappuccino), chocolate, white chocolate, vanilla, mint (créme de menthe), Bavarian cream

Other flavors: cannoli or coconut cream, mascarpone cheese, chocolate ganache

No-nos: lemon curd; mousses such as passion fruit, apricot, Key lime, mango, pineapple

yellow/white chocolate/ vanilla cake

Fruits like raspberry, cherry, orange, strawberry, lemon curd, passion fruit, apricot, Key lime, mango, pineapple

Nuts like almond (including marzipan), pistachio, hazelnut, praline

Mousses and creams like amaretto, mocha, cappuccino, chocolate, white chocolate, vanilla, Bavarian cream

No-nos: mint, mascarpone cheese

lemon/carrot/ poppy seed cake

Fruits like lemon curd, raspberry

Nuts like almond (including marzipan), hazelnut

Mousses and creams like lemon, white chocolate, vanilla

Other flavors: cannoli or Bavarian cream, cream cheese, mascarpone

No-nos: chocolate or coffee-based fillings, mint, coconut, Key lime, passion fruit, mango

choices include marzipan, a paste made from ground almonds, sugar, and egg whites that's used in sheets like fondant; whipped cream, a sweetened, whipped heavy cream (great with fruit fillings—but must be refrigerated, so it won't work for an outdoor affair); and ganache, a rich mix of chocolate and heavy cream (meaning it will soften in very humid weather) that's denser than mousse but less dense than fudge.

MORE SWEET IDEAS

Couples aren't stopping at the cake anymore—from dessert bars and take-home treats to creative groom's cakes, there are more options than just the traditional wedding cake. Cap off your nuptial meal with desserts that express who you are as a couple while giving your guests a sweet reward—whether that's a single cake, multiple cakes, or a display of your favorite sweet treats.

The groom's cake

That other, smaller confection you may have noticed sitting quietly off to the side at wedding receptions in the past (especially in the South) is taking center stage these days. Grooms are getting creative, ordering their cakes in the shapes of guitars, golf clubs, or football stadiums to show off their passions and obsessions. And while the groom's cake used to be darker and heavier (chocolate or, traditionally, fruitcake) than the main wedding cake, today it can come in any flavor.

Some couples decide to slice and box it for guests to take home. (Legend has it that a single woman who sleeps with a slice of groom's cake under her pillow will dream of her future husband.) The bride's cake—the one cut by the couple at the reception—is traditionally eaten

---

PROS AND CONS

buttercream vs. fondant

When it comes to frostings, buttercream and fondant still take the cake. But which one should you choose? We've given you the rundown of the pros and cons of each to help you decide.

BUTTERCREAM	FONDANT
pros	**pros**
Has a smooth consistency	Allows for some of the most gorgeous decorating options
Delicate, delicious flavor	
Easily shaped into swags, borders, and flowers	Yields a perfectly smooth, pristine surface with a porcelain finish
Stays soft so it's easy to cut, color, and flavor	Holds up better in warm weather
cons	**cons**
Requires refrigeration	Not everyone loves the bland flavor
Doesn't hold up well in hot weather	Finish looks almost fake it's so perfect, so you don't get the mouthwatering frosting appeal
Design won't be as perfect but looks more like a real cake	

---

as dessert. But you can also cut and serve both to your guests or save it for the morning-after brunch.

Cake alternatives
If you're not a wedding cake kind of couple, don't feel obligated to have a four-tiered, fondant-covered masterpiece. Some brides and grooms are opting out of serving a traditional wedding cake. Cupcakes on stacked tiers, perhaps with the top tier holding a small cake, are a stylish alternative, or you could serve mini pastries, logo cookies with the bride and groom's silhouette or monogram on them, or miniature wedding-cake-shaped cookies instead. A glam option: individual cakes in the shape of, say, an open Tiffany-style box filled with cream and berries.

Dessert stations—basically a buffet setup that guests visit—are another great cake-free option. Even if you're doing a seated meal, a dessert station gives guests a chance to circulate a bit. We've seen stations that range from totally elaborate Viennese tables with every confection imaginable to simple themed offerings. Case in point: the candy bar filled with sweets you loved from your childhood—like malted milk balls, jelly beans, and caramel popcorn. Include empty bags so guests can take home their favorites. You could also do a truffle station or an ice cream bar. Still, consider ordering a small cake to cut, a timeless and memorable tradition and photo op we love!

TRADITIONS

preserving a slice

Saving the top tier of your wedding cake to share on your one-year anniversary is a treasured tradition. Let your caterer know ahead of time if you want to do so. Have him remove the sugar flowers, wrap it in several layers of plastic wrap, and then seal it in an airtight baggie. (Stay away from aluminum foil, as it might not protect against freezer burn as well as plastic wrap will.) If you forget to tell your caterer and he just sticks it in a box for you, remove any sugar flowers or other add-ons and chill the cake overnight in the refrigerator to harden the icing so it doesn't stick to the plastic wrap. The next step: Place the slice in an airtight Tupperware container or plastic bag and then put it in your freezer when you get home (or have a friend do it for you). One year later, you're ready to thaw, serve, stare at it, decide if you should really eat it, tentatively taste it—and find out it is actually still pretty tasty.

22

favors and welcome gifts

TIMELINE

PLANNING

1 month before
Order favors and packaging

Outline welcome bags

1–2 weeks before
Assemble favors and welcome bags

1–2 days before
Deliver favors to the venue (if nonperishable)

1 day before
Pick up perishable items and deliver them to the venue and guests' rooms

With most of the elements of your wedding, your goal is to make an impression in the moment—or beforehand, it's a chance to give guests a sense of what's to come. With your favors, you also want to leave a *lasting* impression. Your parting gifts should embody the feeling you want guests to take with them while also expressing your gratitude in a personal way. They don't have to be big or outrageous, but they should somehow reflect you and the day.

FAVOR BASICS

Favors have become a staple in the world of weddings. You may not be sold on them yet, but trust us: They're a great way to show your guests you appreciate their support and to give them something to remember the day by. Your parting mementos can also help carry out your reception theme and even add a little extra flair to your tables. So the packaging is important too—it's the final piece of your wedding décor. And like any good gift, you want to put some thought into it and send your guests home with something they'll be excited to use. But before you can start looking for the perfect parting presents, there are some broader questions that you'll need to decide first.

How much? We're not talking about how many to order—we'll get to that next. We mean how much of your budget do you want to devote to favors? The good news is there's no set amount you should spend—a fabulous favor can be as inexpensive as a pretty packet of your wedding flower seeds or as extravagant as a bottle of fine bubbly. The even better news: There are plenty of options that fall somewhere within that range.

Who gets what? Everyone at the wedding should get the same favor—or pretty much the same (maybe you're giving out white and red wines or different types of books). So you shouldn't give "extra-special" favors to the wedding party or to your favorite aunt at the wedding (give them these "extra-special" gifts before or after instead) and you can't skip the favors for the best man's girlfriend you didn't want to invite or for your family who will "totally understand." That's why it's important to find a favor that, like your reception playlist, the *entire* guest list will appreciate. And always order extra (figure about ten backup favors for every hundred guests) in case any get lost or a few guests get greedy and take more than one.

Singles or doubles? You can give favors out by couple—that way people don't end up with two of whatever you're sending them home with. This works best if you're planning on using place cards to designate where people are sitting (you don't want your single friends to leave empty-handed because they sat where a spouse was supposed to sit).

Practicality? You want to make sure your favor won't end up a dust collector or—worse yet—get left behind. Make sure you choose a gift that is one of two things: edible or practical. But if you are choosing

something useful, ask yourself—and maybe a few friends—if you *really* would use that item. And, if you're planning on personalizing it, avoid the common pitfall of turning a practical item into something that guests won't want to use. For instance, guests who enjoy entertaining would find coasters handy, but no one (excluding your mother) will want to display coasters featuring your engagement photo.

DIY or buy?

You can order fully personalized favors online, scout out unique favors at boutiques or specialty food stores, or make them yourselves. While DIY favors may save you money—and can be a fun personal project—beware: Assembling and wrapping two hundred favors is probably a lot more time-consuming than you ever imagined. And if you're not handy with the glue gun, all that effort may go down the drain when you decide you don't like the final products. Make a few samples to gauge whether you're up for the project before you commit. And enlist the troops to help: Throw a favor-assembling party and ply your friends with cocktails and snacks.

Prefer to let someone else do the work? If you're ordering your favors online, from a lesser-known source, purchase a single sample before you hit "buy now" and end up with one hundred. You want to make sure the truffles actually taste good or the pashminas are the right hue (the colors you see on your computer screen may not look the same in person). Some vendors will supply samples for free, so it's worth asking. Even if you're just purchasing personalized favor tags or packaging, ask to see a proof to make sure everything is spelled right and the wedding date is correct. All of the same rules apply if you are having favors designed by a custom invitation or gift designer.

Favorite favor ideas

There is a world of favor options, from home goods and games to tasty treats! To help you narrow down the thousands of choices, pick a direction, a favor "mission," from the list below.

GO PERSONAL Choose favors that express your personalities by sharing something you love with your guests. Are you both into wine? Bottles with personalized labels will go over big, as will wine accessories, like stoppers and bottle openers. Have a unique heritage? Try a tin of Asian cookies, Mexican Talavera pottery candleholders, or authentic olive oil from the region of Italy where your ancestors were born. Obsessed with a sport? Give out golf balls or tees customized with your initials.

the knot NOTE

find fab favors
Browse tons of personalized party favors and packaging to fit your wedding style, plus all the ingredients you need for your welcome bags and great bridesmaid and groomsmen gifts. **TheKnot.com/favors**

welcome bags

Since you won't be able to greet all your guests personally upon their arrival, a welcome bag (or basket) of goodies is a great way to touch base with them right away. This is especially true if you're having a destination wedding or hosting lots of out-of-towners.

packaging

Personalized tote bags are great for beach destinations or cities where guests might do a lot of sightseeing. But cute baskets or galvanized pails work well for a garden or vineyard wedding, and beautiful boxes can work, too. Whatever you choose, make sure it holds everything guests will need, plus a few fun surprises.

key ingredients

Be sure to include a welcome letter and a packet with key information, including an itinerary of the weekend's events, phone numbers for their "weekend contact" in case they have any questions (assign this to a planner, honor attendant, or relative—you're going to have enough to worry about without fielding calls from lost guests in need of directions to the rehearsal dinner). It's also nice to include a guide to the area with local highlights like your favorite restaurants, top sites to check out, and activities to do during downtime. A custom map that shows guests where the wedding events are taking place, as well as where to find the hot spots you're recommending, is a thoughtful touch. It's always nice to include a few

snacks so guests aren't forced to raid the minibar, as well as destination essentials like sunscreen and flip-flops, or metro cards and city maps if you're in an urban locale.

special delivery

Getting these special favors to guests is a little trickier. Shipping welcome bags to your location is a no-fuss option, especially if you're flying to your wedding. You're going to have enough to carry (your dress!) and with fees for checked bags, it may be more economical to send them by mail anyway. If you'd rather transport the favors yourselves, pack them well in a box and have a family member (or a few close friends) bring them as checked bags. (Save stuffing the decorative tissue paper until the last minute or it will get crushed en route to being delivered.) Enlist attendants or family members to help you distribute bags to guests' hotels to be handed out at check-in, or even better, to be waiting in their rooms when they arrive. But be sure to ask the hotel about any charges for this: Some hotels will charge you up to $7 a bag to hold or deliver welcome bags to guests' rooms.

GO FUN If you're the type of couple who just wants to have a good time, throw all the "rules" out the window and find favors that are totally playful. Bring a smile to your guests' face with a middle school throwback like yo-yos or dominos, or keep them entertained before the ceremony starts (or on the trip home) with a book of crossword puzzles, a heap of brain-teaser games, or a deck of cards bearing your wedding date and motif.

GO GREEN Symbolize the idea of marriage as a living, growing entity with potted plants or individual flowering bulbs, the perfect

global gifts

Get inspired by traditional wedding favors from around the world.

Italy: jordan almonds
These candy-coated nuts are gifted in groups of five, representing health, wealth, fertility, happiness, and longevity.

China: double happiness
Display the traditional Chinese wedding character, which signifies a couple's joy and love, on note cards or in the icing of a sugar cookie.

Holland: bridal sugar
Bruidssuiker (Dutch for "bridal sugar") can be five pieces of any type of candy (chocolates, peppermints). The name comes from what these five pieces signify—love, happiness, loyalty, prosperity, and virility. Wrap five of your favorite candy bars together in a kitschy or pretty package for a sweet send-off.

Switzerland: pine tree
Newlyweds plant a pine tree in their backyard to represent fertility. Send guests home with their own pine tree seedlings.

Korea: dates or chestnuts
Traditionally offered by the newlyweds' parents and symbolic of children, these delicacies can be given whole or baked into cookies to pass on the luck to your guests.

Morocco: milk bath
Moroccan custom dictates that before the wedding, the bride takes a milk bath. Pamper guests with small jars of scented milk bath to enjoy when they get home. Make sure to include an explanation!

complement to a beautiful garden or vineyard wedding. Or go with a dozen different individually potted herbs and let guests choose their own favorites for their kitchens.

GO FUNCTIONAL Offer friends and family favors they can take home and start using immediately. Some of our favorite ideas: flip-flops, pashminas, blankets, baseball hats, tins of mints, stemless wineglasses, grooming kits and manicure sets, gourmet coffee beans, luggage tags, chopsticks, martini shakers, picture frames, books, personalized lip balm, or photo albums.

GO LOCAL Give a regional specialty such as jalapeño jelly from Texas, hot sauce or Cajun spice rubs from Louisiana, Vermont cheddar or maple syrup, or Atlantic City saltwater taffy. For a seaside wedding, a beach towel or mesh beach bag are great bets. For a mountain wedding, try lift tickets or hand warmers or neck warmers in your signature colors.

GO FOODIE A practical gift with instant gratification, edible treats are always a winner. Offer a sweet snack like caramel popcorn in elegant goodie bags or truffles in beautifully wrapped little boxes, or even have chefs whip up boxes of warm beignets sprinkled with powdered sugar to hand guests as they leave. Share jars of Grandma's special jam, or bake cookies and include the recipe tied to the top of the bag. Don't forget to personalize your food favors, too—wrap the area's specialty microbrew in custom labels, or stamp jars of local honey with your names and wedding date.

GO SEASONAL Your favors can also be a perfect place to play up your wedding season. Candy apples are a sweet idea for a fall wedding. In winter, help guests keep warm with hot chocolate mix or cider-mulling spices. Protect guests against spring showers with umbrellas in your wedding colors. Summer's obvious options include grilling spices, sun hats, pretty citronella candles, boxes of sparklers, or the hottest beach read.

GO CHARITABLE On a day when you're showered with so much love and affection (not to mention gifts!), think about sharing the spirit of your day with more than just your guests by donating to a favorite charity in your guests' honor. Let guests know about the donation by leaving a note at their place settings; add a small token that references the charity, like a jump rope if you donate to a kids' organization or a dog-bone-shaped cookie if you give to an animal rescue foundation. You can even get guests in on the giving by having them drop their escort cards into decorative bowls that represent a few different foundations you support. Then allocate your donations accordingly.

GO DIY Homemade treats make wonderful keepsakes and fit in especially well with weddings that are filled with other DIY details. For a summertime affair, you could make fans that also serve as programs at your ceremony. Wrap journals or photo albums in fabric that coordinates with your wedding décor and write each guest a note on the inside of the cover for an ultrapersonalized touch.

FAVOR DISPLAYS

Once you choose what to give, your work isn't done yet. Presentation is key. Just like carefully wrapped holiday presents placed under a tree, the way you package and show off your parting gifts helps create a fun surprise and can go a long way toward making your guests feel welcome and appreciated.

Wrapping them up

You can definitely judge a favor by its cover. Packaging says as much about your style as the favor itself and can even be used as part of the décor. So when you're shopping for your favors, think about their outerwear too, and look for custom containers, tags, labels, paper, and ribbons to fit your wedding palette and style. Craft and stationery stores and event- and bridal-supply retailers offer a vast array of packaging in different patterns. Many offer custom gift wrapping and will even do the assembling and wrapping for you. Doing it yourself is also an option if you start early. First, find the right size and type of bag, box, or other container. Next, personalize it with a custom label or tag bearing your wedding date, your monogram or motif, a meaningful quote, or a note thanking your guests.

Creative packaging can be half the fun of the present. Beyond classic favor boxes and cellophane bags, you can use Chinese takeout containers, mini bamboo steamers, galvanized pails, slim silver canisters, or mason jars. If your favor has a pretty shape or fits the theme, show it off at the party and skip the packaging—a ribbon and a personalized tag will be plenty. Beware when packaging food: Paper bags look pretty but can quickly absorb the grease of cookies or custom popcorn, so use a plastic bag inside for a solid seal.

Giving them out

The final piece of the favor puzzle: deciding how you want to hand them out or display them for guests to pick up. Though they're thought of as parting gifts, favors can be given at the start of the reception, awaiting guests at each place setting when they take their seats, or they can come out during the dancing or cake cutting. Favors might also make an early entrance, appearing on ceremony chairs or during the cocktail hour as part of the escort card display. How you distribute them really depends on the rest of the décor *and* the favor itself.

Just tell whoever is setting them out (a planner, site manager, or amazing friend) exactly where you want them. And if you're leaving them out, make sure guests know that they're theirs for the taking by attaching favor tags to each one, or by placing a legible framed sign nearby that says, "Please take one," "Be our guest," or simply "Thank you." Here are some more delivery options to consider.

WHEN THEY ARRIVE Favors might also appear piled in baskets by the ceremony entrance or on their chairs (think parasols to keep your guests comfortable on a sunny afternoon) or by the dance floor to help guests get into the groove (with sunglasses, for example).

CLEVER IDEAS
packaging

Your favor packaging should match the overall feel of your wedding.

classic
Tulle circles tied with ribbon

Organza pouches

Paper boxes

rustic
Burlap sacks

Galvanized pails

Wicker baskets

modern
Acrylic boxes

Cocktail glasses

Silver tins

vintage
Lace pouches

Mismatched teacups

Ornate jars

WHEN THEY SIT DOWN Attach a tag to each favor with each guest's name and table number, and use them as escort cards to lead guests to their tables. Smaller favors that are wrapped in pretty packaging can add to the table décor—arrange them on guests' place settings or prop them on their seats. Just stick with small gifts and do a dress rehearsal first: Ask for samples of your linens, plates, and glasses, plus any other items like menus and place cards, to make sure it all works together and they won't crowd your tables. If your favors are attractive and big enough, you may decide to make them the centerpieces themselves, or a centerpiece component. To let everyone know the centerpieces are their gifts, display a framed sign nearby or have a note printed on the menus that says, "Thank you for being a part of our special day. Please take a piece of it home with you."

DURING THE PARTY For an extra-special delivery, arrange to have them distributed between courses or during dessert by waiters carrying the tiny tokens on silver trays. If you're having a groom's cake, ask the caterer to box up slices and deliver them to each place setting during dessert.

ON THEIR WAY OUT Display guests' gifts on a table or in baskets near the exit with a sign instructing attendees to take one. Giving out favors at the end of the night works especially well if you'll be sending guests home with something that's good-night themed, like a midnight snack: Include a cookie, a mini carton of milk, and a note that says, "Sweet dreams."

23

transportation

TIMELINE

PLANNING

6–8 months before
Start researching your transportation (book your transportation if you're getting married during prom or wedding season)

2–3 months before
Book transportation

1–2 weeks before
Confirm transportation

3–7 days before
Finalize all transportation details, including schedule of pickup/drop-off times

You're going to the chapel . . . but wait! How are you getting there? And what about your maids—or your mom, for that matter? Will you choose a sleek silver Rolls-Royce, a horse and buggy, a party bus, a trolley, or a bicycle built for two? It's not limited to your arrival and exit; consider how you will get your guests around, too. Just remember: Looks aren't everything. The real secret to transportation success is mapping out the timing and the routes down to the last detail.

TRANSPORTATION BASICS

Arranging special transportation for you and all your guests isn't a priority for every couple, and depending on your guest list, wedding location, and budget, you may not consider it a must. However, it is a fun way to take extra care of your guests, ensure your VIPs get where they need to be on time, and stage a spectacular entrance and exit to your party.

Deciding who needs a ride
Start by figuring out the number of people in your bridal party and find a vehicle that will fit them all. The average limo seats eight to ten passengers, so for an oversized bridal party, you'll need a bigger vehicle. Be sure to allow space for the wedding gown—big petticoats, billowy skirts, and long trains need plenty of room (consider your dress as at least one extra person, depending on its size). And if you want your photographer by your side to snap you getting out of the car paparazzi-style or sharing a special moment with your dad or your girls on the way there, you may want to make room for him or her, too. See "Sizing Up Your Ride," opposite, to get an idea of the capacities of various types of vehicles. If you're transporting family and/or guests, you'll also need to determine the number of buses, vans, or trolleys it will take to move them all.

TRANSPORTING YOUR VIPS If your budget allows, providing transportation for the wedding party and your parents is a nice way to take care of everyone and to make sure all the key players are where you need them, when you need them. Start by figuring out who needs to travel together: Treat parents, siblings, and grandparents to private town cars; move attendants en masse in limos, buses, or SUVs. Generally, the bridesmaids ride to the wedding ceremony with the bride, and the groom and groomsmen ride together. Some couples choose to have their parents join their respective parties, but you may prefer to have private time with Mom and Dad on the way to the ceremony and arrange a separate ride for your maids. The groom's parents should arrive stylishly, too, whether with him or separately. If your parents are riding apart from you, they can take the grandparents or other key members of your entourage. Flower children and ring bearers can ride separately with their parents or you can offer their families rides if you have space.

Postceremony, the bride and groom will leave together in their own car while the rest of the wedding party and parents file into the other limos or shuttles (or their own cars). In most cases, the hired rides

sizing up your ride

A breakdown of how many guests fit in some standard vehicles.

rides for two (and maybe a lucky few)

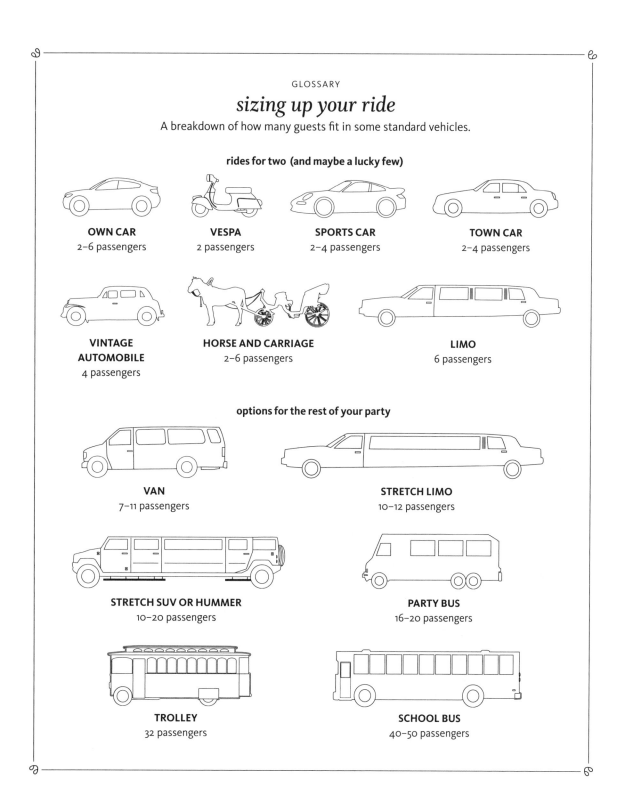

OWN CAR
2–6 passengers

VESPA
2 passengers

SPORTS CAR
2–4 passengers

TOWN CAR
2–4 passengers

VINTAGE AUTOMOBILE
4 passengers

HORSE AND CARRIAGE
2–6 passengers

LIMO
6 passengers

options for the rest of your party

VAN
7–11 passengers

STRETCH LIMO
10–12 passengers

STRETCH SUV OR HUMMER
10–20 passengers

PARTY BUS
16–20 passengers

TROLLEY
32 passengers

SCHOOL BUS
40–50 passengers

that carry the wedding party to the ceremony will wait until after the ceremony and then take them to the reception. If you're providing a shuttle from the ceremony to the reception for all attendees, the wedding party (and even your folks) can just jump on the shuttle with everyone else. If you forgo formalized transportation, the wedding party can tag along with friends and relatives, but be sure that these rides are arranged at least one week before the wedding day. Also, make sure the wedding parties know where to meet and at what time (just in case their escorts want to take a detour on the way) for postceremony pictures.

After the limos or shuttles drop the bridal party off at the reception, one may wait for the duration of the party as the bride and groom's postreception getaway. You're not responsible for arranging postparty transportation arrangements for your bridal party, so they are responsible for making their own plans unless you're providing shuttles to take guests home (in which case, they can just hop on the shuttle with everyone else).

Bola & Gbolabo

SEPTEMBER 18
PHILADELPHIA, PA

The bride arrived in style courtesy of a white vintage Rolls-Royce, which perfectly fit the high school sweethearts' classic-with-a-twist wedding vibe (not to mention provided a timeless backdrop for their wedding pictures). Each of the day's details embodied that same quirky spin on tradition: The escort display featured yellow blooms hanging from manzanita branches, while the cake featured a kitschy 1950s replica of the couple.

GETTING GUESTS AROUND If you have many out-of-towners, are hosting the wedding events at different places, are having the ceremony in a hard-to-get-to location, or just want to ensure your guests don't have to worry about a thing, consider renting vans or shuttle buses to get everyone to each spot on time. It's not only a safe idea, it's also fun (kind of like a school field trip, only your wedding is the planetarium) and a good way to ensure guests won't think twice about letting loose at the party.

If you go the shuttle route, let everyone know you're providing transportation by putting the information on your wedding website. You can also include transportation cards with your invitations (see chapter 19). To make sure no one misses the bus, it's also a smart idea to leave copies of an itinerary with all of the details at your guests' hotels as well. Even if you don't plan to rent a shuttle bus for your guests, you should at the very least provide a taxi phone number so that any guests who've imbibed will make it home safely. You can also plan ahead with a taxi company so that it always has one cab waiting out front and can radio more cars as needed after the party's over. If you're marrying at a hotel, the concierge will take care of this.

CHOOSING YOUR RIDE There are tons of ways to zip off in style, and like everything else, you can personalize your wheels—especially

riding in style

Consider shuttling everyone (including yourselves!) around in something with a little more pizzazz.

best in busing

Hire a double-decker bus, a chartered shuttle, or a vintage trolley to transport all your wedding guests to and from their hotels. The average shuttle holds up to sixty passengers, while trolleys hold thirty-two passengers.

party ride

If just the thought of a limo puts you to sleep, liven things up with a party bus complete with a bar and an array of fun music, ensuring a great ride whether you want to dance your way to the church or just kick back. Party buses can hold up to twenty passengers.

souped-up escapes

For a limolike experience with a little more flash, check out the stretch Hummers, Escalades, and Navigators that come with fiber optics, disco lights, lasers, mirrored ceilings, and full beverage bars. SUVs and Hummers can fit up to twenty people!

sporty send-offs

If you seek a more solitary escape, two-seater sports cars make for a sleek getaway. For this special day, your man's dream car can become a reality. From the Maserati GranSport to the Lamborghini Gallardo, these low-lying, ultra-exotic specialty vehicles will have you speeding off into the twilight. If you're going to be driving one of these fast rides, check on all liability issues before jumping behind the wheel.

two-wheelers

If you're not in the mood to be chauffeured into the sunset, show off your take-charge personalities with a motorcycle, Vespa, or tandem bike. You'll get great picture ops, and it'll be a wonderful memory to look back on.

airlift

If you prefer, you can simply fly away by jumping into a hot-air balloon or escaping in your very own helicopter. You need a certain amount of open land to fly a balloon or land a helicopter safely, so consider your reception location when making your choice. Also, you will need to carefully coordinate with your rental company and your reception venue team once you get the green light.

for your big entrance and exit. Everything from a VW Microbus or a Harley-Davidson with a sidecar (it's hard to make straddling anything in a gown look classy) to an old-school trolley or a cherry-red Lamborghini can work. Don't feel limited to automobiles. A horse-drawn carriage may appeal to the bride looking to complete her fairy tale. And a bicycle for two is a fun touch for a summer wedding. You could also create the perfect thank-you-note photo with one of you sporting a "Just" and the other a "Married" sign on your backs as you hop onto a scooter.

PARKING AND VALETS

Even if you're providing transportation, some guests—and certainly your vendors—will be driving, so don't forget to inquire about parking at your ceremony and reception sites. Ask the site manager what your parking options are, who handles the arrangements, and if they include valet services. Make sure there is enough space for everyone to park, including your vendors, especially if you're not planning to provide transportation.

A massive guest list, meager-to-nonexistent parking facilities, or a complicated location will require more help and add to the cost. If you're hosting a wedding at home or another nontraditional space, you won't want to reenact the famous scene from *Father of the Bride*, scrambling to move cars midwedding. Unless you have the lawn space, you'll need to look into alternative nearby parking lots that you can use. You may be able to rent out a lot at a nearby school or temple or church.

If the parking lot is a long trek and you're concerned about guests having to walk a half mile, consider hiring your own parking attendants. Everyone will appreciate the consideration and convenience, and you won't have to fret over whether your eighty-seven-year-old grandma made it up the hill. In the event that you have to hire an independent valet service, tailor it to your needs. You can choose a full-service team, which will park your guests' cars and retrieve them at the end of the night, or opt for parking attendants that merely direct traffic, hold signs, and guide drivers to empty spaces. The charge is on an hourly per-attendant basis (typically about $20 to $25 per hour per parking attendant), plus a 15 to 20 percent tip (usually tacked onto your total bill). Before you get a price quote, make sure the parking service manager scouts out the location to see how many attendants you'll need, but figure on three to four parking attendants for every hundred guests. When hiring valets, carefully read your contract and ensure that they have adequate insurance in case of an accident (better safe than sorry!). Also, include provisions for attire, and make it clear that you will cover their tips in advance so guests don't have to open their wallets to park.

RENTING YOUR RIDE

If you're planning to rent a fabulous vintage Rolls-Royce for your getaway car or reserve a few party buses to transport your guests between the ceremony and reception location, here's what you'll need to know before you start shopping for the right sets of wheels.

Shop around

Start researching transportation prices about six to eight months before your wedding day. If your ceremony coincides with prom and graduation season in May and June, get started even earlier. Visit at least two companies, and ask for a detailed quote of their services and any special amenities.

BUDGET CONSIDERATIONS When renting cars, you're likely to be charged by the hour (anywhere from $100 to $800, depending on the type of vehicle and wedding locale), and you'll probably be required to contract the cars for a minimum amount of time (typically three hours), as most services don't offer pickup and drop-off options only.

No matter what the wheels, a 15 to 20 percent gratuity will almost always be added to your bill. During prom season, however, you can expect the price to increase by as much as 30 percent and the company to require eight-hour minimum rentals—if you can even find a limo to rent. Some companies offer wedding packages that might include discounts for multiple rentals (so it's usually the most cost-effective to book all your transportation at the same time), as well as perks like champagne. Before booking any package, compare the à la carte costs to make sure it is actually a good deal.

DO YOUR HOMEWORK Although it might not seem like a big deal, it's a good idea to know who actually owns the vehicle you're renting. If the transportation company you're dealing with doesn't have the car you're looking for, they'll often "borrow" a car from another vendor (and basically pay them a rental fee). Here's where it gets sticky—since you're one more middleman away from the wedding car of your dreams, you leave the door open for lateness or, even worse, a no-show. If you have your heart set on a particular car, you'll be better off finding a vendor that actually owns the one you've got in mind.

Also, make sure that they have liability insurance that covers both the passengers and the drivers. And before you book a hot-air balloon, helicopter, or golf cart to whisk you off, make sure that your venue will allow them to park, land, or otherwise arrive on the property. This goes without saying, but any type of vehicle you'll be using on a public street must also be properly licensed.

TEST-DRIVE It can be tempting to sign up for your transportation over the phone or online. But unless you're getting a referral from your wedding planner, don't. You don't want to be disappointed with what shows up at your door or at the wedding to whisk you away for your big getaway (remember: it's a key photo op). Take the time to visit the rental location, see the fleet of vehicles, and sit in one to get a feel for

transportation

Make sure your agreement includes the following key points.

☐ Arrival time to pick you up at the start of the night (pad an extra twenty minutes for safety's sake); do one for each vehicle if you are renting more than one (for the groom and groomsmen, bride and bridesmaids, guests, etc.)

☐ Details of what any wedding package includes, if applicable

☐ Reception departure time at the end of the night

☐ Any other stops, including pickup and/or drop-off times for each

☐ Pickup/delivery times and details for rentals that you will be driving yourselves (like your getaway car)

☐ Addresses of all places where you (or your guests) will need to be picked up and dropped off

☐ The size, color, and model of the exact car(s) (with the license plate number if you've chosen something specific)

☐ Number of passengers

☐ Total number of hours you will need each vehicle and driver

☐ Type of occasion

☐ The name of the driver you want

☐ What you want the driver to wear

☐ Cleaning fees

☐ Any special requests that you have, like champagne or a certain type of music player

☐ Decorating policy (see "Special Send-offs," page 353)

☐ Insurance coverage (including liability insurance for passengers and driver)

☐ Repercussions clause (fees for any damage done to the car—some companies may spell out the exact amount you will owe for different types of damage and can also charge for lost business while the vehicle is being repaired)

☐ Gratuity policy

☐ Deposit amount and date paid

☐ Remaining balance amount and due date

☐ Cancellation policy

☐ Overtime policy and fees

the quality and condition of their cars (including the ones your guests will be riding in—it might be one of their first impressions of the night). Insist on checking out the actual car you'll be using for your wedding. Then copy down the license plate number and include it in your contract to ensure that it's the same vehicle that shows up on your wedding day. Meet the driver and make sure you're both on the same page in terms of his duties and attire, too.

what's your transportation style?

1. Describe your wedding in three words:
A. Classy, understated, modern
B. Rustic, elegant, relaxed
C. Romantic, formal, feminine

2. Let's talk dresses. Your gown is:
A. A one-shoulder sheath with minimal detailing
B. Vintage with sleeves and a demure scoop neckline
C. A sweetheart neckline with a huge, frothy tulle skirt (and a mile-long train!)

3. It's the weekend. What are you and your fiancé up to?
A. Hosting a rooftop party at your downtown loft for a few friends
B. Heading to the country for bonfires, hiking, and delicious grilled food
C. Date night—dinner at your favorite restaurant, then a movie

4. What will your wedding guests be noshing on?
A. Amuse-bouche-style hors d'oeuvres
B. High-end comfort food, like bite-size macaroni and cheese and mini cupcakes
C. Traditional favorites, like filet, roasted vegetables, and chocolate cake

5. Your favorite thing to wear (besides your wedding dress):
A. Sleek black pumps you found at a sample sale
B. Sneakers—you're always on the go
C. A necklace your fiancé gave you for your first anniversary

6. Your fiancé loves planning, of course, but you're sure he'd rather be:
A. Going to a concert
B. Out on the field (football, baseball, soccer, you name it!) with his boys
C. Spending his Sunday mornings drinking coffee and reading the newspaper

7. What are you topping your wedding day look with?
A. A sparkly hair clip or nothing at all
B. A simple, elbow-length veil
C. A birdcage veil with a feather fascinator

8. What are you most looking forward to about your wedding?
A. The live jazz band
B. The food!
C. Seeing friends and family

9. What style is your reception?
A. A cocktail party with gourmet passed appetizers and cupcakes
B. A backyard barbecue
C. A traditional cocktail hour with a seated dinner and dancing to follow

10. What's the one thing you're not stressing over?
A. The flowers. I prefer modern, nonfloral centerpieces anyway.
B. The transportation. Just get me from point A to point B on time.
C. The music. My guests will dance no matter what we play.

Mostly A's: Hire a Convertible
You and your fiancé are always ahead of the trend. A couple as chic as you needs transportation that won't slow you down. Keep it simple by renting an Audi convertible or a European sports car; then switch to a motor scooter or tandem bike for some adorable exit photos. Or if you're partying on the water, consider making your entrance on a sleek yacht or sailboat.

Mostly B's: Hire an SUV
One thing you don't want in your wedding transportation? Fuss. But there are plenty of ways to stay casual while still making a sleek statement. Stretch out in a rented SUV or a luxurious town car. Or, for a more rustic affair, make your getaway in a vintage Ford truck.

Mostly C's: Hire a Rolls-Royce
You're a classic couple, but that doesn't mean you have to default to a horse and carriage (unless that's what you've always envisioned). Opt for an antique car or vintage Rolls-Royce to get you to the ceremony and reception—and to create the perfect backdrop for glam photo ops.

The transportation timeline

When booking your transportation, consider the time your ceremony ends, how long it will take guests to get from one point to the other (allowing for traffic and a late start), and the hour your party is scheduled to start. To keep things flowing, create a detailed schedule with the times that the vehicle should pick up the groomsmen, the bridesmaids, the family, and the bride, plus guests (if applicable). Include any special requests, such as grand entrances or special getaways. Build in cushions, too, for traffic and latecomers (we guarantee you your guests will not all be on the bus at the designated time, so set the departure fifteen minutes earlier than when you actually need them there). If you're having your limo or bus do double duty (for example, picking up the bridesmaids and then meeting the groomsmen elsewhere before heading off to the ceremony), you'll want to allow for double the extra time there, too.

If you are getting ready elsewhere and driving to the ceremony site, do a test drive on the same day and time as your wedding, so you can get a realistic idea of how long it will take you to get to the site. Then budget in an extra fifteen to twenty minutes for traffic and other mishaps. Figure you want to arrive at the ceremony site at least fifteen minutes before it's time to hit the aisle, so count back from there—and you have yourself a departure time. Schedule the limousine to arrive at least twenty minutes before your departure. This timetable will help determine how long you'll book your transportation for, and you'll want to include all the timing info (like the exact time your driver is expected to pick you up before the ceremony) in the contract, so it's important to put together at least a rough schedule before you start researching transportation options.

To make sure everything runs like a well-oiled machine on your wedding day, create a call sheet with the names of guests and all pickup and drop-off addresses and times, and call to confirm those arrangements with the car company the day before or morning of the wedding (or designate a bridesmaid to do it). Drivers should have all of this information in advance, including detailed directions to the ceremony and reception sites (even with GPS, it's important to make sure they have the right information and location). It's also a good idea to assign a few friends or family members to be transportation captains and give them a copy of the directions, including an emergency contact number in case the driver somehow gets lost or stuck.

24

the other parties

We already told you about the engagement party in the prologue, but that early celebration is only the beginning. Similar to the engagement party, planning the shower, the bachelor/bachelorette parties, and the rehearsal dinner doesn't fall on your plate, but you will need to help gather the guest lists and decide on dates, and give your input when it comes to overall direction. In addition, you may also choose to host a welcome party, after-party, and postwedding brunch. Here's what you need to take care of all these peripheral parties.

THE BRIDAL SHOWER

The bridesmaids often host the bridal shower, and the maid of honor puts it all together. But it doesn't have to be this way. Although strict etiquette types say relatives shouldn't host this event—claiming it looks like they're fishing for presents for their own family member—we think it's perfectly fine for your mom or sister to play this role. Your maids will probably appreciate the help. And if a coworker (even one who isn't invited to the wedding) wants to throw an at-work shower for you, that's fine too.

Though you have no official say in this party (sorry), you can let your hosts know whether you'd prefer daytime or evening, as well as how formal you'd like it to be (laid-back barbecue vs. swanky cocktails). Also, let them know how you (or your family) feel about having guys and games involved.

The timeline
A shower can take place six months before the wedding day or at two weeks and counting. The only fixed rule is that the shower should come sometime after the engagement parties but before the big day. (We don't recommend having the shower the same week as the wedding—there will be far too much going on.)

The guest list
Create a list of friends and family you'd like to include in addition to your bridesmaids, such as other close girlfriends and relatives, as well as your groom's close female friends and family. If it's a couple's shower, obviously work with your spouse-to-be to create the guest list. The only rule: Everyone invited to the shower should also be invited to the wedding.

The invitations
From Evites, phone calls, or e-mails to mailed paper invitations, your hosts can go as casual or formal as they want when spreading the word. It's a nice gesture to ask your hosts to still send invites to guests who you already know won't be able to attend (like your college roommate who lives in London). Etiquette-wise, it's 100 percent acceptable for your hosts to include your registry information on the shower invitations—so make sure they have the details.

The scene
Prepare to ooh, aah, and smile—primary activities at any shower are eating, laughing, playing games, and opening gifts. Make sure someone keeps track of all the gifts you unwrap, so thank-you notes are easy to execute. Contrary to what you may have heard, you don't have a year after the wedding to send thank-you cards for gifts, particularly

for shower gifts. In fact, any gift received before the wedding requires a thank-you before the actual day, so get busy. Don't neglect to send out formal thank-you notes and a small gift, like flowers, to the hosts of the party.

THE BACHELORETTE PARTY

Bachelor parties have been a wedding tradition since the so-called olden days, when they gave the groom a chance to "sow his wild oats" before marriage. Now, of course, brides are in on the sowing action. There is no "typical" bachelorette bash. You can paint the town red if that's your style, but there are lots of other ways to celebrate—try a nice dinner, a concert, or a spa weekend. You needn't do anything you don't want to, but be a good sport (just as they were when you asked them to help stuff three hundred envelopes!). The point is to reminisce, laugh, and let them embarrass you (at least a little). It's officially the MOH's job to plan the party, but if one of the maids is more of a party organizer, she'll probably step up. So what's your role (besides wearing a plastic tiara and veil and sipping drinks from a phallic-shaped straw)?

bachelorette party antics

post: snrideout
My bridesmaids are planning my bachelorette party, which I greatly appreciate, but they said they're going to dress me in something funny, but won't tell me what it is. Would it be awful to refuse to wear what they want if I don't like it? I don't want to hurt their feelings, but I also don't want to look like a complete fool.

reply: tlv204
I wouldn't be happy about that, either. I guess just wear something you like on the way there, and then negotiate depending on what they have planned.

post: cew515
There's no way in hell I'm wearing anything with a penis on it during mine. I'm also boycotting tiaras and sashes. Period.

reply: mrs.b6302007
Tell them that you don't want to draw attention to yourself and that you want to keep everything—clothes and paraphernalia included—low-key. It's not like you're taking over planning the party; you're just giving some input on what would make you more comfortable.

reply: catwoman708
You don't get to control the details of the party they're throwing, but you can reserve the right to NOT wear inappropriate clothing.

post: megk8oz
You're an adult, and that means you can dress yourself. Just be honest with your friends and tell them how uncomfortable their plan makes you feel. If they're good friends, they'll understand.

the knot
Like many of these Knotties said, your friends can't force you to wear anything that makes you feel uncomfortable. They shouldn't want to, either. After all, they're throwing this party for you. To avoid sounding like a bridezilla, be super-polite about it. Tell your MOH how you feel and give her a concise will-not-wear list—we're talking two or three vulgar items. Before you two chat, decide on a few silly things you can bear. That way, you aren't shooting down every single one of their ideas. If for some reason your friends don't get the message and show up with some wild gear for you to don during the party, play along for five minutes or casually shed said items and pass them on to your bridesmaids over the course of the evening.

The timeline
Party at least one or two weeks before the big day, though one or two months is probably better. You'll have plenty to do in the final weeks leading up to the wedding (see chapter 25 if you don't believe us). Some brides and grooms prefer to party simultaneously—it leaves no time to wonder (read: obsess over) what the other person is doing. But there's no rule that says you can't combine forces or just meet up at the end of the night if you want.

The guest list
In addition to the bridal party, you can invite other close friends and relatives, though it's usually best to keep this party

pretty small—ten or so is ideal. Chances are that most bachelorette party guests are wedding guests, too, but it's fine to invite coworkers or friends who may not be invited to your small or out-of-town wedding. Just be up-front with them about your limited wedding guest list.

The scene   You can have a "traditional" bachelorette party with barhopping and booze. But if you'd rather do something else, let your friends know early on. Hopefully if you have visions of jetting off to Vegas or South Beach for your bachelorette, your girls are right there with you. But if it's a stretch for them financially—or time-wise—you can't get bent out of shape. Float the idea, but be happy with whatever they come up with.

THE REHEARSAL DINNER

The dinner part of the rehearsal is traditionally hosted by the groom's parents on the eve of the wedding. After the ceremony rehearsal, everyone gathers for a celebratory meal, where the bride and groom are toasted and roasted (go easy on the toasting—you do have a wedding the next day!).

The rehearsal dinner is the perfect opportunity for your two families to get better acquainted before the wedding day (if they don't already know each other well) in a more relaxed atmosphere. The goal here is to relieve some of the prewedding tension and make everyone invited feel comfortable with the impending nuptials while not upstaging the big event. Traditionally, the groom's family organizes and pays for this fete, but you two might take matters into your own hands, or both sets of parents may choose to do the honors together. Even if you're not throwing the dinner, you'll still be involved in the planning.

The timeline   The rehearsal dinner is traditionally held the night before the wedding, most often a Friday, and usually starts at about seven p.m. This leaves time for attendants who cannot take the day off to get out of work, attend the rehearsal itself at around five thirty, and get to the dinner. For a Sunday or holiday wedding, you have more options. Since the rehearsal dinner has become more of a celebration in its own right than just a formality, some couples are holding the event two nights prior to the wedding. This way, there's more time to relax, recuperate, and get ready for the main event. Plus, it can leave you with more room in your wallet, too: For a Saturday wedding, a Thursday-night rehearsal dinner could also mean striking a better deal with a caterer or

the bridesmaid luncheon

Many brides host a bridesmaids' tea or luncheon to thank the gang for all the wedding prep they've put up with and to get in some last-minute bonding. Usually on the casual side, this girls-only get-together is an opportunity to swap stories and for the bride to present each maid with her gift.

The tea or luncheon is usually held a day or two before the wedding and sometimes on the big day itself. This timing works well, especially if your bridesmaids are coming from all over and will be in town for a few days. Feel free to keep it low-key (and to not serve tea at all), hosting brunch or lunch at home, your country club, a restaurant, an event space, or even a suite at the hotel where the wedding will take place.

restaurant. If most attendants won't be arriving until late on the eve of your wedding, a breakfast celebration the morning of the wedding is also acceptable (as is skipping the rehearsal dinner altogether!).

The guest list

Even if you're planning to let your future in-laws figure the whole thing out, you'll want to weigh in on the guest list. The rehearsal dinner is a very good opportunity to maximize your quality time with visiting friends and relatives—you'll be more relaxed than at the wedding, and you'll have more time to chat. As with the actual wedding, deciding just how inclusive to make it is among the toughest decisions you'll face when planning the rehearsal dinner. On one hand, it's an opportunity to have an intimate gathering for family bonding. On the other hand, it's a great excuse to have face time with key friends and extended family who have traveled far.

At the very least, the rehearsal dinner guest list includes immediate family (parents and siblings), wedding-party members and their spouses or significant others, and the parents of any child attendants (inviting the children themselves is optional). You should also invite the officiant and his or her spouse to the dinner (they may not come, but it's the polite thing to do). If your wedding is mostly local friends and family but a few key people traveled far to come to your wedding (those cousins from Hawaii!), extend the rehearsal dinner invitation to them to thank them for their extra effort.

The invitations

If your rehearsal dinner will be a fancy affair with lots of out-of-town guests in a hotel banquet room, a country club, or someplace similarly dressed up, you should send formal invitations. You'll also want people to RSVP so you have a head count for the caterer. If, on the other hand, your rehearsal dinner will be fairly low-key or small—a party at a restaurant or an intimate gathering at your future in-laws' home—then you don't need to be as "official" with your invitations. You can send Evites, use DIY invites, or call to personally ask people to join you. Just make sure it's clear to your guests where they need to be and when. If you're sending out invitations, get them out *with*—or shortly after—your wedding invitations to help everyone keep their schedules straight, book their travel plans, and ensure timely RSVPs. Give far-flung attendants the basic plans far in advance so they can book flights with the proper arrival time.

The scene

Since the rehearsal dinner is more informal than the wedding reception, the food and atmosphere should reflect that. The

SAMPLE

rehearsal dinner invitation wording ideas

Note: Feel free to swap any of the lines of wording between each option
to achieve your perfect sense of formality.

PLEASE ALSO JOIN US FOR A
REHEARSAL DINNER IN HONOR OF
SUSAN AND JOE

FRIDAY, SEPTEMBER THIRD
STARTING AT SIX IN THE EVENING

BLACK FINN RESTAURANT
19 EAST 7TH STREET, SPRINGFIELD

PLEASE REPLY TO AMANDA
(513) 555-8106
OR AMANDA@E-MAIL.COM
BY AUGUST 15TH

**for rehearsal dinner invitations included
with the wedding invitation**

A REHEARSAL DINNER...

IN ANTICIPATION
OF SUSAN & JOE'S BIG DAY,
PLEASE JOIN US FRIDAY, SEPTEMBER 3
AT 6 P.M. FOR GREAT FOOD, DRINKS,
AND CELEBRATION

BLACK FINN RESTAURANT
19 E. 7TH ST.
SPRINGFIELD

RSVP BY AUGUST 15
(513) 555-8106 OR AMANDA@E-MAIL.COM

**for rehearsal dinner invitations as
a separate paper invitation**

PLEASE JOIN US TO CELEBRATE
WITH SUSAN & JOE
AT THEIR REHEARSAL DINNER

FRIDAY, SEPTEMBER 3, AT 6 P.M.
BLACK FINN RESTAURANT
19 E. 7TH ST., SPRINGFIELD

REHEARSAL IMMEDIATELY PRECEDING
DINNER AT ST. ANTHONY'S CATHEDRAL.
(only include this line when you send to
your attendants)

CLICK TO RSVP

**for rehearsal dinner invitations
sent digitally**

wedding should be the climax of the weekend; the rehearsal serves to whet guests' appetites. Ultimately, the setting of the rehearsal dinner depends on the budget, how many guests there will be, and what kind of party the host envisions. While you as the honored couple may have input on the overall direction, if the groom's family hosts, you should really try to let his mom and dad be the creative directors of the evening. If, on the other hand, you are hosting, you get to choose the location and style, so you'll want to give yourselves enough time to scout venues in order to book one four to six months in advance.

While a sit-down dinner at a hotel ballroom or fine restaurant may be the norm, there's no reason to feel hemmed in by that. Couples are getting revved up for their wedding day in backyards, at art galleries, and on beaches. Feel free to use the term "dinner" loosely—cocktails and hors d'oeuvres, a buffet, and even a barbecue are all perfectly acceptable options. (Just be sure you make this clear in your invites so your guests know what to expect.) While you don't have to provide specialty entertainment, here are the typical rehearsal dinner activities.

MEET AND GREET The rehearsal dinner is your chance to welcome everyone. Walk around and catch up with loved ones (and meet more of the in-laws) throughout the evening, because the wedding night will most likely be a bit of a blur.

TOAST As dessert winds down, the toasts begin. As host of the party, the groom's father (sometimes along with the groom's mother) typically goes to bat first, toasting his soon-to-be daughter-in-law and her family. Next up: Traditionally, the groom also toasts his new wife, the guests, and the hosts, but there's no reason both of you can't stand up to thank everyone together, if you'd prefer. This is also an opportunity for the hosts (traditionally the groom's parents) as well as the bride and groom to thank everyone for coming, and for loved ones to say a few words about the soon-to-be-marrieds. Some couples ask their honor attendants and/or other members of the bridal party to speak at the rehearsal dinner, so they have more time for mingling and dancing at the wedding reception. Just don't ask anyone to do double duty—so if you want your sister to speak at the wedding reception, give her the night-before off. Sit back and enjoy the speeches and toasts in your honor. It's not often that you get to hear your favorite people sing your praises. Take any gentle ribbings with grace and laugh along with the crowd.

GIVE GIFTS You may hand out the bridal-party gifts at this occasion, but do it subtly. No matter what, take a moment to stand and thank your bridal party for their support. Parent gifts can also be presented

creative rehearsal dinners

If the in-laws are at a loss for ideas, here are some creative suggestions for the party before the party.

give a nod to the season

Having a winter wedding? Invite guests to a ski lodge with a giant fireplace. Decorate the room with snow lanterns and luminaries. Serve up wintry fare, like stews or soups and a hot-chocolate bar. For a summer celebration, consider using the lawn of your aunt's gorgeous estate for a poolside affair. Hire an acoustic guitarist to play, and serve lighter fare and summery cocktails like margaritas and watermelon martinis.

embrace the local culture

Getting married in New England? Treat guests to a classic clambake with chowder, lobster, mussels, and potatoes. Deep in the heart of Texas, you might consider a down-home barbecue with short ribs, kettle-baked beans, and homemade corn bread.

be entertaining

You don't have to let food be the only guide to creating a memorable rehearsal dinner. Play lawn games like croquet, or hire a favorite bar band or local bluegrass group to play after dinner.

have fun with food

Make it more than just a meal and hire a sushi chef to create custom rolls. Bring in a sommelier to do a wine and cheese tasting, or have chefs whip up crepes for your guests.

preview the honeymoon

Center the party's theme around the couple's honeymoon destination. Hawaii and Mexico are obvious themes, but Italy, Asia, and South America are also fun inspiration.

TIP

inviting out-of-towners

If you're throwing a destination wedding or a party where at least half of the guests are from out of town, show your appreciation by inviting everyone to some kind of night-before festivity. If your budget is limited, stick to a more exclusive group for the rehearsal dinner itself but follow it with a large but informal welcome cocktail or dessert party for out-of-towners later in the evening.

---

at the rehearsal dinner, but we prefer a more private time. Parents will often break down in tears, and the gift exchange can be a nice last moment for you to connect with them before the festivities. Some brides and grooms also use the occasion to present each other with special wedding gifts or surprises.

ATTEND TO DETAILS While everyone is still seated and you have their attention, it's also your chance to slip in a few last-minute reminders about the next day. Before calling it a night, double-check

Here's how to keep
the toasts tasteful and
under control.

the tipsy toast
Try to avoid the situation
altogether by scheduling
the toasting early (at the
start of dinner even), so
there isn't enough time
for any reveler to get
truly intoxicated before
raising his glass.

the endless toast
When you invite
someone to speak,
explain that the toasts
should be no more than
two minutes long to
leave time for all the
other activities.

the roast toast
Before your friend with
the knack for dirty jokes
is standing in front of
your entire family
holding a mic, tell him
(and all other toasters
when you first ask them)
to save any racy material
for the bachelor/
bachelorette party.
Or just cut the friend
speeches and keep it
to family.

that everyone in the wedding party knows exactly where to go the next day, what things they're supposed to bring, and when and where they're expected to arrive to get ready. If you have a broader audience, remind guests about any activities for them the next day, as well as pickup times and locations for transportation you've arranged to get them to and from the ceremony.

THE WELCOME PARTY

If most of your guests are out-of-towners or if there are a lot of people you haven't seen in a while coming to your wedding, a welcome party is a great way to greet everyone in a relaxed, no-pressure atmosphere. Your guests are investing time and money to attend your wedding, so it's nice to make them feel included in all the festivities from the moment they arrive. A welcome party can be a cocktails-only, open-house-style celebration on the hotel patio, something big, fun, and festive like a cruise around the city complete with a buffet dinner, or something as simple and sweet as a dessert-and-champagne party at someone's house. Don't worry about going too formal with this one—unless you want to. The welcome party should be low-key enough for guests to relax and get to know each other without stressing about having a second perfect party dress. As for the hosts, anything goes with this one. You and your fiancé can certainly host, or another family member or close friend can do the honors.

The timeline
Unless your wedding event is four days long, the welcome party takes place the night before the wedding. It can take the place of the rehearsal dinner, it can take place during the rehearsal dinner (hosted by a relative or close friend and the guests of honor making an appearance near the end), or it can be a shorter postdinner cocktail party.

The guest list
In addition to your VIPs, you'll want to invite all of your out-of-town guests, naturally, but you may choose to invite everyone else, too.

The invitations
A printed invitation is not necessary, but you can always print the details on an enclosure card to send with the wedding invitations of whomever you want to include, or if someone else is hosting, they may want to send a completely separate printed invite. Evites, e-mails, or a post on your wedding website will work, too.

The scene Food and drinks are essential at this event, but you won't want everyone to completely overindulge. Hearty appetizers or a protein-filled buffet will keep everyone's stomachs sufficiently full while they're drinking and talking. A sit-down is also an option, but remember that people will mostly want to mingle, so keep it limited to two courses followed by a dessert buffet. A menu tied to the location or region will give out-of-towners a fun local experience. Show off your hometown pride with a pair of signature cocktails named for your respective former stomping grounds, or choose local beer and wine to serve with dinner.

While you don't need a DJ and a dance floor, you will want to have music to add to the festive mood. Live performers are always exciting—and a conversation starter for guests who don't know each other. A smooth trio of jazz musicians, complete with stand-up bass, will set a swanky vibe; a loud and brightly colored mariachi band will add a festive feel. Consider the musical acts or live performers that didn't work for your wedding.

THE AFTER-PARTY

Couples who want to prolong the festivities as much as possible are now capping off the reception with a lively parting song and then leading any guests who wish to continue the merrymaking to the after-party venue. They may still do the reception exit for the pictures and ceremonial effect, or they may skip the official getaway.

The "after-party party" is still a pretty informal gathering, generally thrown for the couple's closest friends and any crazy relatives who want to attend. Some couples are making the postreception blowout official, booking a second location, sending out invitations, and even giving it a theme. If you don't plan to make it into a big to-do, it's a good idea to have an after-hours game plan, even if it's just a nearby wine bar so that you don't wrangle everyone for an impromptu party at the end of the night.

Chances are there will be many friends offering to pick up the bar tab. But between the showers, bachelorette and bachelor parties, gifts, attire, hotels, and travel, your loved ones will have already spent plenty to be a part of your celebration. Covering the cost of the after-party is the perfect way for you to thank your crew for their exertions. No need to go overboard—if you're worried about overspending, just put a cap on the craziness after an hour or two. Or, if someone offers to host, particularly a sibling, by all means let him. But if everyone just decides of his or her own volition to head to the bar after the wedding, don't

---

CLEVER IDEAS
video montage

Short video montages are a popular rehearsal dinner entertainment option to run before dessert. The key word here is *short*. Sure, your loved ones will enjoy a walk down memory lane, watching you and your groom grow up and fall in love, but set it to music and cap it at two songs or five minutes; anything longer and guests will get bored. And use your judgment—any photos that might make your grandmother blush should probably be left out. If you don't want to stop the party for this presentation but still want the personal touch and conversation topic, you can always have a slideshow projected silently on a wall throughout the evening.

feel like you have to open a tab to cover all the drinks (though it would certainly be a nice gesture).

The timeline

While the timing is pretty self-explanatory, you will need to decide how late you want the party to go. It's completely up to you (and when the venue closes), but a good rule of thumb is two to three hours, depending on the time your reception ends.

The guest list

A stringent guest list is rarely adhered to, but some couples aim to restrict the postreception bash to the bridal party and close friends at a hotel suite, while others choose to invite anyone and everyone who's begging for more. You might want to start by determining who will definitely be in tow (your sorority sisters, your brother, and other bons vivants) and then just know to expect other guests who spontaneously want in on the action.

The invitations

If you want to get the crowd psyched up for the festivities, send out invitations. Or just let word of mouth take over. Mention the party at the bachelor and bachelorette bashes, and maybe follow up with invitations in guests' welcome baskets or details posted on your website. You could also just let it happen organically and have your bridal party spread the word.

The scene

Springing for a simple gathering in the hotel bar or bridal suite is standard. Have the bridesmaids and groomsmen tote some of the leftovers to party central for when you get the munchies, and a table centerpiece or two will work wonders for ambience. Another option: Rent out a room at a favorite local watering hole, wine bar, or swanky club (be sure to make reservations in advance). It's perfectly fine to plan the party to contrast with the type of wedding you're having. For example, if you'll be having a buttoned-up evening reception at a country club that doesn't allow loud music, you might want to throw an all-out dance party for your friends later that night at a bar you've rented out.

THE MORNING-AFTER BRUNCH

After the frenzy of your wedding day, this low-key event will give you a chance to thank your guests and say one last good-bye. Traditionally, the bride's parents take the reins, but anyone can throw this get-together. You may, however, decide to do the honors yourselves, with or without the help of your parents, as one last thank-you to your guests. Of course if you're planning to leave for your honeymoon bright and early the next morning, it's totally fine to skip this extra celebration, too.

The timeline

If you're having an evening wedding that runs past midnight, be kind to your guests and don't ask them to set their alarm before 9:00 a.m., which means a 10:00 a.m. or 11:00 a.m. start for brunch.

The guest list

The brunch is usually for the couples' families and any wedding guests who are still in town, but feel free to include attendants, friends, or even the family dog (depending on the location). Basically, anything goes. Of course, that depends on who's paying for it, which leads us to the invitations.

The invitations

A printed invitation is not necessary, but you can always slip a brunch card in with the wedding invitations of whomever you want to include, or if someone else is hosting, she may want to send a completely separate printed invite. Regardless, the brunch invites can also be as informal as phone calls and e-mails, or if everyone's invited, a simple post on your wedding website will work, too.

The scene

Keep this party decidedly low-key with an intimate, completely relaxed setting. A buffet breakfast or brunch laid out in a hotel banquet room or your mom's living room is perfect. The standard brunch fare will do: omelets, French toast, waffles, pancakes, scones, croissants, bagels, coffee, and juices. Since guests may be hitting the road right after, include some heartier dishes to hold them over, like pasta or chicken Caesar salad. Just add Bloody Marys and mimosas to make it a cocktail brunch.

the countdown begins

You've carefully picked the outfits, nailed down your vendor contacts, and pored over every detail of your wedding. Now what? At one month and counting, it is the time to savor the moment. No amount of obsessing will guarantee against surprises, so you might as well just kick back. Trust yourself—the groundwork you've laid and the capable vendors and loved ones whose help you've enlisted will ensure that your wedding is fabulous. At this point, the bulk of your wedding planning has been taken care of. So what's left to do? Mostly calculating final payments, finessing the décor and menu, and confirming plans with guests and vendors. Relish these final tasks; your adventure in wedding planning is about to be over!

THE REMAINING TO-DOS

Don't lose steam as you approach the finish line. There are still some key tasks left before the celebrating begins. Many of these—such as the seating arrangements—can be surprisingly challenging and can be made worse if stress levels are running high. So read up on and accomplish the following as early as humanly possible.

Wedding night accommodations
Whether you make a beeline to your room as soon as you cut the cake or after the last of your guests has gone to bed is your prerogative. Some couples, delighted to spend time with friends and relatives they haven't seen in ages, prefer to hang with everyone else until the wee hours. Hopefully, even your rowdiest relations aren't the types who will have the nerve to knock on your door on your wedding night after you've hung the "Do Not Disturb" sign. But to be on the safe side, when you call to book your wedding-night accommodations, request a room that's far from the ones your guests will be occupying. Reserve the bridal or presidential suite, which is usually the most spacious, where you're more likely to be tucked away from the other hard-partying guests (since there are fewer rooms on floors with these suites).

You should book your wedding-night room two to three months in advance. So if you haven't booked a room already, you'll want to do so now. Without a doubt, the most common wedding-night destination is the most luxe hotel in town. The night is earmarked as one of the most memorable of your life, and special, fancier-than-normal surroundings can set the perfect tone. As we all know, however, not all hotels are created equal—even the four-star kind—so it's important that you do a little prewedding reconnaissance and select your lodgings with care. Visit the hotel in person and ask if you can take a peek at a room or the actual suite you're interested in booking. When you're ready to reserve a room, make sure to mention you're booking it for your wedding night. Most hotels offer some sort of upgrade or thoughtful freebie for newlyweds, from a chilled bottle of bubbly to a better view.

Honeymoon prep
The final few weeks before the wedding are the perfect time to shore up your honeymoon plans: Reconfirm your flight and hotel reservations about five days before takeoff. Even if one (or both) of you is changing your name, make sure all international reservations are in your given names. You can't apply for a passport using your married name until after the wedding; keeping everything consistent will save you big-time headaches. And if you need a passport

the knot NOTE

honeymoon finder
Need help deciding where to go? Find honeymoon-specific reviews of top destinations, from the Caribbean islands and Hawaii to the South Pacific, plus recommendations of the best resorts.
TheKnot.com/ honeymoons

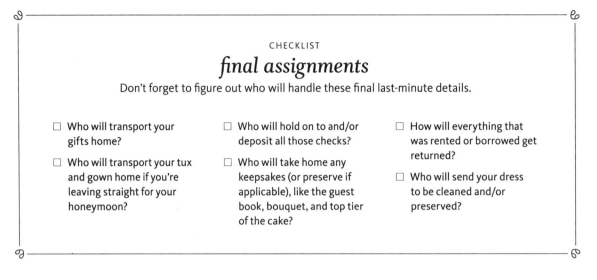

CHECKLIST

final assignments

Don't forget to figure out who will handle these final last-minute details.

- ☐ Who will transport your gifts home?

- ☐ Who will transport your tux and gown home if you're leaving straight for your honeymoon?

- ☐ Who will hold on to and/or deposit all those checks?

- ☐ Who will take home any keepsakes (or preserve if applicable), like the guest book, bouquet, and top tier of the cake?

- ☐ How will everything that was rented or borrowed get returned?

- ☐ Who will send your dress to be cleaned and/or preserved?

(double-check the dates to confirm you don't need to renew yours), make sure to apply at least six weeks before your trip. You'll also want to pack at least several days before your wedding, so you'll have one less thing to worry about. Flip to the appendix for more honeymoon planning help.

Final head counts

Now's the time to find out, once and for all, who's coming and who isn't. The first thing to do just after you hit the two-week mark is to contact people you've invited who haven't sent in their RSVPs yet. Simply inquire whether they plan to attend. Start with e-mail and divvy up any final phone calls with your fiancé, mom, or planner—each of you can phone the guests you're closest to—and you should be done in no time. Once you have your final head count, let your caterer or banquet manager know, as well as your cake baker and any other vendors who need a head count. For the most part, they'll need to have the details at least ten days in advance. Use the final guest count to nail down with your site manager or rental company the exact number of tables and chairs you're going to need (see chapter 7 for a refresher on table sizes).

Seating assignments

Depending on the kind of wedding you're having, you may or may not want to assign your guests reception seats. If you've invited less than fifty people to a low-key buffet, it's fine to let things fall into place spontaneously. You also don't need to worry about a seating chart if you're having cocktails or a casual brunch or lunch. However, if you're serving a seated dinner, do your guests a favor and make a plan. You'll cut down on the overall chaos, inspire great conversation by seating the most compatible people side by side, spare your guests the discomfort of feeling like they need to "save" spots and shoo away strangers, and make everyone feel like you've thought of them (especially once they see those calligraphed place cards).

The easiest way to think of your seating plan is creating mini dinner parties at each table. Say your guest list of one hundred and sixty will be sixteen tables of ten—have each set of parents handle the seating for their guests, so in this formula (assuming you are dividing the guest list evenly in thirds), each would get four tables, and there are eight off of your plate! Now, with your tables, try to think of them in themes and come up with lists, ways to slice and dice your friend sets. Obvious examples are sorority sisters and spouses, soccer club friends, colleagues. Try to avoid the "singles" table and instead intermix two or so singles at each table. If you are having banquet-style seating with long tables, act like each section of eight chairs is a table and seat members of a theme across from one another. (See chapter 7 for the rundown of table types and seating options.)

Try to strike a balance between familiar faces and acquaintances. Every person at the table should know at least one or two of her neighbors, but consider adding some fresh faces as well. After all, the essence of a wedding is bringing people together and taking a leap, neither of which is reflected in grouping people who all know each other. This is an excellent opportunity to get your relatives acquainted with your fiancé's, build bridges between your childhood and "adult" friends, and even play matchmaker.

The next step is determining where the tables go (go to page 93 for more on table layout options). In other words, how to arrange them in proximity to the dance floor, and this is where things get sticky. . . . Someone's guests will have to sit in the back of the room or near the kitchen. Draw straws so it's fair, or distribute it evenly so your tables and each of your parents' tables have a mix of prime spots and not-so-prime placement. In general, the head table (that's where the wedding party sits) and sweetheart table (if you're having one—otherwise, you sit with the wedding party or your families) are centrally located. From there, close friends and relatives are typically seated nearby in a ring around you. Note: It's best to seat the older guests away from the speakers and dance floor and place younger revelers closer to the stage and dance floor.

Once your seating chart is set, you'll want to confirm any last-minute attendance changes and then hand off the final list to your reception site manager and/or your planner for setup. If you're having the escort and place cards done by a calligrapher or printed by your stationer, you'll want to drop them off at least two weeks before to allow for plenty of time, so start on that seating chart right away. Seating-card wording should match the formality of your invitations, so if you sent formal invitations, include full names and titles. For more casual affairs, it's okay to skip the titles.

Checking in with your vendors

You and your wedding vendors have already hashed out all the specifics and signed a contract. Now let them do their thing without breathing down their necks. (You screened these pros carefully—trust your instincts *and* theirs.) That said, you definitely should check in with each vendor during the final few weeks to lock down all the details, answer any last-minute questions, make sure preparations are on track, and get the reassurance you need. There will be some details, like the menu, photo shot lists, ceremony readings, and playlists, that you may not have finalized yet, so you'll need to meet with your vendors to confirm everything first.

FINAL MEETINGS At one month and counting (or even earlier), set up final meetings with all of your vendors to finalize any remaining details. This is the time to make any changes to your orders (make sure they are added to your contract and both you and the vendor initial the changes), work out timing, setup/delivery and breakdown details, and confirm the final amount and due dates for any remaining balances.

Florist Florists will place their orders about two weeks or so before the wedding, so check in just before the two-week mark to finalize all the floral elements, make any changes to your order, and check out a sample centerpiece (if you haven't done so already—some florists prefer to wait until closer to the wedding so they can show you a sample with the flowers that will actually be available). (See chapter 8.)

Music-Makers Meet with your band or DJ about a month before to go over any equipment they will need, setup details and timing, the reception playlist, the do-not-play list, any dress code requirements, break times, meals, as well as any other details that haven't been finalized. If you are hiring ceremony musicians, go over the ceremony playlist, dress code requirements, and other details. (See chapter 12.)

Photographer and Videographer Meet with your photographer and videographer about three to four weeks before to discuss your shot list, your day-of timeline so they know where they should be when to get the shots you want, timing for your portraits, and details like breaks, meals, dress codes, and any other remaining points. You will likely be in contact at least once before the wedding, as your timing and day-of schedule inevitably shift—make sure you know the best way to communicate these last-minute changes, too, during the final days leading up to your wedding so an e-mail or update isn't missed (See chapters 9 and 10.)

Caterer You'll have your tasting about one to two months before the wedding to finalize the menu, so you'll want to make sure to set that up in advance. Also, go over the day-of timeline, the list of items the caterer will provide (like dishes, etc.), and what he/she will need, setup details. Make sure any changes or additions to the menu or other services are added to your contract and signed by both parties. (See chapter 11.)

Officiant Finalize your ceremony lineup and content, including the readings (make sure any readers have copies so they can start practicing), music selections, and of course, your vows. Meet with your officiant to go over the wording of the ceremony, your vows and readings, and musical selections a month or two before the wedding, and practice (and write if you haven't already!) your vows in the final three to four weeks leading up to your wedding. (See chapter 13.)

Cake Baker Confirm your order as well as the delivery time, space needed to store the cake in the refrigerator (if needed), and the details for any final décor elements (like fresh flowers) to be added just before the reception. Make any remaining DIY elements, like ceremony programs, escort cards, favors, etc., about a month before to get them out of the way. If you've had them professionally made, pick them up from your stationer or other store one to two weeks before. (See chapter 19.)

Stationer/Calligrapher You'll place orders for any remaining printed paper elements (like escort and place cards, menus, and favor tags) about a month before the wedding, so they will be ready to pick up the week before. Allow for at least an extra week or two if you're planning to have the escort cards and any other element with guests' names on them calligraphed. The calligrapher will need about two weeks (or more, especially if you're having a large guest list and getting all the envelopes calligraphed) to finish them. (See chapter 19.)

Transportation Confirm transportation details, including arrival times, day-of schedule, and addresses, with the transportation company and driver. (See chapter 23.)

The Rest of Your Team Also confirm timing, details, and balances with the following optional other vendors: event designer, rental company, lighting designer, day-of coordinator, site manager, hair and makeup, and specialty entertainment.

last-minute vendor questions

Here are some general types of issues to address with your team of wedding professionals in the final days leading up to your nuptials.

☐ **Ingredients:** Do you already have the specific blooms, liquor brands, or fresh fruit (or other ingredients) that I ordered? If my picks are unavailable, what replacements will be used? [Some items, like food and flowers, will depend on availability and won't be finalized until the week of your wedding.]

☐ **Legwork:** Have you completed the labor-intensive, complicated tasks? How long will you need to finish the rest and what's there

to do? [Make sure they have the contact information of whomever (site manager, planner, etc.) will be at the site the day-of to let them in and answer any questions.]

☐ **Access:** Are you all set to get into the site(s) when you need to?

☐ **Equipment:** Do you have everything you need?

☐ **Schedule:** [Run over crucial arrival and departure times in writing.]

Logistics In addition to finalizing your orders and details with each vendor, there is some major coordinating and communication you'll need to do (or that you'll want to make sure your planner or coordinator does for you). We suggest a phone call at the two-week mark, a call (or visit) during the final week (if possible), and a last ring the day before the wedding to reconfirm arrival times and other important points. Have contracts on hand so you can go over what needs to be done in an organized fashion. If you can, leave some of the final just-calling-to-confirm calls to a trusted friend or family member who's capable and willing (Mom, you're a saint!), or even better, your planner, so you don't have to tie yourselves up in knots over any last-minute glitches.

Once again, confirm all final payment amounts, details, locations, and delivery times with your vendors. Now is also a good time to prepare a "day-of" package for each vendor. In it, note any last-minute changes you made or requests you have and include any pertinent information, including the following:

■ Give vendors copies of any information they'll need in case they forget theirs (like the playlist for the DJ or band, special food requests for the caterer, and a shot list for the photographer).

■ Give your caterer, cake baker, and reception site manager the final head count.

- Supply the reception site manager with a list of requests from other vendors (such as a table for the DJ, setup space needed by the florist, and so on).
- Distribute a key contacts list including the bride, groom, bridal party members, planner, and key vendors.

Preparing your party

Check in with the bridal party and make sure they have all their attire together, meaning they've picked up their dresses or tuxes—and tried them on to confirm they fit. In addition, make sure they have all their accessories and any other gear. Send an e-mail with their itinerary for the wedding weekend, including times and locations of the rehearsal and rehearsal dinner, where they should meet you to get ready the day of, makeup and hair appointments (if you're having them), and ceremony times. Follow up by phone, if necessary. Provide printouts at the actual rehearsal. (Even though everyone has a smart phone, paper is more reliable every time.) If you are having children attendants, call or e-mail their parents two weeks before the wedding to confirm all the details. You will want them to come to the rehearsal to practice their role in front of a smaller group, so they know where to go on the actual day, but you may want to tell your parents that they can just show up for the last ten or fifteen minutes of the rehearsal so they don't get restless while you're going over altar positions with your attendants.

THE DAY-OF TIMELINE

To make the day manageable, create a play-by-play schedule of exactly what's going to go down and when on the day of your wedding. This timetable will not only keep your whirling head in check (and assure you that everything will, in fact, come together), it will also be a useful tool for your wedding party and vendors, helping them plan and prepare for what they need to accomplish.

Creating the framework

Your day-of schedule should go in order of the events of the wedding weekend, from the first delivery drop-off at the reception site to the returning of the rentals the next day. Your planner or a day-of coordinator can be a huge asset in helping you organize all your vendors and map out your wedding schedule, but you will still need to work with her (and your other vendors and wedding party) to make sure it's feasible and to fill her in on the appointments you booked like hair and makeup timing.

TIP
final payments

Your final payments will likely be due to your vendors in the week leading up to your wedding or on that day. Prepare in advance by sitting down and separating any remaining payments into envelopes for each vendor. Now is also a good time to divvy up the tips for your vendors into envelopes, too. Then give any payments and tips to be paid at the end of your reception to your best man, father, planner, or other point person you've put in charge of handling payments, tips, and vendor issues the day of the wedding.

Make your timeline as detailed as possible—always include the addresses and contacts for each event. Also, list all the phone number(s) and e-mail addresses for all vendors and contacts working on each event, or include a master list of all your vendors and wedding party's contact information at the beginning of the document. Keep in mind: Your day-of schedule will be a work in progress that's constantly changing, so you'll be updating it continuously in the weeks and days leading up to the wedding.

Aim to firm up your schedule two to three days before the wedding, and e-mail it to all your vendors, the site manager, and anyone else involved in the wedding, including the entire bridal party and your parents. If there are any last-minute changes after you've sent it out, highlight them in a different color before sending everyone the updated version. And as we mentioned earlier, bring hard copies of the final schedule to go over quickly at the rehearsal (or to leave in attendant's hotel rooms with the welcome bags), just to make sure everyone is clear as to where they need to be on the actual day.

SCHEDULING YOUR VENDORS Start working on the schedule a few months in advance (or even sooner!), inputting details and events as you work them out. Figuring out how long things will take (and padding in extra time) is key to making your day run smoothly. While you can use our timetable guidelines to get an idea of when things should take place and how long they will take, go over the schedule with your vendors during your final meetings to confirm details like how long it will take to serve and clear each course from the site manager or caterer (see chapter 11), how long the ceremony should last (see chapter 13) from your officiant, how long portraits should take based on your shot list from the photographer, and so on and so forth.

Your vendors can also suggest the best time to deliver certain items (like the cake) and can tell you what they will need to keep deliveries fresh before go-time (like a large-enough refrigerator space for the cake—ask for the measurements so your site manager can plan accordingly). If items need to be installed, such as a dance floor, draping, or a stage, you'll want to find out how much time your vendors will need to set up and factor that into your timetable as well. Don't forget about the breakdown and cleanup details—whether they're taking place the day of the wedding or the day after, work out with your site and vendors all the details for when and how all rentals will be returned and the equipment and décor will be broken down, and who will be responsible for everything.

Coordinate with your reception and ceremony venue contacts to make sure the site will be available for setup and deliveries and to find out where vendors can distribute their items, and for a contact who will be at the site to accept deliveries (you'll need someone to be there for both setup and pickups). A site manager may even be able to coordinate the itinerary directly with each vendor, saving you the hassle.

Once you know how much time you need to get ready or take pictures and how much time your vendors will need to set up, you can work backward from your start time to figure out where everyone needs to be and when. Next, enter your ceremony (chapter 13) and reception (chapter 20) timelines into your schedule and build from there, adding the photo schedule you worked out with your photographer, any appointments your booked (like hair and makeup), delivery details (like cake and flowers), and pickup times (for transportation, for example) as you work them out.

VERIFYING VOLUNTEERS   If you have a family member or friend helping with any of the setup or delivery (dropping off welcome bags at hotels, picking up favors and dropping them at the reception site, picking up your dress and bouquet from the bridal suite to be cleaned and preserved while you're on your honeymoon), reach out two to three weeks before the wedding to confirm that they are still on board with their duties and that they have all the pertinent information they need to perform said tasks. You'll also want to work out the timing for each and coordinate with any vendors or with your site, if applicable. Then, add that information to your itinerary as well.

The ingredients   Though every couple's wedding schedule is unique, here is a general list of what any day-of timeline should contain. Of course, the order in which the events take place will vary—arrange yours in chronological order.

CONTACT INFORMATION
- All vendors' contact information (including all phone numbers where they can be reached, as well as e-mail addresses)
- Ceremony and reception site managers' contact information
- Planner's (or day-of coordinator's) contact information
- Contact information for all members of the wedding party, including your day-of (or weekend-of) point person (this honor should go to your parents or MOH—you'll have enough to worry about)

ADDRESSES AND DIRECTIONS
- Address of ceremony and reception site(s)
- Directions to ceremony site, to reception site, and from ceremony to reception site

SETUP AND DELIVERIES

- Reception setup and deliveries (include name and contact information for the person who will meet the vendors at the site and anything they will need, like refrigerator space for the cake)
  When: 3–6 hours before reception start time; if you are having a tent wedding, bringing in Porta Potties, or installing flooring or draping, setup will take longer and may need to begin the day before
- Ceremony setup and deliveries (include name and contact information of site manager or day-of site contact)
  When: 2–3 hours before the ceremony start time
- Flower delivery and setup (include arrival times and locations of all flower elements for the ceremony and reception; we recommend having your florist handle all deliveries and setup to ensure that everything is fresh and looks amazing for the wedding)
  When: 1–4 hours before ceremony start time (allot extra time for more elaborate floral installations)

GETTING READY

- Bridesmaids and groomsmen arrive at location where everyone will get ready; bridesmaids begin hair and makeup (allot 30 minutes each)
  When: 3–5+ hours before ceremony start time
- Lunch delivered to bride's and groom's locations (if your ceremony will be later in the afternoon or evening you will need the energy)
  When: 2–4 hours before ceremony start time
- Photographer and videographer arrive at bridal suite for getting-ready pictures (if you're including preceremony footage in your package)
  When: 20 minutes before bride's hair and makeup begins
- Bride's hair and makeup begins (allot 45 minutes for each)
  When: 90 minutes to 2 hours before you plan to start taking preceremony pictures (or before the ceremony if not)
- Bride and bridesmaids begin getting dressed (allot at least 45 minutes to get your gown on and 30 minutes for your maids)
  When: 45 minutes before the preceremony photos are scheduled to begin (or before the ceremony if not)
- Groom and groomsmen begin getting dressed
  When: 30 minutes before the preceremony photos begin (or 60 minutes before the ceremony start time if not)

PHOTOS

- Take any preceremony portraits, including group bridesmaid, group groomsmen, and respective family portraits, as well as first-look photos (if you are doing them) (include time, location, participants, and other relevant details for preceremony photos in the schedule)

When: 1–2 hours before ceremony start time; allot 2 to 3 hours if you are doing all portraits before the ceremony, including family and wedding party (45–90 minutes) and first-look photos (at least 30–45 minutes)—plus, travel time if taking pictures in more than one location

CEREMONY

- Ceremony vendors (officiant, musicians) arrive (include setup details, such as contact information for the person who will meet them at the site); groom and groomsmen arrive, as well as everyone else who will be involved in the ceremony, including ushers, parents, flower children, ring bearers, readers, and attendants (be sure to indicate where they should congregate before the ceremony and details about any tasks or props, such as where to find the ceremony programs or the location of a room where the groomsmen can hang out until go time)
  When: 60 minutes before ceremony start time
- Leave for ceremony (include transportation pickup times and addresses as well as the driver's cell phone)
  When: 30–60 minutes before ceremony start time (depending on how far away ceremony is)
- Doors to ceremony venue open and guests begin to enter
  When: 30–45 minutes before ceremony start time
- Bride, bridal party, and bride's parents arrive (if all riding together)
  When: 20 minutes before ceremony start time
- Processional music begins, followed by the ceremony; include ceremony start and end times and rundown of ceremony events (processional and recessional lineups and everything that will happen in between and who will be doing it—see chapter 13)
  When: 10–15 minutes after ceremony start time

RECEPTION

- Reception vendors such as the band or DJ arrive and begin setting up
  When: 2–3 hours before cocktail hour begins
- Transportation arrives for getting everyone from the ceremony to the reception site
  When: 20 minutes before ceremony ends
- Receiving-line participants line up (include where each member should stand), if you're having one (see chapter 13)
  When: 10–15 minutes before cocktail hour begins (immediately following the ceremony if the reception is at the same location)
- Cocktail-hour begins (include setup times for cocktail hour bar, music [if applicable], and stations [if applicable], as well as when guests will start being ushered into the reception and who will do the honors)
  When: 45–60 minutes before reception begins

- Reception begins; include timeline for meal service and cake cutting (see chapter 11) and all activities, such as when the band/DJ will take a break, when the spotlight dances will happen along with the names of participants and songs to be played, what the bandleader/DJ/other emcee will be announcing and when, and details about stop time and breakdown (see chapter 12)
  When: 3–5 hours before end of reception
- End-of-night transportation for couple, wedding party, and guests arrives (include times and addresses for pickup and drop-off locations as well as reservation confirmation for the wedding-night suite)
  When: 20–30 minutes before end of reception (if you are providing rides home for guests, consider staggering transportation, with a bus leaving every 30 minutes, starting about an hour before the reception ends)
- After-party begins (include details like location, timing, and directions)
  When: Immediately following reception (typically lasts anywhere from 1 to 3 hours)

BREAKDOWN AND CLEANUP

- Reception breakdown and cleanup begins (include pickup times and who will be responsible for returning rentals; which vendors will be responsible for cleaning up or returning each element; who will pick up the groom's tux and where it should be returned; who will pick up the bride's dress and bouquet and take them to be preserved)
  When: Immediately following reception

Run-through
To help ensure everyone is on the same page, to work out any wrinkles in the day-of plan, and to make sure all your vendors are familiar with the site and where they will be setting up, ask your reception manager if it's possible to set up a reception rehearsal with relevant vendors at the venue a few days before the wedding. (You can use your ceremony rehearsal to do this with your florist, ceremony musicians, and any other ceremony vendors who will want to be familiar with the site in advance.)

Use this time to introduce your site manager to make sure everyone knows who their point person will be for day-of deliveries and setup, to familiarize everyone with the space and where things will take place, and to confirm that they will have the equipment they need to set up (such as tables, outlets, etc.). Also, run through the schedule of events, including setup and breakdown details, so you can introduce and coordinate with vendors who will be working together (like the cake baker and florist if you're decorating your fondant tiers with fresh flowers). On your list of invitees: lighting designer, rental company, caterer, florist, event designer, band/DJ, site manager. If you have a planner, let her handle the run-through, or your site manager may even be willing to do it for you. You can also do site visits separately during your final meetings with each vendor if you prefer.

WELCOMING THE TROOPS

Now's the time to do the prep work that makes out-of-town guests feel welcome. A few weeks before your wedding, check with the hotel(s) where your guests have booked rooms to make sure everyone's rooms and rates are set. Make a round of calls/e-mails to find out how and when your faraway guests are coming into town—consider hiring a car service to pick them up at the airport or train station, or arranging to have nearby family and friends fetch them in shifts. Make sure everyone has rental-car and hotel-shuttle information, too, or any other information they may need to get to your wedding. Also confirm a time to drop off welcome bags and anything else you want to leave for guests.

Jenn & Christopher
SEPTEMBER 25
CRIGLERSVILLE, VA

When Jenn and Christopher decided to get married on the bride's parents' farm, they let the natural, rustic environment set the tone for the day. The couple went for an eclectic look that incorporated lots of DIY and repurposed vintage elements, like escort cards made out of shipping tags and strung up with clothespins. Colorful wildflowers were used for the bride's bouquet and the table arrangements.

day-of wedding kit

Be sure to pack everything on this list (or have your MOH do it) to ensure your wedding goes off without a hitch.

- ☐ Pain reliever (for headache or cramps)
- ☐ Clear Band-Aids/ blister pads or moleskin
- ☐ Bottle of water
- ☐ Corsage pins
- ☐ Dental floss/ toothpicks and to-go toothbrush
- ☐ Eyedrops
- ☐ Extra earring backs
- ☐ Extra panty hose (if wearing any)
- ☐ Baby powder (it does wonders on white dress stains and can sop up any oil or sweat)

- ☐ Hairpins/ponytail holder
- ☐ Hand sanitizer
- ☐ Shoe pads
- ☐ Safety pins
- ☐ Makeup remover Q-tips (for any smudges)
- ☐ Clear nail polish
- ☐ Crochet hook (for button or loop closures and bustiers)
- ☐ Lint roller
- ☐ Stain removal wipes
- ☐ Oil-blotting sheets
- ☐ Fashion tape
- ☐ Static-cling spray

- ☐ Dry mascara wand (for declumping and brushing eyebrows into place)
- ☐ Tissues
- ☐ Tweezers
- ☐ Breath mints
- ☐ Cell phone
- ☐ Comb/brush
- ☐ Cash (just in case)
- ☐ Hair spray
- ☐ Makeup (include powder, lipstick, concealer, blush, and mascara for touch-ups)
- ☐ Mirror
- ☐ Nail file

- ☐ Nail polish (in same shade as on your fingers and toes)
- ☐ Perfume
- ☐ Moisturizer
- ☐ Tampons
- ☐ Granola bars
- ☐ Krazy Glue (for nail fixes, shoe heels, decorations, even jewels)
- ☐ Sunblock (for a destination or summer wedding)
- ☐ Your inhaler, EpiPen, or other medications
- ☐ Change of shoes

Speaking of which . . . now's also the time to get busy working on those favors and gift bags (see chapter 22, page 339). Pick up (or order) all the ingredients and start stuffing them about two weeks before the wedding (hint: bribe your bridal party with wine to get them to help). On the day before the wedding, drop off the welcome bags at your guests' hotels, or enlist your wedding crew to assemble and distribute all these treats.

We know you'll be busy in the days leading up to your wedding (and your guests know this, too). Try to get as much done before everyone arrives so you can spend quality time with them. Remember, the reason that these intrepid travelers have made this trip is to see *you*.

THE NIGHT BEFORE . . .

How you spend the night before the wedding is entirely up to you—the key is to get as much sleep as possible. If you and your spouse-to-be live together, it can seem kind of weird and old-fashioned to suddenly move out for the night, but most couples enjoy the ritual of dividing up for the night. Do what feels right for you (and your fiancé!), and you won't have to worry about yawning during your vows. If you go the sleep-apart route, get separate hotel rooms or each crash in the extra bed in your honor attendants' room. For girls who love a slumber party, the bridal suite can serve as a crash pad for you and your bridesmaids. But make sure after all the gossip and giggling, you get some beauty rest.

MAKING IT OFFICIAL

One of your most important eleventh-hour missions is getting your marriage license. This state-issued permit to wed is proof that you two are fit to marry each other (that is, officially single, divorced, or widowed, and of legal age). You obtain it by going in person (both of you) to city hall, the city or town clerk's office, or the local marriage license bureau. Check online or call the appropriate office in advance to find out about operating hours and whether you need an appointment. See which

marriage license

To apply, you may need the following (requirements vary per state and city, so check).

- ☐ Birth certificate (proof of age)
- ☐ Proof of citizenship and/or residence
- ☐ Photo identification

- ☐ Parental consent if underage (legal age is usually sixteen or seventeen; you may also need court consent)
- ☐ Death certificate if widowed

- ☐ Divorce decree if divorced
- ☐ Blood test results (if needed; only a few states still require this, so check; also, ask how long results are valid)

documents you need to bring along and to find out whether a blood test is required. See "Marriage License," above, for a list of the typical required documents. In most states, you can walk in to apply, but some offices require an appointment, and some states also require you to bring a witness, so look into that, too. There is a fee for your license, which typically ranges from $25 to $100, again depending on the state.

Timing is key when it comes to getting your license—most states have both a waiting period between the time you get the license and the time you actually can say your vows as well as an expiration policy that dictates how long the license is valid. In other words, a marriage license allows you a specific window of opportunity. (For many states, it's thirty days.) So it's crucial to find out the rules in the state (or country) where you're getting hitched. If you're getting married in a state other than the one in which you live, you'll have to wait until you arrive in your wedding town/city to get your license. Be sure to leave time for this crucial task.

The marriage license is basically permission to get married. At the ceremony, your officiant and maybe two witnesses (typically your honor attendants), will sign the certificate and your officiant will submit it for you. A few weeks later, the certificate will be mailed to you.

CHANGING YOUR NAME

One of the most important logistical decisions you two need to make— before you get hitched, ideally—is what to do on the last-name front.

the knot NOTE

name-change help
Crazy busy catching up with postwedding life? For a reasonable fee, several websites will do 90 percent of the name-changing paperwork for you.
TheKnot.com/ namechange

To change . . . or not to change

Once upon a time, wives had no choice but to adopt their husbands' names, but today's couples have many options.

WIFE TAKES HUSBAND'S NAME The traditional way, which will make your old-fashioned relatives happy and keep the question-asking to a minimum. Many couples also see this choice as a sign of real togetherness.

HUSBAND TAKES WIFE'S NAME A twist on the conventional decision, this can work especially well if the man dislikes his last name or the woman is the only child of her clan. It's a pretty rare choice, though. And his family might be miffed. Just keep in mind that it can be much harder (and more expensive) for a man to change his name legally.

WIFE TAKES HUSBAND'S NAME (SORT OF) Some women choose to adopt their husband's name socially but continue to use their given name for business purposes, even legally. This is a good option if you're a professional who relies on name recognition for your livelihood.

YOU BOTH KEEP YOUR OWN NAMES You've spent your lives "building a name" for yourselves; changing what people call you may be hard. Bonus: You'll avoid the long lines at the DMV. Drawback: You may have to deal with in-laws who question your reluctance to take "their name," and you'll also have to figure out what you want to do about the kids, if you have them.

YOU JOIN NAMES Adopting a double or hyphenated surname is an increasingly popular option. A hyphen ensures that people use both names, although the bride might prefer using her given last name as a middle name (Tina Brown becomes Tina Brown White). Sometimes only the bride does the sandwich last-name thing, but you can also both do it.

YOU BOTH DO THE SWITCHEROO You may decide to adopt a whole new name for yourselves. This is a good idea if your names don't go together (like Kerry-Berry) or if you want to revive an extinct family name. You could also artfully combine your last names (Yasser and Warner become Yasner, for example), or choose the name of a personal role model, or a name you just happen to like.

How to change your name

You can't start filing the name-change paperwork until you're officially married, but you'll want to start thinking and talking about it before then, because there's a place on the marriage license where your officiant will write your new name (if you're changing it). You'll need additional copies of your license to change your name, so ask your officiant to request four copies when he submits it (one for you, one for the DMV, one to change your social security card, and one to get a new passport). You can also request additional copies from the courthouse where your license was issued.

To make your new identity official with the rest of the world, there's some paperwork you'll need to do after the wedding. Start by going to the Social Security Administration's website at SSA.gov for step-by-step name-change directions and to download the necessary forms. (Once you change your Social Security information, make sure to change your contact information with the payroll department at work—they have to match or you won't get paid.)

Once you get your new Social Security card, visit the Department of Motor Vehicles to get your driver's license and other identification changed. This agency requires you to make a personal appearance when recording a name change. Bring your original marriage certificate (with the official-looking raised seal that you'll get in the mail), your current license, and your new Social Security card. Double check your local DMVs website to make sure you have the correct forms. Some require

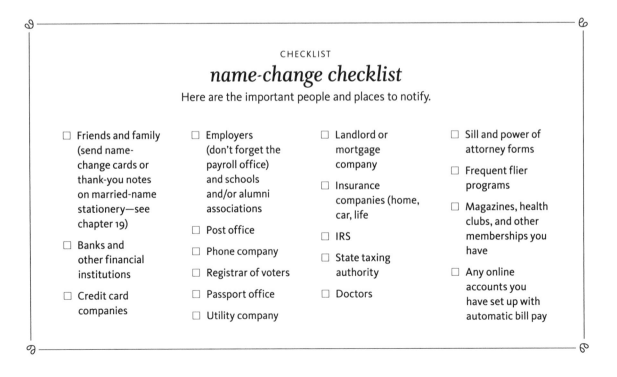

CHECKLIST

name-change checklist

Here are the important people and places to notify.

- ☐ Friends and family (send name-change cards or thank-you notes on married-name stationery—see chapter 19)

- ☐ Banks and other financial institutions

- ☐ Credit card companies

- ☐ Employers (don't forget the payroll office) and schools and/or alumni associations

- ☐ Post office

- ☐ Phone company

- ☐ Registrar of voters

- ☐ Passport office

- ☐ Utility company

- ☐ Landlord or mortgage company

- ☐ Insurance companies (home, car, life

- ☐ IRS

- ☐ State taxing authority

- ☐ Doctors

- ☐ Sill and power of attorney forms

- ☐ Frequent flier programs

- ☐ Magazines, health clubs, and other memberships you have

- ☐ Any online accounts you have set up with automatic bill pay

proof of address (like a phone bill), too. Note: In some states, you must visit the DMV before you can file for a new Social Security card, so confirm with both offices before you file paperwork for either.

For your passport, go to the post office or USPS.com to download the forms you'll need to submit along with your old passport and a certified copy of your marriage license. Again, if you will need your passport for your honeymoon, wait until after you get back to change your name (the name on the reservation and on your passport need to be the same) and it typically takes a few weeks to get a new passport bearing your new name.

Next up? Tell the world. Once you have a Social Security card and a driver's license in your married name, making the other changes should be fairly easy. Some institutions require only a phone call; others may ask for more (to see your marriage certificate, Social Security card, and so on). See "Name-Change Checklist," left, to get a rundown of who else you'll want to tell.

26

the day of . . . in detail

Your big day will come and go like a beautiful, blazing comet. If all you're doing is obsessing and fretting, you'll miss its fleeting glory. So, now that you've planned ahead and know what to expect, it's time to revel in every moment. Focus on the amazing parts—when you're pronounced husband and wife, your adoring guests, the scrumptious food, watching your friends dance—and don't worry about any glitches or slipups. Not only will this make your day that much better and put your attendants and guests at ease, it will also be good practice for marriage—and life (that is, always look on the bright side). There are just a few final steps to take before arriving at the altar.

6–8 hours before
Eat a hearty breakfast with protein to sustain you (you're going to need the energy, especially since you probably won't get a chance to eat at the reception)

Introduce your reception manager and consultant or maid of honor (if that hasn't happened already) so they can deal with any questions during the party

4–5 hours before
Give bridesmaids their gifts (if you haven't already)

Meet bridesmaids at the bridal suite (or other spot where you're getting ready)

Present parents (and each other) with gifts or at least a big hug and kiss

Have lunch delivered for the groom and his men

Have the groom give the best man and/or maid of honor your wedding rings

Have the groom give his father or the best man the officiant's fee envelope, to be handed off after the ceremony

Have lunch delivered for you and your maids if the ceremony is later

3–4 hours before
Have your hair done (see chapter 18 for tips on timing your hair appointments right)

Have your makeup done (see chapter 18 for more on having your makeup done)

1–3 hours before
Put on your gown (go to the bathroom first)

Take first-look photos (optional) and pictures with your attendants and family

45 minutes before
Groom, ushers, groomsmen, and groom's parents arrive at the ceremony site (if getting ready somewhere else)

20 minutes before
Bride, father-of-the-bride, ring bearer, flower child, and bridesmaids arrive at the ceremony site

go time
Savor every minute of your ceremony and reception!

GETTING READY

It may seem like getting ready will only take a couple of hours—especially if someone else is doing your hair and makeup. But allow three to four hours of prep time altogether (including hair and makeup and getting dressed) for yourself and four to six hours if you and your bridal party are all getting ready together, so that you're not rushing, you can stop for photos, and you can take the time to relish every second with your bridesmaids, mom, and future mother-in-law.

Setting up the bridal suite   Decide where you want to get ready and who will join you. Getting ready near the ceremony site will make your preceremony moments a lot easier if you're running late. Some sites provide bridal suites where you can spend the day prepping. This is great because you don't have to get into a car and risk wrinkling or dirtying your dress before the ceremony. If you reserved a room at

Some say it's bad luck for the bride and groom to see each other before the ceremony. We say it's bad luck to do something just because it's tradition. Go with your gut—breakfast together might be just what you need.

a nearby hotel for your wedding night, you can request an early check-in time and prepare there. That way, you don't have to worry about transporting all your stuff after the ceremony—you can just have one of your maids pick everything up after you check out if you're heading to your honeymoon right away.

Who you invite to join you in the bridal suite is completely up to you—but trust us, even if you have nerves of steel, you'll want (and need) someone there to help you get into your dress (it's not as easy as it looks—see "Putting On Your Dress," below). Many brides like to spend the hours before they walk down the aisle with their bridesmaids by their side. It's a great way to bond and have some final single-girl fun while you get ready. Order breakfast or lunch for you and your girls and maybe pop a bottle of champagne for a quick pre-ceremony toast. If you're close with your mom, you may want her to be there, too, and if it won't make you any more stressed out than you'd already be anyway, it's always a nice gesture to invite your future mother-in-law (and sister-in-law if you have one) to join the party.

If you want to spend the hours before you walk down the aisle alone, you might prefer to ask just your maid of honor (or close family members) to help you get ready a few hours before and have your maids (and moms) meet you at the ceremony site. You want the hours before the main event to be as stress-free as possible, so choose your company based on who will help you to stay calm and enjoy every moment of this special day.

Putting on your dress
As we eluded to, putting on a wedding gown isn't like putting on any old dress. There's prep work involved. The main goal is to keep your gown clean, so wait until the last minute to put it on. You'll also want to arm yourself with the following advice to get into and get around in your gown.

ASSEMBLE THE ACCOUTREMENTS Before you even start getting your hair or makeup done, have your mom or one of your bridesmaids inspect your gown; use the instructions your seamstress gave you at your fitting to deal with any wrinkles or loose threads before you put on the dress (see chapter 15). You'll need to have a few things ready, starting with your undergarments, your garter (if you're wearing one), and your shoes. In general, wedding dresses are stepped in to, but if your gown needs to be slipped over your head, have a scarf on hand to put over your face and hair while you slip it on. If your gown has a lot of buttons, make sure you have a crochet hook to help pull the loops over them. (Note: Similarly, it's best for the groom to leave his shirt and jacket off until the last minute, too.)

STEP RIGHT IN   When it's finally time to get dressed, place a sheet on the floor and set your shoes down on top of it. Then follow these steps:

- Put on all your undergarments (including your garter, if you have one); then unzip or unbutton your gown and position it over your shoes
- Have your mom or an attendant hold the dress open and support you as you slowly step into it one leg at a time, placing your feet in your shoes as you go
- Have your mom or an attendant zip or button the gown
- If your shoes have clasps, ask your mom or a friend to buckle them

GET INTO POSITION   Examine the gown to make sure every fastening has been secured, every inch is lying smoothly, and there are no last-minute smudges or spots. If you need to sit down for a moment before hitting the aisle, perch on a backless stool with your gown fluffed out around you—not scrunched under you. If you can't find a backless stool, pull your gown up before you sit, and ask an attendant to drape your train over the back of the chair. Finally, turn toward a full-length mirror and take a long moment for yourself. If you have a silk sheath dress, you have no choice but to stand until you walk down the aisle, so plan accordingly.

LIFT IT UP (SLOWLY)   Try not to do much moving in your gown before the ceremony, but when you do move around, gently lift your gown to avoid last-minute tears and stains. To do so, bend just a tiny bit at the knees and gently gather a piece of your skirt in each hand (if you carelessly grab a fistful of fabric, you'll wrinkle it). Then slowly lift your skirt up and away from the ground.

If your dress is super-full or designed with a train, try not to walk or step backward (again, you'll risk ripping the fabric). Instead, reach behind yourself and delicately lift the back of your skirt with your hand, or enlist the help of an attendant. When you arrive at your destination, simply drop the skirt behind you, and it will naturally fluff itself out as you take your first few steps. Your attendants can help you hold your dress while you walk and smooth out the back and train before the ceremony and even when you get to the altar, so make sure they read this section, too.

BUSTLING YOUR DRESS   Decide in advance when you'll bustle the train. Though some brides wait until after the first dance, most choose to bustle their train right after the ceremony. It helps to have a designated bustler, like a wedding planner, family member, or maid of honor, who accompanies you to your last fitting to learn the ins and outs of your gown. Once you've been bustled, have the bustler check to make sure the entire hem of your gown is even and that the fabric drapes gracefully (but isn't so poufy that you can't sit comfortably during dinner).

KEEPING IT CLEAN We highly, highly recommend that you not eat or drink (or do pretty much anything) in your gown before the ceremony. Avoid sitting in your gown, too—the back of your dress is highly visible (and photographed) during the ceremony, so you don't want it to be wrinkled. If you need a final makeup touch-up or want to have a sip of water (seriously—water marks will show on certain materials), cover the front of your dress with a sheet first.

Transporting you and your dress If you're driving to a different location for your ceremony, you'll need to get in and out of the car slowly, taking care to avoid greasy door locks, dirt, and dust. You should also avoid sitting on the back of your gown if possible. Instead, pull it up behind you and lean forward in your seat. If you're wearing a gown with a big skirt, save an extra seat or two in the car just for your dress—this isn't the time to pile in with your maids. Even when the ceremony is over, you'll still need to take care when moving around in your dress—at least until after you finish taking formal pictures.

For those who want to wait to bustle until after the first dance, your bustler will need to take charge of your train in the meantime. She'll need to help you in and out of the car, drape your train over your chair when you sit, and help transport it when you walk. You can also ask your seamstress to attach a loop to your train that you can slip over your wrist, allowing you to carry it all night, or you can just change into a second reception dress that's bustle-free and easier to move in.

Wearing your dress Forget about modesty: Going to the ladies' room in a classic wedding dress is a two-person job. Assign your bustler or another attendant to bathroom duty, as you'll need help lifting your gown. If you're wearing a vast ball gown, don't be shocked if you actually have to step out of your gown altogether for that trip to the toilet, which means your bathroom buddy will need to help you get both out of and back into your dress.

Finally, when you get to your reception and start making the rounds, remember all that great advice your mom gave you. You know—stand up straight, keep your shoulders back, don't chew gum, and smile. From the moment you step onto that aisle, all eyes (and camera lenses) will be on you. But don't worry so much about your dress once the festivities have begun. You look beautiful, we promise!

TROUBLESHOOTING

The sun's up. Your vendors are getting ready to do their thing. Your mothers are having a cry. It's all come down to this. The big day. Just a few more hours until all eyes are on you two. Problems will arise on your wedding day, some serious and some silly. Most will work themselves out before you walk down the aisle. Some you'll never even know about. For the ones you do, here's how to keep your cool.

Heat wave
If your idea of a perfect wedding doesn't include a sweltering meltdown, beat the heat by having huge water coolers (and cups!) on hand at your ceremony and reception, heavy-duty electric fan action, and paper fans as favors. (Ceremony programs will double in a pinch.) For outdoor affairs, make sure there's ample shade by hanging fabric among the trees, setting up an airy tent, or supplying sun umbrellas to guests. Make sure air conditioners are on early enough to get your sites cool before the crowds arrive. This is particularly important for early-morning events.

Rain or snow
In case of rain, bring as many oversize umbrellas for your guests as you can and move the festivities indoors as quickly as possible. (That backup site we recommended comes in handy right about now.) For snow, hire a plow operator to clear access roads and parking lots (or make sure your sites do), rent four-wheel-drive vehicles to transport guests, and bring space heaters to your sites. In both cases, stock bathrooms with grooming products so guests can counteract weather damage. You should also be prepared to play appropriate songs during your reception, such as "Singin' in the Rain," "It's Raining Men," and "White Christmas."

Family emergency
If a close family member falls ill and is unable to attend your wedding, the show should go on (unless, of course, things look really, really bad and you're too upset). Your loved one probably would want it that way. Find opportunities to include this person in the proceedings. Have him write something you can read during the ceremony; have your officiant lead a prayer for his recovery;

ASK CARLEY
GIFT EXCHANGE

Is a wedding gift exchange between the bride and groom a time-honored tradition or no big deal?
It's an optional tradition for the bride and groom to exchange gifts the night before the wedding, the morning of, or once the festivities are over. You could give each other something to wear for the wedding itself (cuff links, a necklace), or maybe something for the honeymoon (a great pair of sunglasses, snorkeling gear). It doesn't have to be anything major—a photo frame or a treasured book of poetry can make a great gift. Our favorite by far: a handwritten note. Honor this tradition in whatever way you two desire!

play the absentee's favorite song in his honor during the reception. Send flowers and a card on the morning of your wedding and then make sure to visit your loved one at some point before you leave for your honeymoon (if at all possible).

Tight ring
It fit perfectly in the store (and two days ago!), but between the heat and your nerves, your fingers have grown to monstrous proportions. This common ailment can be prevented easily by running your hand under cool water and coating your ring finger with Vaseline just before the ceremony to ensure a smooth, easy glide.

Man (or woman) down
A wedding is a highly emotional event for everyone, and depending on the season, it can get hot in that house of worship, so it's not uncommon for someone to pass out midceremony. Don't panic. Have someone attend to the fallen guest; once the person has been revived, he should sit with his head down until he feels better. Offer ice water or lemonade outside the ceremony location as well as chilled washcloths to keep guests cool.

Hangover
While you'll be tempted to stay out late drinking and catching up with friends at your rehearsal dinner, we can't stress enough the importance of getting a good night's sleep and not drinking too much. Another solution: hosting your rehearsal or welcome dinner two nights before the wedding so you have time to catch up with everyone and still recover. But if you get caught up in the moment and wake up on your wedding day feeling slightly less than your best, here's what to do: Drink lots of water from the moment you wake up. Amazingly enough, greasy foods will help calm your stomach, as will a bottle of Coke (regular—not diet). Take a long, cool shower and take some aspirin if you need to. Even though we know it will be the last thing you'll feel like doing, consider fitting in a morning workout—there's something to be said for sweating out the toxins (just make sure to hydrate before, during, and after).

Overimbiber
Every party has at least one guest who goes overboard. Designate one of your assertive attendants with sober (okay, almost sober) duty to take care of disruptive behavior. If necessary, identify a designated driver to take beyond-drunk guests home or back to the hotel. In general, it's a good idea to close the bar an hour before your reception ends so people can't have "one for the road."

Vendor issues Most wedding vendors are complete professionals and 99.9 percent of the time, weddings go off without any major hitches. That said, things happen. On your wedding day, it's too late for your vendor to undo the damage if he or she brings the wrong order, sends a less-qualified replacement, shows up late (or never!), or otherwise fouls up your agreement. Careful screening and contract-writing are important preventive measures against vendor mishaps. However, even the best of vendors can have unforeseen emergencies. Most professionals have an entire network of resources and colleagues who will take over in case of disaster, but just in case . . . Here's how to deal with major day-of vendor mishaps and the steps you can take immediately to help you settle up after the wedding. In the short run, you need to do the following.

- Let your planner handle it!
- Take a deep breath.
- Point out to your vendor the items or services that are not satisfactory.
- Try to track down a missing-in-action vendor.
- Either return unsatisfactory orders or get a verbal (or, even better, handwritten or e-mailed) commitment to be compensated financially.
- In addition to your photographer, ask your planner, a parent, or your honor attendants to take pictures of any visible evidence that your vendor delivered an unsatisfactory product.

If you have a clear and precise contract and have paid your deposit using a credit card (we can't emphasize enough the importance of this), you're fairly safe as far as getting your money back in the case of a no-show or an unsatisfactory job. Either your vendor will do the right thing by reimbursing you or your credit card company will take up your case if you dispute a charge. Worst-case scenario: You can take the negligent vendor to small-claims court.

FOOD FIASCO If your caterer crashes and burns, order in from a nice restaurant nearby (or from a bunch of nice restaurants, depending on how many mouths you're feeding), preferably one experienced in catering for parties. Have friends and relatives run out for hors d'oeuvre platters, as well as dessert and anything else you need. Who knows? Your makeshift cuisine might be an even bigger hit than the catered fare would've been.

FLOWERS FUMBLE If your florist flakes, call around to local florists and flower shops and see what they can pull together. You can also raid the nearest farmer's market or flower mart for the day's best blooms and enlist the help of crafty attendants or relatives to make tons of small arrangements in different-sized glasses. Stick with a single bloom or color to make it all tie together. Potted flowers can also work. Candles—all shapes and sizes—are quick fixes and can turn an ordinary space into one that's moody and romantic, making up for the oversize centerpieces you'd envisioned.

PHOTOGRAPHY/VIDEOGRAPHY DISASTER If these crucial professionals are no-shows, call around to a few different local photographers or videographers to see if any are available. You never know—your second choice may have had a cancellation and be free for the day. After the wedding, you can follow our tips (see "Vendor Issues," page 399) to recoup your money from the no-show "professional." If no one is available, it's time to figure out which of your guests is an amateur photographer or videographer and ask him or her to fill in. Better yet, ask a few friends who count photography or videography as a hobby to help record the day, so you can get as many great images as possible.

TRANSPORTATION TROUBLE If your limo never arrives, it's time to hail a cab (they'll stop in a heartbeat for a chick in a wedding dress) or hitch a ride with the bridesmaids or Mom and Dad. Know someone with a fancy set of wheels, like a sleek sports car or a vintage vehicle? Now's the time to hit them up for a getaway ride. Promise to take them out for lunch when you come back from the honeymoon.

If your limo is running late, tell the driver to meet you at the ceremony and hitch a ride with your maids and parents. It's better to arrive on time than in style (no one will even see you coming in).

SHOWTIME

Now it's time to forget the preparations, the decisions, the agonizing, the coordinating, the orchestrating, the finessing. Your most critical task at this point is having the time of your lives. This is what it's all about: love, happiness, fun, good friends, and family. And, of course, how simply amazing the person you're marrying is. Enjoy!

epilogue
you're married!
... now what?

TIMELINE
TYING UP LOOSE ENDS

1–2 days after
Return tux if it's a rental

1–6 weeks after
Write thank-you notes

Take your bouquet
to be preserved

Thank vendors

Make any final payments

Preserve, donate,
or sell your dress

Change your name
(see page 388)

6–8 weeks after
Order or create your
wedding album

Order wedding video(s)

Congratulations! All those details you spent months agonizing over miraculously came together; you said your vows (nice job if you wrote your own, by the way), had your party, and somehow, here you are—married! But wait, not so fast . . . you still have a few things to wrap up. Attend to these final postwedding to-dos during the first few weeks (or even days) after your wedding, so you can enjoy the memories of your special day for decades to come.

WHAT TO DO WITH YOUR DRESS

You spent months (or maybe even years) dreaming of your wedding dress. Here's how to make sure your gown's greatness will live on. Your first step, regardless of what you plan to do with your dress next: Have it professionally cleaned. While it's generally safe to wait as long as six weeks after the ceremony to have your dress preserved, it's best to take it to be cleaned a few days after the wedding if there are noticeable stains (like wine, juice, or ink). If you're leaving on your honeymoon right away, have your maid of honor or mom take your gown in for you. Until then, store your dress in a dark, dry place, rolled or folded in a clean white sheet.

Preserving your dress

A simple dry-cleaning and storage box are not enough to keep your gown preserved for years. Don't just drop your dress at your usual dry cleaner. The chemicals dry cleaners typically use to clean your suits and cocktail dresses are too harsh for your wedding dress. If you decide to go the preservation route, you'll need to enlist a wedding-dress specialist. They'll analyze the fabric, dyes, weaves, and ornaments of your gown, as well as the composition of stains, in order to formulate a customized cleaning plan. In removing invisible soils and other stains from the gown, they prevent the potential damage that results when these substances embed in the fabric and undergo chemical changes.

To find a skilled wedding-gown preservationist, ask the store where you purchased your dress or your seamstress to recommend a cleaner who specializes in dress preservation. Ask about pricing, procedure, and warranties before entrusting your one-and-only gown to any dry cleaner. Keep in mind: The price of cleaning and preservation will also vary with the complexity of a gown's beadwork, train length, and stain damage. But cleaning and preserving your gown can run up to several hundred dollars, so request an estimate first.

After cleaning, the gown is carefully wrapped in stable archival materials and packaged in an archival box like the ones museums use to prevent mildewing, discoloration, and disintegration over time. All storage materials, including the tissue paper and box, should be acid-free. Then it's your job to find a safe place to keep it so that it's protected from extreme temperatures, moisture, and exposure to direct sunlight, which can cause discoloration and mildewing. (In other words, the basement is not a good place to keep your dress.)

ASK CARLEY
ORGANIC GOWN PRESERVATION

I want to keep my gown as an heirloom. Are there any environmentally friendly gown-preservation options?

Many dry cleaners use green practices they call "organic gown preservation" to preserve wedding dresses. Green cleaners use nontoxic, odor-free chemicals that don't create harmful emissions, or nonhazardous liquid silicone, to clean and preserve garments. The results are the same, and green methods may be gentler on your dress's delicate fabric. The prices can vary depending on the dress, stains, and city. Go online to find a green cleaner near you that specializes in organic dress preservation or ask the store where you bought your dress.

Selling your dress

If you aren't planning on saving your gown for your daughter to enjoy one day but hate the idea of such a beautiful dress wasting away in the back of your closet, let another bride get just as much enjoyment out of it as you did by selling it after the wedding. Contact nearby consignment shops that will either sell the gown for you and keep part of the profit or buy the gown directly from you (often at a much lower price than what you paid for it) for resale. You can also sell your dress online, using an auction website like eBay or one of the many sites dedicated just to buying and selling used wedding dresses and accessories (like veils and shoes).

Donating your dress

Maybe you don't have an emotional attachment to your dress, but you want to keep the positive vibe and love you felt on your wedding day going. Give your dress to a charitable organization like Brides Against Breast Cancer (bridesabc.org). Don't forget your maids: We know they'll love the dresses you choose, but if they don't foresee using them postwedding, ask them to donate their dresses to the Glass Slipper Project (GlassSlipperProject.org) or the Fairy Godmothers Inc. organization (FairyGodmothersInc.com), both of which work to put dresses in the hands of underprivileged teens who can't afford prom dresses.

WEDDING KEEPSAKES

You worked so hard to decide on and create all the details of your day. Here's how to save them for years to come. And for tips for saving a slice of your cake, turn back to chapter 21.

Preserving your bouquet

Not only can you preserve your dress, you can also save your bouquet by drying the flowers—by yourself or via a professional service—before they begin to brown or wilt. There are a few different methods you can use: silica gel (a quick-drying mode that involves immersing the blooms in a sandlike silicon substance in an air-tight container for two to seven days) or pressing (flattening flowers using a flower press and then framing them). With both methods, once the flowers are dried, they must be kept in glass frames or domes so they don't reabsorb moisture. If you're going the DIY route, you can find silica gel at hardware or gardening stores, or you can air-dry the blooms yourself.

Another option: freeze-drying (a method used by professionals that involves spraying the blooms with a starch to set the colors and then flash-freezing the bouquet). This method takes about four weeks and will give you the most true-to-life results in terms of maintaining the flowers' shapes and colors. It's also the most expensive method (some brides choose to freeze just a few select blooms instead of the full bouquet), but preserved flowers can last until your golden anniversary and maybe even longer, as long as humidity, direct sunlight, and bright halogen lamps are avoided.

Decide whether you want to preserve your bouquet and, if so, which method you want to use before your wedding day. That way, you can assign a bridesmaid to take care of your bouquet after the ceremony so it's in prime condition when you hand it over to the preservationist. Check with your site manager to see if you can store it in a refrigerator during the reception, or if it's a hand-tied bouquet, have one of your maids stick the stems in water. For best results, drop your bouquet off at the preserving establishment (or have someone do it for you) the day after the wedding (or begin drying the blooms out yourself) as soon as possible after the wedding. Many professional services will be unable to work with your blooms if they've been too badly dried out, bruised, or otherwise damaged. So be careful with them if you plan on having them preserved. Store and transport your flowers in a cooler with sealed ice packs covered in wax paper on the bottom. (Pack tissue paper around the bouquet to prevent it from moving and bumping.)

Preserving your photographs
While photographs are the most obvious way to preserve wedding memories, there are specific strategies required to make sure that your prints and album will be available to show your children and grandchildren one day. Carefully compiling and packaging your photos will prevent common damage such as yellowing, fading, or disintegration.

ORDERING ALBUMS Most wedding photography packages don't include prints and albums, so after the wedding, you'll need to settle down to the hard work of selecting which photos you want to keep and how you want to preserve them—put this on your to-do list or we promise you, it will be two years and you still won't have a wedding album. Ask about album options and costs when hiring a photographer and choosing a package, so you can budget for it. Depending on the type of cover (linen, leather, or metal) and binding, the total cost can run anywhere from $500 to as high as $5,000.

ORDERING PRINTS Even if you don't order an album from your photographer, think twice before choosing to buy a DVD of the images or the rights to them to print at home or at the drugstore. Final prints from your photographer will be retouched and printed professionally on high-quality, archival paper to ensure your photographs will still be around in twenty years. If you choose to print them yourself, keep in mind that you'll have to buy the rights to the photos. If you print them on regular drugstore printing paper, they won't stand the test of time. Your wedding photographer is a major investment—don't let it go to waste by skimping on the prints. If budget is an issue, splurge on the professional prints and make the album yourselves.

When ordering prints, keep longevity in mind: Black-and-white prints generally last longer than color ones—though a good professional photographer can produce color prints that will be equally durable. The materials used in color prints are more susceptible to fading from surrounding conditions, such as temperature and moisture. Be careful when handling any photos. Both touching them and resting them on newspaper can taint them with oil and acid that will speed the aging process. Store any leftover prints that didn't make it into an album (or that are waiting to be put into an album) in an archival box (you can find one at any photo and art supply store or mass retailer like Target, and many stationery stores sell them, too) to prevent any damage or fading.

ORDERING THE ALBUM If you order an album from your photographer, expect to wait up to a few months. If you think your parents or grandparents will want one, it can save you money to order them all at once. If you decide to do the album yourself, make sure the one you choose is made with acid-free prints, acid-free paper, acid-free adhesive, and even acid-free photo corners. As with your dress, acid will damage and discolor your pictures over time. Choose an album with a strong binding that's handcrafted—inexpensive albums will begin to disintegrate much earlier than ones made from sturdier materials. Store your wedding album in a cool, dry place, away from bright sunlight.

SAYING THANKS

Among the top postwedding activities to look forward to (besides the honeymoon): opening all your gifts—and playing with them. But first, you have one final chore—writing thank-you cards for all those gifts. We know writing personal notes to a hundred and eighty guests is just about the last thing you want to do, but the sooner you get started, the sooner it will be done and you can go back to enjoying your new toys. So limber up those wrists—it's thanks-for-giving time.

The recipients

Simply put, you've got to thank every single gift giver for each and every gift. No exceptions: Engagement, shower, and wedding presents all apply. Thanking people for their specific gifts reassures them that you got what they sent. And since most people have their gifts shipped (unless we're talking about engagement-party or shower goodies), your thank-you cards are their only way of knowing you actually received the goods. Sorry—generic "thank you" e-mails aren't sufficient. Likewise, preprinted thank-you cards are a major etiquette faux pas.

The timeline

Do yourselves a big favor from the start, and before you begin opening gifts, open your guest-list manager or spreadsheet and record each gift next to the giver's name and address. Include a few words about the gift so you don't get confused. You'll never remember which of the ten crystal vases your aunt Amelia gave you, so be specific: "Waterford Balmoral vase." Then put a big check mark next to the guest's name when the thank-you note has been signed, sealed, and delivered.

Don't save them all for after the wedding. We know you have a million other tasks to do while planning your wedding, but try to write thank-you notes as soon as you open gifts. You've probably heard the rumor that you have up to a year after the wedding to send your thank-yous. Forget it. While better than nothing, sending a thank-you note a year after someone gave you a gift is rude—and your wedding is no exception. The actual rule: For all gifts received before the wedding, thank-you notes should be sent within two weeks of their arrival. For all gifts received at or after the wedding, you have up to three months once you return from the honeymoon to write them (if you go on your honeymoon right after your wedding—otherwise, it's three months after the wedding). But the sooner you get them done, the better.

The approach

Both of you are responsible for sending out thank-you notes. We don't care how bad your handwriting is or how much stress you're under at the office, the gifts you've received were intended for both of you, so you should both reciprocate. To establish equality on this front, divvy up your thank-you list. You send notes to your friends, family, and family friends; he does the same for his posse. Guests who "belong" to both of you get split down the middle. And you both sign all of them.

Don't attempt to get them all done in one sitting. Trust us—it won't happen and you'll likely give yourselves carpal tunnel syndrome in the process. Your best bet: Divide and conquer. If you each put aside fifteen minutes daily (or every other day) toward this end, you can probably bang them out at a rate of ten a day and have them done in under two months. Open a bottle of wine, do it together, and you'll find you won't dread thank-you-writing time nearly as much.

The design
Traditional thank-you notes are written in blue or black ink on simple ecru sheets or folded cards that match your invites. You can also ask your stationer to create cards with your married names, new monogram, or wedding motif—or make them yourselves. Note: You shouldn't use notes with your married name on them until after the wedding. So if you choose monogrammed cards, order some notes with your maiden name or initials and some with your married name or initials. You can also buy boxed sets to use before.

The wording
Personalize each note by mentioning the present by name and addressing your unique relationship with the giver. Explain how you plan to use the gift or why it's perfect for you. You also should be specific when thanking someone for a gift of money—give as much detail as possible.

SAMPLE

thank-you note wording ideas
Here's how to say thanks for every type of wedding gift.

Dear Elizabeth and Tom,

Thank you so much for the gorgeous crystal wineglasses. We now have a complete set! We were both sorry that you couldn't be with us, but thank you for thinking of us on our wedding day. Derek and I are looking forward to your next visit, when we can enjoy a drink together. Thank you again for thinking of us at this special time in our lives.

Warmest regards, Lila and Derek

gift from the registry

Dear Aunt Sue and Uncle Tom,

Thank you so much for your generous gift. Lila and I are saving for a new home, and thanks to you, we'll be moving into our dream house very soon. We're so glad you could share our special day with us. Uncle Tom's dance moves were a hit and really got the party started. Again, many thanks for thinking of us.

Love, Derek and Lila

a cash gift

appendix
budget

ESTIMATING YOUR WEDDING BUDGET

Don't drive yourselves or your family into debt over your wedding! Use this formula as a guide to help you figure out how much money you can save or your families can contribute. These estimates are not for everyone. You need to assess your other financial pressures, such as loans, debt, and so on before you fix on a number.

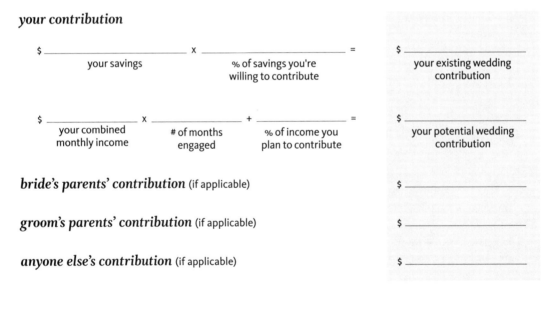

your contribution

$ _____ x _____ = $ _____
your savings   % of savings you're   your existing wedding
willing to contribute   contribution

$ _____ x _____ + _____ = $ _____
your combined   # of months   % of income you   your potential wedding
monthly income   engaged   plan to contribute   contribution

bride's parents' contribution (if applicable) $ _____

groom's parents' contribution (if applicable) $ _____

anyone else's contribution (if applicable) $ _____

total wedding budget $ _____

ESTIMATED WEDDING BUDGET BREAKDOWN GUIDE

Depending on your priorities, use this chart to estimate your budget per category. If you know you want to spend more on a category, you'll have to account for it someplace else.

total budget: $ _____

category	%	example	your estimates
		($30,000)	
Reception site, rentals, food, drink, cake	x .50	$15,000	$ _____
Wedding dress and formalwear	x .10	$3,000	$ _____
Flowers and decorations	x .10	$3,000	$ _____
Photo and video	x .10	$3,000	$ _____
Music and entertainment	x .10	$3,000	$ _____
Invitations and guest details	x .05	$1,500	$ _____
Ceremony site and officiant	x .05	$1,500	$ _____

When you get a price quote from a vendor, don't forget to factor in taxes and tips.

NOTE: The following big-ticket items are not included: honeymoon (can run upward of $3,000); wedding consultant (up to 10 percent of total budget); rehearsal dinner.

the knot NOTE
Track all your expenses online (and set up reminders for yourself) at **TheKnot.com/budgeter**

YOUR WEDDING BUDGET BREAKDOWN

Now that you have an idea of what you're going to spend, it's time to start working it out on paper. One of the best ways to stay on track is to organize all of your wedding-related expenses. Use this line-by-line worksheet for your itemized wedding budget.

total budget: $ _____ ← all reception items should add up to this!

category	your estimates	actual cost
reception (50%)	$	$
site rental	$	$
food	$	$
cake & cutting fee	$	$
bar	$	$
rentals (table, chair upgrades)	$	$
lounge furniture	$	$
late-night food	$	$
food tax and service fee	$	$
ceremony & officiant (5%)	$	$
location rental	$	$
officiant fee or donation	$	$
rings	$	$
marriage license	$	$
special décor (unity candle, ring pillow)	$	$
wedding dress & formalwear (10%)	$	$
wedding dress & alterations	$	$
accessories (veil, shoes, jewelry)	$	$
hair & makeup	$	$
formalwear	$	$

category	your estimates	actual cost
photo & video (10%)	$	$
photography	$	$
videography	$	$
album	$	$
flowers & décor (10%)	$	$
flowers	$	$
lighting	$	$
additional décor rentals	$	$
music & entertainment (10%)	$	$
ceremony musicians	$	$
reception band or dj	$	$
other special music	$	$
invitations & guest details (5%)	$	$
invitations	$	$
save-the-dates	$	$
ceremony programs	$	$
extra stationery (menu cards, favor tags)	$	$
postage	$	$
wedding favors	$	$
welcome bags	$	$
transportation	$	$
parking	$	$
additions	$	$
	$	$
	$	$
	$	$
total cost:		$

registry checklist

KITCHEN ELECTRICS

- ☐ Blender
- ☐ Coffeemaker
- ☐ Coffee grinder
- ☐ Espresso maker
- ☐ Tea kettle
- ☐ Juicer
- ☐ Food processor
- ☐ Stand or hand mixer (with attachments)
- ☐ Slow cooker
- ☐ Pressure cooker
- ☐ Rice cooker
- ☐ Toaster
- ☐ Toaster oven
- ☐ Waffle iron
- ☐ Electric grill and griddle
- ☐ Electric wok
- ☐ Panini press
- ☐ Microwave
- ☐ Deep fryer
- ☐ Ice cream maker

KNIVES

- ☐ Steak knives
- ☐ Chef's knife (6–12")
- ☐ Paring knife (2.5–4")
- ☐ Utility knife (4–7")
- ☐ Kitchen shears
- ☐ Sharpening tool

COOKWARE

- ☐ 4-to-5-inch skillet
- ☐ 10-to-12-inch skillet
- ☐ 2- or 3-quart saucepan with lid
- ☐ Sauté pan
- ☐ Stockpot with pasta and steamer inserts
- ☐ Double boiler
- ☐ Stir-fry pan/wok
- ☐ Dutch oven
- ☐ Grill pan
- ☐ Griddle
- ☐ Roasting pan
- ☐ Casserole dish
- ☐ Cast-iron skillet
- ☐ Pot rack
- ☐ Fondue pot

BAKEWARE

- ☐ Bakeware set
- ☐ Baking sheets (2–4)
- ☐ Cake pans (2–4)
- ☐ Muffin tins (2)
- ☐ Cooling racks (2)
- ☐ Cookie cutters
- ☐ Trivets (2)
- ☐ Mixing bowls
- ☐ Rolling pin
- ☐ Rolling pin mat
- ☐ Cake decorating kit
- ☐ Cake stand

KITCHEN TOOLS

- ☐ Measuring spoons and cups
- ☐ Spatulas (2–3)
- ☐ Whisks (2–3)
- ☐ Tongs
- ☐ Cheese grater
- ☐ Zester
- ☐ Peeler
- ☐ Can opener
- ☐ Garlic press
- ☐ Pizza wheel
- ☐ Slotted spoons (2)
- ☐ Ladles (2)
- ☐ Salad spinner
- ☐ Mortar and pestle
- ☐ Colanders (2)
- ☐ Ramekins/Prep bowls (6–8)
- ☐ Cutting boards (2–3)
- ☐ Cruets
- ☐ Ricer
- ☐ Ice cream scoop
- ☐ Pepper mill
- ☐ Kitchen timer
- ☐ Basting brush
- ☐ Paper towel holder
- ☐ Soap pump
- ☐ Trash can
- ☐ Aprons (2)
- ☐ Dishtowels/cloths (6–12)
- ☐ Dish rack
- ☐ Mitts/Potholders (2–4 pairs)

DINNERWARE

- ☐ Casual place settings for 8–12
- ☐ Salt and pepper shakers
- ☐ Serving platter (s)
- ☐ Sugar bowl and creamer
- ☐ Serving bowls
- ☐ Salad bowls
- ☐ Serving trays (2)
- ☐ Soup tureen
- ☐ Butter dish
- ☐ Cake plate
- ☐ Espresso cups and saucers (8)

FINE CHINA

- ☐ Formal china place settings for 12
- ☐ Accent plates (12)
- ☐ Formal rimmed soup bowls that double as pasta bowls (12)
- ☐ Chargers (decorative plates)
- ☐ Coffeepot
- ☐ Teapot
- ☐ Gravy boat and stand
- ☐ Creamer and sugar bowls

FLATWARE

- ☐ 5-piece flatware sets (formal and casual)
- ☐ Butter knife
- ☐ Salad servers
- ☐ Serving spoons (2)
- ☐ Slotted serving spoons (2)
- ☐ Serving forks (2)
- ☐ Demitasse spoons (8)

GLASSWARE

- ☐ Wineglasses (14) (2 extra for breakage)
- ☐ Water goblets (14)
- ☐ Champagne flutes (12)
- ☐ Double old-fashioned glasses (12)
- ☐ Iced-beverage glasses (12)
- ☐ Margarita glasses (6)
- ☐ Martini glasses (6)
- ☐ Dessert-wineglasses (6)
- ☐ Shot glasses (6)
- ☐ Highballs (12)
- ☐ Juice glasses (6)
- ☐ Beer mugs or pilsners (6)
- ☐ Casual drinking glasses (12)

BARWARE

- ☐ Wine chiller
- ☐ Cocktail shaker
- ☐ Ice bucket and tongs
- ☐ Jigger and bar tools
- ☐ Coasters
- ☐ Carafe
- ☐ Wine fridge

TABLE LINENS

- ☐ Napkins and napkin rings (12)
- ☐ Large formal tablecloth
- ☐ Smaller tablecloths
- ☐ Casual napkins and placemats (12)
- ☐ Cotton or pad liner for tablecloth

BEDDING

- ☐ Sheet sets (4)
- ☐ Duvet
- ☐ Down comforter
- ☐ Bed skirt
- ☐ Mattress pad
- ☐ Blankets (2)
- ☐ Pillows (6)
- ☐ Decorative pillows (2 or 3)

BATH

- ☐ Bath towels (6)
- ☐ Bath sheets (6)
- ☐ Hand towels (6)
- ☐ Washcloths (4)
- ☐ Guest towels (4)
- ☐ Bath mat
- ☐ Shower curtain
- ☐ Scale
- ☐ Hamper

DÉCOR

- ☐ Vases and frames
- ☐ Table lamps
- ☐ Pillows and throw blankets
- ☐ Decorative accents (candles)
- ☐ Furniture
- ☐ Electronics (speakers, TV)
- ☐ Outdoor/gardening supplies

honeymoon help

You've agreed on the perfect honeymoon place, bought the books, and registered for luggage you had to have. Now all that's left between you and euphoria is the details—booking the trip, packing your bags, and finding someone to feed Fido while you're gone. To help you plan the trip of a lifetime, start early (six to eight months or more in advance) and keep reading for everything you need to know to plan an amazing honeymoon.

HONEYMOON BUDGET

Unless your honeymoon is a gift, you need to factor it into your budget. So just how much will it cost? An average eight-day honeymoon can cost anywhere between $5,000 and $30,000. Remember in your budgeting process to include not only airfare and hotels, but also taxis, meals, alcohol, snacks, and souvenirs. Plane tickets and hotel costs will be more than half of the total. Always overestimate honeymoon expenses and leave padding for an unexpected splurge. Plan to take along a few hundred "safety" dollars and a credit card for emergencies and extras.

If the trip of your dreams is slightly out of reach, shop for online deals, and let your friends and family help by registering for your honeymoon. You can also take advantage of all those wedding-related purchases you charged by signing up for a credit card that gets frequent-flier miles, and cashing those in for the flight to Fiji. Another option: Consider honeymooning during the "shoulder season"—the week or two before and after a destination's peak season—and take a mini-moon immediately following your wedding to someplace nearby. Don't be afraid to work the honeymoon angle either: Tell everyone it's your honeymoon and ask about specials. You may at least get an upgrade.

CHOOSING YOUR TRIP

Once you have your budget settled, it's time for the fun part: deciding where to go. There are a number of ways to narrow down your choices, depending on your priorities. Keep in mind that whatever you do, you're going to be tired after the wedding, so build in plenty of time for rest and relaxation.

In season vs. out of season

Great weather and optimal sightseeing opportunities—as well as high room rates and more crowds—often go hand in hand during a destination's high season. (Low season is when seasonal businesses—restaurants and island ferries, for example—shut down and attractions may close for renovations.)

High season in Hawaii and the Caribbean, where the weather doesn't change that dramatically, runs from January to April simply because people from colder climes flock to their sunny beaches to flee the winter chill. Conversely, Disney World is packed in the summer despite the searing heat because kids are out of school. The months immediately preceding and succeeding a destination's prime time are often called "shoulder" seasons and usually boast good weather, as well.

Package possibilities

For easy booking and great deals, there are countless online travel sites that offer "package" deals, which include airfare, hotel rooms, airport transfers, tours and excursions, and so on, for a better price than you would otherwise get if purchasing everything à la carte.

A package may mean restrictions on dates, so you may not be able to leave for your honeymoon right after the wedding. And if you miss a connection or have to make changes to your travel plans, there may not be much flexibility. Also, your upgrade options may be limited if you book a package deal.

Tour trips

A tour is a package that generally includes a guide and other travelers. It may be a huge trip with hundreds of people or a small, specialized group. You may have to take a tour if you're going somewhere remote, like the Himalayas, and it can be a great option if you're headed someplace far-flung where you don't speak the language or where you don't feel comfortable traveling on your own, or when you want to visit multiple cities without worrying about making all the arrangements on your own. There are also adventure tours that will take you on a hike to Machu Picchu, for example, which can be worth considering if you are looking for a once-in-a-lifetime adventure.

honeymoon by season

CARIBBEAN AND SOUTH AMERICA

best dates to go: December to May, when the area is coolest and enjoys the most wind, but average temperatures year-round hover between 78 and 88° Fahrenheit

dates to avoid: Official hurricane season runs from June to November; the worst months are August, September, and October

HAWAII, ASIA, AND SOUTH PACIFIC

best dates to go: March to July; October and November

dates to avoid: December and January are the coolest (75° Fahrenheit on average); August and September are hottest (92° Fahrenheit on average); the wettest months are November to March

EUROPE

best dates to go: May through September. Shoulder season is springtime

dates to avoid: It gets cold throughout most of Europe so avoid December through February if possible

MEXICO, BAJA, AND CENTRAL AMERICA

best dates to go: Anytime between October and May

dates to avoid: Rainy season runs June through September and the area hottest during the summer months

AFRICA

best dates to go: Spring and fall (May through October)

dates to avoid: It's hottest between April and May; rainy between June and September

USA AND CANADA

best dates to go: Of course it depends on where exactly you're going but in general, March and April as well as October and November

dates to avoid: June through September tend to be the hottest

But think seriously before signing on for a honeymoon tour. Not only can traveling en masse make it hard to get to know a place, but it also means forced togetherness with people other than your new spouse. This is your honeymoon, after all—do you really want to spend it with thirty strangers? Of course, an organized tour does mean less planning—and you may want the security of that big group in a remote destination where you don't speak the language. Some companies offer private tour guides, which you may want to consider if privacy tops your priorities.

The all-inclusive option At an all-inclusive resort, you pay one price for your room, meals, entertainment, activities, and (sometimes) alcohol. Everything is within the resort's compound, so

you never have to leave. These resorts vary in price, size, ambience, and degree of luxury—an all-inclusive can be a private, sixty-room hideaway where you'll eat meals alone, albeit in a dining room with other vacationers, or it may mean three hundred other couples, poolside drinks and games, and group excursions. Some all-inclusives are "couples only," meaning it's just you two and a bunch of other lovebirds. While all-inclusives once had a bad rap for being somewhat cheesy, that's not the case anymore. There are many amazing four- and five-star all-inclusives that offer luxe suites and amenities, amazing food, and plenty of privacy. You'll find all-inclusives throughout the Caribbean, and, increasingly, in Mexico, Europe, and the South Pacific, as well as a scattering in the United States, and they are becoming more popular all over the world.

On the glass-is-half-full side, an all-inclusive is easy, easy, easy. You roll out of bed and start playing. It's nearly impossible to get bored or lonely, and there are plenty of other people to swap wedding stories with. Because you pay one price, you can try every activity included— from swimming, boating, parasailing, and water-skiing to dining and dancing till dawn—without ever thinking about cost while you're there.

On the half-empty hand, staying at a self-contained resort may prevent you from getting to know the local culture. You can explore the island outside your resort, of course, but since you've already paid for all your meals and activities, you may not be motivated to leave. If you're not joiner types, a huge all-inclusive with "manufactured fun" (volleyball around the pool, evening activities) may be more annoying than entertaining. And some resorts charge extra for premium drinks and activities, so find out what's actually included when comparing resorts.

Cruises If crashing waves, the wind in your hair, and salt in the air appeal to your free spirits, setting sail on a cruise ship and exploring new worlds might be your ticket to paradise. Cruise ships are no longer just floating buffets with some gambling and Vegas-style entertainment thrown in. Of course, there's plenty of time to lounge on the lido deck and sip piña coladas, but it's hard not to be enticed by what cruises have to offer. These mobile luxury hotel-and-spas can transport you to such exotic locations as Sri Lanka, the Galápagos, or Antarctica. Cruises make it easy to visit a bunch of different destinations without the hassle of coordinating transportation, activities, and itineraries—or unpacking and repacking on your trip. As with ports of call, onboard activities are boundless. Partake in workouts from yoga to tai chi. The more adventurous can rock-climb walls, parasail, or kayak.

honeymoon planning checklist

6–8 months or more ahead

Set a budget.

Start trading honeymoon fantasies.

Research potential destination options.

If the price tag for your dream trip is off the charts, brainstorm ways to save money like frequent-flier points or honeymoon registry options.

Book your flights and/or cruise, get seat assignments, order special in-flight meals, and check luggage allowances.

Research hotels, check room availability, and reserve a room.

Reserve a rental car (if necessary).

Visit the CDC Travelers' Health site (wwwnc.cdc.gov/travel/) to check whether certain vaccinations are recommended or required before visiting your destination.

3 months ahead

Obtain your passports and visas, if necessary.

Research travel insurance and purchase if you decide to get it.

2 months ahead

Buy luggage—or register for it before your bridal shower!

Research and book tours, theater tickets, hot restaurant seats, and any other activities that require advance reservations.

Get certified to scuba-dive or begin lessons for any other activity you hope to pursue on your trip.

1 month ahead

Make a packing and shopping list.

Reconfirm all reservations.

If you have a pet, make kennel reservations or contact your house sitter or pet sitter to make sure they're available.

Book transportation for getting to and from the airport.

2 weeks ahead

Exchange about $50 (or at least enough to get you to your hotel from the airport) into small bills in the currency of the country you'll be visiting. There is usually an exchange counter or ATM at the airport, but it can be nice to have cash in hand when you arrive.

1 week ahead

Arrange to have mail held at the post office during your trip.

Stop newspaper delivery.

Make two to three sets of photocopies of your passport, credit cards, insurance cards, wills—basically any paperwork people would need if your wallet were stolen or something happened to you. (Give one set each to a parent and/or a relative or friend, pack one set in your luggage, and leave one set in your safe-deposit box.)

Ask stores where you've registered to hold orders so gifts don't pile up on your doorstep, or ask a relative to collect packages.

Set out clothes to pack; buy what you need.

Make sure you have extras of everything you can't live without: medicines, glasses or contacts, etc.

3 days ahead

Reconfirm any flights.

Order champagne to await you in your hotel room.

Leave a copy of your itinerary and a set of house keys with a relative or close friend in case of emergency.

Check weather forecasts for your destination.

Prepare your home for your departure—water plants, dispose of perishable food, etc.

1 day before

Reconfirm flights and check for any delays or upgrade options.

Make sure your luggage (carry-on and checked) is labeled.

honeymoon tipping table

DINING
United States and Caribbean: 15 to 20 percent of total pretax bill

Mexico: 20 percent of total pretax bill

Europe and Canada: 10 percent of total pretax bill (gratuity is often included)

South Pacific: 15 to 17 percent of total pretax bill

TRAVEL
Airport porter: $1 to $2 per bag

Train porter: At least $1 each night in a sleeper car

HOTEL
Bellman: $1 to $2 per bag

Maid service: Leave about $2 per night in the United States and Caribbean; in Europe, it varies, so ask at the front desk

Room service: About 20 percent of the bill in the U.S., 10 percent in the Caribbean, and nothing extra in Europe

Special service: If someone from the housekeeping staff brings you an iron or a bottle of champagne, give them $2

All-inclusives: Check the information in your confirmation package

CRUISES
At least $20 for each day aboard when averaged out among all the people on staff who will take care of you regularly during your stay (waiter, person who cleans your room, etc.)

CABS
United States: About 15 to 20 percent of the fare

Caribbean: About 10 percent, generally; no tipping in the Dominican Republic or the British Virgin Islands

Europe: Generally, just round the bill up to the nearest dollar; in Italy, Portugal, and Britain, go with the 15 percent rule

destination directory

We have information on all these honeymoon hot spots (plus tons more) on TheKnot.com, but here is the contact information for the most popular honeymoon destinations.

U.S.
Arizona: ArizonaGuide.com
Colorado: Colorado.com
Florida: VisitFlorida.com
Hawaii: GoHawaii.com
Las Vegas, Nevada:
VisitLasVegas.com
Napa Valley, California:
VisitCalifornia.com
New York City: NYCVisit.com

CARRIBBEAN, MEXICO, AND LATIN AMERICA
Anguilla:
Anguilla-Vacation.com
Antigua and Barbuda:
Antigua-Barbuda.org
Aruba: Aruba.com
Bahamas: Bahamas.com
Barbados: Barbados.org
Cayman Islands:
CaymanIslands.ky
Costa Rica:
VisitCostaRica.com
Dominica: Dominica.dm
Dominican Republic:
GoDominicanRepublic.com
Grenada:
GrenadaGrenadines.com
Guadeloupe:
Go2Guadeloupe.com
Jamaica: VisitJamaica.com
Martinique: Martinique.org
Mexico: VisitMexico.com
Montserrat:
VisitMontserrat.com

Nevis and St. Kitts:
StKittsTourism.kn
Puerto Rico:
SeePuertoRico.com
Saba and St. Eustatius:
StatiaTourism.com
St. Barthelemy:
St-Barths.com
St. Croix: VisitUsVI.com
St. John: VisitUsVI.com
St. Lucia: StLucia.org
St. Maarten: St-Maarten.com
St. Martin: St-Martin.org
St. Thomas: VisitUsVI.com
St. Vincent and The Grenadines:
DiscoverSVG.com
Tortola and Virgin Gorda:
BVITourism.com
Turks and Caicos:
TurksandCaicosTourism.com

EUROPE
Italy: ItalianTourism.com
France: FranceTourism.com
United Kingdom:
VisitBritain.com

PACIFIC RIM
Fiji: BulaFiji.com
Tahiti: Tahiti-Tourisme.com
Australia: Australia.com
Indonesia:
Indonesia-Tourism.com
New Zealand:
NewZealand.com
Thailand:
TourismThailand.org

AFRICA
Morocco:
Moroccotouristguide.org
South Africa: Southafrica.net

CRUISES
Carnival Cruise Lines:
Carnival.com
Celebrity Cruises:
CelebrityCruises.com
Disney Cruise Line:
Disney.com
Mediterranean Shipping Company (MSC) Cruises:
MSCCruises
Norwegian Cruise Line:
NCL.com
Princess Cruises:
Princess.com
Regent Seven Seas:
RSSC.com
Royal Caribbean International:
RoyalCaribbean.com
Seabourn Cruise Line:
Seabourn.com
Wind Star Sail Cruises:
WindStarCruises.com

ALL-INCLUSIVE RESORTS
AM Resorts: AMResorts.com
Beaches: Beaches.com
Breezes: Breezes.com
Couples: Couples.com
Dreams: DreamsResorts.com
Grand Velas:
GrandVelas.com
Secrets: SecretsResorts.com
Sandals: Sandals.com

year-by-year anniversary gifts

Ideas for what to get each other for your first and fiftieth anniversaries and everything in between.

first
PAPER: deluxe stationery set, hand-bound photo album, antique book of love poems, gift certificates.

second
COTTON: luxurious bathrobe, chenille sweater, sexy undergarments, pajamas.

third
LEATHER: cool pants or coat, nice bag or briefcase, fancy organizer, exquisite belt.

fourth
LINEN: luxury bedding, nice summer outfit, hammock.

fifth
WOOD: handcrafted bowl, antique chest, trip to the woods, rocking chair.

sixth
IRON: wrought-iron bed frame, fancy candlesticks, gym membership (iron abs and buns!).

seventh
WOOL: cozy blanket or shawl, month's worth of warm socks, trip to Wales (lots of sheep there).

eighth
BRONZE: deluxe cookware (bronze, copper—close enough), sculpture, piece of jewelry.

ninth
POTTERY: art class, certificates for mud mask (and other spa treatments).

tenth
ALUMINUM: set of fancy silverware, fireplace tools.

Other important anniversaries
FIFTEENTH: crystal
TWENTIETH: china
TWENTY-FIFTH: silver
THIRTIETH: pearls
FORTIETH: rubies
FIFTIETH: gold
SIXTIETH: diamonds

additional resources

FOR THE LATEST WEDDING TRENDS
Wedding Obsessions Blog: TheKnot.com/blog

FOR ENGAGEMENT RINGS,
PARTIES, AND PROPOSALS
Just Engaged: TheKnot.com/justengaged

FOR INSPIRATION
Photo Galleries: TheKnot.com/photos
Invitations and Stationery:
TheKnot.com/invitations
Wedding Cakes: TheKnot.com/cakes
Wedding Flowers: TheKnot.com/flowers
Reception Ideas: TheKnot.com/reception
DIY Wedding Ideas: TheKnot.com/diy
Wedding Favors: TheKnot.com/favors
Wedding Style: TheKnot.com/style
Wedding Colors: TheKnot.com/color
Real Weddings: TheKnot.com/realweddings

FOR PLANNING HELP
Wedding Planning: TheKnot.com/planning
Budget Weddings: TheKnot.com/basics
Ceremony and Vow Ideas:
TheKnot.com/ceremony
Your Guests: TheKnot.com/guests
Wedding Traditions: TheKnot.com/traditions
Wedding Programs: TheKnot.com/programs
Destination Weddings:
TheKnot.com/destination
Rehearsals and Brunches:
TheKnot.com/rehearsal
Luxe List: TheKnot.com/luxelist

FOR VENDOR HELP
Music and Dancing: TheKnot.com/music
Photo and Video: TheKnot.com/photography
Transportation: TheKnot.com/transportation

FOR "WEDIQUETTE" ISSUES
Sticky Subjects: TheKnot.com/etiquette
Ask Carley: TheKnot.com/askcarley

FOR FUN
Take a Quiz: TheKnot.com/quizzes

FOR THE WEDDING PARTY
Grooms and Guys: TheKnot.com/grooms
Maids and Moms: TheKnot.com/bridesmaids

FOR YOUR HONEYMOON
Hot Spots: TheKnot.com/honeymoons

FOR YOUR LOOK
Fashion: TheKnot.com/fashion
Beauty: TheKnot.com/beauty
Dress Search: TheKnot.com/gowns
Bridesmaid Dresses:
TheKnot.com/bridesmaiddresses
Accessories: TheKnot.com/accessories

**FOR REAL BRIDE ADVICE AND
RECOMMENDATIONS
(OR JUST PLAIN VENTING)**
Community: TheKnot.com/talk

FOR REGISTRY HELP
Registry Center: TheKnot.com/registry

FOR YOUR GUESTS
Going to a Wedding?:
TheKnot.com/guestguide

PLANNING TOOLS AND APPS
Wedding Planner: TheKnot.com/planner
Checklist: TheKnot.com/checklist
Budgeter: TheKnot.com/budgeter
Guest List Manager: TheKnot.com/guestlist
Registry Manager: TheKnot.com/registry
Save-the-Dates: TheKnot.com/savethedates
Wedding Websites:
TheKnot.com/weddingwebsites
Inspiration Boards: TheKnot.com/inspiration
The Knot TV: TheKnot.com/videos

THE KNOT MAGAZINE
The Knot regional magazines include:
Boston, Chicago, Colorado, Georgia, Florida,
Michigan, Missouri/Kansas, New Jersey, New York,
North Carolina, Northern California, Ohio,
Pennsylvania, Southern California, Texas, Twin Cities,
Washington D.C./Maryland

OTHER BOOKS FROM THE KNOT
The Knot Guide to Destination Weddings
The Knot Ultimate Wedding Lookbook
The Knot Book of Wedding Lists
The Knot Guide to Wedding Vows and Traditions
The Knot Ultimate Wedding Planner
The Knot Book of Wedding Flowers
The Knot Guide for the Groom
The Knot Guide for the Mother of the Bride
The Knot Bridesmaid Handbook

NEWLYWED RESOURCES
The Nest Home Design Handbook
The Nest Newlywed Handbook
TheNest.com

acknowledgments

A large team of insanely talented people helped to create this book. I want to thank Kristin Koch and the rest of The Knot staff: Rebecca Dolgin, Rebecca Crumley, Kelly Crook, Danielle Lipp, Alice Stevens, Anja Winikka, Amelia Mularz, and Brooke Alovis for their fast, wonderful work on this updated edition. Thank you for your tremendous effort and time dedicated to researching, writing, editing, and designing all the wedding know-how we've gathered over the past sixteen-plus years.

In addition to the in-house team, I also want to thank all the genius wedding planners who shared their ideas, advice, and support: Lindsay Landman, In Any Event, JoAnn Gregoli, Marcy Blum, Annie Lee; and the incredible wedding vendors and experts who contributed their insights and inspiration: Stacey Weinstein, Lisa Zagami, George Kyriakos, Elizabeth Messina, Reem Acra, Melissa Sweet, Sylvia Weinstock, Amsale Aberra, Michael Stuart, Boutique Bites, Great Performances, C&J Catering, Blue Plate Catering, Mel Barlow, and the many others who are always willing to offer their expertise and support in a pinch. We'd also like to show our appreciation to all the photographers who shared their work with us .

A special thanks to our team at Clarkson Potter; our agent Chris Tomasino; and our patient families. And finally, thanks to all the wedding-obsessed Knotties who spend their days clicking around TheKnot.com and inspired us to create this book.

photo credits

Page viii: Laura Dombrowski Photography
Page 7: Sergio Mottola Photography
Page 14: Emilie Inc.
Page 44: TJ Cameron Photography
Page 52: J. Perlman / R. Lutge Photography
Page 58: Visionari
Page 71: Jonathan Canlas Photography
Page 108: Jesse Leake Photography
Page 113: Kim Mendoza Photography
Page 117: Broxton Art
Page 120: Lunaphoto
Page 128: Apertura
Page 130: Artisan Events, Ashley Garmon Photographers, Docuvitae, Verité Boutique Photographers
Page 155: Kari Kochar Photography
Page 192: Jen Kroll Photography
Page 200: DJK Photography
Page 203: Jodi Miller Photography
Page 243: Ira Lippke Studios
Page 258: Judith Rae Photography
Page 263: Marni Rothschild Pictures
Page 266: Jennifer Lindberg Weddings
Page 289: Brian Dorsey Studios
Page 302: Judith Rae Photography
Page 331: KT Merry Photography
Page 346: Kristin Spencer Photography
Page 350: Michael Norwood Photography
Page 354: Candice K Photography
Page 385: Cramer Photo
Page 391: KT Merry Photography
Page 394: Ira Lippke Studios

index

A

Accommodations
  accommodation cards, 297
  for out-of-town guests, 59
  for wedding night, 373
Afternoon tea menus, 157
After-party, 369–70
Aisle runners, 192
Altar arrangements, 194–99
Anniversary gifts, 421
Announcements
  engagement, 3–6
  save-the-date, 286–89
  wedding, 313–14
Ask Carley
  black tie vs. black tie optional, 12
  cash gifts, 213
  choosing honor attendant, 69
  choosing special song, 171
  communicating with vendors, 82, 85
  double-booked venue, 45
  dress codes, 269
  father-daughter dances, 72
  financial help from parents, 20
  friend's music performance, 173
  hiring local bands, 170
  inviting plus-ones, 55
  let guests know tips are covered, 25
  male maids of honor, 65
  multiple wedding showers, 361
  not changing names, 389
  obligatory bridal party members, 72
  organic wedding dress preservation, 402
  paying for maids' styling, 275
  paying for transportation, 351
  paying for wedding attire, 262
  portrait photos, 127
  pregnant maids, 268
  rehearsal toasts, 366
  same-sex wedding wear, 246
  small weddings, 53

  taboo clothing colors, 264
  telling friends they are not bridesmaids, 70
  walking down the aisle, 194
  wearing gloves during ceremony, 244
  wedding band placement, 242
  wedding gift between bride and groom, 397
  when to register for gifts, 8
Attendants. *See also specific attendant names*
  bridal party shorthand, 67
  budget considerations, 70
  choosing, 68, 69–71
  list of, 63–69
  numbers of, 70, 71
  pets, 71
  very important extras, 68–69

B

Babysitters, 320, 366
Bachelorette parties, 361–63
Bands, 176, 182, 183
Bar
  cash bar, 152–53
  décor for, 109
  limited bar, 152
  nonalcoholic offerings, 153
  open bar, 151
  signature cocktails, 152
  signature mocktails, 153
  staffing guidelines, 154
  supplies checklist, 152
Bartenders, 154
Bathrooms, 97, 109
Beauty and fitness, 270–81
  beauty blunders and fixes, 274
  booking beauty pros, 272
  choosing bridal look, 275–76
  classic makeup looks, 277–81
  do-it-yourself hair and makeup, 277
  extra beauty to-dos, 280
  finding a hairstylist, 271

  finding makeup pros, 271
  getting in bridal shape, 279
  hair and makeup trial runs, 272–73
  scheduling beauty pros, 273–75
  up vs. down hairdo, 278
  wedding day beauty timeline, 275
  wedding day hairstyle, 276–77
  wedding day timeline, 382
Best man, 66–67
Black tie vs. black tie optional, 12
Bouquets
  bridal, 117–19, 323, 324, 403–4
  for bridesmaids, 119
  shapes for, 118
  tossing at the reception, 323, 324
Boutonnieres, 119–20
Bracelets, 244
Bras and bustiers, 245
Breakfast receptions, 156–57
Brides. *See also* Beauty and fitness; Wedding dress
  bridal bouquets, 117–19, 323, 324, 403–4
  bridal showers for, 360–61
  giving gift to groom, 366–67, 397
  portraits of, 137–38
  transporting, in wedding dress, 396
  wedding day bridal suite, 393–94
Bridesmaid dresses, 261–69
  accessorizing, 266–67
  color and fashion rules, 264
  contract checklist, 265
  key considerations, 262–64
  maternity options, 268
  measuring for, 265–66
  for preteens, 268
  shopping for, 264
  who pays for, 262
Bridesmaids. *See also* Bridesmaid dresses
  bouquets, 119
  color themes for, 15
  confirming details with, 379